THE GREAT

APOSTASY

The Deceived People

BY

M.A.NOBLE

LAST CHANCE SERIES

The Great Apostasy The deceived People

CONTENTS

INTRODUCTION

This book entitled 'The Great Apostasy' The Deceived People', is written from a psychological perspective which is vital to understanding how the concept of apostasy has come about in a 'so-called' civilized and intellectual world.

Some of the content can be disturbing, and controversial. The book borders on what may appear to be extreme and irrational. It discloses information not easily digested by some readers.

However, In Part 2, the author provides logical answers and solutions to the subjects so the reader is not left with fear and uncertainty, but with hope and assurance of a happy ending, however, the guarantee of a happy ending depends entirely on the individual's choice!

The Author has spent many years watching events taking place worldwide, and connecting these events to past, present and future prophecy. The author's life has been shaped, since early childhood, towards a ministry as a watchman and a modern time spokesperson to forewarn people of the pending troubles about to befall the world! The author has been trained and directed towards this goal through life experiences, a spiritual awareness and a daily walk with the Creator of the Universe. This may sound strange to the reader yet many people can testify to the same sort of relationship with the God of the Universe! It relies on an initial step of faith to enter into such a relationship but then after the first step it becomes as natural as taking a walk in the park!

This relationship with a Triune God (meaning there are three parts: God, the Son and Holy Spirit) is not the disturbing and irrational phenomena referred to in the above passage, far from it, this relationship with God is the most natural, the most rational and the most wonderful experience anyone could ever have!

No! The strange and illogical phenomenon I refer to is so evil, so opposite to the Holy God, so unbelievably diabolical that it has taken control of people's minds in such a way the

5

world has been conditioned to believe the Creator God and His Son are to be avoided at all costs! People are being fed a LIE! People have been conditioned to accept the LIE! As a result people have been denied the wonderful experience of a loving God and instead have settled for the counterfeit force!

The author has studied many subjects such as: New Age, Humanism, World Affairs, Sociology, Economics, Biology, Neuroscience, Psychology, Social Science and Health Care and acquired various qualifications along the way, including a BSc in Psychology as well as specialising in Counselling people with Phobias and Exit Counselling those trapped and controlled by a religious cult.

This background of experience and learning, over 40 years, qualifies the author to write <u>rationally</u> on what appears to be <u>irrational</u>, yet makes perfect sense when the reader is presented with the true facts.

This book is relevant to every individual, regardless of status, rank, intellect, age, culture or faith.

It is a reality check! A book of reflection and life changing decision-making! The author's goal is to present true facts so the reader and many people from all over the world will have access to these facts; that provide evidence of current events taking place, the consequences of these events and through this knowledge may be given the truth that will set them free! What do I mean by this? Well read the book to find out but it is suffice to say that there is a pending danger –a terrifying danger much greater than Noah's Flood, much greater than the destruction of Sodom and Gomorrah and much more horrific than the Holocaust or the modern day Ethnic Cleansing or the current chemical warfare taking place in the Middle East!

***

I, the author feel compelled to speak to the people of this world via the written word because of the message in Ezekiel 3: ***"I have made you a watchman for the house of Israel…"*** God also says clearly in verses 18-22 that if a watchman does not warn a wicked man to mend his ways that wicked man will die and if a watchman doesn't warn a righteous man, who commits evil to repent of his sin and turn back to righteousness he will also die! And if the watchman doesn't fulfil these obligations he will be held accountable! Many believers would state this does not apply because Christ forgives all sin –if that is true then the apostasy God mentions in the end times must be a lie? I do not believe God contradicts himself or that he lies!

My heart is stirred by a noble theme as I recite
My verses for the King,
My tongue is the pen of a skilful writer
Psalm 45

The reader can obtain further information about the Triune Godhead in Book 1 of the Last Chance Series below:

Christ Yeshua Jesus from Genesis to Revelation by M.A.Noble (2013) ISBN 13- 9781484136386,

PART 1

PART 1 PROVIDES EXPLANATION AND EVIDENCE, CONCERNING THE NATIONS AND INDIVIDUALS, UNDER THE CONTROL OF ONE, ELITE, POWERFUL GROUP FOR THE PURPOSE OF A ONE WORLD SYSTEM UNDER THE DICTATORSHIP OF A ONE WORLD RULER. IT IS THIS RULER THAT INSTIGATED THE GREAT APOSTASY!

The LORD looked down from heaven upon the children of men, to see if there were any that did understand, and seek God. (Psalm 14:2 KJV)

BUT GOD FOUND THERE WERE NONE!

The world has become APOSTATE! They have all turned their backs on Him – the one who created the universe, who created mankind and gave them life on this earth! They have chosen an alternative for their worship!

CHAPTER 1

APOSTASY EXPLAINED

Events are occurring in this world; unusual phenomena, causing drastic changes to human behaviour, and to the environment such as widespread mental health issues, new life threatening diseases, continuous disasters, civil unrest, wars and rumours of wars. Many ordinary folk just living their daily lives, going about their business are unaware of these events or the future consequences of these, or how relevant historical events have effected these changes. All of these factors are still changing our world, –right before our eyes.

Sadly, much of this change has taken place unchallenged because the majority of the population do not acknowledge there is such a concept as the duality of 'good and evil' Many people acknowledge that there may be a superior being up in the heavens who is responsible for creating this world and the people in it, yet many more people do not believe anything. The majority of people have either been born into, or chosen to follow, the concept of the 'Big Bang Theory which is a THEORY, not FACT! This theory has been confirmed to be UNTRUE over and over again!

More importantly, although some believe in a superior being and call him by different names i.e. YHWH, Jehovah, God, Cosmic consciousness, many deny the existence of an evil superior being or demonic forces or that evil exists. Some people may even blend both good and evil together, saying God is good and evil.

This confusion is part of the great lie!

This lie is deceiving many into believing satan the serpent, the devil and ultimately lucifer does not exist! There is also a universal ignorance to the reality of hell. Other words associated with hell are Hades, Abyss and the Underworld. Biblical references indicate hell to be in the centre of the earth.

This makes sense when you think of the magma chamber of a volcano. The centre of the earth therefore must produce this magma which is also underground! The earth consists of a circle of fire which is a circle of volcanos that also exist under the sea. This circle of fire will be part of the Great End Time Fire that destroys this earth, prior to the New Earth (the third and final one) God is going to create!

Because of this determination to believe an evil being does not exist, or that hell or final judgement is a myth, people choose to ignore God's warnings, pushing these into their subconscious archives of their minds.

People tend to look at all phenomena on a humanistic level, rationalising every unusual or unanswerable event. Instead of accepting a 'miracle producing' God who works among us to make things good, to provide blessings and answer prayers with action, people deny His actions by labelling them 'coincidences, or find a 'humanistic and practical solution. Yet when these same individuals experience phenomena that are orchestrated by demonic forces they call it miraculous!

This behaviour has happened for so many years (during the past 100+ years) it has been transferred from generation to generation until this 'anti God' behaviour has become firmly rooted! So much so that this generation find it impossible to break the habit of humanising everything. Hence apostasy becomes deeper and deeper ingrained into the persons soul!

The greatest stumbling block to mankind (apart from rejecting the Son of God Christ Yeshua) is to ignore the fact there are hidden forces at work and these are being orchestrated by a 'currently' hidden leader called satan!

Now if you flinched when you read the words 'the Son of God, Christ Yeshua', if your body suddenly shook, when you read those words, or if your mind went dizzy or felt strange or if you felt a feeling in your stomach as though someone had punched you, then these and other reactions are telling you that you are probably one of the apostate people. This tells you that you have been conditioned over the years to reject the **only one** that truly loves you and cares what happens to you, the only one who can save you. You have been prevented from accepting God's gift of eternal life of peace and happiness! You have been conditioned to follow the wide path that leads to destruction!

Unfortunately, unless people face this fact, the apostasy would continue and many people would be left behind after the Rapture of God's people. They would be left behind to face the leader of this evil force and accept his mark of ownership; this will lead to eternal damnation!

Unless people take their heads out of the sand and face the facts, things will continue to escalate to the Great Apostasy that has been predicted to happen in the Great Tribulation. This period will arrive shortly after the rapture of God's people.

Within the Christian world there is great naivety about evil forces at work. So much so believers are blinded from seeing prophecy at work.

Every adverse issue is dealt with on a human level for example, many divisions of the Christian church do not currently recognise how close we are to the period of the Great Tribulation or that we are in the End Times period. The leaders continue to teach the people basic 'milk' teachings instead of preparing them for the oncoming dangers and return of the savior.

Christ Yeshua gave many parables about being prepared and ready for these times, yet still preachers are preaching about Christian marriage or tithing etc. By now the Christian church should be actively showing great power in the Spirit of God, ready to stand strong against the evil forces at work. Ready to receive the Messiah when he returns for them. But this is not happening, instead believers are going about their daily business ignoring the signs and just living 'carnal and secular lives'. All of this is part of the apostasy!

It is vital individual's open up their minds to go beyond what they see as reality to understanding the duality that exists between what is seen and what is not seen, to understand, (this comes from the gift of wisdom) to accept there are things happening that are hidden from view yet they are very real! There is a very real duality of forces between Good and Evil! These two forces are uneven in power yet still at war with each other. They are uneven in power because one of these forces

created the other and therefore the created can never supersede the Creator!

The Creator is God who created all of this world, and the previous world (before the flood when God saved Noah and his family to survive as a remnant to continue into this world), and the heavens above.

The evil force was created originally as a pure and holy being in the heavens but later fell from God's grace, through rebellion, and became the enemy of everything good. Hence we have the two forces at war good and evil at work; the difference is it has already been decided who will win the war. God sent Christ Yeshua to call the people away from evil into God's grace to be saved from this corruption that came from the evil force known as satan.

Until people recognise these facts the apostasy will continue resulting in many lost and condemned souls!

Although so far the reader has read about what seems illogical and irrational i.e. about God and a fallen angel called satan. The realities however, consist of a world of evil and violent wars and starvation in third world countries because of human greed for money and power. The majority of the world population have chosen to blot out the Creator God from their thoughts, their hearts have turned cold on hearing about such things and they are blind to what is happening in the world. They are unable to see how corrupt the world has become; how justice has become perverted and how innocent people have been persecuted and destroyed. This is direct proof of how irrational and illogical the world has become. The world has turned upside down!

Apart from people's blindness towards a Creator God, it is also difficult for people to accept and to be aware of hidden forces at work, or of conspiracies, or of long term plans to restructure the world ready for a totalitarian ruler. It is difficult to recognise these things when you are under severe pressure to survive each days challenges.

When you hear others laughing, smiling, enjoying themselves – everything seems 'normal'. When you see people sitting on a bus, going somewhere, doing something normal like shopping, theatre or dinner in a restaurant- it is life as normal.

People appear normal yet if these same people were approached on these matters, particularly if you mention God; their reactions would highlight their determination to harden their hearts, to close their ears to avoid hearing the truth!

Normality (status quo) and avoiding anything that makes us 'uncomfortable' provides us with an inner security to believe all is normal! Avoidance of truth becomes a security blanket a pacifier!

As human beings it is 'normal' to want to feel secure, safe and happy. We are social beings therefore need to socialise. This socialising is an outlet from the stresses and strains of life. However, this scenario of 'life continuing as usual' also occurred just before the flood came upon the people and destroyed all but Noah and his family! You say 'you don't believe in the bible story of Noah! Well, it happened! The world was destroyed, just like Sodom and Gomorrah was destroyed – these are historical facts. These places existed in Israel and the uninhabited area of these two cities still exists. Just as Pompeii and other ancient historical cities of sin were destroyed yet evidenced they existed!

The 'normality' scenario mentioned, also took place just before the Holocaust. The Jewish people endured throughout Europe, Pogroms, (Pogrom's are acts of violence, disruption and persecution). The Jewish people rationalised these pogroms, convincing themselves these incidents were nothing to worry about, they told themselves these pogroms were isolated incidents of racism, so they buried their heads in the sand in the hope it would all sort itself out and return to 'normality'. But of course these pogroms were just the beginning of their troubles. It was also a sign to the world trouble was brewing but they went on burying their heads in the sand until they had to face WW2!

Exactly the same is happening today, people are not recognising the signs of trouble ahead! The signs are there in full view of us, yet they are being ignored. One of those obvious signs is the worldwide apostasy, the theme of this book.

To begin on the subject of apostasy, it is necessary to explain the concept of Apostasy. Below are five explanations/definitions for the reader to choose one which makes sense personally. There will be a summarized, easy to understand, version of the definition of Apostasy from the author's perspective based on the events taking place in the world and how this relates to biblical interpretation and biblical prophecy.

It is important to recognise the apostasy goes beyond religion or Christianity. It involves the whole of humanity.

The first two definitions are an example of apostasy defined in a humanistic (non-religious) way, using complex wording that confuses rather than explain, almost as a means of misleading the reader into fully understanding what the true definition is. This is an important point to note as it will be revealed that this avoidance of truth is a common method used today to mislead the people of this world! The other three definitions lean towards the truth but narrow it down to specifics; however, the key concepts are there i.e. rebellion, a falling away and adultery.

The following definitions are from the free Wikipedia webpage entitled 'Apostasy'.

http://en.wikipedia.org/wiki/apostasy#cite_note-29

1. **The American sociologist <u>Lewis A. Coser</u> defines an apostate to be not just a person who experienced a dramatic change in conviction but "a man who, even in his new state of belief, is spiritually living not primarily in the content of that faith, in the pursuit of goals appropriate to it, but only in the struggle against the old faith and for the sake of its negation."** [2][3]

2. **The American sociologist <u>David G. Bromley</u> defined the apostate role as follows** [3] **Apostate role: defined as one that occurs in a highly polarized situation in which an organization member undertakes a total change of loyalties by allying with one or more elements of an oppositional coalition without the consent or control of the organization. The narrative is one which documents the quintessentially evil**

essence of the apostate's former organization chronicled through the apostate's personal experience of capture and ultimate escape/rescue.

3. The Christian understanding of apostasy is "a willful falling away from, or rebellion against, Christian truth. Apostasy is the rejection of Christ by one who has been a Christian....", though many believe that biblically this is impossible ('once saved, forever saved').[29] "Apostasy is the antonym of conversion; it is de-conversion."[30] The Greek noun apostasia (rebellion, abandonment, state of apostasy, defection) [31] is found only twice in the New Testament (Acts 21:21; 2 Thessalonians 2:3).[32] However, "the concept of apostasy is found throughout Scripture."[33]

4. The Dictionary of Biblical Imagery states that "There are at least four distinct images in Scripture of the concept of apostasy. All connote an intentional defection from the faith."[34] These images are: Rebellion; Turning Away; Falling Away; Adultery.[35]

a) Rebellion: In classical literature apostasia was used to denote a coup or defection. By extension the Septuagint always uses it to portray a rebellion against God (Joshua 22:22; 2 Chronicles 29:19).

b) Turning away: Apostasy is also pictured as the heart turning away from God (Jeremiah 17:5-6) and righteousness (Ezekiel 3:20). In the OT it centers on Israel's breaking covenant relationship with God though disobedience to the law (Jeremiah 2:19), especially following other gods (Judges 2:19) and practicing their immorality (Daniel 9:9-11).Following the Lord or journeying with him is one of the chief images of faithfulness in the Scriptures. The Hebrew root (swr) is used to picture those who have turned away and ceased to follow God ('I am grieved that I have made Saul king, because he has turned away from me,' 1 Samuel 15:11).The image of turning away from the Lord, who is the rightful leader, and following behind false gods is the dominant image for apostasy in the OT.

c) Falling away: The image of falling, with the sense of going to eternal destruction, is particularly evident in the New Testament. In his [Christ's] parable of the wise and foolish builder, in which the house built on sand falls with a crash in the midst of a storm (Matthew 7:24-27), he painted a highly memorable image of the dangers of falling spiritually.

d) Adultery: One of the most common images for apostasy in the Old Testament is adultery.[37] "Apostasy is symbolized as Israel the faithless spouse turning away from Yahweh her marriage partner to pursue the advances of other gods (Jeremiah 2:1-3; Ezekiel 16). 'Your children have forsaken me and sworn by god that are not gods. I supplied all their needs, yet they committed adultery and thronged to the houses of prostitutes' (Jeremiah 5:7, NIV). Adultery is used most often to graphically name the horror of the betrayal and covenant breaking involved in idolatry. Like literal adultery it does include the idea of someone blinded by infatuation, in this case for an idol: 'How I have been grieved by their adulterous hearts which have lusted after their idols' (Ezekiel 6:9)."[35]

5. Speaking with specific regards to apostasy in Christianity, Michael Fink writes: Apostasy is certainly a biblical concept, but the implications of the teaching have been hotly debated.[38] The debate has centered on the issue of apostasy and salvation. Based on the concept of God's sovereign grace, some hold that, though true believers may stray, they will never totally fall away. Others affirm that any that fall away were never really saved. Though they may have "believed" for a while, they never experienced regeneration. Still others argue that the biblical warnings against apostasy are real and that believers maintain the freedom, at least potentially, to reject God's salvation

Versions 3,4 and 5 provide a clear definition of the meaning of the word apostasy however, it is restricted to Christians only, whereas this book is based on the biblical meaning which applies to the 'last days' and includes every individual and every nation throughout the world, Jew, Christian, Muslim, Gentile, regardless of religion, status, position, or political persuasion! The religious viewpoint as stated in the Christian definition is a major part of the Great Apostasy, however many Jewish communities should also be included as part of the apostate world, but more importantly religious and non- religious have blended in together to produce this 'worldwide' apostasy!

According to the New Bible Dictionary, apostasy always relates to rebellion against God (Jos 22:22;2 & Ch.29:19) originally instigated by satan, the apostate dragon of Job 26:13 This suggests then that apostasy is not just about the believing population who have fallen away, backslidden or rebelled against God, it is also in relation to the non-believing population!

2 Thessalonians 2:3 describes the Great Apostasy prophesied to occur, alongside or prior to the revelation of the man of lawlessness (Mt 24: 10-12). And the passage refers to a 'final catastrophic revolt' against the authority of God, which in apocalyptic writings is a sign of the end of the world. This prophecy refers to God having provided prophecy, within his bible scriptures, as a means of communicating with the people of this world. He provided, through his chosen prophets such as Isaiah, Daniel and Ezekiel, information to the people of all nations. He also provided physical and experiential examples in the Old Testament books through his chosen people –the Jews. They were examples of the consequences of rebellion and wickedness! God disclosed through his prophecies, not only the consequences of a sinful world but a solution to it through salvation from it!

The definition of apostasy used within this book is that of a worldwide rebellion against God which includes a 'turning away from' God in various forms and by all peoples, including rich or poor, powerful or weak, religious or secular!. Ironically, the wealthy western countries have become poorer than the

Third World Countries. Those who suffer poverty, famine and diseases often know and worship God- therefore they are spiritually rich, whereas westerners have turned their backs on God and Creationism which makes them spiritually poor! They are spiritually poor suffering a famine of the truth and of a spiritual connection to God! The third world poverty nations have a great desire to find the true God! There is a spiritual hunger within the starving nations yet the western countries are too proud to acknowledge the existence of a Holy Superior, 'Spiritual' Being! However, the apostasy demonstrates how serious it has become when it has infiltrated into Christianity and Judaism bringing about rebellion and the turning away of the believing population so that they too, reject the Holy God that they had once accepted. This has produced a large number of backsliding Christians and Jews!

This apostasy has particularly occurred among carnal (worldly) Christian's (not born again), those who lack a firm foundation, weak in faith and disobedient, walking in the world instead of with God! These people found the worldly pressures and temptations too difficult to resist – it is much easier to fall back into what you are familiar with –even though it has serious consequence – even though it means eternal death! Many Christians have been misled and deceived away from the truth, turning onto the 'wide' road which leads to destruction.

It has the same consequences for rebellious Jews who have turned their back on Hashem (God) and His covenant choosing to follow the path of unrighteousness.

The Great Apostasy involves non- religious individuals who have chosen to reject all aspects of God such as the triune God, creationism and prophecy, regardless of all the evidence, signs and warnings that have been provided by God. These people are aware of this indisputable evidence yet do all they can to discredit that evidence, placing their trust in Man, science and humanism, rather than God.

Finally, all of the above mentioned groups of people, religious and secular, who have taken part in this apostasy, turning their backs away from God, have committed adultery! This term adultery refers to turning away from respecting or loving God in order to love and respect another (in this case –

satan!) The individual may not be aware of satan's existence but because of the 'duality' of life on this earth, if an individual rejects God they automatically 'by proxy' become adulterous with satan (as he is the master of this world) by involving themselves totally in humanistic activities. The person committing adultery has rejected a relationship with the Creator in preference to the respect and love for other gods such as satan who controls and rewards the adulterer with money, status, power, and pleasure, capturing them in a web of deceit.

Instead of entering into a covenant with God where he offers eternal life, everlasting peace and security in exchange for loyalty and faithfulness, the adulterer prefers to sell his soul for prosperity and worldly pleasures which are temporary!

The Great Apostasy also includes all nations. Many nations that were once strong in Christian or Judaic values, have turned away to adopt humanistic values instead.

The Great Apostasy incorporates a new religion Humanism! Humanism is everything opposite to God! Humanism is when Man and Woman decides to follow human theories, trust in humans to provide their needs including protection from poor health, suffering, poverty and mortality. Humanism is about trusting scientist and new technology and pleasurable experiences to keep them happy and secure!

The first man and woman to become humanists were Adam and Eve, when they chose to follow a serpent's suggestion to ignore God and do what they want! They hungered for knowledge and so gave up their relationship with God their Creator!

Excluding the Creator God from your life has always been called 'secular'. That is when people know there is a God but chose not to follow him, they know of him, attend church for weddings etc, they know the moral codes, would live regular lifestyles that consist of a fairly moral form of righteousness until eventually some crisis would occur and suddenly they remembered God and turn to him for help.

However, apostasy is much deeper than secularism. It consists of a people who have been born into a society where God is never mentioned or acknowledged- where he is considered taboo and anyone who follows God's son Christ

(Jesus) is ostracized, persecuted, ridiculed and scoffed at. Believers are often seen as eccentrics, crazy, weird etc. The world has become so apostatized that any mention of the word God or Christ, people respond by making an outward statement of distaste! Their behaviour is automatically and commonly standard! It is to change the subject quickly or to mock or worse to become aggressively abusive! Interestingly, the majority of western populations use the same tones of defence, usually by firstly attacking the bible as being contradictory or made up of stories and written by ordinary men. The second key response is by arguing that God cannot be seen so He cannot exist, is not real or that Christ was an ordinary man and is now dead! All of these arguments are conditioned reactions implanted by the apostate world mind controllers who planned it that way over 2000 years ago. Many people also argue that Christianity is no better than any other religion.

All religions have a god figure, an assistant i.e. prophet or equivalent and their followers. Today's Christianity is quite correctly the same as any other religion (excluding the remnant, the minority 'born again' believers).

Apostasy is when the majority of the population say that those who believe and have faith in an invisible being is desperately trying to find a way to avoid the sting of death or they are weak because they cannot survive by themselves (this is the survival of the fittest concept). Of course these views are totally opposite to the truth. True followers of God, through his son Christ, are actually very strong! It takes courage to live a Godly life amongst those who would easily prefer them not to exist!

Throughout the history of this world, the fight between the Godly and the ungodly has been continuous. Many Jews and Christians throughout the world have been martyred, murdered for their faith, refusing to convert to Catholicism (which is a pagan religion that incorporates Christian concepts) or Islam. Today many believers are still being murdered because of their faith and refusing to denounce their Heavenly Father God and Christ Yeshua (Hebrew name). This subject will be covered in more detail later in the book.

Satan's long term plan is to rid the world of his opposition which is God and his people. This commenced from the day Adam and Eve decided, on the serpent's suggestion, to disobey God. From the time they were cast out of the Garden of Eden the world became cursed and gradually the world became divided into those who had faith in God and lived righteous lives and those who had faith in objects i.e. pagan gods, and lived humanistic lives. Gradually, after Christ Yeshua's ministry and his crucifixion many people became His followers – Jew and Gentile followers. The Romans (a pagan nation) decided to try and destroy these Christians and managed to martyr many of them. Later the Roman Emperor Constantine with his wife's help introduced a new pagan/Christian religion and called it Roman Catholicism. Gradually this Roman religion replaced Christ's Hebraic Christianity with a gentile/pagan counterfeit which has become a major influential, wealthy and powerful religious and political tool world-wide. The purpose of this new religion was to mislead people, to force conversions and compliance to a religion that offered no salvation, no forgiveness of sin and no future eternal life! Today many Catholics have moved on from the original false church and become 'born again' believers. However, there are still thousands of people who believe they are saved and forgiven; they are being misled away from the truth!

A remnant of Christ's followers who survived the Roman persecution went throughout the world, to preach the Gospel of Christ to the people. As a result thousands of people became believers worldwide despite the many attempts to destroy these Godly people. As soon as the enemy martyred one believer, many more would rise up to replace him! Same with the Jewish nation, Hitler and the Arab nations have attempted to completely annihilate them from the earth, but the Jewish nation are stronger and increased in greater numbers than ever before and God has sent them back into their own nation Israel. The nation of Israel that was given to them by God himself!

Believers have paid a severe price for their faith and endured suffering for thousands of years but still the following generations walk with God in faith, because they have a personal relationship with him their heavenly father, guided by

Yeshua and the Holy Spirit who teaches them all they need to know! Does that sound like weakness? Believers are certain of their future, the promise of eternal life in the presence of God! As certain as God's past prophecies and promises which have been fulfilled, therefore future prophecies and promises will also come to pass!

Today, the world has become separated from God, through a subtle introduction of pagan culture, of THEORIES (not facts) based on evolution, humanism and secular philosophies which has infiltrated the Jewish and Christian faith by planting 'wolves' to try to deceive the faithful! In many cases this infiltration has been successful.

Those carnal or secular Jews and Christians who did not have a firm foundation in their faith have weakened and fallen into the trap of deception planted by the infiltrators (the wolves dressed in sheep's clothing that go amongst the sheep). These infiltrators introduced pagan practises such as celebrating the pagan festivals of May Day pole dancing, Easter, Christmas, St Georges Day and Halloween.

Celtic and Egyptian symbols (used in satanism, occult and witchcraft) have increasingly been introduced to society as ornaments or as symbols in synagogues and churches. They are used as jewellery, seen in films and games. More recently, during the past few years, pagan symbols such as the Buddha or African idols have found their way onto people's shelves in their homes and into shops and restaurants throughout Western society. Everywhere you look today there are statues of pagan gods and goddesses in public places.

This subtle take over has been so successful that the majority of people, including Jews and Christians have accepted paganism and occult practices as part of their daily lives and their religion. The infiltration has become so effective that there is now **no division between** the secular and the religious!

It has become a worldwide mix of both paganism and religion which will soon amalgamate into a ONE WORLD RELIGION where it will not so much be a religion as a political force!

There are only a small minority (a remnant) of true believers in the world, compared with the world population. The rest of the believers are being deceived and have merged into the apostate world (without them realising it), either by following a false manmade religion or following the humanistic philosophies. The majority of believers have been saturated and absorbed into the worldly behaviours and attitudes which have negatively affected their lives, becoming part of this world instead of separated from it as commanded by God.

Society today has become so humanistic and pagan that the total environment consists of selfish interest, selfish ambition, super egotism, narcissism and a return to subtle pagan worship.

Gradually over the past 150 years there has been various methods used to <u>exclude God</u> in order to introduce satan as the 'new' god. He has many names, i.e. satan, serpent, dragon, lucifer, antichrist and beast. These last two names apply to these times – the Apostate Age.

God foreknew this would happen and he wrote in his bible, through his faithful servant Paul, who wrote a letter to Timothy a young believer (Paul was an Apostle of Christ Yeshua). Paul wrote according to God's inspired guidance:

"There will be terrible times in the last days. People will be lovers of themselves, lovers of money, boastful, proud, abusive, disobedient to their parents, ungrateful, unholy, without love, unforgiving, slanderous, without self-control, brutal, not lovers of the good, treacherous, rash, conceited, lovers of pleasure rather than lovers of God having a form of godliness but denying its power…. 2 Tim 3:1-5

"They are the kind who worm their way into homes and gain control over weak-willed women, who are loaded down with sins and are swayed by all kinds of evil desires, always learning but never able to acknowledge the truth….These men oppose the truth – men of depraved minds, who, as far as the faith is concerned, are rejected. 2 Tim 3: 6-9.

God also said to his believers, *"Stop trusting in man, who has but a breath in his nostrils. Of what account is he?* Isaiah 2: 22.

The meaning of this is relevant to all mankind not just to believers. God is saying in the verse that He created mankind; therefore man cannot be greater than his Creator! Why follow someone who has limited power and authority rather than a limitless Creator God?

The following chapters will discuss in depth the concept of satan, people being controlled by him to the point of desensitization towards anything relating to God and about other forces at work to confuse and deceive the world, drawing them away from the truth! All will be explained. It will involve a journey back in time, before these last days when apostasy is nearing its peak! Journeying back to the time when people were 'normal. People lived moral lives, cared about each other and had time for each other because there wasn't the same kind of pressures that exists today. It was a time when people knew what was good and what was evil!

We will then journey forward in time when people stopped acknowledging God, accepting evolution and humanism as truth! This will bring us up to date with the Apostate Age which has not yet reached its maximum level until the 7 years Tribulation Period soon to come!

CHAPTER 2

PSYCHOLOGY OF APOSTASY

How can there be a psychology of apostasy?

Psychology is the study of the mind that results in behaviour. The mind is a complex part of the human soul! The brain sends messages to the body according to stimuli from the environment (whether internal or external) and this ultimately determines our behaviour. Internal (body and mind etc) and external (environment and social etc) influences our actions. No scientist, psychologist, or neurologist can explain how the mind works or its function. It is a separate entity from the brain or the body; it is totally independent and unpredictable. For example, you may one day be working on your car and suddenly for no connective reason you may have a thought pop into your head that is totally irrelevant to the current situation and you wonder how the thought came to your mind. You may be having a conversation with someone and at the same time you may have a thought pop into your head that is totally irrelevant to your conversation with that person. You may be walking along the road on a warm Sunday afternoon, and a sudden thought pops into your head about how God created the sun, the moon and the stars, now a humanistic person would react to this thought by consciously changing that thought to something else to avoid feeling 'uncomfortable!' However, a person whose mind is on Godly things would realise this sudden thought is the Holy Spirit teaching or speaking or guiding the believer's way. There is a link between the believer and God's kingdom that through faith has a direct line to Christ. Humanists cannot grasp this concept and dismiss it has Hogwash! Yet thousands of believers of all different cultures, status or age experience this Holy Spirit connection and it is a normal everyday occurrence!

The focus of this book is on human behaviour that brought about the apostasy and the behaviour that will bring about the

Great Tribulation period prophesied for these end times. The human mind is so intricate and can be abused or manipulated in negative ways. This mind control is relevant to the apostate time. There is a silent war which will take over the minds and souls of secular mankind!

Historically, the world has always consisted of two groups, those who believe in God and those who do not, or to put it another way, the religious and secular. However, even those who claimed to disbelief in a creator usually believe in something i.e. mother nature or reincarnation. Or they may worship something such as a statue, money, sex, power. So the world has always been partially apostate! However, in these last days the apostasy becomes more obvious, when every inhabitant of the earth who accepts the 'Mark of the Beast' (described in the book of Revelation), curses God and turns their back on Him! This is to happen in the near future. Rev 16:9

When the whole world turns totally anti-Semitic and anti-Christian (very close to this point already- with worldwide massacres or persecution of Jews and Christians) it then becomes obvious it's an apostate world! Another obvious step is when all nations including Britain and USA have removed their support of Israel and its people. These are specific biblical prophetic signs to all that the 'End is nigh'. Remember years ago when men walked around with a sandwich board stating 'THE END IS NIGH! Well it is now on the doorstep to becoming true!

Looking back to the 1990s the most obvious sign of the apostate age was when people started leaving the churches, when churches became social clubs instead of places that gave praise and glory to the one who blessed them! These churches never opened a bible, yet claim to be believers! Many church buildings were turned into casinos or dwelling places or literally 'social clubs'.

This evidenced the period of change, of the religious sector stepping over the line into secularism!

When churches allowed freemasons and those involved in witchcraft to become part of the congregation, and when believers sought after miracles instead of having faith and preferred to follow the false religion of the Toronto Blessing and Pensacola movement then God's Holy Spirit left those churches! The church building had willingly changed its landlord!

For it to become a total apostate world there must be many forms of influences to develop it. Apostasy cannot form itself; it cannot just happen over-night. A world population of people cannot suddenly become rebellious or become adulterous and turn completely away from God and Creationism. It has to occur over the span of many years and it has to consist of a gradual, subtle input of a variety of influences to change the world's population thought patterns, emotions and behaviour in order to achieve a complete turnaround. It has to be orchestrated over a period of time to prepare the people for the ultimate apostasy of the 'End Time Tribulation Period' whereby apostasy will be at its highest level involving a multitude of people!

To put it into perspective, today's apostasy is a much greater apostasy than the one that existed in the biblical cities Sodom and Gomorrah. Those cities consisted of a small population of apostate people who indulged in every form of wickedness and perversion possible. So much so that God destroyed them swiftly! They were completely annihilated. What was their crime that led to their destruction? They committed terrible acts such as bestiality (sexually perverted acts with animals) they practiced sodomy (homosexual behaviour) they raped and brutalised people within their community. More importantly they practiced paganism which meant they rejected the one true God in favour of idols! This was a small population, now we are talking about worldwide apostasy! How does a whole world suddenly start performing the same acts and worse, as Sodom and Gomorrah?

It all started with the human sin and the desire to be self-sufficient, to live by man's rules rather than by the Creator's rules. The ability to be deceived, misled and manipulated by man is already in the hearts and mind of the individual who was born into a sinful world. The individual has the ability to be the deceiver or the deceived, the manipulator or the manipulated. Throughout the world there are victims and perpetrators, the controlled and the controllers.

Psychology has become hugely popular over the past 10 years. Hitler, a known controller, recognised the value of Psychology as a tool for applying immense suffering, degradation and emotional traumas to the Jews during WW2. This evil dictator and manipulator, used psychology to understand the mind and emotions of Jews as parents, so that he could cause immense psychological pain when he had the children watch their parents being killed or visa versa! He tortured his victims by playing mind games, he would reduce his victims to a human shell after stripping them of every ounce of dignity and emotion, starved, naked and weak, and they were at the point of hopelessness and helplessness. He was determined to destroy their very soul! This man set the trend for future evil that produced the Ethnic Cleansing atrocities – the Mass Genocides that still secretly, and in some cases 'openly,' occur throughout the world.

Hitler has set the precedent through his psychological research and experiments on human behaviour, he had acquired expert knowledge of how the mind works and how to achieve compliance from a large number of victims using just a small number of henchmen.

In 1974 a psychological research experiment took place to find out why Hitler had such an influence on his men that they could impart such evil on the Jews, and not show any mercy or guilt! I have enclosed an extract of the Milgram's experiment written in Wikipedia (a free online encyclopaedia):

The Milgram experiment on obedience to authority figures was a series of <u>social psychology</u> <u>experiments</u> conducted by <u>Yale University</u> <u>psychologist</u> <u>Stanley Milgram</u>, which measured the willingness of study participants to <u>obey</u> an <u>authority figure</u> who instructed them to perform acts that conflicted with their personal <u>conscience</u>. Milgram first described his research in 1963 in an article published in the <u>Journal of Abnormal and Social Psychology</u>,[1] and later discussed his findings in greater depth in his 1974 book, <u>Obedience to Authority: An Experimental View</u>.[2]

The experiments began in July 1961, three months after the start of the trial of German <u>Nazi</u> <u>war criminal</u> <u>Adolf Eichmann</u> in <u>Jerusalem</u>. Milgram devised his psychological study to answer the question: "Was it that Eichmann and his <u>accomplices</u> in <u>the Holocaust</u> had mutual intent, in at least with regard to the goals of the Holocaust?" In other words, "Was there a mutual sense of morality among those involved?" Milgram's testing suggested that it could have been that the millions of accomplices were merely following orders, despite violating their deepest moral beliefs. In Milgram's first set of experiments, 65 percent (26 of 40) of experiment participants administered the experiment's final massive 450-volt shock, though many were very uncomfortable doing so; at some point, every participant paused and questioned the experiment; some said they would refund the money they were paid for participating in the experiment. Throughout the experiment, subjects displayed varying degrees of tension and stress. Subjects were sweating, trembling, stuttering, biting their lips, groaning, digging their fingernails into their skin, and some were even having nervous laughing fits or seizures.[1]

Milgram summarized the experiment in his 1974 article, "The Perils of Obedience", writing:

The legal and philosophic aspects of <u>obedience</u> are of enormous importance, but they say very little about how most people behave in concrete situations. I set up a simple experiment at Yale University to test how much <u>pain</u> an ordinary citizen would inflict on another person simply because he was ordered to by an experimental scientist. Stark authority was pitted against the subjects' [participants'] strongest moral imperatives against hurting others, and, with the subjects' [participants'] ears ringing with the screams of the victims, authority won more often than not. The extreme willingness of adults to go to almost any lengths on the command of an authority constitutes the chief finding of the study and the fact most urgently demanding explanation.

Ordinary people, simply doing their jobs, and without any particular hostility on their part, can become agents in a terrible destructive process. Moreover, even when the destructive effects of their work become patently clear and they are asked to carry out actions incompatible with fundamental standards of morality, relatively few people have the resources needed to resist authority.[6] *Professor Milgram elaborated two theories:*

- *The first is the theory of conformism, based on* <u>*Solomon Asch conformity experiments*</u>*, describing the fundamental relationship between the group of reference and the individual person. A subject, who has neither ability nor expertise to make decisions, especially in a crisis, will leave decision making to the group and its hierarchy. The group is the person's behavioral model.*
- *The second is the agentic state theory, wherein, per Milgram, "the essence of obedience consists in the fact that a person comes to view themselves as the instrument for carrying out another person's wishes, and they therefore no longer see themselves as responsible for their actions. Once this critical shift of viewpoint has occurred in the person, all of the essential features of obedience follow".*[17]

In his book Irrational Exuberance, Yale Finance Professor <u>*Robert Shiller*</u> *argues that other factors might be partially able to explain the Milgram Experiments:*

[People] have learned that when experts tell them something is all right, it probably is, even if it does not seem so. (In fact, it is worth noting that in this case the experimenter was indeed correct: it was all right to continue giving the 'shocks' — even though most of the subjects did not suspect the reason.)[18]

A partial replication of the Milgram experiment was staged by British psychological illusionist <u>Derren Brown</u> and broadcast on Channel 4 in the UK in <u>The Heist</u> (2006).[26]

Another experiment, 'The Stanford Prison Experiment', was performed to examine how people would respond when placed in authoritative positions:

The Stanford prison experiment (or SPE) was a study of the <u>psychological</u> effects of becoming a <u>prisoner</u> or <u>prison guard</u>. The experiment was conducted at <u>Stanford University</u> from August 14 to August 20 1971 by a team of researchers led by psychology professor <u>Philip Zimbardo</u>.[1] *It was funded by the <u>US Office of Naval Research</u>*[2] *and was of interest to both the <u>US Navy</u> and <u>Marine Corps</u> as an investigation into the causes of conflict between military guards and prisoners.*

Twenty-four male students out of seventy-five were selected to take on randomly assigned roles of prisoners and guards in a mock <u>prison</u> situated in the basement of the Stanford psychology building. The participants adapted to their roles well beyond Zimbardo's expectations, as the guards enforced <u>authoritarian</u> measures and ultimately subjected some of the prisoners to <u>psychological torture</u>. Many of the prisoners passively accepted psychological abuse and, at the request of the guards, readily harassed other prisoners who attempted to prevent it. The experiment even affected Zimbardo himself, who, in his role as the <u>superintendent</u>, permitted the abuse to continue. Two of the prisoners quit the experiment early and the entire experiment was abruptly stopped after only six days.

These experiments demonstrate how easily an individual can slip into a different role when in a specific environment, when prompted by an authority figure who provides the right 'triggers' to induce certain behaviour This is how world domination is achieved! This is how individuals throughout the world are manipulated, controlled and programmed to perform certain tasks. It is also how the world has been programmed to turn their backs on a Creator God and His Son Christ Yeshua (Jesus) particularly over the past few centuries.

It was gradual, it was planned, and it was orchestrated to take place over the past 2,000 years, the pursuit to pervert, corrupt and annihilate the Messianic Judaism [Jewish Christendom].

This plan has significantly increased over the past 13 years, since the millennium year 2000, and escalated during the past two years. This means we are getting closer to the end times - to the 7 years of Tribulation! This Tribulation is prophesied by God's prophets in the bible. It is a 7 year period when the world population will be faced with devastation, wars, famine and other plagues. It has been prophesied in God's Word –the Bible, that there will be a world dictator who will be in a position of great authority (not necessarily obvious to the world during the first 3yrs and 6 months). This humanistic dictator will dominate the world!

At the start of the Great Tribulation, which is the second part of the 7 year tribulation, the last 3yrs and 6 months, events will escalate even more rapidly!

Until this point what has been written in this book can be accepted as rational truth because most of what has been mentioned is historical fact, the events actually occurred and evidence is easily obtained by the reader to confirm and rationally assess what has been written in this book. However, now we enter the realm of something that has not yet happened which is the 'seven year tribulation'?

It appears irrational to speak of a seven year Tribulation period, but when you look back on history to the Iron Age, The Reformation and the Enlightenment period, these were all significant periods of change! So a final end time change is not so abnormal or unrealistic.

However, we are about to tread on unprecedented territory and enter the realm of beasts and dragons, now this may appear 'mythical' and you are right to think this, but 'go with it'. Read on as it will all eventually make logical and feasible sense.

The following verses speak of a beast that will be taken over by the second beast who will demand all people worship the first beast and his image! They will be forced to take his mark.

*"**He** (*the beast) ***ordered them** (people of the world) **to set up an image in honour of the beast who was wounded by the sword and yet lived. He was given power to give breath to the image of the first beast, so that it could speak and cause all who refused to worship the image to be killed. He also forced everyone, small and great, rich and poor, free and slave, to receive a mark on his right hand or on his forehead, so that no one could buy or sell unless he had the mark, which is the name of the beast or the number of his name.*" Rev 13:14-18

This verse is found in the last book of the Bible (the New Testament part of the Bible) and the book is called Revelation. The book of Revelation speaks of the End Times and describes the events to take place during the 7 years Tribulation Period. Many people attempt to read this book and either gives up after the first few imagery passages or they read it and totally misinterpret its true meaning. Many scholars suggest it's an allegorical book and they couldn't be more wrong!

It is interesting that in some books of the bible there are mentioned beasts that represent nations; however, in the book of Revelation it has a dual context. It appears to have a dual meaning as it still represents nations but more specifically it refers to two world leaders. Firstly the beast (also known as the antichrist) is then superseded by the devil himself who possesses the first beast's body. In the book of Revelation chapter 13:4, it states, *"**Men worshiped the dragon because he had given authority to the beast, and they also worshiped the beast...**"*

Further in the verse it speaks of the second beast, this beast *had two horns like a lamb* (goats horns) [but appears innocent like a lamb], *and spoke like a dragon.* This suggests the first beast was taken over by the dragon. He appears to be as a lamb but is actually a beast! In simple language this means he will appear to the world to be the Messiah – to save the world by bringing peace, but he is in disguise! He is actually a false messiah bringing destruction!

It is interesting to note that the book is full of ancient and mythical descriptions such as a dragon, a harlot and mystery babylon. These all represent key figures or nations actively in existence during these last days. [Note: the author deliberately avoids using capital letters on any word that opposes God, such as dragon, illuminati and antichrist except at the start of a sentence.]

The verses stating beasts can be a little confusing to understand until you put it into context as an opposite to God and goodness. Christ Yeshua was sent to this world by God to represent Him and to inform the world that through Christ each individual can have a relationship with the Almighty God, not only this but through Christ the Messiah, they can receive eternal life. This means that via Christ, people would receive forgiveness and cleansing from their sinfulness to bring them back into a relationship with their Creator. It was their sin that separated them from God, but once they return to Him, through their faith, they will gain a new life in the Kingdom of God.

Therefore Christ was sent as a savior for the people. He was then crucified, suffered a wound that bleed, as atonement, for Man's sin. This act of love produced the forgiveness (atonement) for sin. After the crucifixion, Christ rose from his tomb, returned to God, where he waits for the time when he returns again (second coming) to this world to claim his inheritance which is the world and its people.

In contrast to this, the evil force produces his own savior that becomes accepted as the messiah! Lucifer the fallen angel (the dragon) from heaven, sends his antichrist to take control of the world, the antichrist suffers a fatal wound, then is replaced by the second beast (second coming). As the previous verse stated both beasts are worshipped. Does the reader see the mirror imagery here between good and evil, God and satan?

In chapter 13 it also mentions *"the beast's number is of his name"*. This number of the beast is 666; ***"This calls for wisdom. If anyone has insight, let him calculate the number of the beast, for it is man's number. His number is 666."***

Man was created on the 6th day therefore it is the number of Man (and humanity), therefore humanism.

The Hebrew letter for the number six is the vav ꜱ. People may be given a mark that consists of or includes the Hebrew letter 'vav ꜱ. Three of these vavs represent the 666 numbers.

Hebrew letters each have a numerical value. The Vav's number is 6. The number of man is 6 therefore humanism is 666 and also represents the unholy trinity of the dragon, antichrist and false prophet. More will be explained on this later, [note: it is customary to use capital letters for anything pertaining to God].

The beast has a double meaning. It is the name of the antichrist, the lawless one, prophesied to become the world leader during the 7 years Tribulation, but it also represents a nation, made up of many nations, more powerful than ever before in history! 2 Thess 2.

*"I saw a beast (*Leviathan*) coming out of the sea (*out of the people*) He had ten horns (10 Kings) and 7 heads with ten crowns on his horns and on each head a blasphemous name. .....The dragon gave the beast his power and his throne and his authority. One of the heads of the beast seemed to have had a fatal wound, but the fatal wound had been healed. The whole world was astonished and followed the beast. Men worshipped the dragon because he had given authority to the beast..."* Revelation 13

To explain the above verse; this beast was given authority by the dragon to take authority over the world. He became the authority over all the nations. The nations were controlled by the beast, therefore became possessions of the beast, duplicating his power in the same way that hitler and his henchman controlled the nations in WW2 by propaganda, mind control and authoritarian leadership. The nations were so much under hitler's spell that the people of these nations ignored the evil going on in concentration camps. And even after the war had come to an end, nations still persecuted the Jewish people and refused them entry into their homeland, Israel, which was given to them by God.

Also in the same chapter a second beast came out of the earth, called Behemoth, this beast literally possesses the first beast, taking over his body! This second beast is lucifer himself who from that point reveals himself to the world, publicly announcing himself as the new god! Lucifer attempts to imitate everything that God, Christ Yeshua and the Holy Spirit does but with an upside down (or mirrored version), that never equals God's power and sovereignty!

This 'possession' of the first beast simulates [but as a mirror image] the triune of God the Creator, Christ his son and Holy Spirit, the latter performs miracles. These three are part of one spirit –the Creator God.

Lucifer therefore 'simulates' this binding together of all three Godheads but in an unholy humanistic way, by possessing the body of the antichrist and through this act creates his own 'unholy' triune system, with him (the dragon) as the new god, his son the antichrist (first Beast who died and was resurrected) and the false prophet who performs great miracles.

This unholy triune is the power involved with orchestrating the great apostasy which seals 'the possessed people of this world' by receiving the mark of the beast! What do I mean by 'possessed people? Well many people have chosen evil and these have become the property of this unholy triune. We have seen many people who have performed the most evil acts and we have wandered how they could be so evil – well the answer is now clear- they are possessed by satan's demonic beings! More about this later.

The mark of the beast is considered to be a microchip that is inserted into the body. The first stage of its introduction into society was piloted as a Smart Card. Bank cards, employee ID cards, the new library cards, passwords, driving licence and many more were smart cards. They hold all your personal details which confirm your identity. The second stage is currently activated as a more advanced Smart Card that holds your bank details so you may purchase items without using cash and omits the need to sign for goods or services purchased and eliminates long queues. The trial is currently used on selected people such as school children and business people. A subtle form of this smart card has been produced by certain banks i.e.

HSBC recently issued a cashless card which allows the purchase of items that would normally require the customer to use small change such as coins. Examples of this are a cup of coffee at a vending machine or take away café, or purchasing a newspaper from the corner shop. If it has the new system installed the shop would just issue you with the goods or you could pick them up yourself and walk out the door without queuing or signing as the system will pick up your details if you wave the card in front of the detector. In some places the latter is not even necessary; customers have opted for an implant whereby when they enter a shop and purchase something it is automatically charged to the person. This is the third stage, the implanting of a microchip!

The chip contains all of the individual's personal data and there are plans to use it (currently on trial in USA on schoolchildren and employees) to hold bank details so that no one can buy or sell without a chip to identify them. This chip is part of the process of taking the mark but there is to be a visible mark. It would be on the same basis as the yellow star Jews were forced to wear during WW2 that led up to the Holocaust period where they were singled out for destruction. The star was to inform everyone that they were Jews and therefore no one was permitted to sell to the Jews or buy from them! They were separated, ostracized and left to die of starvation and sickness, in the ghettos!

However, the beast's mark will be opposite to the yellow star, that is, instead of exposing the Jew and the Christian that way, satan uses a method that by 'default' exposes all those who are righteous and who refuse to follow the dragon or accept him as their new god. There will be no need to mark them as it will become obvious who they are – they will stand out from the rest of the population because of their refusal to comply.

There will be only a remnant that stay loyal to God and Yeshua, these believers will already be marked with the seal of ownership and protection by their Creator God. Therefore satan cannot claim ownership on them! During this time it will not be difficult to divide the peoples into two groups, the compliant and the non- compliant.

The yellow star was the outward sign obvious to all peoples that the Jews were different to the rest of society. However, they also had a mark that singled them out! They had a tattooed number on their arm that identified who they were.

What happened to the Jews was a forerunner of future events that would happen to the inhabitants of this world! This time not only the Jews will be enslaved and persecuted or controlled, it will apply to every human being on this earth! Even those who take the beast's mark will be enslaved, controlled and eventually totally destroyed!

[None are exempt from destruction accept the remnant sealed by God! The remnant are thought to be the 144,000 Jews mentioned in Rev 7. Yes, they are the Post Rapture remnant, but there is also a remnant of 'born again' believers prior to the Rapture whether these remnants are the same believers is not clear. The Rapture is when Yeshua returns quietly to collect the remnant of loyal believers and takes them to the heavens. The 144,000 are said to remain after the rapture to witness to the world. However, later the 144,000 who were sealed by God are at the end taken and seen with Yeshua on Mount Zion in Jerusalem]

What happened to the Jews was a sign to the rest of the world that they would be next in line to become victims of evil!

Now it's the world's turn to be marked and singled out for enslavery! It has already started; people are enslaved in many ways, financially, through materialism, sexual addiction, bondage to immorality and many other forms of slavery.

Through the witness of the events, that took place during the war against the Jews, we have a real testimony of the events (only there's worse to come) that will take place during the 7 years Tribulation. The start of this period will see a change in the atmosphere; it will darken and grow cold because of the lack of the holy presence of God, and his people! There will be an overwhelming presence of evil instead!

Christ Yeshua speaks of the End Times. He says in Matthew 23:10 *"At that time many will turn away from the faith and will betray and hate each other, and many false prophets will appear and deceive many people. Because of the increase of wickedness, the love of most will grow cold, but he who stands firm to the end will be saved. And this gospel of the kingdom will be preached in the whole world as a testimony to all nations, and then the end will come."*

He also says in verse 21, *"For then there will be great distress, unequalled from the beginning of the world until now-and never to be equalled again. If those days had not been cut short, no one would have survived, but for the sake of the elect those days will be shortened."*

The last days will be the worst ever in the whole history of the world! It will be worse than the wickedness and destruction of Sodom and Gomorrah and the first world through flooding. It will be worse than the Second World War (WW2) and the Holocaust, or ethnic cleansing or the genocides taking place today!

To return to the mark of the beast, the microchip is only part of the process, the initial part that allows the beast access to each individual's personal details and therefore control over his/her finances etc, but more importantly he will have direct control over your MIND, BODY and SOUL!.

The second part of the mark is the most crucial part and that is the voluntary part whereby the inhabitant chooses to willingly worship satan. Some may need a bit of persuasion some later may submit to the beast through brute force. But the key point is that they will reject or deny allegiance to Christ Yeshua and God! This is done as an open confession followed by a visible mark on the hand or forehead. Many people have already done this part willingly and therefore they will actively respond to the microchip! Many people who have automatically turned their backs on God will automatically be responsive to receiving the microchip and probably already have the mark! These marks may simulate the Jewish tattooed numbers or some other form of tattoo!

The author believes that the **visible** sign, the visible mark will be a tattoo! But this tattoo would be the reverse of that which identified the Jews. The number tattoo was forced on them as a means of identifying and separating them from the rest of the population. Instead this 'End Time' Mark of the beast – the tattoo would be a mark of ownership of all those **non-Jews** and **non-Christians** that belong to satan and who have become his property. In other words the tattoo will suggest loyalty to satan. The tattoo will be a way of visibly seeing who worships satan and who doesn't. But also distinguishes them from those without the tattooed skin! How easy it would be to detect the minority without tattoos when the majority are covered in them! [Because the church has chosen to reject God's Torah Law they failed to know of the Law that stays *"Do not put tattoo marks on yourselves"*. Leviticus 19:28.

The tattoo would be a mark placed on every inhabitant, those who choose it freely or forced on them, (the indecisive non-believers) and it represents those who are (unknowingly) enslaved, to follow and worship satan! The price of this will be the loss of the person's soul and eternal death in hell! During this time there will be a massive worldwide delusion where all inhabitants will believe the great lie! [More about this in my book next year entitled 'Worldwide Delusion'].

"All inhabitants of the earth will worship the beast – all whose names have <u>not</u> been written in the book of life belonging to the lamb that was slain from the creation of the world." Revelation 13:8

What the reader needs to understand before we go any further is that throughout history, the Almighty God has always ALLOWED punishment of sinful behaviour! People have the choice to behave righteously or wickedly, the latter would be vulnerable to punishment. When you realise that the whole world has become 'adulterous, (follow other gods), rebellious, (opposing God and anything good, preferring evil) and turning their backs –having fallen away from God, you realise that the world is obviously, as the historical pattern suggests, going to face the same judgement and punishment.

God always provides opportunities for people to return to him by showing signs and forewarnings through prophecy and other methods prior to an event. God has provided evidence throughout his word, through bible prophecy, which has been introduced in this book. He has forewarned the world of the pending Tribulation and the one world leadership of the dragon, described as the lawless one!

It is for the person to decide whether to accept these warnings and do something about it or just ignore it!

God sends out or allows evil leaders of nations to bring about his Will. Such as the time when God's people 'Israel' rebelled against God so he sent the Babylonian's to invade Israel, to take them captive, (Before Christ (BC). Later the Roman invasion on Jerusalem (AC (after Christ) Era) took place for the same reason. So it is not irrational or unreasonable to expect the same thing to happen to the world today, a world that is so corrupt that poverty levels increase daily along with millions of starving and sick within their own ghettos! People suffer while the powerful elite look on from their luxurious dwellings. This prosperity is short lived in these end times and then its eternal damnation!

God allows his enemies (nations and individual groups) to punish his own people, who have betrayed him; however, those who have turned against God's people do not go <u>unpunished</u>! These perpetrators will be cursed!

God says to his people Israel *"May those who bless you be blessed and those who curse you be cursed!"* Numbers 24:9

God uses nations to bring about his retribution but he also judges the nations regarding <u>their</u> behaviour <u>towards Israel</u>. Many nations have gone beyond retribution and desire the complete annihilation of the Jews and the State of Israel. This was not part of God's plan and therefore the enemy nations will be cursed! We are seeing this taking place during (2013) when the Arab nations are being massacred by their own people! They are also killing Christian Muslims and therefore there will be retribution on these nations for the shed blood of these saints!

God allows his own people to be punished by allowing enemies to perpetrate the punishment. This is done for many reasons, one of which is so that God can gloriously intervene, which will demonstrate to the world that He exists and is in control of events. This will happen when Yeshua intervenes during the attempt of the enemy nations to take over Jerusalem, God's beloved city!

The difference between punishing God's people and punishing those selected to instil the punishment (who are not God's people) is the former are reminded through the punishment or trial that God is still available to return too! He allows these trials so his people will TURN BACK TO HIM!

Whereas, the punishment of those who are sent to punish God's people depends entirely on whether they confess and repent from their sin towards Israel and God's people, that is, if the country goes beyond the Lord's command to punish His people i.e. kill them instead of just punishing them, then they are not given the option to turn to God. They are condemned to eternal punishment!

This all seems very complicated, but if you use the analogy of a loving father, whose children are continuously rebelling against him, bringing him to shame amongst his people, then he would be an uncaring and foolish father to do nothing about it. The bible story of the prodigal son is a good illustration of this principle, Luke 15:11-32.

The prodigal son, (a simile of rebellious Israelites, Jews and Christians) chose to leave his father, after taking gifts from him (inheritance money, etc) to go into the world to find his own way. This meant the son chose not to follow his father's plan for his future, but rather to pursue his own destiny in the world.

The father allowed his son to go. The father loved his son and patiently waited for his return.

The son was away for many years and during this time he had many bad experiences, he eventually lost all of his money, suffered severe poverty and hunger and loneliness all of his own making because he chose to leave the safety and security of his father. The son thought the world and mankind could provide better than his father but he discovered that was not so! Instead the world stole from him, cheated and deceived him, he lost everything – he was broken!

Now his father could have intervened, he could have sent someone to search out his son and to report back on his status or even to rescue him. But he didn't, he just waited patiently for his son's return which he knew would come because the world is corrupt and mankind has nothing to offer in comparison to his father's land of plenty! He allowed his son to go through these trials and experiences to discover for himself about the world, and about the differences between good and evil. See Luke 15:11-32

From this story we can see that when we leave the safety of our father's protection we become vulnerable to world events. In the case of Israel when they are in rebellion they are vulnerable to attack from the enemy, however, God allows the enemy free reign up to a point! Then He intervenes!

We can only appreciate the good things and God's blessings once we have experienced the bad things.

The prodigal son eventually reached 'rock bottom' in his life, lost everything, his clothes were rags, his body thin and he was weak, so he returned to his father willingly, having lost all interest in a world that had let him down! His father welcomed him and he received great blessings because he fell at his father's feet and asked for forgiveness for the things he had done!

God is this father who allows his rebellious children to choose their destiny either the world or his heavenly kingdom.

As an example, in the Old Testament part of the Bible, God's people the Israelites (Jews) became rebellious and sinful against God and His commandments; this meant they broke their part of the covenant between them and God. As a result God sent the Babylonians to seize the Israelites removing them from Israel. They became captives of the Babylonians for many years.

However, eventually God chose Ezra a priestly man of God, to lead the people back to the Holy Land, to return to Israel, to rebuild the temple in Jerusalem. He encouraged the people to repent of their sins and return to God! But more importantly their capture and removal from their beloved land Israel was a punishment that brought them back to repentance! Again in Isaiah 8 Assyria, was chosen to be the Lord God's instrument to punish Israel, because of their sin of idolatry and occult practices.

In the end times God turns the refining and punishing period of his people into a time of revenge on their oppressors! God is now turning the world upside down, figuratively speaking. It is now the time of judgement of the nations for their sin against Israel and his people (Jews and 'Born Again Believers). He writes in His word in Jeremiah 50:33,

"This is what the Lord Almighty says:
'The people of Israel are oppressed, and the people of Judah as well. All their captors hold them fast, refusing to let them go. Yet their Redeemer is strong; the Lord Almighty is his name. He will vigorously defend their cause so that he may bring rest to their land, but unrest to those who live in Babylon....' "

This Babylon refers to the last days (as well as the previous ancient Babylonian oppression). This modern second Babylon deceives Israel into a false peace – a seven year peace which lasts only three and a half years. Then the new Babylonians try to 'drive the nation of Israel into the sea'. The sea usually represents the population of peoples; therefore to drive those into the sea also mean to drive them to dispersion amongst the nations as before with the diaspora that took place during the Roman invasion of Israel.

This Babylon is the one mentioned in the book of Revelation and is the name that represents the era of evil – Babylon is full of sin, corruption and evil. It is the preferred place of the Beast!

So we can see from all of this that the oppression of God's people had a purpose. There are many reasons and many biblical references (particularly Isaiah) to explain this.

In summary: God allowed oppressors to oppress His people for correction and refining purposes and to encourage His beloved to return to him. Unlike the devil (satan/lucifer), whose goal it is to enslave and destroy.

God does not force people to do anything, it must always be their decision, to return to Him, all he does is provide situations to encourage the person to make a decision by becoming aware of good and evil. This is the true love of a father to his children.

However, the oppressors assumed incorrectly, that because they were allowed to inflict punishment on God's people that they were in God's favour and it was then assumed that the Israelites (Jewish people) were therefore not in God's favour. The oppressors became proud and pursued God's people but instead of being oppressors they became assassins, murderers and destroyers!

Therefore God in these end times does a complete turnaround and He will pour out his blessings on His people but the oppressors will receive God's vengeance!

This is the promise from God for these End Times.

"The oppressor will come to an end, and destruction will cease; the aggressor will vanish from the land. In love a throne will be established; in faithfulness a man will sit on it – one from the house of David – one who in judging seeks justice and speeds the cause of righteousness." Isaiah 16:4.

This verse refers to the land of Israel whereby in the last days, Christ Yeshua will sit on the throne as Judge! Yeshua is referred to as a man because that is how he came the first time, born as a human child of the line of David, and came as the savior! However, he is part of God; therefore he has the power and authority of God!

Unfortunately, many Jewish people then and now have rejected Yeshua as the coming Messiah and particularly because of this verse are expecting a human messiah to suddenly arise. It is because of this misinterpretation of scripture and of God's prophecy that many Jews will believe the antichrist to be their messiah!

Also as ancient Babylonia was chosen to be God's instrument to oppress His people as a punishment for their idolatry, so it will happen again in these last days. Babylon will rise again but this time greater than ever before and will consist of many nations who will come against Israel! It is Israel who must come together as a people and return to their God (Hashem or YHWH –the names preferred to be used for God) before this happens. The majority of Jewish people are secular and it is the secular who will cause the judgement on the nation.

How is this relevant to non- Jews? Well those enemy nations will include your nation, as in the last days ALL the nations will come against Israel! Therefore all the nations will come under the wrath of God!

The same thing is replicated as above, in these last days, satan is allowed, given authority (by God) to punish God's people who have fallen away from him, so that they may return to him. However, satan goes after God's people and destroys many of them instead! I have simplified this so that any non-biblical scholarly readers may appreciate the events written. If you are not familiar with the bible this reading can be very heavy and fill the reader with many questions, one of which has already been partially explained: Why would God allow the beast, satan to destroy His people?

The answer of course is that God never intended His people to be destroyed but they chose their own destiny! They chose to ignore God's warnings and His call back to Him and His gift of eternal life and forgiveness through His son Christ Yeshua! Yeshua was sent for the Jews AND THE GENTILES so they may receive forgiveness and salvation.

No one can enter heaven or God's presence, unless they are purified from sin. God sent Yeshua to provide this purification. Through Christ Yeshua's death on the cross, we are able to go through him (spiritually) and become cleansed of sin, hence purified! This also explains why Christ will be the judge of all those not written in the book of life – those who chose to reject God! Christ as a mediator is able to receive the sinful and impure before him on judgement day, whereas God cannot receive any impure object or person before him – he is too holy!

[Reference to the book of life can be found in the book of Revelation 20:11-15.]

During the Great Tribulation, the time of receiving that salvation and purification will have changed. Up until the point of the rapture when all the believers will be taken out of this world, the Holy Spirit will also be removed, along with all righteousness. It will be a time of darkness and evil! Some of those left behind in this dark world, will realise their error in rejecting God's gift of salvation through Christ, and go down on their knees, seeking his forgiveness! They will make a decision to follow Christ and reject satan and they will receive the seal of ownership placed on them by God. However, their purification will come through their endurance of the hardships during the 7 years tribulation period and this will be their purification process; *Those who endure until the end! They will receive the crown of righteousness!* During this purification process they will be made ready, holy and acceptable to enter the presence of the Sovereign Lord God, when they enter His kingdom!

Everyone has to be refined, purified through life experiences and trials so that they fully understand the difference between good and evil; this is inevitable to come to this phase before they enter the kingdom of God. Individual believers do not have to do anything to achieve this wisdom, holiness or cleansing as God provides this transformation himself through his teaching and guidance and the person's life experiences, as well as the trials of life!. The Holy Spirit also guides and teaches them what they need to know. You cannot enter the kingdom of heaven by works and it is only possible to enter the Kingdom of Heaven through Christ Yeshua. These trials and training sessions of good and evil cannot be self-made through works or doing good deeds. Why is it so important to understand the principles of Good and evil? It is the knowledge, through experience, of these two concepts that enables you to become holy but also provides you with a firm foundation so you last the course. When you fully understand that evil exists and you experience or witness it, then and only then can you fully appreciate the opposite to evil. You then appreciate God's holiness and goodness and His Kingdom. It is this knowledge that opens the door to wisdom so you do not repeat the same mistake Adam and Eve made!

Now back to the mark of the beast. As mentioned above it is becoming a reality, it has already been piloted for many years. As mentioned earlier many people will accept the microchip to be planted in the hand or forehead. This is because it will be presented to the people as a benefit to mankind, probably for health reasons i.e. so that in emergencies the person's personal details can be detected via the microchip using a microchip reader, or the latest is that a missing child may be detected and tracked down using the child's implanted microchip, or your elderly parent suffering from Alzheimer's Disease may be found when they reach the 'wandering stage.

American news reported recently that the microchip (considered to be the means of inserting the mark on the right hand or forehead) is now ready and the date was originally set for March 2013 but postponed until 2017. Although people are volunteering to have the chip implanted during 2013, especially in USA and mostly employees of associated research and business organisations.

Many people in America have already willingly offered themselves as guinea pigs and taken the chip in their hand. People are being made ready to accept willingly this microchip by breaking down the NHS service and centralising the emergency services so that people do not receive the support or a service they need during an emergency, people then demand a solution which is provided by introducing the microchip as a means of improving the emergency system. This is how manipulation and mind control works 'en mass'. The focus is on those services that are important to people, including basic needs such as the provision of finances to provide the basic needs and security needed during a crisis.

Take for example if satan wants to make the police more powerful than the 'bobby on the beat' he must change the system so that the police officer is isolated from the community and retrained to a 'closed rank' system,. He would then put him in a patrol car and at the same time increase the pressure to perform administrative tasks to certain deadlines, and he would also reduce police authority over the criminal. This causes officers to be angry, frustrated and stressed and leads to aggression and tougher policing which we see today! Later satan would centralise all the towns and cities police stations so that it takes an unreasonable time to respond to an emergency, this offers a two –pronged advantage as crime increases, the public feel vulnerable and therefore welcome new solutions to these problems. Hence the microchip solution! So when a solution to these problems is offered to the public and police officers, it is accepted willingly!

The solution to the problems of high crime rates and not enough police force to deal with the amount of crime, will be introduced to the microchip as a solution, the police would then be programmed as 'enforcers' and finally involved in 'martial law' including a Nazi style (brutal) police force that will use weaponry against those who refuse the mark of the beast.

This change from a friendly policeman available to help the community, has gradually been conditioned, through specific training, work pressure, and traumatic situations (as the world has become more violent and aggressive) to become an aggressor and a controlling force. This is seen when peaceful demonstrations have been turned into riots, usually by police acting as catalysts of violence because of their attitude and bias reaction towards protestors!

To return to the mark of the beast, during the last 5 years or so, there has been a craze throughout western society, affecting young and old alike. This craze is visible everywhere. The craze is to have as many tattoos as possible all over the body and many of the tattoos are figures of serpents, dragons, skulls, and occult symbols!

Already people have been subconsciously manipulated to have these tattoos, people who you would never imagine, people who are timid, and appear to be morally upright, even older women in their eighties! It is as though they have taken leave of their senses!

Where the Jewish people during WW2 were forced to have a number tattooed on their arm as a means of identifying who they were, all peoples today are willingly tattooing themselves that also distinguishes who they are! These people show themselves to be worldly and humanistic, therefore already under the influence of satan! They may not be aware of this fact but their actions determine where their heart and mind is – it is not centred on Godliness –therefore, must be humanistic!

Those who have tattoos are already being accepted by many of the population as the norm! They stereotype themselves willingly and identify themselves as willing subjects to follow satan! Many of those with serpent or dragon tattoos are involved with the occult one way or another and often involved in all sorts of violent crimes, drugs, gang warfare. They are ideal candidates!

These tattoos are an initial identification of the type of person who will easily accept the rest of the initiation process. These tattooed individuals will be the easy prey selected to be an example to the world (as admired individuals because of their body art), on humanism and submission to the beast's demands for compliance. These people will be, and already prove, they are easily manipulated and mind controlled to be compliant with the emergence of the apostate age!

The division between believers and humanists has widened so that believers are exposed! Soon it will be so obvious who is a believer by their appearance and attitude, compared with the lawless, unruly, blasphemous and marked individuals.

Those singled out by the beast for destruction i.e. Jews and Christians, are not given a yellow star to wear, or a number tattoo, the rest of the unbelieving inhabitants are given the yellow star in the form of a microchip and numerous tattoos with a choice of designs – as the mark! The people willingly fall into the trap and by doing so are on the brink of losing their souls! The next stage is to evidence allegiance to the devil and worship of the beast. Many of society's subjects with tattoos have already completed this stage. Think how easy it would be to spot those with clean, unmarked skin!

People who cover their skin with dark tattoos have deliberately made their bodies look unclean; the ink gives the impression of dirtiness. Some tattoo designs make the skin look almost reptilian, which is scaly, dirty and dark. The serpent, the devil and the dragon all give an image of reptilian creatures with scaly skin!

God gives what the world want, they choose not to acknowledge God therefore they are allowed to pursue their goal.

God foreknew what the dragon had planned and wrote in advance to warn his people, informing his people through the scriptures of the events to occur. Now most non-believing readers would ask the question, why did God allow this to happen? Why did he not stop it? The answer is because good can come out of bad, many people may turn to God and be saved, when they realise how evil the beast is!

Many people with tattoos have already 'woken up' before it is too late and realised they were on the road to destruction. They have become born anew into God's Kingdom of safety. And they always have their tattoos removed when they realise it was wrong. There will come a time soon when this rebirth and removal of tattoos will not be able to occur.

There will come a time when it will be too late to change or seek God, as he removes his Grace from a humanistic world of evil!

God is a **Just** God and where evil dwells God must punish those involved. These end times, particularly the last seven years, are times of worldwide judgement for sin and rebellion on those who have chosen not to accept God and Christ, even after many warnings, signs and prophecies, they chose to rebel! Mankind has rebelled for thousands of years and soon it is to end!

God's people (believers – Jews and Christians) will have left in the rapture whether this is before or midway during the 7 year tribulation (and some say believers may have to go through the whole Tribulation –this may be so for some people who may be lukewarm believers- who need to go through trials to determine their loyalty). At this point those left on earth are those who have chosen allegiance to the devil and those who have managed to avoid the mark of the beast but also haven't made a decision to follow Christ! They are still sitting on the fence unable to make a decision. It is the latter who become the 'Tribulation believers' because they refuse to worship the beast or take his mark! Instead, they eventually accept Yeshua and receive eternal life.

"Men worshiped the dragon because he had given authority to the beast, and they also worshiped the beast and asked, 'who is like the beast? Who can make war against him?'

The beast was given a mouth to utter proud words and blasphemies and to exercise his authority for forty-two months. ... He was given power to make war....and he was given authority over every tribe, people, language and nation. All inhabitants of the earth will worship the beast...

This beast is replaced by a second beast –more powerful than the first. *He deceived the inhabitants of the earth and ordered them to set up an image in honour of the beast (1ˢᵗ beast) that was (fatally) wounded by the sword and yet lived. He was given power to give breath to the image of the first beast, so that it could speak and cause all who refused to worship the image to be killed. He also forced everyone, small and great, rich and poor, free and slave, to receive a mark on his right hand or on his forehead, so that no one could buy or sell unless he had the mark, which is the name of the beast or the number of his name."* Revelation 13.

Everything that has happened and is happening now in the world is linked to the above events and the end of the world.

Now it is becoming clearer as to why there is a great apostasy already in existence and why it will become worse as time moves on. We also can see who is responsible for this apostasy and why. Lucifer is planning his take over- he must have the people under his control and ready to serve him before he can take over as ruler and king of this world. The majority of the population must want him in power, and must willingly support him. All of this is the beginning; this is satan's own form of the 'sifting of the wheat and chaff'; sifting out the loyal and disloyal subjects.

Later after the first three and half years have passed lucifer will reveal his TRUE identity and demand loyalty to him and this act of submission is finalised by all willing subjects taking the mark and unwilling subjects being <u>forced</u> to take the mark or die! This is a reality in Syria (Sept 2013) when Christians have been beheaded after they refused to convert to Sharia rule!

Although the above sounds extreme and unbelievable it is nevertheless very real and happening now! The evidence supplied in this book will prove without a doubt the existence of the beasts, the dragon and the plot to introduce a totalitarian world leader! The apostasy is fact and it was instigated as part of the worldwide plan to introduce the totalitarian world leader.

The Great Apostasy consists of the covert (secret underground work) planning to take control by performing worldwide pilot studies, research and practice for the Great End Time Event!

Lucifer knows he has a limited time, therefore he has rapidly moved forward his plans, hence the rapid changes taking place in people. Crime such as rape, murder, pornography and war crimes have escalated during the past couple of years. All this is a hint to the world that something is going on! Why is lucifer rapidly moving forward? Because he knows God is real and Yeshua is returning to claim the throne of the world! Therefore lucifer has to claim as many people as he can to form his great army against Christ Yeshua! However, have no fear for he is doomed!

These events were forewarned by God in his Bible many centuries ago, so far everything he prophesied has taken place and in the process of taking place therefore, logically it can be said that these end time events will also come true!

The previous bible verse from the book of Revelation appears extreme because it speaks of beasts and a dragon but that is because we have only ever known about mankind, in human form. We were not born into a world of dinosaurs, giants or dragons; however that does not mean they do not exist!

In the heavens God dwells, and with him are angels, these do not all have human forms, therefore if we saw them we would find it frightening. Anything not of human form would frighten us. Horror films are evidence of this. Therefore, it is not so incredible that there will be a dragon or a beast ruling the world in the future. You only have to look at a lizard or a chameleon to see that these dragon-like creatures exist!

However, the bible is God's Word and therefore spoken from His perspective not ours. God describes two beasts, one from the sea and the other from the earth.

This is significant, one beast comes from normal birth lineage (from the sea meaning the people and the nations) as a human, yet he would originate from God's heaven (as a fallen angel). The second beast comes from the earth. He is a resurrection or possesses the body of the first beast that died of a fatal wound and therefore resurrected. This is to simulate Christ's death on the cross and resurrection in order to deceive the people!

The word used to describe these two dictators (as beasts) will become clearer later. But the term 'beasts' is not imagery; it is a true description from God's perspective! The beasts of the bible are always described as animals yet are nations, such as the bear represents Russia. So it is the beasts that represent specific powerful leaderships that control all nations. It is by this description of such power and control that makes these beasts unique to any other previous power that has attempted to take control of the nations, i.e. the Greek and Roman Empires.

For now it is necessary to return to the world we know – or knew!

There are many factors which have turned our world upside down from a 'normal' existence to the world of chaos, wickedness and evil, beyond anything ever experienced before in history!

We have always had wars, there has always been poverty, sickness, and disasters, during our lifetimes, however, there was also a moral code that was followed – In Christian communities it was The Ten Commandments, in Jewish communities it was The Torah Law and in secular communities they also had their own moral code - an awareness that there was a 'right' and 'wrong' behaviour!

Seculars had a code of practice. An example of this is prior to the 1990s. Criminals had their own ethical/moral code whereby they would never commit crime within their own community; they would never harm children or women! Most criminals would have a rule never to maim or harm an innocent person. Even gangs had their own moral standards such as these.

However, today these standards do not exist as we see children abused, used for pornography, sold into slavery or prostitution! We hear stories of children being used as frontline shields in war, trained as drug dealers or thieves and some are bred purely as a future sacrifice for satanic rites. Children are targeted at an early age to become rebellious against their parents, to cause chaos within their community and to accept that there is no hope for a future; therefore the only way to deal with it psychologically is to immerse themselves in sin, drugs and drink to drown out the pain of life!

Many people are involving themselves in a life of sexual promiscuity/depravity, drug taking, binge drinking, game addiction, music and materialism, using these as their comforters until the inevitable day of death! That is the hope young people of today have been given –to live selfish lives of self- indulgence until the end! Their lives are full of hopelessness!

How did the world get to this?

It was a gradual process of subtle 'subliminal' mind control, manipulation, trapping and power/authoritarian control instigated within the education system, government restrictions on parenting and criminalising ordinary law abiding people.

In order to understand the psychology of Apostasy we need to take a journey back in time.

For those who were born before the 1990's it would be easy for you to recall the memories of how life used to be then and how much has changed in the western countries.

Just in 20 years, society has been encouraged to accept the following:

- to abort unborn babies
- to artificially produce babies, (ironic isn't it, destroy and then produce babies)
- clone animals
- accept homosexual behaviour as the norm
- encourage gay marriages
- encourage heterosexual couples to co-habit or have a humanistic (civil) wedding
- give the criminals and murderers rights while the victims suffer
- victims of crime are criminalised when they protect themselves while the perpetrator is granted compensation.

In the past when a person had a problem there was always an organisation (not regulated by strict unrealistic rules) to provide help and support. People displayed compassion and concern, unlike today when robotic people look straight through you, quoting rules as to why they cannot help!

Readers can probably remember when a community was supportive of its people, neighbours were close to one another, watching out for those in need, helping neighbours during illness or difficulties and sharing food with the poor, this still happens within the older generation today and certain charitable organisations. Kindness is rare today, compassion and concern is very superficial or done only when seen by others.

Almost every household grew their own fruit and shared the fruit with others, now the fruit is left to rot! Many fruit trees were chopped down by local governments which deprived people of free fruit.

Today, fruit is controlled by retailers; large supermarkets fill the shelves with goods they want us to buy. Much of it is genetically modified foods and foods that have been deliberately infused with additives, colourings, or flavourings to make them more appealing, they ignore all warnings of the potential harm it may cause to our bodies! In some cases the additive has been introduced into foods, deliberately, as part of the mind controlling plan to bring people under the directive of the future world leader.

Allergies, illnesses, food intolerance, and psychological disorders have increased throughout the western population because of the ingredients put into food, to yield higher financial profits for the business and all done legally!

A great deal of research has been done on the diets of autistic or disabled children and those suffering other behavioural or physical diseases. It has been found that many foods cause the symptoms and when the child's diet has been controlled, symptoms disappear.

There are plans to control our food supply. The time will come soon when we have to grow and eat what the manufacturers dictate – it is not only about supply and demand and the need to deal with the worldwide famine we already have, and soon to become worse, which God prophesied would happen. This GM food is the excuse used to instigate the next stage of control.

Genetically modified foods are soon to become our only food source, a large New World Order (N.W.O.) seed company Monsanto is to take control of the seed production worldwide.

They have been given the power to prevent farmers from growing their own crops from non GM seeds. These farmers will soon come under the control of the EU regulations. The excuse [there is always a publicly acceptable reason given for any action, but the true underlying reason is never exposed] is to feed the current starving populations.

What you are not being told is that there is to be a world famine which was prophesied in the bible, to occur in these last days. This world famine will affect all nations including the wealthy ones. Satan tries to prevent God's prophecies from taking place by introducing solutions, in this case GM foods. But he also as a dual motive which is to affect humans health and mental attitude. For example, what you are not told is that GM wheat crops are bad for your health and contain a substance called Gliadin, which acts as an Opiate. This Opiate is a means of controlling the mind, through drug addiction. Constant intake of Gliadin, **or to put it in perspective; to eat regular amounts of bread, pasta, biscuits, cake etc** ensures a constant mind controlling addiction that is difficult to give up. Especially when the victim is unaware of the addiction.

People are not willing to accept they have an addiction and therefore would continue under the power of Opiates, triggered by Gliadin. There are other harmful additives in wheat.

Below is an extract written by Dr Davis. There are many other websites that offer further information – look it up for yourself. The subject of Monsanto and GM food has been discussed on TV news channels, in the newspaper and Journals.

The Gliadin Effect. Posted on <u>January 14, 2012</u>

By <u>Dr. Davis</u>

Gliadin is a protein found within wheat gluten. It is, from a cold scientific viewpoint, a fascinating issue, a protean protein capable of incredibly varied biologic effects in humans. Among the things we know about gliadin:–Gliadin is the most abundant protein in wheat, contained within gluten polymers. –Gliadin of 2012 is different from the gliadin of, say, 1960, by several amino acids, part of the genetic transformation of wheat introduced to increase yield-per-acre.
–Gliadin is degraded to a collection of polypeptides called *exorphins* **in the gastrointestinal tract. Exorphins cross the blood-brain barrier and bind to opiate-receptors to induce appetite, as well as behavioral changes, such as behavioral outbursts and inattention in children with ADHD and autism, hearing voices and social detachment in schizophrenics, and the mania of bipolar illness.**
–People who consume gliadin consume 400 calories more per day; people who remove gliadin reduce calorie intake by 400 calories per day. Incidentally, antibodies to gliadin are capable of binding to nervous system tissue and may contribute to immune-mediate neurological impairment, such as cerebellar ataxia and gluten encephalopathy. Gliadin, particularly the omega fraction, is also responsible for allergic responses, including Bakers' asthma and the odd wheat-dependent, exercise-induced analyphylaxis (WDEIA).) The high-yield, semi-dwarf strains of wheat, invented in the 1960s and 1970s, was introduced to North American farmers in the late 1970s, who adopted it over the next decade. By 1985, virtually all wheat farmers were growing this high-yield strain.

This is the true reason for gross obesity of American and British citizens! It is the eating of genetically modified wheat found in almost every food product i.e. processed foods such as ready meals often contain gravy or other wheat containing products. Fast foods i.e. the burger contains wheat as well as the bun. Many breakfast cereals contain wheat. Beer contains wheat and many confectionary sweets also contain wheat so that all ages may be influenced by opiates in their food! All people are being addicted subconsciously! Also many peoples are becoming obese which effects their mind and behaviour!

More importantly Gliadin acts on the Opiate transmitter to increase the effect of the addictive drug opium. It produces euphoria, extreme relaxation and decreases any sensation of pain. It controls movement, mood, digestion, body temperature and breathing and ultimately could affect the immune system. This is certainly the ingredient one would expect to be useful to anyone attempting to perform mass mind control. What better way than to introduce a substance into the food that makes a person feel good, feel content with life, feeling euphoric. A person in this state would accept wickedness and evil because they would be oblivious to emotion, just living from day to day in contentment, induced subconsciously through food additives! You think this is farfetched? What about prisoners and soldiers given Bromide in their tea to reduce their sexual ardour? It happened! It was real! So there is no reason why this food additive is not real!

Food will be used as a weapon for controlling every individual who consumes the food. More on this subject later.

Now to return to memory lane and the past community life.

Can you remember when it was safe for children to play outside in the street, to walk to the shop, and of course in those days children wore sensible clothing that made them look like children not porn stars!

Can you remember when you would walk into your neighbour's house, calling out to them "to put the kettle on?" There were no locked doors, no standing on ceremony to avoid offending them in case they decided to take you to court for financial gain!

Do you remember when people understood how it was impossible to manage on dole money and so they were allowed to earn a little extra cash for those 'important extra's which made life worth living for, and the neighbours would happily understand, not point an accusing finger at them calling them 'benefits thieves?"

Do you remember the rare occasion a single woman would become pregnant? The baby would go out for adoption to a loving family who longed for a child. It was a 'win- win' situation. Unlike today when women are manipulated into having abortions, which leaves her 'subconsciously' traumatised and guilt ridden for the rest of her life! Today many women have become so mind-controlled they cannot experience emotion or guilt about terminating their baby. They lack awareness or the emotion to convict them of wrong doing. Society, peers and education have desensitized them to the importance of what they have done. It is a terrible sin, there is nothing worse than an offence against children particularly abortion. It is a double offence because there is no reason (other than serious medical reasons) for the woman not to carry the baby full term so that it can be a gift to others who long to have a baby!

Do not misunderstand what is being said here! There is no condemnation on the woman who aborted her baby if she was a victim – she may have been manipulated through subliminal and subtle mind control techniques to take this option- she only knows (through ignorance of the facts) what she has been conditioned to know! If however, she knew and understood that she was committing an act of murder and deliberately and willingly agreed to this then she would be accountable!

This principle of being 'mind controlled, produces a new perspective on why God loves everyone. It is a concept not fully understood by many. People say how can God love those people who are wicked and perform evil deeds? When you look at mind control whereby a person is behaving as they are, because someone is working their mind like puppets on a string, you can see that the individual, under the influence of opiates from eating a lot of wheat products, could be excused!

When you look at the overall picture from God's perspective many people have been influenced and therefore have become 'victims', vulnerable to unforeseen influences and hidden forces. However, there are those people who are not victims, they have evil hearts, and they chose to do wicked deeds!

So that is why God has extended his Grace and the gift of salvation to the Gentiles, because of the power of sin and the curse of this world as well as the hidden forces at work! There are people who are destined to do evil –they chose this way of life and therefore are accountable! There are those who are coerced into committing sins and therefore may be victims, and therefore eligible for God's Grace. This does not mean that a wicked person is not eligible for God's Grace. Biblically, there are many testimonies of people who performed wicked deeds, yet through repentance received God's Grace.

When someone is being manipulated covertly, when they are unaware of deception affecting them, altering their behaviour, their thinking etc – and then it is easy to see how God can love all people! Many people who were once good, morally upright people have joined the ranks of the wicked! Some however, will be accountable others not so, it all depends on the inner heart of the person and the circumstances – hence God's judgement day! This is a complex subject that requires a lot of discussion but not in this book.

Those who are written in God's Book of Life will be saved. Those who commit deliberate evil knowingly will be blotted out of the Book of Life! Rev 20:11-15.

Back to nostalgia!

Do you recall the past when newspapers reported on very rare occasions, a rape, or attack on a person; usually it would be a prostitute or a gangland victim, rarely a member of the public. The Bobby on the beat would walk around the community dealing with petty incidents such as drunkenness or clipping a youth's ear for using a pea shooter! The biggest news article was the Great Train Robbery!

Now however, on a daily basis, there's constant news reports of innocent victims of rape, violent acts and murder! Police today would drive pass a youth with a pea shooter to avoid the paperwork! Now they save their energy to deal with youth gangs with knives and guns!

So how did Britain, America and other western countries come to this? Psychological manipulation over the years, a gradual introduction to the acceptance of change of the boundaries of what is good and what is evil. This method of manipulation has become effective. Many of the older generation have meekly submitted, rather than challenge the New World that's developing before their very eyes. If you speak to older people most of them will tell you how they long to die because the world they are experiencing is the worse they have ever known! It is a world of confusion, selfishness, violence and pure evil!

They find their personal liberties stolen from them; they are forced to live on a small pension which has decreased instead of the promised increase as agreed that guaranteed them a secure financial future. Their earned and saved money for all those years has suddenly become controlled by the government who then decides what they can and cannot have! The Government dictates that their pension is now considered as EARNINGS and therefore TAXED. Originally it was TAX FREE! Now they receive a pay slip every month like an employee and are bombarded with paperwork to sort out, tax codes etc, causing the pensioner enormous stress in the days that should have consisted of happiness, leisure, and freedom from insecurity, fear and stress!

Another area under control and used to manipulate young minds, is education. Gradually over the years education has been used as another method of mind control, the school system changed, dividing classes between private funded schools and Government funded schools (secondary schools – even the title suggest it is second rate to the schools provided for the wealthy). The curriculum also changed. Gradually Christian studies were phased out along with Assembly which involved a Christian prayer and singing of Christian hymns. Eventually it became outlawed completely and replaced by a secular assembly. As we know today only interfaith teaching is permitted in schools. God and Biblical Teaching have been deliberately removed from schools so that the young people could be conditioned into a secular way of life. The curriculum instead taught evolution and humanism!

It is unlawful to wear a Christian cross or to teach Christianity in (the British 'Christian' Country) schools or the work place, particularly to older people in care homes who are to die without knowing the hope of eternal life!

Jews are not allowed to wear a skull cap in a non -Jewish school yet Muslims and Hindus are permitted to wear their headwear in schools and workplaces. So here we have an obvious pattern of discrimination of Britain's own people in favour of interfaith practices which deliberately censor Christianity and Judaism.

To write fully on how the apostasy came into being would produce a huge volume. It is a complex subject with many factors involved and span over many years. The reader should research these subjects further to extend their awareness of what is going on behind the scenes!

As mentioned previously the apostasy began in the Garden of Eden when Eve was persuaded by the serpent that she had misunderstood what God had said about the tree, she was easily convinced because of her rebellious heart! Interestingly, he introduced Eve to the concept of good and evil. He said to her, "No! You won't die; you will acquire knowledge of good and evil'! This tempted Eve into rebellion which led to the turning away from God and acceptance of satan which is the act of committing adultery! So you see the key points were there; Rebellion, Turning away and Adultery, these three would lead to a falling away which is the falling away spiritually – dying a spiritual death- to a final destiny of eternal physical death!

It is this spiritual death (a detachment of a person's spirit from God) that has occurred and is still the problem today and the next stage is physical death leading to judgement.

Throughout the historical years after the incident with Adam and Eve, the world became cursed (as a punishment for the sins of Adam and Eve) and the people were divided between those who were pagan and those who were righteous.

This continued throughout history whereby these two groups were rivals, and the innocent righteous were constantly attacked and pillaged by the pagan tribes. In retaliation the righteous defended themselves and with God's intervention had victory over their enemies many times.

These events are evidenced in many ways i.e. writings from the books written by ancient Jewish scribes, by Enoch and Elijah, Dead Sea Scrolls and other ancient Scrolls, the Septuagint, Apocrypha, texts from Josephus and Philo and the Bible's 66 books.

Apostasy existed prior to the flood and Noah's Ark, which saved only 8 righteous people out of the whole world population (which was significantly small in number than today). God destroyed the world by flood because it had become so wicked and evil, so much so that God could only find 8 righteous people, Noah and his family, who acknowledged the Creator God. We are coming to a time when this will happen again! Soon God will not find many people on this Earth who will acknowledge him as the Creator God or acknowledge the giver of Eternal Life Yeshua! – Eternal life comes through the acceptance of Christ Yeshua, His son- the savior!

Soon all those who are righteous will be taken from this earth in a Rapture. This has been prophesied to occur, when suddenly in a twinkling of an eye people (including children) will be taken up to heaven. At this time the Great Apostasy will occur throughout the world! There may however, be some who become 'born again believers after the rapture occurs, but the period will consist of mostly apostate and lawless people, depraved and wicked as in the time of Noah and as in the time of Sodom and Gomorrah when God said to Lot and his family, 'leave this place because I am about to destroy it, for it has become wicked!'

At this point let the reader take a moment to reflect on the changes that have taken place, think about how sin has escalated over the past 20 years, how desensitised people have become towards wickedness, how people have a desire to watch horror films, to listen to head banging music, to watch pornography as everyday entertainment, to speak coarse language in public, to murder someone in daylight in public view where there are children watching! Think about what causes a person to do such things, what causes someone to take a baby and sexually abuse that baby? What causes someone to walk into a school and shoot down many infants and teenagers? What causes someone to walk onto a bus and blow up themselves and others?

What causes thousands of people to commit suicide and take their families with them? What causes the majority of teenagers to have under age sex and relationships, before marriage, which involves committing murder of innocent babies?

Why are the majority, including people aged 70+, so determined to tattoo their bodies, when not long ago it was considered antisocial, unacceptable and only for service men or criminals. Tattoos were a rare occurrence a decade ago except with service men who wore one on their arm as an insignia to their service. Other questions on changed behaviour are; what makes so many children and adults addicted to either drugs, alcohol, food etc? Why has so many families been made homeless - losing their homes because of debt?

This chapter has become a mere introduction to the methods used to bring about this apostasy; we have barely begun to explore the causes.

Throughout the book you will be introduced to further methods used, along with evidence, and links to the bible that would confirm God knew this apostasy would develop. God watches from above and records every detail ready for the time to 'call in' revenge! He will raise his hand to herald in the four horses of judgement upon the nations!

Apostasy, the rebellion and the falling away from anything that relates to a Godly being, consists of a variety of causes, some of which have already been mentioned i.e. changes in education, particularly religious studies and the introduction to humanism within psychology and science, changes in food production and long term deliberately orchestrated adjustment of thinking and behaviour to the acceptance of evil and the rejection of good.

The point of all this? The goal is to open the way for the dictatorship of lucifer himself, to take control of all the inhabitants of the earth. Currently, Lucifer is gaining world control through the concept of a New World Order (N.W.O). This consists of a global government structure that implements changes and the gradual takeover of people's liberties.

It needs to be understood that there are a number of groups involved with the transition of the N.W.O, i.e. the illuminati, freemasons, leaders of the nations via UN, EU etc, the vatican, scientists/ researchers, new age organisations and others. They all have their own agenda towards the N.W.O and all have a role to play to make it happen! Therefore, the mind control comes from different directions, using different methods to achieve the same goal – to control the majority into submission and slavery! To achieve this several things must happen:

- Reduce the world population to a more manageable size.
- Desensitise the people. Desensitization is when the emotional responsiveness to a negative or aversive stimulus, after repeated exposure to it, is not even noticed. In other words if you see a murder being committed often enough, it becomes an acceptable part of behaviour, 'The Norm'. You stop feeling emotion about the evil deed and accept it as the normal process of everyday life. You start to lack compassion, and empathy. You have an inability to feel the suffering of the victim and eventually your appetite increases for such activity as it becomes a pleasurable experience. This is what God calls the 'hardening of your heart,' you feel nothing; you are dead inside, emotionless! This emotionlessness effect can be achieved when an emotional response is repeatedly called into play in situations whereby the action associated with the emotion proves irrelevant or unnecessary. Desensitization is a process used to assist individuals to unlearn certain behaviour, such as lose their ability to rationalize what is going on in the world today along with the inability to assess what is right and wrong and lacking in awareness of the ' mind controlling' activities that are taking place.
- Introduce regular mass mind control techniques and regular programming to bring about worldwide compliance of the people.
- To control the world population via the individual nation's leadership authorities, as chosen by the N.W.O. Elite.

- The nations are to be joined together to form 4 key powers: Asian Union, African Union, European Union and the North American Union, these may also be referred to as Hemispheres.
- The people of the nations are to receive a microchip under the skin of their hand or forehead which is to be used to store information about the person, to track them and control them like slaves.
- A different type of slavery to the past slavery. This new slavery will not be so noticeable. People will be going about their normal business but they will be enslaved in their minds, doing what they THINK they want to do but actually doing what is expected of them! They will also be enslaved by the heavy burden of sin and wickedness. Eventually 'freedom of choice' will no longer exist – we are being piloted in European countries already for this.
- There is to be a one world bank, a one world religion, a one world currency, a one world leader (Dictatorship).

Most of the above list have already occurred or in the process of occurring and will increase in severity.

To sum up so far, the world is in an apostate age whereby the majority have turned their backs on their Creator God and rejected His Son Christ Yeshua (Jesus). Even those who once believed have turned to the world for their pleasures, guidance and security.

This turning away comes from a person's heart turning from what is right and good to complacency and an acceptance of what is **not** good, accepting wickedness and ignoring its consequences that lead to eternal death in hell! This behaviour is 'Rebellion!

Christ says in Matthew 24:10 *"At that time many will turn away from the faith and will betray and hate each other and many false prophets will appear and deceive many people. Because of the increase of wickedness, the love of most will grow cold, …"*

Apostle Paul writes in Romans 3: that all are sinners, Jew and Gentile. *"There is no one righteous, not even one; there is no one who understands, no one who seeks God. All have turned away, they have together become worthless; there is no one who does good, ... their tongues practice deceit, ... their mouths are full of cursing and bitterness..."*

Those who once believed in their Heavenly Father and Christ Yeshua have committed 'Adultery', by turning from following God's Way to following the way of the world, and because the devil (lucifer- the serpent) is in control of this world, they have chosen to follow satan's way.

Many people were born into this secular world, yet all are also born with an internal awareness of a creator, therefore still have the ability to make a choice whether to be secular or follow the faithful path!

"This is how it will be at the end of the age. The angels will come and separate the wicked from the righteous and throw them into the fiery furnace..."

Matthew 13: 47 -51. This is a parable of the end times when God will divide the people according to their hearts, of rebellion or faith. During the time of judgement, the faithful are rewarded and the 'rebellious wicked' are cast into hell!

Originally, the serpent manipulated the mind of Eve, but Eve chose to take note of the serpent and disobey God. This was an act of rebellion by Eve and Adam. The same situation occurs today. There is no excuse for mankind who has seen the evidence, knows God and Christ are real and yet prefer to accept what is being presented to them through the deceiving tongue of satan! The hidden dark forces are manipulating minds through everyday methods i.e. propaganda, but also through subconscious level i.e. subliminal messages. There are many other methods also used to reach every human being according to their age, intellect, values and beliefs as well as the level of rebellion, or desire for materialism, power and success etc.

The serpent in the Garden of Eden is also the dragon spoken of in Revelation 12. He has many other names: beelzebub, bell, baal, devil, satan, preacher of lies, fallen angel, prince of darkness, and lucifer.

Revelation 12 speaks of how the dragon (lucifer) was sent down to earth and leads the world astray.

"And there was war in heaven. Michael and his angels fought against the dragon, and the dragon and his angels fought back. But he was not strong enough, and they lost their place in heaven. The great dragon was hurled down –that ancient serpent called the devil, or satan, who leads the whole world astray. He was hurled to the earth and his angels with him," Revelation 12:7.

So we have it! Satan and his fallen angels are here on earth and have been here for a very long time! Their presence has helped to produce the apostasy! [Some scholars place the above verse as relating to the last days, but this doesn't make sense when satan was cast down to earth in several verses in the Tanach (Old Testament) i.e. Ezekiel 28:11 & Isaiah 14:12-15.]

This rebellion and falling away has come about because the hearts of mankind have become selfish, rebellious, desiring wickedness and pleasures rather than righteousness and contentment in Christ that surpasses all the worldly pleasures! However, this rebellion was also instigated through subtle manipulation and mind control over many centuries to bring mankind to where it is now!

The duality between mankind's rebellion and satan's rebellion equates to a mass falling away from all things Godly!

It is easy to put it into perspective when you realise the war that took place in heaven between Michael and the dragon ended with the serpent being sent down to earth which was a cursed place because of the sin from his tongue of deceit to Adam and Eve. It is also easy to accept that he would then be a superior being roaming the earth, taking charge and deceiving the earth! He had his fallen angels with him, who also roamed the earth causing havoc and provoking evil! These fallen angels chose to sleep with human women and therefore produced offspring of combined 'human and superhuman' personalities.

It is these two key factors, the devil and his demonic force, which are controlling the activities of this world and leading Mankind into satan's traps of lies and deceit. Mankind through their desire for power, money and materials are easy prey for such a world under the leadership of a dictator who is determined to control every man, woman and child, every business and institution, every nation and city.

Now it is not all bad news, although mankind is wicked, rebellious and commits adultery against God, he has allowed these things to take place to provide mankind with the information that will bring them to an understanding regarding good and evil, to decide and to make a choice! To decide whether they prefer good or evil, God or Satan! Depending on that choice, God refines and purifies those who choose good, to enable them to return to Him in the Garden of Eden (which is symbolic of the new future world to come). God cannot accept anyone back into His kingdom unless they are purified and made clean (from evil) they need to be consecrated –made holy – to come into His presence as He is a Holy Awesome God!

Of course this is the purpose of sending his son Christ, as the way to acquire the first step of this cleansing and purification process. Christ is the forgiver of sins and through his crucifixion he provides a way for people to claim this forgiveness. Their rebirth into God's Kingdom is aided by the presence of the Holy Spirit who teaches and trains the 'new born' believer directing their path that leads to eternal life!

This holiness and purification is achieved through recognition of our sinfulness and uncleanness, so that when we are put through terrible trials and difficulties we learn from this experience what is right and wrong. Those who are wise and sincere would learn through suffering that the world and mankind provide **no** peace or safety. It doesn't prevent the individual from sinning or protect the person from self –harm or destruction through drug abuse, immoral living, and criminal acts or from committing murder. What this world has to offer does not satisfy the soul! The activities just take a person deeper into sinful, evil acts until there is no return!

God sent His son Christ Yeshua to earth as a man so that he could walk among men and women to guide them away from the serpent's influences, to bring those out of the evil that chained their souls! Mankind is steeped in sickness, pain, and chains; they do not know what it is to be free!

The majority of the world population have never known true freedom. Mankind believe freedom is to do what you like, drink, party, have sex with anyone you like heterosexually, homosexually, or other immoral acts etc. To have no rules is considered freedom, yet it is a **slavery to sin!** Sin controls you, your behaviour, your mind and in turn it affects your relationships as well as your lifestyle and more importantly it affects your final destination.

When these people confront their deep inner being, there is a deep dark void of depression and unhappiness that cannot be lifted no matter how much drink or drugs they take!

Many who have felt this way have ended taking their own lives- they would rather end their life than to submit to a loving Saviour Christ Yeshua, who takes away all sin from a person so that they can start anew, become cleansed and purified!

To conclude this summary, we have also discussed how covertly satan is working to manipulate the inhabitants of this world. His time is limited; he knows God's prophecies for the end times and the end of the world. He knows that he has to move fast to complete his plans of conquering the world to become its new god. To achieve this he must have maximum control over all the inhabitants and to destroy all those who are enemies of his plan i.e. Jews, Messianic Jews, Christians and any others who refuse to denounce God and Yeshua.

Satan therefore is working fast! He is ready to finalise the stages of his plan. This plan is to gain maximum control over the inhabitants within the next few years.

He has already managed to encourage many young people to commit suicide by controlling their minds through hallucinatory drugs, excessive drinking and subliminal messages in music, games and films and computer websites.

Many of the older generation have died, or rendered incapable of resistance or have become desensitized to what is happening around them. This has been achieved by the introduction of specific cell damaging or cell destroying drugs that also produce other medical or psychological conditions to accelerate death or suffering, as well as weakening their spirit to resist! The older generation do not present a problem to satan and his plan, unlike the younger generation those who are independent thinkers and doers, intelligent, able to rationalise what is going on in the world and willing to do something about it!. The young are also the last generation on this earth, therefore vital to his plans.

As for the in-betweens, the family units, they are so bogged down with debt, and trying to keep up with technological advances and maintaining their nuclear paradise (their home environment) that they are totally oblivious to what is going on around them, they believe what they are told by the media, they moan about the pressures of life but accept it as 'inevitable progression', they have become so complacent, and compliant! Many of them have accepted the first stage of the identification process that suggests allegiance to lucifer; many have already marked themselves with a tattoo!

Keep in mind the fact that satan is described as a dragon. Dragon's breathe fire (and hot air) they are angry and devour their enemies. Dragons have long tails used as weapons to swipe their prey. They have piercing, hypnotic eyes, and scaly skin. This description simulates reptiles of today and is akin to the snakes (serpents) and lizards. A dragon's offspring would also simulate these characteristics.

His fallen angels would have a slightly different appearance to the dragon, though it is difficult to define their appearance as it may vary. They have the ability to change their appearance.

The scripture below describes these fallen angels as men so they are in the form of men and we know that mankind have different characteristics such as body and facial differences just like humans.

"Certain men, whose condemnation was written about long ago have secretly slipped in among you. They are godless men,...and the angels who did not keep their positions of authority" Jude verse 4

It is important to keep the above description in mind as further in the book it will describe something incredible!

CHAPTER 3

PSYCHOLOGY OF THE MIND

Psychology over the years has transformed enormously, from the time when it consisted of philosophical debates and the attempts to cure what was considered demonic possession by boring a hole in the brain to let out the demon, to developing into a science using scientific research to justify the findings and to set precedents.

The scientific approach is a form of control as it is difficult for anyone without a doctorate or some recognised status, to have an influence on changing research findings. Those with particular influence setting theories are, humanistic researchers i.e. evolutionists, which consists of most psychologists, biologists, and other researchers.

These theories have 'irrationally' been accepted as facts and well established into societies thinking to the extent that no one challenges them as theories! Today theories are still accepted as facts and psychology has become a powerful tool to deceive the masses.

Psychology is used in business, particularly advertising. Adverts are suggestive and powerful, controlling an individual's mind by inducing a set behaviour. It may induce a temptation to follow what has been portrayed in the advert. For example, men must show masculine tendencies (Alpha males) women are depicted as the weaker, 'dolly bird' types who are an extension to man's ego and seen as their property. These women are expected to submit to man's desires and to indulge in promiscuous sexual behavior etc. They are expected to maintain their image of sexiness and to remain an attractive submissive status symbol in support of the male's image as an Alpha Male.

Apart from the power of advertising, retail outlets are trained to seduce customers into buying their products, either through sales representative's persuasive techniques or displaying the goods in a particularly enticing manner or advertising strong messages that influence decision making. Advertising today usually contain a strong message within a message and may also have subliminal messages. For example a Coca Cola advert may send a message to young people that it is trendy to drink Coke but also to party, to be trendy, and use all the latest gadgets, subliminally it is also saying it is cool to take Coke (another name for the drug Cocaine). These types of advertising are known to influence behavior and the evidence is all around you with the increase in drug crime and lawless behavior!

The underlying power of advertising is to direct an individual's behaviour towards the desired goal not only to purchase the advertised goods and services but to also manipulate the mind to behave in a specific way – ultimately altering societies thinking, culture, beliefs and expectations. Advertising has the power to instigate change!

Supermarkets use psychological manipulation to persuade customers to buy certain products, using tactics such as placing candy or toys near the cashpoint knowing that children would be drawn to the items and parents would not be able to refuse the child's request. Another example is the' buy one get one free'. It is amazing how many people fall for this trick. No one seems to notice that the price of the one item has doubled since before the promotion, so that the customer gained nothing by purchasing two items instead of one – but the customer has paid out 50% more than originally intended, whereas the shop has gained an extra sale.

Psychology has split into many divisions such as biopsychology, sociopsychology, abnormal psychology and cognitive psychology. All of these are used to direct human behaviour towards the ultimate goal of a world dictatorship and a New World Order. All of the psychological subjects, perspectives and approaches at educational level and beyond are research based and focused on Darwin's evolutionary perspective.

God's word says, **"See *to it that no one takes you captive through hollow and deceptive philosophy, which depends on human tradition and the basic principles of this world rather than Christ.* Colossians 2:8.

Within the category of psychology is Counselling, which is also taught from the evolutionists perspective. Psychologists and counsellors promote and use religion as part of their solution to psychological problems such as stress or depression, however, the techniques used are not from Christianity or Judaism, which use concepts such as prayer, forgiveness of sin, seeking God's forgiveness, and receiving healing and eternal life. The key religious concepts used by psychologists and counsellors are made up from sections taken from humanism, new age, hinduism and other faiths.

In Nexus magazine [Aug-Sept 2013, Vol 20 number 5] Psychology has introduced a new treatment for phobias, dysfunctional thinking, emotional and physical traumas etc. It's called Energy Psychology. It originated from Chinese medicine {it is yet another new age enticement into a situation whereby the mind is played with.} It is similar to the Toronto Blessing /Pensacola false religious leaders who zap innocent people with the 'energy'. This energy has been described as electricity going through the body and mind. It is a satanic replica of the True Holy Spirit of God!

Satan's (replica of God's Spirit) energy entices people further into humanism, the more that humanism is seen to provide 'miraculous healings etc' the more people are lured away from the (unseen true healing spirit of God) towards the 'physically observed' healings of satan!

This new energy therapy treatment involves touching and tapping the body to stimulate energy. The aim is to heal the subconscious mind where 95% of thoughts and behaviour originate. See Appendix 1 for further information on Energy Psychology.

There are four types of treatment:
1. EFT – Emotional Freedom Technique
2. TFT – Thought Field Therapy
3. MR– Matrix Reprinting- [originates from shamanism- which is occult]
4. PK – Psych-K

The key method, that is the most dangerous, is MR, it's purpose is to encourage the patient to look within themselves, (into their inner self) to find a way to 'self- actualise'-as an independent being, [this means away from God], to find themselves as a god or goddess, therefore having no need for the true God in their lives, this equates to narcissism! A definition of narcissism .according to Wikipedia includes one from S Hotchkiss who identified what she called the seven deadly sins of narcissism:

1. *Shamelessness: Shame is the feeling that lurks beneath all unhealthy narcissism and the inability to process shame in healthy ways.*

2. *Magical thinking: Narcissists see themselves as perfect, using distortion and illusion known as magical thinking. They also use projection to dump shame onto others.*

3. *Arrogance: A narcissist who is feeling deflated may re-inflate by diminishing, debasing, or degrading somebody else.*

4. *Envy: A narcissist may secure a sense of superiority in the face of another person's ability by using contempt to minimize the other person.*

5. *Entitlement: Narcissists hold unreasonable expectations of particularly favorable treatment and automatic compliance because they consider themselves special. Failure to comply is considered an attack on their superiority, and the perpetrator is considered an "awkward" or "difficult" person. Defiance of their will is a narcissistic injury that can trigger narcissistic rage.*

6. *Exploitation: Can take many forms but always involves the exploitation of others without regard for their feelings or interests. Often the other is in a subservient position where resistance would be difficult or even impossible. Sometimes the subservience is not so much real as assumed.*

7. *Bad boundaries: Narcissists do not recognize that they have boundaries and that others are separate and are not extensions of themselves. Others either exist to meet their needs or may as well not exist at all. Those who provide narcissistic supply to the narcissist are*

treated as if they are part of the narcissist and are expected to live up to those expectations. In the mind of a narcissist there is no boundary between self and other.

There has been a noticeable increase of narcissistic tendencies within the young generation, over the past few years. This is seen in an attitude of superiority among both male and female and in bullying types who believe they are a superior race to those who are 'nice' and 'different' and those who do not behave according to the narcissistic code. Young people have become so self- obsessed and self- important that they have no respect or tolerance of older people; they disrespect their parents and the 'normality' of society. Yet they DEMAND respect from others and become abusive, violent or aggressive if they are disrespected! This is particularly found among the gangland culture or high crime areas.

The following verse was Christ's words to his followers then and today, about the future end time rebellion, which is taking place now in a mild form and will transcend to the betrayal mentioned in the verse!

"Brother will betray brother to death, and a father his child, children will rebel against their parents and have them put to death." Matthew 10:21

This is the reason for the narcissistic children! This is why satan has turned the children to rebellion so that they will in the near future turn against their own 'believing parents' to have them killed. Satan is producing an army of whistle-blowers, [Just as hitler did when the German citizens betrayed the Jews]. Satan is training people to betray those who do not worship him, who are followers of Christ!

We live in a society where people are encouraged to inform on people they believe are 'benefit cheats', tax evaders, and possible terrorists. These appear worthwhile causes however; innocent people are also being targeted.

Ordinary innocent people, out of fear for their own safety, are whistle-blowing without thinking through the consequences.

I am not saying we should not be vigilant or report suspicious activity; however, we must be aware of where this is leading. The more this activity takes place, the more the goal posts move so that eventually it will be innocent people being arrested because they have a bible in their home, they attend church, they are preaching the Gospel or they do not have the mark of the beast!

Trauma is a major cause of change in personality; take for example, a soldier on the frontline of conflict. That soldier may experience colleagues and friends killed, in barbaric ways, he may be injured himself and returns home on compassionate leave. His personality [before he signed up] has been lost in the archives of his subconscious, replaced with images of destruction and fear! He would suffer many flash backs of the horror he experienced. These flashbacks would haunt him daily. His identity has changed from an enlisting teenager to an edgy, depressed and confused man who cannot control his emotions or memories – he has no peace! He is unfortunately an ideal vulnerable candidate for this dangerously new energy therapy. This soldier has a deep inner feeling of alienation from the world, he feels his inner being is split apart and disassociated. MR is used to put this right.

Psychologists claim that trauma produces a feeling of splitting /dissociation with the body and the mind and therefore hypnosis is used to reintegrate these dissociated parts. MR appears to be a modern version of depatterning which was a method once used to completely clean out the memories [so that the patient lost their entire identity and the neurologist then reintroduced new memories] Obviously because this soldier has already lost his identity it is easy to replace it with a new one. The new identity will be fashioned on the illuminati's design for mankind, in the same manner hitler attempted to fashion an Aryan race. Sadly, the soldier would not be informed that all he needs is to turn to God and ask for healing. He would not only receive healing of his wounds, memories, emotions, but also his soul would blend with his spirit making him complete and whole! He would then experience true peace! God takes charge of the safety of the body, mind and soul of those who totally trust in Him, God guarantees the renewed person would not be destined to hell! The soldier would be completely set free from all fear and entrapment and assured of eternal life.

Counsellors now suggest yoga, transcendental meditation, mindfulness and other such soul destroying techniques that entrap people (UNKNOWINGLY) into mind control through the emptying of the mind during meditation and submitting themselves to dark forces and demonic influences used in witchcraft, séances, occult practices etc.

*"But there were also false prophets among the people, just as there will be false teachers among you... They will secretly introduce destructive heresies, even denying the sovereign Lord...*2 Peter 2

In their greed these teachers will exploit you with stories they have made up. 2 Peter 2: 3

The mind is a very intricate part of a human being; it consists of the soul and spirit part. The soul is the intangible part of the human being that links the body and the mind to the world beyond the material substance of flesh. The Spirit is the intangible part of the body and mind that links to God and Christ Yeshua and the Holy Spirit. .

If there is a natural body, there is also a spiritual body. The first man Adam became a living being, the last Adam, a life giving spirit. ....The first man was of the dust of the earth, the second man from heaven. (Christ Yeshua) 1 Corinthians 15

"For who among men knows the thoughts of a man except the man's spirit within him? In the same way no one knows the thoughts of God except the Spirit of God." 1 Cor 2

The above piece of scripture suggests clearly, that our thoughts are linked to our spirit and that each human has an earthly body and a spiritual body.

The mind links to God through his Holy Spirit, and it is the mind that allows us to contact him through prayer to Christ

Yeshua, (Yeshua is Jesus true Hebraic name) as we link to Yeshua through God's Holy Spirit.

The mind also links the soul of man to the dark forces, unless the individual belongs to the Kingdom of God by being 'spiritually reborn, then and only then, is the individual protected from the dark forces! These dark forces and evil powers can only access (internally) the individual who does not have God's seal of protection that comes from an acceptance of God and his son Yeshua - Savior and Messiah.

These evil forces are able to take control of a person's mind, body and soul and this is exactly what has driven this apostasy plan into action.

"He *who does what is sinful is of the devil, because the devil has been sinning from the beginning. The reason the Son of God appeared was to destroy the devil's work. No one who is born of God will continue to sin, because God's seed remains in him, he cannot go on sinning, because he has been born of God. This is how we know who the children of God are and who the children of the devil are...* 1 John 3:8

In the bible the book of Jude states:

"Certain men, whose condemnation was written about long ago, have secretly slipped in among you. They are godless men,...and the angels who did not keep their positions of authority but abandoned their own home- these he has kept in darkness, bound with everlasting chains for judgement on the Great day."

".....In the last times there will be scoffers who will follow their own ungodly desires. These are the men who divide you, who follow mere natural instincts and do not have the spirit."
Jude verse 4.

If an individual chooses to follow the humanistic world rather than live in righteousness then the individual is susceptible to worldly events such as the pre - orchestrated plan for mass mind control. Not only this but the individual opens the door and invites demonic influences into their lives, for example, a person may get drunk on alcohol or high on drugs or absorbed in music or watch horror movies or play mythical games etc, the mind becomes so absorbed in the fantasy world or far removed from reality that the mind becomes vulnerable to invasion or possession from a demonic influence.

If this happens (which is highly likely) it is often evidenced by a change in the individual's personality (which can only be noticed by other people, the individual is usually unable to analyse themselves) and the person's circumstances usually change i.e. unsociable behaviour, withdrawal from others who are good and righteous, an affinity with those who are evil or wicked, crisis situations develop, a darkness overwhelms the person or they become suicidal or take on symptoms of mental disorder! Society labels these demonic possessions as mental disorder however; this is a way for the individual to remain in the clutches of humanism rather than a saved soul in the kingdom of God!

Do not misunderstand the above; there are mental disorders that are just that, it does not mean a person is possessed. They are usually people who have become ill because of biological factors i.e. stress and post traumatic disturbances which affect the neurotransmitters, causing chemical imbalance in the brain which then effects behaviour.

Most of the demon possessions occur because of addiction to something which makes the individual easy to control. It can be seen by their shabby appearance, there is a strong sense of darkness engulfing them and they demonstrate aggressive behaviour. They are quite different in appearance from those suffering from mental disorders.

When you watch ordinary folk going about their daily lives, talking to friends, having lunch, going to work, playing footie with their children, it doesn't make sense or even seem possible that horrific things are happening behind the scenes in this world. However, when you watch the news bulletins and see the daily world disasters, famine and diseases and civil war in other countries and when you see that children cannot play because they are too weak from hunger, and when you hear news reports that children are forced to marry old men and are giving birth at age 12 or younger, and when you hear of Christians beheaded because they were once Muslims and refuse to bow down to Islamic leaders, you cannot help but realise the world isn't so good after all. The reality of a corrupt world hits home!

It is far more difficult to accept that hidden forces are at work when western civilisation offers materialistic happiness. Nevertheless, the reality is that <u>now</u> even western society is starting to suffer poverty and deprivation!

Global Shift in Finances and Banking - During the past ten years, society, political leadership, local governments, social sectors and health organisations have changed enormously in Britain, America and EU Countries.

Around a decade ago the news channels reported a Global Financial Crisis within various countries, including Britain. Taxes were increased to bring in new revenue while interest on savings decreased; wages were frozen, while utility bills and food prices rose along with petroleum to retain financial equilibrium.

Interestingly the people suffered financial hardships, yet the different cities throughout the countries suddenly started building, renovating broken down cities and towns. Where did the money come from?

Towns and Cities all around Britain which had been in a sad, derelict condition, with old grey concrete buildings suddenly became flush, vibrant, modern places with state of the Art designs along main public areas! Businesses suddenly became bigger and more professional with lavish décor and designs, including civil service buildings which had previously been draughty and dilapidated.

What was going on? Where did this sudden funding come from that allowed a country to suddenly make such expensive improvements which would cost millions of revenue?

The answer to that question is debateable, but certainly appears, using basic logic, based on the facts of world domination; it is possible the money was a pay-out (a loan) for joining the EU or an equivalent global authority.

Just in the last two years we have seen affluent countries suddenly collapse because of serious debt problems. This came about from the demands placed on the government and local councils to make improvements and to bring about changes and reductions in their services etc. These demands were usually unrealistic and pressure was exerted on the government to meet these demands within a certain time scale or pay a penalty!

During this period the public found that companies were under pressure to meet certain regulations imposed by the EU that would cost huge sums of money to make such changes particularly within the required deadlines. These demands usually meant redundancies. This in turn placed pressure on the remaining staff and so it went on. Pressure on top of pressure until breaking point! People can take no more of it so the pressure lid bursts off and there's civil unrest, riots, protests and so on.

We have seen this with our very eyes, Greece, and Italy are examples. Terrible riots took place then suddenly it went quiet, no longer in the news, what happened? They were offered financial help that would take that pressure off, but at what price? We shall have to wait and see!

Britain, is experiencing the same pressures and demands, the same massive debt, the sectors have each been placed under huge financial pressure and forced to meet high unrealistic goals in a very short period of time!

As a result public and private services have changed their policies, reduced their staffing levels therefore increasing the pressure on the remaining overworked, overstressed workforce,

Since writing this chapter further information has come to light. Nexus magazine, August 2013 (vol 20) issue, wrote an article in the Global News Column, reporting on the Bank for International Settlements (BIS) headquarters in Basel, Switzerland, which is the central bank for the World's Central Banks. (New World Order World Bank). *The latest Basel 111 Accords 2010 are to be implemented over the next few years.*

This Accord is a system of pacifiers (now that most banks are in debt) *to resolve the debt problem and to maintain the banks in a stable condition by providing solutions to remaining solvent,* (the phrase 'To Pacify' is significant). It was necessary for the N.W.O. to come up with something to instil trust in the banks and the nations, as the people were becoming restless, civil unrest needed to be dealt with and banks needed to feel secure after the 'roller coaster' events of the financial crisis. The huge restructuring of the banking system which involved nations parting with huge sums of money, shares and investments, has left the banks totally dependent on the World Bank to prevent them from sinking!

[Incidentally, the general public have never actually been informed that all the banks throughout the nations, including Britain and USA, are under the control of the World Bank (The New World Order Banking System), however, that is this situation, you will hear often the words 'World Bank' banded around by politicians and others, on a regular basis – it is real!]

The article also described how Cyprus came to financial collapse. It was the smallest EU member yet had a huge financial pot of money from Russia, Britain, money launderers etc until 2009 it went into recession [like many other EU countries]. In 2012 it went into total collapse to 'junk status. It had accumulated 22 billion euros of Greek debt so requested help from the EU, [oh! Surprise surprise!] The Troika (a trio group) which is the European Commission (EC), the International Monetary Fund (IMF) European Central Bank (ECB) this group imposed **CONDITIONS** called 'Austerity Measures'.

These conditions involved cutting:

1. **Civil Service Salaries**
2. **Pensions**
3. **Social Benefits**
4. **And implementing Taxes**

In return Cyprus was given a 10 billion Euro 'bail-out' deal, after which the Cypriot Government was forced to **RESTRUCTURE** and **AMALGAMATE** the Bank of Cyprus with Laiki and the latter was a scapegoat bank made to fail so that all the money could be taken over by the main bank. Prior to the actual amalgamation, billions of euros were withdrawn by Russians and associates of the President Anastasiades (newly elected President of Cyprus).

[The bold and underlined words are significant and should be remembered by the reader as these concepts are mentioned later].

In Nov 2010 all major governments of G20 agreed at the Seoul Summit to implement the new 'Bail – In' Regime. This is Russia trying different methods and policies to pacify nations who have been taken over and controlled by these conditions and obligations since accepting financial help from the TROIKA. A website called Globalresearch.ca provides an excellent explanation of this 'Bail-in' regime. Basically what it means is the N.W.O. took all of the banks money in the first place to make them bankrupt, then gave them money to re-establish the large banks, using the assets from 'failed banks' to build up these main banks. Then to keep them solvent they take away the customer's savings by bankrupting these failed banks which robs the saver of their savings. The banks then are 'bailed in' by the customers!

It is the individual consumer who now bears the brunt of the financial losses. It is the customer who now finances the large businesses and organisations that supposedly serve them.

The customers have recently been informed that all interest on savings is to be drastically reduced (to the point where it is actually pointless saving for a mere pittance of interest on offer today). Also included in this reduction of interest is the ISA which has become regulated so much that it is too complicated to follow, and the Savings Bonds (Ernie) which offers a lower return on winnings.

So basically it is the consumer who once again is paying out and losing out = bailing in the banks!

It is interesting how the above report came to light as this very subject has been written about in future chapters of this book, particularly of a report by Barry Smith, from New Zealand, on video which was recorded in year 2000.

Barry a teacher and author of many books on Eschatology (End Times Prophesy) and the New World Order pointed out that these things would take place and now in 2013 they are happening before our very eyes and everything he said was accurate.

The author of the Last Chance series discovered, through personal experience and watching world events (Eschatology studies) and linking this research to biblical writings, that this research has led to the same conclusions as Barry mentioned, these have all come to pass; the prophesied events have already occurred!

Shift of power - Further worldwide and societal changes have involved a focus on a shift of power between customers [consumers] and large business organisations, which has already been demonstrated above. This involved passing accountability and responsibility, from the organisation onto the individual, (who has no power to fight). The time when businesses would do all they can to support the customer and offer a fair deal, that concept has disappeared. There has been a removal of responsibility, accountability and liability which has now shifted from the large organisations, and placed on the consumer, so that the customer is not protected against unfair treatment, instead they are now vulnerable to unfair deals and can do nothing about it. Like the bank savings 'bail-in' system, consumers are always paying out and losing out, so that large businesses can acquire huge wealth! We know this to be fact by the huge salaries paid out to directors of such companies. Many have become millionaires over night!

In the past, customer complaints were dealt with and compensated; now complaints are often overridden with political and repetitive legal jargon to dissuade the customer from pursuing the complaint. Large organisations have legal backup and easily find ways to scheme out of responsibility! This has given them greater powers! As a result, the individual is powerless to fight injustice or corruption!

Accountability and responsibility has transferred onto the individual customer who are powerless to resist as they do not have the financial capability or professional expertise to resist or fight! A few years ago in the UK a free legal aid service was available for those on a low income to receive free legal representation on all matters of injustice. Today there is no such service except for family matters.

Society has become strongly divided between the provider of goods and services and the consumer. Power lays with the providers not the receivers!

All inhabitants' young and old have been manipulated 'covertly' into becoming consumers, even the elderly drawing their pensions. Older people in Britain are forced in many cases to organise their own health care and pay for it under a government funding scheme called 'Direct Payments'. These old people become employers, hiring an employee to care for them! Older people feel when they reach 80 yrs of age; they do not want responsibility but to be left to retirement in peace! But they are forced to be part of consumerism!

Pensioners are now seen as earners and receive a pay slip instead of a pension statement; they are taxed on their pensions.

The unemployed and disabled or mentally ill are forced to work and therefore become contributors (consumers) funders to the N.W.O. activities. Some will argue that it is good for people to work and that is true however, choice is replaced by enforcement!

All of the above, put individuals, into a power struggle they know they cannot win- they become victims of the elite! It produces a feeling of helplessness and hopelessness and a feeling of entrapment! Compassion has disappeared replaced by dictatorship already!

This is dangerous it could bring the person to a point of despair where they are likely to become passive and withdrawn into themselves , eventually taking their own lives or react in a negative way by turning violent, aggressive, taking their anger and frustration out on others. Certainly we have experienced a huge increase in violent behaviour during the past few years.

The inhabitants in the third world countries, who are weakened by poverty and disease, are willing to submit/ comply for food to feed their children whereas in western society they will submit in order to sustain their standard of living, entering into huge debts to do so!

All will become compliant under the stress and strain! These unfortunate people enter into a state of utter helplessness and hopelessness as they struggle to survive, many sadly fall under the pressure and either submits to the call of self- induced harm, insanity or deep depression. Interestingly, they still refuse to turn to God for help!

A person who is in a state of helplessness and a feeling of low worth is susceptible, therefore placed in a vulnerable position through bad debts, poverty and so on. Placing such pressure on a human, particularly those responsible for the welfare of their families have often resulted in the person taking their own lives rather than face seeing their children suffer. Many just cannot cope with these trials of life.

This is useful information to those who plan to control the inhabitants of the world. The more susceptible people are to traumas or crisis resulting in depression, the more vulnerable they become to the influences used to take control of their lives! Hitler knew all about this. He knew how to place a person into a helpless state so that they became fully submissive to whatever was their fate; they were unable to fight because they lost the will to live. The Jewish people are witnesses to this, 6 million Jews tortured and slaughtered, while the rest of the world sat back and watched!

Win or Lose? - If a person is placed in such a situation it is a psychological battle to fight without faith! If an individual does not have a relationship with God then there is no hope in them. They can see no future, no happy destiny. They therefore loose the battle.

Atheists have won many souls into the world of humanism by telling people that to believe in God is escapism from reality, a crutch for people who cannot face the thought of death. But that is the most stupid suggestion ever! And the most ridiculous excuse for rejecting God! Which is better, to have hope or hopelessness?

Believers are on a 'Win Win' situation because of the knowledge and experiences they have through a personal relationship (evidenced relationship) with God who guarantees an afterlife. This is factually, proven, by the resurrection of

Christ, which was witnessed by many people at that time and recorded, as well as the many testimonies from people today, who experience daily that Christ Yeshua is alive and real today! There were many other biblical figures taken to heaven or resurrected from the dead and many people today have experienced near death or other traumatic occasions when they have seen or heard or felt the presence of Christ.

Yet humanists are on a 'lose lose' situation they have no such hope –only a definite finality in eternal death! Suggesting that to accept there is no afterlife, death is the end and there is no hope for a future is just plain foolishness! It offers nothing! And more importantly it's a LIE!

There is an afterlife for those who reject God – Its life eternal in Hell! But people are not told this! *"Sodom and Gomorrah and the surrounding towns gave themselves up to sexual immorality and perversion. They serve as an example of those who suffer the punishment of eternal fire"*.
Jude verse 7.

People are told only what they can bare to hear! The thought of dying and being placed in a box for burial or cremated is acceptable to many as they see this as the end. What people are *not* told by humanists is that you have a soul and that soul does not die! The soul is you! The soul is your personality, it is who you are! The body, an empty shell, is what is buried or cremated! The soul, if not saved by Christ, prior to death, or the person's name is not written in the book of life by God, goes before God on judgement day to be punished according to the person's deeds. Punishment consists of different levels and it lasts forever, unlike a prison sentence when you are set free after a period of time. Punishment is forever!

Placing yourself into a position where your mind, soul and body is susceptible to abuse is the door opening to trouble! When it is open anything can happen.

Here is a scenario:

A husband goes into a newspaper shop to buy a newspaper, he sees a magazine with a nude woman on the front page, he decides to have a quick peek through the magazine, thinking 'it's okay, no one will know, 'besides', he says 'it's what men do!' Then later that evening his wife goes out with her work mates while he decides to watch some television, as he flicks through the channels his thoughts fell on the image of the nude woman in the magazine and it excited him, he continued flicking the channels and came across an adult channel so he watched it. On his wife's return he was keen to experience some of what he had watch on the Adult TV. However, his wife was tired and wanted only to sleep. Next day the husband went to work and discussed the TV program with his colleague who then offered to bring him some DVD's he could watch. The following evening he watched the DVD's and he was mesmerised by the various scenes even when it showed young Asian girls who looked no more than 14 or 15 years old. He found himself quite excited about his new hobby and could not wait to get home after work so he could go onto the computer to buy some more DVD's and that night he found some DVD's entitled 'Virgins', this was the start of a deeper level of perversion seeking thrills from young girls of 13 enslaved in pornography against their will, yet he was enjoying it!

He was gripped in sin! This sin sent him far away from the hands of God into the clutches of the devil himself! This man who started looking at a nude woman sunk to the depths of depravity and sold his soul for lust! The mind is weak when there are many temptations about and when people are feeling despair in their lives they become vulnerable to closing the doors to righteousness and taking in the lusts and pleasure, seeking these as a comforter.

In this scenario that man's destiny was to seek pornographic material of young children and the next stage would be paedophilia. He would be trapped! Satan captured the man and held him to ransom!

That is how it works. Open the door to evil and your world could change overnight!

Open the door to righteousness and your world could change overnight! It is a matter of receiving blessings or curses (curses mean no God-given blessings and a life of trouble). The choice is available for the individual to take.

Manipulation of the Mind - With the advancement of research, on the workings of the human brain, comes the ability to manipulate the brain and therefore the mind. Because they are linked it is easy to affect the brain function and therefore affect the memory, particularly, the storage and retrieval of information and also perception.

During the 1950's Wilder Penfield performed surgery on an epileptic patient and discovered he could manipulate the brain to produce memories. This opened the door to brain manipulation through surgery but also knowledge gradually developed to understand how 'environmental influences' can also affect behaviour and memories. For example a great deal of research was performed to find out how a person behaved under pressure, as evidenced in the previously mentioned Milgram and Stanford experiments. Derren Brown on his Television show, demonstrated during his series, how it was possible to control the mind of an individual. He experimented on a young man and conditioned him to take on the role of an assassin which was obviously done as a safe and controlled experiment so that he would not actually commit the assassination, although he reached the point where he entered the premises of the (volunteer target –a VIP) and pointed the gun at him.

Derren also demonstrated on another program how easy it is to control the minds of a mass audience!

Physical stimuli on our bodies is what generate our mind into thoughts, feelings and consciousness as well as our subconscious. Stimulation from external stimuli produces our perceptions and therefore our actions. E.g. if we see the sun shining we perceive the sun is too bright for our eyes so we put on our sunglasses. This is a conscious action. However, in our subconscious level there may be a buried memory that is triggered by the sun which brings to the surface the memory of sunstroke several years ago which led to hospitalised, so instead of putting on sunglasses, we may drink a glass of water.

This is how the mind can be controlled by an anonymous method. Implanting thoughts, creating new memories that trigger behaviour, these are the methods used for mass mind control which is discussed and evidenced throughout this book.

Derren Brown used every day, regular behaviour that would be performed by any person in any circumstances, like walking along the road, making a cup of tea etc. He would use these normal familiar events to plant key 'trigger words' or phrases or he would give the person a gift i.e. the assassin was given a toy gun as a joke. Later a real gun would be planted ready to be found by the assassin when the assassin was given the key trigger to perform his task. All of this was achieved without the participant being aware he was selected to assassinate a VIP; instead he had been given a completely different scenario. All during the process the participant was in his normal conscious state until he was triggered into a trance like state and controlled via triggers, into performing the (simulated) assassination.

This suggests under the right conditions, using the appropriate methods, it is possible to control an individual's mind and force that person to commit a criminal act without them being aware. It is important for the reader to hold onto this concept as it will be useful later to make sense of other concepts mentioned.

The mind is intangible and invisible and therefore difficult to research. Many philosophers and psychologists have debated the subject at great length. Plato suggested the mind was the 'soul', separate and different from the rest of the body. He also suggested the mind and brain existed separately.

The Christian Philosopher St Augustine (A.D. 354 -430) believed the forming of ideas in our mind was a gift from God; he called this gift 'illumination'.

Since Plato and Augustine's insight to the mind, humanists have attempted to distort this reasoning and replace it with evolutionary explanations such as, environment decides a person's thought patterns based on learned behaviour or genetically transferred knowledge. Others suggest knowledge can be gained by thinking and reasoning, removing completely the spiritual element of the mind that links us to the Spirit of God.

Sensory experiences are important and determine our perceptions. If we hear a high pitched sound that after a short while gives us a severe headache, we are likely to investigate the source of the problem. If it stops and our headache immediately goes away we would assume the headache was caused by the high pitched sound. If we ate a particular food containing wheat and we suddenly felt ill we would assume we had an allergic reaction or intolerance to the wheat, even though the real problem is a substance added to the wheat. If we smelt gas but the property only had electricity we may possibly assume the smell was something else or outside of the property. These are common sense thoughts, to rationalise the stimuli received to the brain and based on your perception of the situation. However, if the brain is programmed i.e. by hypnotism or by using autosuggestion or specific classical conditioning, it is possible to react or perceive differently to the stimuli.

It has become possible to convince people that white is black and black is white or that good is evil and evil is good. People have come to a 'complacency level' where the majority believe everything they hear on the news without questioning its authenticity. Not so long ago people would be able to question things and stand outside the box to look in at what is really going on. However, more and more people are becoming entrapped in their minds so that they become complacent and accept the untruth that good is evil and evil is good!

Instead of looking deeply into a cause, people today tend to go for the easy option and accept the most obvious answer for example the wheat allergy mentioned above. If a person feels ill after eating a wheat product and this occurs several times over a long period of time, logically, it must be the wheat that is the cause of the illness. However, if the person was to investigate further they would discover that a product called Gliadin had been artificially introduced into the wheat and this would produce opium type symptoms that not only produce the symptoms causing ill health but also produced an addiction to wheat, so that wheat is craved for and therefore continued to be eaten, the illness and the effect of the opiate keeps you and your mind under constant control of those who processed the scheme to achieve mass compliance of the population! But humanity tends to accept what is obvious and easiest to accept, they avoid delving deeper! So the truth is never discovered –they continue to eat wheat, continuing their addiction to it, so they eat more and more absorbing more of the opiate derivative which produces a state of acceptance, compliance and submission. It also increases the lack of desire to use the mind to analyse what is going on! It plays games with our conscious level.

Consciousness is very significant in relation to hypnosis, meditation, psychoactive drugs and sleep patterns. These can influence the way our brain processes 'conscious' thought. Consciousness is being aware of our subjective (internal) experiences.

In the bible God often says he has closed the eyes and ears and the mind of certain people, so they cannot know the time or the secrets of God's word. This is referenced to those who practice evil! But in those who are loyal to him he opens their minds to understanding and provides them with wisdom and discernment.

The unconscious mind is necessary, people cannot remember everything all of the time, it would be too exhausting. Therefore every day experiences or repetitive events may be pushed back into the subconscious memory store, rather like the archives in a government department. It is the brain's way of avoiding overload. It is usual for unpleasant events to transfer to the subconscious level. Specific triggers or signs may later recall the stored event to the front of the memory.

It is the unconscious mind, emotions, judgement and reasoning, that can be affected by traumatic experiences and therefore subdued and hidden in the depths of the subconscious.

This is what happened to a woman called Arizona who testified to her childhood experiences as a young child, born into a demonic family (whether fallen angels or cross bred descendants– this concept is explained later in more detail).
Arizona and other children were conceived and born specifically chosen to be the property of the Illuminati, (a powerful elite group (see Appendix 2). Arizona discussed how she was tortured, starved, sexually abused and trained to perform terrible activities against her will. She discovered that this abuse was deliberate to create a traumatised mind which made it easier to control and program her to do what they wanted. If we look back at what was stated above about subconscious storage of unpleasant experiences, these were

triggered to the forefront of Arizona's mind to bring her into a vulnerable state and susceptible to mind control!

When a person suffers a trauma there are several biological events taking place in the mind and body, particularly chemical changes. Depending on the severity of the trauma, the body goes into a state of anxiety which produces high levels of cortisol. This has the effect of causing confusion, passivity and physical weakness, there is an inability to fight or resist, as the memories take over the mind and the powerful emotions associated with the traumatic event produce fear, insecurity and helplessness. People today are suffering the same traumatic effects from excessive anxiety because of severe debt, ill health, unemployment, poverty etc.

An altered state of awareness is the term given to the period when you may watch a TV program and not notice someone walk into the room or speak to you. This is when you are so engrossed in the program that you lose conscious awareness of your surroundings. This is what happens when hypnotised and when asleep or taking drugs.

People are most vulnerable when over stretched mentally or under a lot of pressure or perhaps anxious about debts, their safety or health, these people are susceptible to mind control i.e. hypnosis.

The hypnotist creates an atmosphere to induce relaxation and deep sleep or a trance state. The person is then ready and susceptible to the autosuggestion put forward by the hypnotist, and the mind is shifted from the focus of the environment during this process.

There are many methods used to manipulate a person's mind:
- Media i.e. propaganda, advertising, specific storylines, distorted news reports, censorship.
- Social and hard drugs and other prescribed medication.
- Environment i.e. external stimuli used to produce desensitization, that is, people become emotionless, or unaffected by horrific scenes such as murder or victimisation. Desensitisation produces a nation of bullies and cold hearted people! Reality TV programs whereby contestants compete against each other and the audience make hurtful comments and vote people in or

out. This is based on the Roman Gladiator sport when the audience 'thumb up' or more commonly 'thumbs down' (meaning kill) the loser of a Gladiator fight. Life had no value! Today humans are treated the same way—life has no value!

- Authority figures, as in the Milgram experiment and Hitler's Regime.
- Leaders of power.
- Political pressure.
- Economic restraints.
- Subliminal messages

And many more methods used to bring the inhabitants to submission, to a helpless and hopeless state, ready to receive and accept whatever is asked of them!

Arizona, the woman mentioned earlier, was under total control of her programmer, an ex-hitler psychologist who experimented on the Jewish victims during WW2. His name was Mengele (however, he used many different false identities)! It was when he died and there was no replacement programmer that Arizona was able to escape and fight against her captors-the illuminati. She now spends her time spreading the word about this organisation which she describes as alien creatures. However, Arizona is not familiar with God's prophecies or the bible references mentioned earlier. These aliens that look like reptiles (as she describes them), with their piercing eyes and scaly skin, sound very much like the dragon's offspring. She also mentions demons but she describes them as unseen. They are hidden in the spiritual world as well as those who have possessed human bodies. The latter would be those demons that have human form and dwell among us.

Incredible stuff yet as we work through the evidence it becomes more feasible!

The mind is a precious gift from God when used correctly. To seek goodness, to desire knowledge of and a relationship with, Christ and God, to look up to the promise of everlasting life where life is uncomplicated, safe and secure, free from corruption and evil, where there is no disease, no stress, no poverty or starvation, where there is perfect peace!

As we have read so far, the mind can also be misused and abused by self- abuse (drugs and alcohol etc) but also by others when placed in the right environment with the right triggers. The mind is an important commodity to those who intend to control the world. It is a commodity that can be sold, used and abused and robotically controlled to perform outrageous wicked and evil deeds.

We have a responsibility to protect our minds and those of our loved ones so that we do not enter the slavery which is intended as our future destiny by satan. He is working to either destroy human life and to capture those who remain alive, to serve his purpose – that purpose is to destroy Israel, God's people the Jews, Messianic Jews and Christians and to cause everyone to deny Yeshua and God and instead worship the devil (lucifer), pronouncing him as god.

Within the Great Tribulation the dragon's goal will be to destroy God's people, the Jews [those who were not taken up in the rapture]. Satan will also take control of Jerusalem.

"Don't let anyone deceive you in any way for that day (of the Lord) *will not come until the rebellion occurs and the man of lawlessness is revealed, the man doomed to destruction. He will oppose and will exalt himself over everything that is called God or is worshipped, so that he sets himself up in God's temple, proclaiming himself to be God."* God's temple is in Jerusalem.

The book of Ezekiel and Revelation are worth reading as there are dual references to the end times. Lucifer and his army take over Jerusalem and the land of Israel will be subjected to lawlessness beyond imagination. Then the time will come when God says *"Disaster! An unheard of disaster is coming!"* Ezekiel 7:5- 27

In Ezekiel chapter 8 Ezekiel was given a vision. He was taken to the entrance of the North Gate of the inner court of the Temple near the alter where the idol that provokes to jealousy stood, *"Son of man, do you see what they are doing –the utterly detestable things…"* Ezek 8:4: This refers to the Great Tribulation period when the third Temple is built and terrible idolatry and rebellion takes place. In Chap 9 God tells his messenger to go into Jerusalem and put a mark on the foreheads (with God's holy mark of protection) on all those who detest what is happening in the temple!

All of this was also the time of the Babylonian invasion and this is a simulation of the end times soon to come when Lucifer and his followers (the new Babylonian Empire – an amalgamation of many nations) will repeat history! Then after this time God has set a promise for his people Israel. He will gather them all to Israel where they will dwell as one undivided nation. Christ Yeshua will be their king. God will save them from their sinful backsliding! Israel is the remnant of Jews and Christians (joined as one man) during the Great Tribulation period. Chapter 43 describes the heavenly temple that comes down from heaven to the New Jerusalem on the New Earth as prophesied in Revelation 21.

The whole of chapters 43, 44, 45, 46, 47 and 48 prophesy the 1,000 years which takes place as a transition period and a 1,000 years Sabbath rest for those who are saved! During this time Christ reigns and the Law of God will come out of Zion!

Let it be known that in those days although Yeshua is king the TORAH LAW will still be relevant! It is never made obsolete! Be sure to understand that Christians have never replaced the Jews!

Finally, understand that Jews will be saved by God's Grace in the same way as the Christians! Jews were promised eternal life, their names were written in the book of life and they were offered eternal life long before Yeshua came as Savior! Yes he was sent for the Jewish people to be saved (not converted) and yes he was sent for the Gentiles to be saved, because the time of deception had commenced and therefore for salvation the Jews and Christians needed Christ! However, eternal life is a different matter! Salvation and Eternal Life are two different words with different meanings. One applies to the present situation and may be temporary and the latter is everlasting.

CHAPTER 4

INFLUENCES PRODUCING COMPLIANCE

We have already discussed a few of the influences that produce a situation of compliance of individuals and communities as well as nations. These influences appear to the complacent and willingly compliant 'law abiding' individual, as normal events which is part of life's progression and evolution of mankind. Such naivety is dangerous, as it leads to deception and enslavery of the mind!

Let's look at some of these influences in more detail.

1. TECHNOLOGY:

At the moment, the subtle, gradual take- over of the human mind is achieved by using normal everyday common sense methods the individual is familiar with. It is this familiarity that mind control becomes unnoticed, nevertheless it is still there! Just like electricity is there, in the hidden atmosphere, yet we know it exists because it provides us with the energy needed to switch on the kettle, to give us light, to work the heating systems etc.

The 'take-over' is done covertly behind attractive items that offer excitement, gadgetry, status and a competitive stance, particularly among the young.

Technology has made huge advances in mind control as it is able to reach the minds of a large number of the population worldwide; again it particularly burrows into the brains of the young mind! This can be seen today by the fact that almost every young person has the latest mobile phone that does everything for them. They use it to socialise with friends, listen to music, play games, find directions, set a wakeup call, and use a dictionary or language translation and shop! These young people spend hours thumbing on these mini computers and they do very little else!

Technology i.e. computers, mobile phones, internet, wireless systems, all of these, through the invention of the microchip, has introduced all the nations to the concept of a global world called the global village. Using this term was chosen to create an image of a small world, a village type community! Ultimately, the plan for the N.W.O is to make it small so that it is feasible to have one leader to rule the world –the small global village. Notice how different it sounds to the words 'world, universe or global!

Nexus Magazine reported on its global page (2013) *Wireless technology emits electromagnetic radiation that effect fauna and flora near mobile phone masts. The microwave and radiofrequency pollution create long-term health issues. It affects bees, worms, birds etc. It interferes with bird's magnetic navigational function.* Source of information: http://www.wifi-in-schools-australia.org

[This explains a lot, over the years birds have just flown straight into car windows, planes and telegraph poles etc. There's a shortage of bees in UK and once common birds have now become scarce!]

To lead up to this point of global control, the computer has been a significant piece of technology. It is essential, for a future world leader to have control, not only of the people, but also of world finance and commerce, world military and nuclear power, distribution and production of goods and services, religion, communications and of course political power. Control of communication happened many years ago with the censorship of the news, in favour of Arab nations and propaganda against Israel. Controlling the film, television and advertising industry, ensures people are educated to receptiveness; to receive massive world changes, using a variety of mind control techniques, via the media and computer internet making it possible to reach the whole world. Language is no longer a problem with applications (apps) that translate.

Computers are bombarded with advertisements and scam emails often infiltrating our emails daily. All of these influence our thinking, our purchasing, our trends, and our likes and dislikes. It also shapes our image and culture. If you stand back and look at the people around you, (particularly the young) you would be able to see how uniformed society has become, how people behave alike, wear the same style of clothing, do the same hand gestures, speak the same trendy jargon and all have the same style of mobile phone with the latest up to date applications. People have become so involved with material goods and keeping up to date, it is an obsession!

The need to communicate with each other has become vital to our existence, through these little hand held computers.

When you walk through the streets and see many people holding mobile phones to their ears, it is evidenced how easy it is to communicate to each other across the world and within the local community, not only that, many people have ear phones so they can listen to music while exercising, walking or driving the car.

Communication through other media such as television, cinema and theatre, is a vital instrument for instilling messages, and mind changing triggers as well as propaganda, through the films watched, the plots used, subtle advertising and trends of behaviour in TV programmes such as soaps and reality TV. Many adverts, films, etc are about murder, witchcraft, sexual permissiveness or satanism and horror.

Very few are straight forward family entertainment, Even Disney films (since Walt Disney's death) has taken to produce films that are no longer cute but have a theme involving witchcraft, or scary scenes or underlying themes of disobedience and chaos or subtly present evil! Many animated films today contain friendly dragons and friendly scaly creatures that are at war with unfriendly creatures.

Today after years of programming the public to become desensitized, (become complacent to and therefore accepting what would normally be considered evil), to whatever is presented to them, the entertaining media i.e. TV, Films, computer applications, mobile phones and games are all used as mind control instruments to transmit subliminal commands, instructions or triggers to perform certain behaviour. More importantly it does the job of desensitising the viewers to accept all things wicked and evil and instil an aversion to all things good and righteous! It is quite acceptable and the 'norm' for every household to watch Harry Potter films or read the books, including young susceptible children. Whereas a few decades ago anything to do with witchcraft would have been frowned upon and there would have been an uproar if it had become part of the school curriculum or shown on television.

Now people salivate (like Pavlov's dogs) while waiting for the next book to be published! People have been conditioned to acceptance and to dismiss all previous reservations about witchcraft and occult, so many symbols and idolatry figurines have been in eye view for so long that people now desire to have these in their homes. It is the 'done' thing, the fashion, the latest trend to have a Buddha statue or an African witchcraft artefact on the shelf, in their homes, where a wooden cross once sat! This is how apostasy came about, from transforming the minds to accept these evils as the 'norm' and desirable possessions!

Many PC Games, particularly hidden object games where you have to search for objects hidden amongst a mass of other objects in a particular setting, have a mind control element also. These 'Hidden Object' games are great fun trying to find hidden items, yet many of the games are themed on witchcraft, occult or ghosts. Within the scenes, the hidden objects are usually among many other objects, all of which are typically objects of the Babylonian era or the Egyptian era, and also contain occult objects and satanic symbolism. While searching for these objects, the brain is focusing so hard that it goes into an 'altered state of consciousness'. It is impossible for the brain not to register the repeated images of occult, new age or ancient mystical symbolism! These games can become addictive and control the mind so much that these games take over your life! You find yourself wanting to play more and more of these games and so you frantically hunt for new games and feel withdrawal symptoms when there are no new games available. It becomes an obsession.

The same happens with other technology including music and mobile phones. These small mobile computers are a pilot for the soon to be launched 'Google glasses (details on this later). Why are the mobiles so popular? They have created a simulation to addictive behaviour. But more importantly where ear phones are used, this is a direct line into the brain and therefore the mind! Total focus on anything to the point of 'selected concentration' can be dangerous and place the person in a vulnerable position.

People have already been programmed and conditioned to use the mobile phone constantly. They have been classically conditioned like the Pavlov dogs experiment. Dogs were trained to perform certain behaviour after hearing a bell ring, they became so accustomed to the bell which meant they would receive food whenever they heard it, and eventually it triggered another response – salivation. Every time the dogs expected the bell to ring they salivated! They had been conditioned to new behaviour by using the bell to stimulate a change in their behaviour. Young people have been conditioned in the same way to use their mobile phones, watch films and TV or using the computer, for the same reasons as Pavlov's dogs-expectation of satisfying their addiction needs! Young people have been trained into using the instruments that can alter their behaviour and ultimately control their minds!

Take a look at the youth of today and see how they are constantly fiddling with their phones, sending and receiving messages, playing games, going on the internet, searching web pages, it has taken over their lives! Look at business people who use their phones constantly day and night for business purposes as well as personal use. People have become addicted and controlled by these small hand held instruments of mind control!

2   EDUCATION:

It has already been mentioned about educational influences which have led to the world apostasy, particularly in western countries, such as Britain.

Recently there was an article in a daily newspaper confirming the reduction of sponsorships and bursaries which had previously allowed the lower income students opportunity of an education, these young people have been squeezed out.

There is gradually a widening gap between upper and lower incomes in all sectors, particularly within the private and public education sector. Entrance to schools, (and grant applications) are now only offered to secular schools, therefore excluding religious schools.

On the news recently (July 2013) it mentioned that the number of students from poor families have dropped from University places and the number of bursaries available were also reduced.

In the past, sex education was never part of the school curriculum for infant or junior school; parents were expected to prepare their children for such knowledge. Sex before marriage was never a problem as moral teaching was commonplace in all homes including secular ones. Obviously there were exceptions, but not common everyday problems like there are today, therefore sex education was not necessary until senior school and even then it was a basic 'need to know' teaching not explicit detail encouraging sexual activity and providing contraception to under age schoolchildren *WITHOUT THEIR PARENTS KNOWLEDGE OR CONSENT*! This sex education has become part of the school curriculum, like many other SECULAR subjects i.e. evolution, multi-religious teaching and computer training.

These and other subjects are the new 'required' curriculum for the N.W.O. Whereas previous (pre 1970's) the educational curriculum was based on living skills, the 3 R's, home economics, religious education (Christian teaching which included morality teaching such as appropriate sexual behaviour).

Television programs, films, clothing industry and advertising all encourage pre-marital under age sexual promiscuity. It is seen as the 'norm' and endorsed by Government law that says under age children can go to the doctor without the parents knowledge for contraception and the 'after' pill to induce a quick miscarriage.

3   MEDIA AND PROPAGANDA

As already mentioned, media can be used to instil into the person, by manipulation of the mind, an acceptance of specific messages, themes, patterns of behaviour, and propaganda that causes change to the individual's belief system and input new values systems, including the acceptance of the changes required for total population compliance!

Here is an example of propaganda **by _NTEB News Desk_**

Is the Obama administration at least partially responsible for turning the George Zimmerman trial into such a huge national spectacle? Judicial Watch has obtained documents which prove that the Community Relations Service, a division of the Department of Justice, was sent to Sanford, Florida in late March 2012 "to help organize and manage rallies and protests against George Zimmerman". This included spending quite a bit of money, arranging meetings between the NAACP and local leaders, and providing police escorts for protesters.

Someone needs to ask Obama why the federal government was doing this. A story that should have never made national headlines now threatens to unleash a firestorm of racial fury unlike anything we have seen since the Rodney King verdict. One young man, a neighbourhood watch captain, shot and killed another young man. This kind of thing happens in American cities every single night. George Zimmerman says that he did it in self-defence. He should be allowed to have his day in court and that should be the end of the matter. But instead, this thing has been hyped into a massive national spectacle and it is being used to divide us along racial lines. And it appears that we have clear evidence that the Obama administration was involved in doing the hyping.

The documents that Judicial Watch was able to obtain contain some absolutely startling information. Apparently the role of the Obama administration in these protests was quite substantial...

JW filed a Freedom of Information Act (FOIA) request with the DOJ on April 24, 2012; 125 pages were received on May 30, 2012. JW administratively appealed the request on June 5, 2012, and received 222 pages more on March 6, 2013. According to the documents:
March 25 – 27, 2012, CRS spent $674.14 upon being "deployed to Sanford, FL, to work marches, demonstrations, and rallies related to the

shooting and death of an African-American teen by a neighbourhood watch captain."

March 25 – 28, 2012, CRS spent $1,142.84 "in Sanford, FL to work marches, demonstrations, and rallies related to the shooting and death of an African-American teen by a neighbourhood watch captain."

March 30 – April 1, 2012, CRS spent $892.55 in Sanford, FL "to provide support for protest deployment in Florida."

March 30 – April 1, 2012, CRS spent an additional $751.60 in Sanford, FL "to provide technical assistance to the City of Sanford, event organizers, and law enforcement agencies for the march and rally on March 31."

April 3 – 12, 2012, CRS spent $1,307.40 in Sanford, FL "to provide technical assistance, conciliation, and onsite mediation during demonstrations planned in Sanford."

April 11 – 12, 2012, CRS spent $552.35 in Sanford, FL "to provide technical assistance for the preparation of possible marches and rallies related to the fatal shooting of a 17 year old African American male."

But the involvement of the Department of Justice went far beyond just spending money and helping to organize and manage the protests.

Apparently, the Department of Justice was involved in setting up meetings between the NAACP and local officials, and the Department of Justice even arranged police escorts for protesters…

On April 15, 2012, during the height of the protests, the Orlando Sentinel reported, "They [the CRS] helped set up a meeting between the local NAACP and elected officials that led to the temporary resignation of police Chief Bill Lee according to Turner Clayton, Seminole County chapter president of the National Association for the Advancement of Coloured People." The paper quoted the Rev. Valarie Houston, pastor of Allen Chapel AME Church, a focal point for protestors, as saying "They were there for us," after a March 20 meeting with CRS agents.

Separately, in response to a Florida Sunshine Law request to the City of Sanford, Judicial Watch also obtained an audio recording of a "community meeting" held at Second Shiloh Missionary Baptist Church in Sanford on April 19, 2012. The meeting, which led to the ouster of Sanford's Police Chief Bill Lee, was scheduled after a group of college students calling themselves the "Dream Defenders" barricaded the entrance to the police department demanding Lee be fired. According to the Orlando Sentinel, DOJ employees with the CRS had arranged a 40-mile police escort for the students from Daytona Beach to Sanford.

Under what conditions is it ever acceptable for the federal government to arrange police escorts for protesters?
And why did the Obama administration want to help them?
What was the goal?

As a result of all of the hype that this case has been given, we now have more racial tension in the United States than we have had in a very, very long time.

And it is becoming apparent to everyone what could potentially happen if George Zimmerman is acquitted. In fact, law enforcement officials are so concerned about violence in the aftermath of the verdict that they have released a video encouraging young people not to commit violent acts...

On Monday, the Broward County Sheriff's Office released a video calling on the public not to riot in the wake of the George Zimmerman verdict, expected this week or next in Florida. The Sheriff's Office released a statement explaining that it was "working closely with the Sanford Police Department and other local law enforcement agencies" to coordinate "a response plan in anticipation of the verdict."

The video, titled "Raise Your Voice, Not Your Hands," focuses on attempting to channel reaction into non-violent response. It depicts two youngsters, one black teenage boy, one Hispanic teenage girl. "Raise your voice!" says the girl. "And not your hands!" says the boy. "We need to stand together as one, no cuffs, no guns," says the girl. "Let's give violence a rest, because we can easily end up arrested," says the boy. "I know your patience will be tested," says the girl, and then both conclude, "but law enforcement has your back!"

This never should have happened.

This case should never have been hyped like this.

Instead of being encouraged to look at each other as individuals and fellow American citizens, our politicians and the media continue to hype racial division and strife. Are we ever going to learn how to love one another? source - End Of The American Dream

NTEB News Desk | July 12, 2013 at 6:48 am | Tags: George Zimmerman, Obama Organize, Trayvon Martin | Categories: Headline News, Obama | URL: http://wp.me/p1kFP6-3J0

Another propaganda news report came in:

by NTEB News Desk

Understanding the Smith-Mundt Modernization Act

For decades, a so-called anti-propaganda law prevented the U.S. government's mammoth broadcasting arm from delivering programming to American audiences. But on July 2, that came silently to an end with the implementation of a new reform passed in January. The result: an unleashing of thousands of hours per week of government-funded radio and TV programs for domestic U.S. consumption in a reform initially criticized as a green light for U.S. domestic propaganda efforts. So what just happened?

Until this month, a vast ocean of U.S. programming produced by the Broadcasting Board of Governors such as Voice of America, Radio Free Europe/Radio Liberty and the Middle East Broadcasting Networks could only be viewed or listened to at broadcast quality in foreign countries. The programming varies in tone and quality, but its breadth is vast: It's viewed in more than 100 countries in 61 languages. The topics covered include human rights abuses in Iran; self-immolation in Tibet; human trafficking across Asia; and on-the-ground reporting in Egypt and Iraq.

The restriction of these broadcasts was due to the Smith-Mundt Act, a long standing piece of legislation that has been amended numerous times over the years, perhaps most consequentially by Arkansas Senator J. William Fulbright. In the 70s, Fulbright was no friend of VOA and Radio Free Europe, and moved to restrict them from domestic distribution, saying they "should be given the opportunity to take their rightful place in the graveyard of Cold War relics." Fulbright's amendment to Smith-Mundt was bolstered in 1985 by Nebraska Senator Edward Zorinsky who argued that such "propaganda" should be kept out of America as to distinguish the U.S. "from the Soviet Union where domestic propaganda is a principal government activity."

Zorinsky and Fulbright sold their amendments on sensible rhetoric: American taxpayers shouldn't be funding propaganda for American audiences. So did Congress just tear down the American public's last defence against domestic propaganda?

BBG spokeswoman Lynne Weil insists BBG is not a propaganda outlet, and its flagship services such as VOA "present fair and accurate news."

"They don't shy away from stories that don't shed the best light on the United States," she told The Cable. She pointed to the charters of VOA and RFE: "Our journalists provide what many people cannot get locally: uncensored news, responsible, discussion, and open debate."

A former U.S. government source with knowledge of the BBG says the organization is no Pravda, but it does advance U.S. interests in more subtle ways. In Somalia, for instance, VOA serves as counterprogramming to outlets peddling anti-American or jihadist sentiment. "Somalis have three options for news," the source said, "word of mouth, Al-Shabaab or VOA Somalia."

This partially explains the push to allow BBG broadcasts on local radio stations in the United States. The agency wants to reach diaspora communities, such as St. Paul Minnesota's significant Somali expat community. "Those people can get Al-Shabaab, they can get Russia Today, but they couldn't get access to their taxpayer-funded news sources like VOA Somalia," the source said. "It was silly."

Lynne added that the reform has a transparency benefit as well. "Now Americans will be able to know more about what they are paying for

with their tax dollars - greater transparency is a win-win for all involved,"
she said. And so with that we have the <u>*Smith-Mundt Modernization Act of*</u>
<u>*2012*</u>*, which passed as part of the 2013 National Defense Authorization*
Act, and went into effect this month. But if anyone needed a reminder of
the dangers of domestic propaganda efforts, the past 12 months provided
ample reasons. Last year, two USA Today journalists were <u>*ensnared*</u> *in a*
propaganda campaign after reporting about millions of dollars in back
taxes owed by the Pentagon's top propaganda contractor in Afghanistan.
Eventually, one of the co-owners of the firm <u>*confessed*</u> *to creating phony*
websites and Twitter accounts to smear the journalists anonymously.
Additionally, just this month, The Washington Post <u>*exposed*</u> *a counter*
propaganda program by the Pentagon that recommended posting
comments on a U.S. website run by a Somali expat with readers opposing
Al-Shabaab. "Today, the military is more focused on manipulating news
and commentary on the Internet, especially social media, by posting
material and images without necessarily claiming ownership,"
reported The Post.

But for BBG officials, the references to Pentagon propaganda efforts
are nauseating, particularly because the Smith-Mundt Act never had
anything to do with regulating the Pentagon, a fact that was misunderstood
in media reports in the run-up to the passage of new Smith-Mundt reforms
in January.

One example included a <u>*report*</u> *by the late Buzzfeed reporter Michael*
Hastings, who suggested that the Smith-Mundt Modernization Act would
open the door to Pentagon propaganda of U.S. audiences. In fact, as
amended in 1987, the act only covers portions of the State Department
engaged in public diplomacy abroad (i.e. the public diplomacy section of
the "R" bureau, and the Broadcasting Board of Governors.)

But the news circulated regardless, much to the displeasure of Rep.
Mac Thornberry (R-TX), a sponsor of the <u>*Smith-Mundt Modernization Act*</u>
<u>*of 2012*</u>*. "To me, it's a fascinating case study in how one blogger was*
pretty sloppy, not understanding the issue and then it got picked up
by Politico's Playbook, and you had one level of sloppiness on top of
another," <u>*Thornberry told*</u> *The Cable last May. "And once something*
sensational gets out there, it just spreads like wildfire."

That of course doesn't leave the BBG off the hook if its content
smacks of agitprop. But now that its materials are allowed to be broadcast
by local radio stations and TV networks, they won't be a complete mystery
to Americans. "Previously, the legislation had the effect of clouding and
hiding this stuff," the former U.S. official told The Cable. "Now we'll have
a better sense: Gee some of this stuff is really good. Or gee some of this
stuff is really bad. At least we'll know now." <u>*source - Foreign Policy*</u>

<u>*NTEB News Desk*</u> *| July 15, 2013 at 7:29 am | Tags:* <u>*Broadcasting*</u>
<u>*Board of Governors*</u>*,* <u>*Middle East Broadcasting Networks*</u>*,* <u>*Radio Free*</u>
<u>*Europe*</u>*,* <u>*Smith-Mundt Act*</u>*,* <u>*Voice of America*</u> *| Categories:* <u>*CIA,*</u>

Department of Homeland Security, FBI, Internet, New World Order, Obama, Washington | URL: http://wp.me/p1kFP6-3Ja
***

The point about the media is that it's a powerful commodity used to fool the public. It can be a smoke screen to cover the real issues, sometimes it's used to deceive the public into believing 'everything is fine' 'all is under control' whereas the reality is quite different! Sometimes news reports can be so ambiguous, that the reader is not sure if it is a good or bad report in fact not sure what it's about! People can be fooled by false conceptualisation, by a message which could appear to say one thing, but the listener or watcher could perceive something completely different acquiring a false concept of the truth; this is used to instil a lie into the brain to make it seem a truth!

A strong example of this is that the world has become anti-Semitic. Why? No one really knows. In the same way the world has become anti God. Why? No one really knows. The possible answer is because it has been orchestrated throughout the years by implanted false concepts about Israel and God, which have been internalised by the majority of world population. All it took was a number of news reports, stories by professional figures, figures of authority who were convincing enough for people to accept what was said without checking the facts – and that was the start of the apostasy!

Media in Britain i.e. newspapers, magazines, advertisements are all used to bring about a general consensus, throughout the various communities. For example, there was huge publicity on gay rights, and every soap opera on television had a strong story line that involved gay relationships, so much so that it was 'in your face' every day! Now people have come to accept it as part of their society and even treat gay people as celebrities!

Reports in newspapers were a regular occurrence on the injustices suffered by gay couples! It was so implanted on our brains that homosexuality was okay and good, that it has now been welcomed with open arms by those who are already conditioned to compliance! Now whenever a gay celebrity appears on the screen there is a huge uproar of applause and shouting of approval and acceptance that is not heard for heterosexual acts. People today, go hysterical when a gay person appears on a talent show, and the more perverted their act the more the audience shouts approval! Politically, people are also afraid that if they did not respond they would be accused of discrimination, of homophobia or even breaking the law! It has now become law for gay couples to marry.

Many people (mostly Christians) have protested and refused to acknowledge homosexuality as legal and therefore they have been ostracised publicly because of it. We now have a society that 'BOOS' objectionists, accusing them of homophobia (which means 'fear of homosexual people) and PRAISES Gay Rights!

Interestingly, the rights of non-homosexuals have been squashed in favour of Gay Rights, hence the TRUE DISCIMINATION whereby ordinary folk have been denied their rights. For example, in 2012 the news whereby a gay couple were refused a room at a bed and breakfast guest house, eventually won the case and were compensated £1800 (Oct 2012) The owners of the B&B, a Christian couple, were denied the right to refuse homosexual couples. It was their B&B business yet they were prevented from saying who could and couldn't stay in their home! Never heard of such a thing! Whose rights were really deprived here? Always B&B owners had the right to select their own clientele!

Ironically the rights of heterosexual couples have been deprived when they have applied to adopt or foster children. Many Christians or low income couples/single persons, disabled, or other minor reasons such as age, these heterosexual couples have been refused as foster parents. They were denied this based on the most ridiculous reasons, as mentioned above, particularly because of their Christian faith!

Yet homosexuals have been granted privileges and given the opportunity to adopt children into a home that has two men or two women behaving as a married couple! How confusing is that for a child! Social services who remove children from their natural parents for the most ridiculous reasons i.e. a little bruise found on the child's leg so an investigation starts or because they have difficulty with finances, they are considered unfit parents. A particular target of the SS (social services) are one

THE GREAT APOSTASY The Deceived People

parent families. The SS show concern for the physical wellbeing of a child but not the psychological, (mental) wellbeing of the child.

Social services contradict themselves when they place a child into a same sex home. They have no problem with the child's psychological development in an environment where two men behave like a man and a woman, and psychologically that is considered acceptable for a child's welfare! Whereas a single heterosexual person may be refused on the grounds that the child is deprived of a balanced relationship, even though the one parent consists of either the father who is a MAN or the mother who is a WOMAN, and therefore offers a psychologically healthy concept. Even though the child may have only one parent, that parent is able to define the difference between a mother and father by inference, in a world where a male is a father and a female is a mother, whereby the child is taught obvious boundaries of male and female and their individual roles as such! Whereas, in the gay world that is not the case, it is an environment of mixed roles, no boundaries of identification and total confusion!

One thing is for sure, that God is watching all this and waiting for the day of vengeance! God records every deed that corrupts an innocent child.

The media has always been used to relay propaganda, particularly during wartime, so nothing knew there, except now the propaganda is used to cover up the truth and to deceive. It isn't about war enemies, as it was during the war, but the propaganda is used today to bring ordinary folk into compliance through manipulation and mind control. To program the individual's mind in order to accept evil for good and good for evil!

The world views have 'turned upside down- taken a reversal – so that wickedness has been accepted as the norm and become the 'status quo' and good has become taboo. People of faith are now ridiculed, laughed at and considered weird or extreme!

4   MUSIC:

Young people are bombarded with all sorts of music. It is not news to say that subliminal messages exist within this music that has an effect on behaviour. This was a major issue many years ago when it was thought that subliminal messages were introduced into advertisements on television. These ads were fairly innocent then, which prompted you to go out and buy a chocolate bar or a beer after seeing it advertised. Today however, it is a different story; the messages are much more sinister! Check out 'Mark of the Beast' YouTube video's on subliminal messages where there is evidence of satanic hand signals and satanic messages are revealed. See appendix 6 for backmasking. This technology of introducing an underlying message within the music or wording on a record exists – it is a reality! It is not fiction! Appendix 6 on subliminal messaging and backmasking explains in detail. Vinyl records in the past when played back were used to induce subliminal messages to the subconscious level of the listener. Disc jockeys often used the technique of play back. Today the CD's are used in the same way. When slowed right down (and also video's) and played back, satanic messages such as 'he is god' worship satan' and 'worship satan'. Now you can understand why so many young people have become atheists, satanists, cruel bullies, violent and narcissistically evil.

That is how today a young person can so easily stab another without guilt or remorse that is how a teenager kidnapped and killed a little boy a few years ago without any thought or hesitation!

Today the addiction to music, particularly, rap, head banging music and deep base drum music are the main ones used for subliminal messages or triggers to control and manipulate behaviour.

A great deal of research has taken place on the dangers involved however; most of the research has denied its harmful effects. The research findings were misinterpreted or 'doctored' to avoid the truth coming out. Some of the research was poorly performed, misdirected or invalidated.

It has been disputed many times that television and music do not affect children, yet many children have been found to take their own lives because they went onto a particular website that encouraged suicide. It has been researched and findings have proven that children, including teenagers are very susceptible to addiction through gaming. So why not music? Why not films? If they all have a common denominator which is 'mind control' and possible subliminal messages, then they will all have the same effect on the child!

The hand held gadgets were created so that music can be played anytime, with earplugs constantly in place; young people play over and over again their favourite music. So when the words (that often cannot be understood) have to be listened to with full concentration in order to understand the words that is when it's dangerous! Anything that requires full attention produces susceptibility similar to that of meditation. The mind is focused on one thing- the music. This not only is dangerous when a person is unaware of their environment and susceptible to muggings, attack or worse, their minds are susceptible to the subliminal messages within the music as well as the obvious song theme that also contains a message. This obvious message is usually either about drugs, sexual promiscuity or violence and the subjective message would be about satan and encouraging allegiance to satan. You can find many 'YouTube' videos to evidence this. There is one that slows down the video of famous singers or speakers who when in slow motion are saying something about satan being god or similar. They can also be seen to do the hand signal of a goat with horns and a beard, which is symbolic of satan.

Rap in particular has become a powerful medium for antisocial behaviour, aggression and anti- everything that is 'normal' and 'good'. Gang culture now dominates the rap music sector! And its gang culture that portray the concept that scars are good, tattoos of satanic symbols are good, secret coding and sign language using satanic hand signals are good! Belonging to a gang that portrays 'safety and protection to the new recruit is enticing when so many young people are being bullied, threatened and abused. They crave love and a sense of belonging and therefore find it in gang culture, (even though it is all a lie).' To belong to the gang comes a sinister price tag!

The gang requires from the new recruit, 'loyalty unto death'. Each gang has their own insignia flag (usually a piece of clothing of a particular colour or a design logo on the jacket. They have their own secret initiations and culture. Gang culture is sweeping the youth culture throughout America and Britain!

Racism has increased between blacks and whites and evident in the gangland world; it's what drives them on a daily basis. Their minds can think of nothing else! From morning to the next morning 24/7, their mind is set on gang warfare on destroying the enemy gangs and picking on an innocent, decent person as their target victim during the initiating process of a new recruit, who has been frightened into harming that innocent person or suffer violence to themselves from the other gang members.

Fear and coercion, rules over the enslaved gang members who are bound to a life of hell on earth! The sad thing is they do not realise what is happening to them. They eventually lose all conscious awareness of their previous lifestyle! After they have maimed, or killed so many people or after committing terrible violent acts, they withdraw into themselves and deny any chance of memory of what they were like BEFORE they became a gang member. They often separate themselves from their families (unless the parents are gang members); they alienate themselves from their previous lifestyle. Eventually they become so narcissistic that they have completely changed their identity! Their hearts have hardened towards anything good! Sadly these young people have been pushed in this direction by mind control techniques. It has been deliberately orchestrated this way.

What has happened to them? They had become traumatised by what they had experienced as a gang member, often violent gross acts of a sexually perverted nature, as well as violent acts of bullying and worse, these experiences have a huge traumatic effect on a young mind, so that the experiences permanently damage their emotional status. They then become vulnerable to brainwashing, manipulation and control in every way i.e. mind, body and soul, by their gang leader and ultimately the illuminati mind controllers.

These young people become exactly what the illuminati want them to become-thugs! When you see a gang member they all behave the same, they look the same, and they think the same. They all have tattoos, they take drugs and drink, they all commit crime, they all spend time in prison and they are all 'anti-establishment yet ironically they (without realising it) work for and are controlled by the establishment.

The illuminati can easily provoke gangs into creating violent acts against innocent people as they all belong to satan! Harsh words! Today, in these last days the majority of gang members have crossed the line, there is no return! What I mean by that is- these last days, if you attempt to talk to a gang member about changing his life and leaving the gang he would probably go into a hysterical rage! To him this has become his religion! He is like a member of a religious cult whereby the belief is if he leaves the cult he will surely die! The difference between the religious cult and a gang is that the latter usually does end up dead. It is seen as an act of disloyalty and a threat to the secrecy of the gang, therefore no one can leave the gang.

The member has been so effected by the gang that his or her mind no longer is able to make an assessment of right or wrong, they have no conscience of the terrible things they have done to others, they have no ability to recall the evil murderous deeds as a breaking of a law of the country or a commandment of God or that its morally wrong. Therefore they lack the ability to feel guilt or seek forgiveness from God. Instead they justify their deeds as a means of survival against rival gangs, that they are fighting to survive in a corrupt world, yet they contradict themselves because they are contributing to it!

It is only through a miracle by God, His divine intervention, through the Holy Spirit, that could save a gang member. God can transform a person from being an evil murderer to a Holy disciple if he so desires. He did just that with Saul, (later renamed Paul) a Jewish rabbi who persecuted and killed many Christians, during the period after Christ was crucified. One day while he was on his way to Damascus to persecute more Christians. God stopped him and said 'Saul why do you persecute me?' At that Saul fell to his knees and he was transformed immediately into a faithful, loyal servant of God who travelled the world preaching the Gospel to all men! Paul became a great Apostle and through his biblical writings inspired by God, many have come to believe also. It is this sort of miracle like Paul's, that could save a gang member- but it can only be a miraculous change ordained by God! Prayer and fasting as well as denouncing satan and instead announcing Christ as their savior can a gang member be saved!

It is God who determines the heart of mankind and how much the person has to endure before he can perform such a miracle. Sometimes people are allowed to enter into a situation of evil in order to learn about it. If they repent (turn from this evil lifestyle and turn back to God) they will be saved.

A demon possessed person can only be released by prayer and fasting, repentance and forgiveness and a true 'spiritual rebirth' (which is the miracle of God) to save and reclaim a lost soul!

Currently, it is still possible to achieve redemption and God's Grace but not for much longer. When God's people are removed from this world, taken in the Rapture, the Holy Spirit and anything pertaining to goodness and righteousness will also be gone from the world and that is when it will be too late for these already lost souls who have given allegiance to satan!

5   DRUGS AND MEDICATION

Research is on-going regarding the effects of certain drugs on behaviour. Common sense alone would suggest that mind altering drugs such as LSD (hallucinatory drugs), amphetamines etc would have an adverse effect. The side effects of antidepressants are said to increase the potential to commit suicide particularly within the teenage group. See Appendix 3 regarding LSD. Some medications affect the balance of chemicals in the brain so that behaviour changes i.e. excess dopamine may produce schizophrenic behaviour.

Drugs are easy to misuse by the individual but also as a means of control globally and this has been found in the case of specific chemicals placed in food and water to bring about certain behaviour. For example Bromide was put into the tea of prisoners to reduce their sexual ardour, Gliadin in wheat to induce compliance and submission.

6 GAMES:

There has already been some mention on games addiction earlier, so to recap: there is on-going debate and research taking place regarding the effects of games on behaviour and whether it is addictive. Much of the symptoms of addictive behaviour found in drugs and alcohol abuse can also be seen with young children and teenagers when playing computer games. The aggression is seen when they play the game, their whole attention span is submerged into the game. There is a strong desire to play for hours suggesting it is difficult to leave the game, and eventually the game becomes too easy, so they search for further challenges, which demands even more of their time and focus. All of this behaviour is typical of someone who has become fixated or addicted (depending on the stage they have attained). It is dangerously alluring to the child and their world becomes very small as they refuse to socialize with the rest of society, isolating themselves. Many game themes are violent, involved in war games, fighting or murder, such scenes are highly influential on a young mind who has not yet had the opportunity to develop their own identity. The peak age to do this is during their teen years, this is the time when they are constructing their identities. So common sense tells us that these violent games are going to be internalised and become part of their identity! It becomes difficult to separate reality from fantasy once something has become internalised. Hence we have a distorted mind bent on scenes of violence, aggression and trauma!

7 COMPUTERS AND TELEVISIONS:

Computers and television have been mentioned already, particularly subliminal messages within adverts to encourage buying. These subliminal messages still exist but the messages are not about buying products (that was just a practice pilot study) it has become more advanced now –the focus is direct mind control to alter behaviour and to induce compliance!

There are many YouTube videos by professional organisations (as well as the small timers who make it their hobby to disclose this mind control to the world) that evidence the subliminal messages have reached a different sinister level. Many of these messages now have direct links to worshipping satan. Some demonstrate famous singers or other infamous people either doing the satanic hand sign of the goat with horns (a satanic symbol of the devil as a goat with two horns and a beard) or when their words are played backwards contain a hidden message such as "I love satan, or satan is your god". This would explain why young people suddenly change their behaviour from a sweet attentive, caring person towards wickedness, particularly once they become involved in teenage culture which involves following peer trends such as fashion and music. Even the clothing labels or the inside of the clothing have subliminal messages or directly within the name are some link to immorality i.e. sex or encouragement to an evolutionary lifestyle and more seriously a message that continues the brainwashing.

Some clothing labels have written 'Red Dragon' or logos or slogans that are directing the young person subconsciously to behave a specific way or to have a specific mindset i.e. one logo inside a T Shirt said 'I love my environment'. There was a period where everywhere you looked people were wearing T Shirts with FCUK which was a play on words.

Although on the surface many of these labels are considered just harmless fun, yet subconsciously, mind control is taking place. When you are continually bombarded with symbolism and triggers on a particular theme, it becomes part of your subconscious and conscious level. Eventually desensitisation takes place.

Most people when they buy clothing rarely read the labels or slogans consciously. However, that is why they are subliminal! Every time the T shirt is put on and taken off, washed or ironed, the logo is subconsciously seen and read! It is the trigger that instigates the action or behaviour. As mentioned previously hypnosis and ultimately mind control is dependent on placing words or images into the subconscious that can be recalled at any time and these images or words trigger an action or behaviour that has also been implanted into the subconscious mind by previous autosuggestion and triggers.

Everything looks innocent – it is meant to, otherwise it would not work! There are many YouTube videos that demonstrate the subliminal messages in children's Disney films or other TV programmes. Subliminal messages are not fiction they are FACT! It started many years when Black and White TV and Films existed! It started off as a means of enticing people to buy their products, it was later made illegal but now it is more powerful than ever before and much more dangerous. It has a real effect on the subconscious mind; it is powerful enough to direct your behaviour into taking drugs, committing sinful acts, becoming a sexual predator, or taking your own life! It is powerful enough to direct your mind to rejecting God, pledging allegiance to the devil instead! The power of suggestion in any form can turn anyone to take a tattoo!

The majority of films shown in cinema's and on television are action films and horror, such as the 'Aliens' film! Many films consist of explicit sex scenes, violence, vulgar language, heroes with tattoos, the Alpha Male imagery, and of course the horror films usually to do with witchcraft, zombies, and occult practices and often involves demonic beings, dragons or monsters. All of these films have desensitized people ready to receive the end of day's beast – the antichrist! People still respond to these films with emotion, but at the same time new images are being placed into their minds, images of Alpha Males, for example. Since that concept came into vogue, it has been used everywhere, and now we see men focused on having muscular bodies (the six pack as the ultimate goal) covered in tattoos, dominating women and behaving like narcissistic leaders!

What has actually happened is these men have been mind-controlled into becoming warriors for lucifer's army. They already have the tattoos to mark this and will be ready in their minds to feed their narcissistic hunger for power and leadership!

The films have also implanted into their memories, images of dragons and demons, so when the time comes the beast and his team will be able to reveal their true identity without any horrified looks, they will be accepted willingly, as the individual is unable to separate reality from the film fantasy! It is implanted in their mind that it is normal because they have seen dragons and reptilian creatures for such a long time, in books, films, TV, clothing logos, on T Shirts, on CD labels, etc. That is what happens, the fantasy world is so impacted into the brain that reality and fantasy become one! By the time the second beast is in full power as world leader everyone will have merged fantasy with reality so that they readily accept the dragon as their leader!

Yes! This all sounds fantastic! Too weird to believe? Take time out to reflect, think it through, see how everything covered so far in this book, links together and form a pattern. The information in this book also answers many questions people have been trying to answer for many years.

8   LARGE ORGANISATIONS

Large organisations have been selected specifically to produce global control e.g. British Telecom and the complex telephone system using a variety of different numbers so that you do not know which to use and what the difference is.

Many telephone numbers are now charged at different rates according to the area, length of time etc even though you have paid a high premium package for anytime calls! The packages are the biggest con ever. People are said to benefit from these yet they often pay for calls outside of the specific numbers covered by the package. BT knows that certain numbers will have to be dialled, and this raises a lot of extra cash! They have created a system where you are charged as soon as you dial the number, unlike the past when you only started to pay for the call when you actually spoke to someone.

They also created the option system, the public were told this would reduce waiting time by directing them straight to the person they need, yet you can spend up to an hour waiting for a response and never actually speak to anyone, for this you are left with a high charge on your bill without achieving the goal of talking to someone! Delaying tactics such as being asked to repeat security checks several times during this call option process. And you are paying call fees while you wade through these options!

Large organisations have power and control over the consumers in many ways. For example If you buy a washing machine, and find it was not as described in the instructions, such as the economy wash takes two hours to wash and dry the laundry and then it comes out all wrinkled, needing ironing then it is not an economy wash after all. The inclination is to make a complaint and request the washing machine is collected and a full refund made. However, the response to that would be "sorry cannot do – as you have unwrapped the goods and used it, rendering it as 'used goods."

It was suggested the only way that it could be returned was if it was faulty! But the manager points out that "if they find it isn't faulty there would be a charge for the work done! So you as the customer have obviously been conned into buying goods that you do not want and can do nothing about it – you are in 'catch 22' as they say. Trading Standards are not interested, neither is your local MP, or the Ombusman, neither is Head Office of the Company or the manufacturers or any other organisations involved in consumer complaints, therefore the company is given full authority to sell goods they know to cost the consumer more money to run, even though there is supposedly an energy conservation policy. You are then left with a machine that cost you more in electricity and time, and does not do the job you originally bought it for! This is an example of the power of businesses over the consumer, today! The ridiculous thing about it is there is no way you can know if a purchase is appropriate for your needs until you unwrap it and test it!

9   FOOD AND WATER:

For years people have been aware of food contaminated by pesticides and fertilisers which has an adverse effect on the body's systems that may cause allergies, diseases and a poor immune system. Water has also been an issue with additives such as Chlorine. Soon all worldwide seed production will be controlled by N.W.O. system. Soon farmers will be prevented from planting seeds that are not GM. Soon we will be eating or growing only GM foods. These foods are genetically modified, altered scientifically according to a pre agreed design.

These foods are already in abundance in our shops and restaurants. Rice, soya, corn and wheat are the most common GM's but it has also been quite obvious (although not openly declared) that many fruits and vegetables are being sold in the open market. Farmers are perhaps unaware they are using GM seeds!

It is possible to determine between natural foods and GM. Usually GM fruit and vegetables are larger than normal and feel like plastic, they have very little odour or taste and very little juice, which is often difficult to extract., i.e. if you scratch an organic lemon the juicy lemony smell hits your nostril when you smell it, if you do the same with the GM lemon, nothing happens.   These foods tend to be much firmer than normal foods, and do not bruise easily, lasting several days /weeks before there's any sign of deterioration.

Food is used in many ways to implant harmful or controlling substances into our bodies, such as mentioned in the clip on wheat and Gliadin, see also Appendix 4 concerning GM Rice.

10 RELIGION

During the 1990s the Council of Churches changed their policies. Churches started to adapt to New Age Religion. This was the beginning of a noticeable 'turning away' and 'rebellion' within Christianity. Jewish synagogues had already fallen away from God's directives by incorporating Babylonian religion into the synagogues. Still the Babylonian (pagan) names are used for each month, i.e. Tammuz is the name of the Babylonian god of fertility. Barren Jewish women used to pray to this god; today they are still using this name in the Jewish calendar.

New age concepts have seeped into all religions whether Jew, Christian, Hindu, Muslim, Atheist, Evolutionist, each can find something within the new age religion to meet their perception of their god. New age is a religion that takes concepts from each religion and incorporate these as their own. Therefore they are able to entice people of faith into the entrapment of a false religion.

Those who are truly born again would be able to recognise this false religion, as the Holy Spirit discloses such information to the faithful. However, to those who are carnal Christians, and those with head knowledge (intellectual assent) only, who lack a firm foundation in Christ Yeshua (son of God, the forgiver of sins and the coming Messiah), will be easily misled! If you are unfamiliar with the allegorical story of Pilgrim's Progress it is a good example of how easily a person can be led astray if they do not have a firm foundation in Christ!

People are manipulated through these false religions; they are persuaded that peace can be obtained through Yoga and transcendental Meditation. Mindfulness is an extension of meditation used to encourage total focus on one thing i.e. your breathing or a noise in the background and to accept it into part of your inner being. There are many dangerous practices that allow total vulnerability of the mind to become entrapped, and sadly Mindfulness is used as a counselling method on vulnerable, emotional people.

People's mental health and medical needs are to become a powerful source for gaining further control. Initially making people ill through preservatives and additives to foods, they are now able to manipulate patients into accepting various forms of treatment most of which are accompanied by drugs.

Over the past few years there has been a change in the National Health Service in UK and the USA. They are currently in the process of introducing a new NHS type system in both countries. However, this has meant for the UK, selling parts of the NHS, which started with a 'sell off' of the administration departments. Now it's a 'sell off' of the actual hospitals to private companies. In 2013 the focus is on discrediting the NHS, suggesting poor service (which is true because the N.W.O (via EU) made it impossible to give good service). The hospitals had demands imposed on them, to increase the quality of service delivery, at the same time the hospitals had their funding reduced which made it impossible to provide a quality service. This was deliberate so that NHS would be forced to sell to a private business which is under the control of the illuminati (N.W.O).

At the present time July 2013, UK government is under the directive of the EU (ultimately the illuminati) to focus on discrediting the NHS so that they can have full control over the system and eventually replace it with **CORPORATIONS!**

First they started the process by grading the various hospitals, choosing certain hospitals as the main central 'Foundation' Hospitals, (similarly to the methods used to introduce the New World Order World Bank). These chosen ones were then given grants and supported by the government, while other hospitals had pressure applied to meet unrealistic goals within an unrealistic timescale; government funding was withdrawn or reduced, putting excessive pressure on the trustees or directors. Staff numbers were reduced to minimal levels to save money but increased the pressure of extra work on skeleton staff so that patient care suffered. This was the same plan to sift out the older peoples care homes, using the same tactics instigated by the CQC (an organisation called Commission for Quality Care). They applied bullying tactics and the nursing homes were forced to spend large sums of money on improvements within a short period of time while CQC and Social Services (SS) prevented new customers from moving in to the home or large numbers of residents were taken out of the home (regardless of the resident's needs). This meant the home was either paying out enormous sums of money or getting no return as the resident's income was removed! Many of these good homes were made bankrupt! Many good homes where residents were settled and happy with their care where forced to leave because CQC and SS decided the home was unsuitable. Yet other nursing homes known by many families of residents have testified to these homes being given a high star rating, even though many residents were undernourished and lacked basic care!

Specific care homes were selected to succeed and others were selected to close down. Many care homes were poor quality and not all of those closed down. Many good care homes gave excellent service and were closed down.

Therefore one would assume it was either a post code lottery or a random selection or specific selection based on certain criteria only known to the elite, whatever the reason behind their strategy it has an air of gestapo type tactics and demonstrates the same nazi attitude and behaviour used towards the Jewish people. There was a definite and a deliberate discard for the residents and their family's opinion in which neglect and poor service was actually created by CQC and SS because of the bullying tactics and interference! Instead of gentle encouragement and support to make improvements, giving reasonable timescales and taking into account the homes' budget constraints, then the ideal solution (if CQC and SS really cared about the resident's needs) would have been to assist management to achieve the goals without removing or putting a stop to income from new residents, so that management could meet the financial demands for the required improvements. Instead gestapo tactics were used which disrupted many people's lives! The same is happening with the **RESTRUCTURING** of the NHS.

To summarise: There are many more methods, than those listed in this chapter, which are used to influence the public into performing certain behaviour and to change the social, political and spiritual attitude of each individual, which then alters communities, cultures, moral codes, etc. The boundaries of behaviour gradually decrease until they disappear altogether!

Individual people are bombarded, on a daily basis, with propaganda, subliminal messages in advertising, music and films which also have a huge influence on the changing of behaviour. For example, when every film or program consists of foul language, sexual immorality, evolutionary concepts and gay relationships, it becomes commonplace and therefore the mind becomes complacent. Eventually, the mind and our emotions become desensitised. We may still 'out of habit' react to shocking things, we may still feel a slight twinge of sadness or anger but we soon forget it and move back into our safe, secure internal mode of self- reassurance that keeps us going on. The self –reassurance tells us it won't happen to us. It happens to others, therefore 'I am safe!' Our minds shift back to our daily tasks or interests which act as a pacifier to help us cope. This is called 'burying your head in the sand, not facing up to reality or dealing with it! It is also called immaturity and sometimes selfishness or ignorance. More importantly it demonstrated a movement towards submission, compliance and being controlled like puppets on a string.

God tells us 'we should look out for one another, care for each other, take care of the widows and orphans, to rejoice with those who rejoice and weep with those who weep'. In other words, we should be aware of what is going on in the world and do something about it. Yes, this world domination and mass mind control is huge! It seems too big for mere individuals to do anything about it. But you are wrong! There is a solution, there is much that can be done and this is discussed in Part 2.

Not only do 'mind controllers' use the visual sensors, they use the other senses as well. Mind control affects what you hear and what you DON'T hear. What you see and what you are expected to see (false memories or perceptions). Mind control also uses the senses of smell, taste and feel, through advertising and through additives in food and through GM products.

People have forgotten what it is to have tasty, wholesome food, we have become a junk food world full of additives, chemical pesticides and chemical preservatives, particularly those on a low income, whereby GM foods are cheap and sold in low priced food stores. These foods contain mind controlling drugs or harmful substances that direct the individual's behaviour and produce a sickly weak and therefore submissive body. One of the tricks in food industry such as a retail business is to use enticing smells. If you walk past a sweet shop or a shop selling different soaps or perfumes etc you may smell an enticing smell to encourage you into the shop. Have you noticed that certain coffee shops ooze out an amazing coffee smell yet when you actually drink the coffee it often tastes bitter!

The N.W.O uses many companies, organisations, groups and individuals (who are easily controlled through greed, love of money, of material things and fear of the removal of these). These groups were acquired by the New World Order, after they were placed in a vulnerable financial position where they had been forced to become part of the overall plan. The companies are controlled by financial blackmail. If they comply and work for the N.W.O they will receive sufficient funding to keep them afloat, if they do not work for them they will be deprived of funding and exposed publicly in such a way that would lead to disgrace and ruin and of course the loss of their affluent lifestyle!

Many small businesses have deliberately been placed in a position of financial hardship and forced out of the market so that large corporations have total control, over the population, controlling what is purchased, and advertised, as well as food distribution and selection (as well as deliberate contamination) and financial control.

These large businesses are now merging with other powerful businesses gaining even greater control! These large corporations work in league with the N. W. O.

There was the introduction of concepts to bring about public awareness for the purpose of spying and reporting others and to monitor and control each person's spending, i.e. Whistleblowing, labelling innocent people as 'Benefit Cheats', loyalty cards that record what you buy on a regular shopping trip, so they can send you coupons to tempt you to buy more of the same within a set timescale., reducing pensions and disability benefits etc, taxing everything and government given the power to look at individual's bank accounts etc.

For many years Western countries have looked at Third World poverty and their suffering and said, 'well we can never be like that'. Now God has turned it around so that the wealthy countries are also suffering, rightly so, Western civilisation has become greedy, misusing their affluence and freedom, as they have turned their backs on God who gave them their wealth in the first place! They have also sealed their fate because of the lack of support for His land and for His people Israel!

CHAPTER 5

ARE WE BEING CONTROLLED?

Are we being controlled? Are our minds being conditioned? Is it possible?

Rationalists and realists would state categorically that this is a ridiculous question only an extremist or crazy person would suggest! However, many people are becoming aware of what is happening in their personal lives and in their communities. They are aware of strange things happening to people and their surroundings, signs in the heavens, changes in the atmosphere and in the environment as well as unexplained phenomena occurring globally. Others are reporting their long kept secrets of childhood abuse, committed by relatives or by influential, well-known people or within secret societies, occult sects etc. These have been well kept secrets for many years only to be revealed during these end times.

There is a great deal of evidence to suggest we have slowly become subjected to a subtle form of exposure to mind control, which occurs daily in our lives to influence our behaviour. Some of this exposure has been natural and fairly innocent, for example, retail advertising to tempt customers to buy certain goods. Also biased news reporting has influenced our thoughts and directed our loyalties. These can be quite innocent influences that direct our culture and values within a specific society. However it is when the influences go beyond the social awareness level and enter into the subconscious level that it becomes more sinister and dangerous!

God himself has written way in advance that this mind control and apostasy will happen! He doesn't use the words, mind control, but the inference is in scripture where he states, through the words of his servant Jude in verse 4, *"For certain men whose condemnation was written about long ago have secretly slipped in among you. They are godless men, who change the Grace of our God into a license for immorality and deny Christ Yeshua our Lord.*"

Also in John's second letter, *"Many deceivers, who do not acknowledge Christ Yeshua as coming in the flesh, have gone out into the world. Any such person is the deceiver and the antichrist".*

More specifically in 2 Corinthians 4:4 it states, *"The god of this age has blinded the minds of unbelievers, so that they cannot see the light of the Gospel of the Glory of Christ, who is the image of God".*

Another verse that suggests mind control exists is the reference to Eve and the serpent in 2 Cor 11:3, *"But I am afraid that just as Eve was deceived by the serpent's cunning, your minds may somehow be led astray from your sincere and pure devotion to Christ".*

Apostle Paul says: *"I urge you, brothers, to watch out for those who cause divisions and put obstacles in your way that are contrary to the teachings you have learned...By smooth talk and flattery they deceive the minds of naïve people...* Romans 16:17 -19

The whole bible by inference suggests a divided world, a world divided by those who are righteous, belonging to God and those who are not!

The fact that the bible also mentions an apostate world suggests there were methods that made it that way. Also throughout the scriptures it suggests that many of the inhabitants were predestined to be good while others were predestined to be evil as suggested in the verse written by Jude. We also know from the verses already introduced, that many fallen angels ascended on earth to wreak havoc. To do this they are going to introduce ways of creating this havoc and common sense would tell us that they will do this in the name of their leader the fallen serpent satan! We also have evidence that this havoc includes the destruction of the Jews during WW2 in the holocaust, the ethnic cleansing in Bosnia and more recent atrocities in the Middle East, and of course the centuries of martyrdom of Christians! Only evil could do such things! Only evil could destroy good! This suggests there is a plan and has been a plan of destruction for centuries.

We also know that the world was so evil at the time of Noah and later in the cities of Sodom and Gomorrah that God destroyed the first world and those two cities! This also, by inference, suggests God is not going to sit back and ignore the evil taking place today!

So these assumptions lead to the fact that there is an evil force at work and it is working against the force of good which is God, Yeshua and his chosen people, the remnant, the elect and the saved!

Now this does not remove from people their accountability for sin. The fact that there is a hidden dark force at work as stated in Ephesians 6:11-17; this evil force is part of the delusion as described in 2 Thessalonians 2: 11.

The reader must understand that those who are easily deceived and therefore susceptible to mind control are mostly those who already have a rebellious heart; they have already made their choice to be directed away from God and goodness. However, as already mentioned those sitting on the fence, those who submit to temptation, and those who allow themselves to be misled because they do not have a firm foundation in Christ Yeshua, lay themselves open to psychological abuse. There are many people who have chosen to reject God who also either ignore satan's presence or reject him as an influence in their life. These people are sitting on the fence. There are only two ways to go, left or right, Good or evil, God or Satan. Anything in the middle is vulnerable to being controlled and eventually these people will be forced to make a decision to follow either God or Satan! Always there is a choice to be made!

Over the past few decades pilot studies and pilot projects have taken place. These pilots are a small version of the bigger project to come.

The pilot study for example regarding the NEAR future, when every human being receives the mark of the beast, begins with the smaller study to gradually introduce people to the idea so they willingly accept it. The initial pilot is to accept identification cards i.e. loyalty cards, bank visa cards, credit cards and of course the driving license and passport. All of these contain a small microchip with all of your personal data in it, i.e. address, identification features such as a mole on left cheek or a specific birth mark. The next stage is to receive a microchip that doesn't involve a Smartcard; it is placed inside the body! The microchip has been piloted on animals under the guise of a tracking devise, to track a lost pet.

This microchip was successfully piloted and now manufactured ready for humans to receive for the same reason, to track terrorists, escaped prisoners and parole prisoners etc. That is not the only reason however, they would also give the excuse to the public that it would be a useful tool for monitoring an individual's health.

There have been other pilots, such as introducing the public to food additives, GM foods, and drugs that control the mind as already mentioned.

There has been a long term pilot to adjust the money system, first it was to change the individual country's currency and introduce a new currency - the Euro. This is to be followed by a world currency which has already been made and ready for use as internet money. This is a means of using something tangible in a cashless society where purchases can only be made in shops using the plastic card (later to be replaced by the microchip implanted in the body of every human which automatically pays for goods in the same way as the credit card or bank card. This will be achieved by using the argument that identity fraud, stealing cards to use the owner's identity, can be stopped by introducing the card details i.e. bank details on a microchip under your skin of your right hand or forehead, where no crook can get hold of your information!

On August 1st 2013, another pilot scheme commenced which will gradually introduce the 'Cashless Society' and is a prelude to the mark under the skin. On this day 1st Aug, the banks have introduced a new scheme called the Contactless Visa Debit Card. The leaflet says the following:

"Contactless readers are popping up all over the country. This method is the new way to pay for small things like magazines, or coffees. Contactless payments can be made for purchases up to £20 wherever you see the contactless logo.

Who like to fiddle about with loose change? Most payments take less than a second so there's little chance of your coffee getting cold when there are contactless readers about. ..Hold your card in front of the reader. Your payment will be confirmed, and then you're good to go."

It all sounds so good, no need to punch in your number code or sign for purchases, it is going to be so much more convenient to just call in for a 'take away' and within seconds continue on your journey with breakfast in your hand. But wait a minute? This is a pilot for something much bigger!

They are already piloting the next stage in America. School children have been issued a cashless ID card they must use for buying their school dinner. The card must be carried at all times. It contains the child's personal details, identification details, etc.

Nexus Magazine – Global News wrote an article about a Biometric ID Card and the Cashless Society in Nigeria. It was announced at a recent World Economic Forum in South Africa. The NIMC (Nigerian National Identity Management Commission under the Government of Nigeria would form a partnership to distribute a new ID card to every Nigerian citizen which is aimed towards a new cashless society. President Miebach agrees with this move and stated *'the cashless policy is a shared vision of a world beyond cash.'*

This new smart card will contain a unique national ID number of the registered person in the country, demographic data and biometric data including fingerprints, facial picture and digital signature. The National ID Database will hold other information such as ID authentication and verification. [You can see how the ability to buy and sell only if you have the mark, comes into play. All you will need to do is walk through a store where your ID is checked along with your financial status and if you have any anti -compliance information i.e. if you do not have the mark, you will not be authorized to buy any goods!]

On the surface 'superficial level' these schemes are preparing people to accept a new system of payment, which erases the use of cash and notes. Instead of countries printing their own notes or minting their own coins, they will use

N.W.O. cashless methods. This would diminish problems such as inflation, financial crisis and recessions.

The bigger picture however, is the worldwide cashless society which is due to take place during the 7 year tribulation period. The new world currency mentioned earlier, is ready to go. It will be an electronic currency which is used instead of actual copper, silver and paper notes. The cashless society has to be introduced so that only those with the 'mark' followers of lucifer (he changes his name from satan to lucifer once he has his place on the throne) will be able to buy or sell. Only those with the microchip can do business! All those who do not have the microchip or mark cannot buy or sell! This is to happen during the three and half years of the Great Tribulation. This is the last three and half years of the seven year period.

All of this can be confirmed by prophesy found in the Bible. These events can be logically explained when the bible is used as a reference point.

One of the ways of being controlled is for the controller to try to control our minds in a subtle way so we are unable to continue our usual routine lifestyle but gradually changing direction towards compliance to the N.W.O. REGIME.

For many years Psychologists and Neuroscientists have researched the human memory system. More recent research has focused on whether it is possible to change an individual's memories and whether it is possible to implant 'false memories. It was mentioned briefly earlier, that a woman named Arizona was raised in an environment where she was subjected to experiments which played with her mind. She and many other children were deliberately traumatized and this was used to control the children, forcing them, through fear, to perform terrible acts of violence and murder. More on this in further chapters.

We know from news reports that many horrid events are happening throughout the world which are hard to believe.

For example, the incident in Cleveland (2013) where three women were kept prisoners for 10 years in a home of a man who admitted he was addicted to sex. He along with his two brothers subjected these women to torture, rape, murder of their unborn babies, until the women managed to escape!

Women held captive for 10 years in Cleveland kept diaries about their lives as 'prisoners of war'

New York Post Thursday 1st August, 2013 Amanda Berry, Michelle Knight, and Gina de Jesus in a video thanking well-wishers. Three women held captive in a run-down home for a decade kept diaries documenting the horrific physical and sexual abuse they suffered on a daily basis, prosecutors said Wednesday. The women's kidnapper was Ariel Castro.

There are many such incidents of pure evil whereby women and children are submitted to cruel acts of abuse, too many to evidence in this book. But there's evidence in daily newspapers and media reports on horror stories of abuse and evil everywhere in the world! These have increased 100 fold during the last 5 years or so. The level of cruelty and abuse however, has noticeably increased over the past 10 years. Why has the world suddenly become so evil! Often people say evil has always existed; it just wasn't publicized as it is today! Well that is nonsense; there has always been publicity about major events. It was because many child sex abuse incidents were hushed up, that we are only now hearing about these things but the abuse occurred during the last 50 or 60 years. The levels of abuse and evil during our civilized Western error (since WW2) has been a gradual increase in levels in line with the mind controlling experiments which commenced in the 1970's and of course not forgetting the 1960's 'Power Flower' period with the introduction of hallucinatory drugs such as LSD and the social drug Marijuana. This was also in line with the period when the mind control experiments were in there first stages and these two drugs were the key to the following experimentations. The Flower Power period was the pilot study!

To return to the previous point of tampering with people's memories which sounds far-fetched; the following clip may put it into perspective.

A report has just been written by NTEB News Desk stating that Neuroscientists have successfully implanted false memories into mice.

by NTEB News Desk

The sinister implications of this story are so great that it boggles the mind. We live in a day and age where even our thoughts will no longer belong to us. Certainly, this unsaved world we live in is preparing itself to meet Antichrist...

From MIT: The phenomenon of false memory has been well-documented: In many court cases, defendants have been found guilty based on testimony from witnesses and victims who were sure of their recollections, but DNA evidence later overturned the conviction.

In a step toward understanding how these faulty memories arise, MIT neuroscientists have shown that they can plant false memories in the brains of mice. They also found that many of the neurological traces of these memories are identical in nature to those of authentic memories.

Whether it's a false or genuine memory, the brain's neural mechanism underlying the recall of the memory is the same," says Susumu Tonegawa, the Picower Professor of Biology and Neuroscience and senior author of a paper describing the findings in the July 25 edition of Science

The study also provides further evidence that memories are stored in networks of neurons that form memory traces for each experience we have — a phenomenon that Tonegawa's lab first demonstrated last year.

Neuroscientists have long sought the location of these memory traces, also called engrams. In the pair of studies, Tonegawa and colleagues at MIT's Picower Institute for Learning and Memory showed that they could identify the cells that make up part of an engram for a specific memory and reactivate it using a technology called optogenetics.

Lead authors of the paper are graduate student Steve Ramirez and research scientist Xu Liu. Other authors are technical assistant Pei-Ann Lin, research scientist Junghyup Suh, and postdocs Michele Pignatelli, Roger Redondo and Tomas Ryan.

Seeking the engram

Episodic memories — memories of experiences — are made of associations of several elements, including objects, space and time. These associations are encoded by chemical and physical changes in neurons, as well as by modifications to the connections between the neurons.

Where these engrams reside in the brain has been a longstanding question in neuroscience. "Is the information spread out in various parts of the brain, or is there a particular area of the brain in which this type of memory is stored? This has been a very fundamental question," Tonegawa says.

In the 1940s, Canadian neurosurgeon Wilder Penfield suggested that episodic memories are located in the brain's temporal lobe. When Penfield electrically stimulated cells in the temporal lobes of patients who were about to undergo surgery to treat epileptic seizures, the patients reported that specific memories popped into mind. Later studies of the amnesiac patient known as "H.M." confirmed that the temporal lobe, including the area known as the hippocampus, is critical for forming episodic memories.

However, these studies did not prove that engrams are actually stored in the hippocampus, Tonegawa says. To make that case, scientists needed to show that activating specific groups of hippocampal cells is sufficient to produce and recall memories.

To achieve that, Tonegawa's lab turned to optogenetics, a new technology that allows cells to be selectively turned on or off using light.

For this pair of studies, the researchers engineered mouse hippocampal cells to express the gene for channelrhodopsin, a protein that activates neurons when stimulated by light. They also modified the gene so that channelrhodopsin would be produced whenever the c-fos gene, necessary for memory formation, was turned on.

In last year's study, the researchers conditioned these mice to fear a particular chamber by delivering a mild electric shock. As this memory was formed, the c-fos gene was turned on, along with the engineered channelrhodopsin gene. This way, cells encoding the memory trace were "labelled" with light-sensitive proteins.

The next day, when the mice were put in a different chamber they had never seen before, they behaved normally. However, when the researchers delivered a pulse of light to the hippocampus, stimulating the memory cells labelled with channelrhodopsin, the mice froze in fear as the previous day's memory was reactivated.

"Compared to most studies that treat the brain as a black box while trying to access it from the outside in, this is like we are trying to study the brain from the inside out," Liu says. "The technology we developed for this study allows us to fine-dissect and even potentially tinker with the memory process by directly controlling the brain cells."

Incepting false memories

That is exactly what the researchers did in the new study — exploring whether they could use these reactivated engrams to plant false memories in the mice's brains.

First, the researchers placed the mice in a novel chamber, A, but did not deliver any shocks. As the mice explored this chamber, their memory cells were labelled with channelrhodopsin. The next day, the mice were placed in a second, very different chamber, B. After a while, the mice were given a mild foot shock. At the same instant, the researchers used light to activate the cells encoding the memory of chamber A.

On the third day, the mice were placed back into chamber A, where they now froze in fear, even though they had never been shocked there. A false memory had been incepted: The mice feared the memory of chamber A because when the shock was given in chamber B, they were reliving the memory of being in chamber A.

Moreover, that false memory appeared to compete with a genuine memory of chamber B, the researchers found. These mice also froze when placed in chamber B, but not as much as mice that had received a shock in chamber B without having the chamber A memory activated.

The researchers then showed that immediately after recall of the false memory, levels of neural activity were also elevated in the amygdala, a fear center in the brain that receives memory information from the hippocampus, just as they are when the mice recall a genuine memory.

These two papers represent a major step forward in memory research, says Howard Eichenbaum, a professor of psychology and director of Boston University's Center for Memory and Brain.

"They identified a neural network associated with experience in an environment, attached a fear association with it, then reactivated the network to show that it supports memory expression. That, to me, shows for the first time a true functional engram," says Eichenbaum, who was not part of the research team.

The MIT team is now planning further studies of how memories can be distorted in the brain.

"Now that we can reactivate and change the contents of memories in the brain, we can begin asking questions that were once the realm of philosophy," Ramirez says. "Are there multiple conditions that lead to the formation of false memories? Can false memories for both pleasurable and aversive events be artificially created? What about false memories for more than just contexts — false memories for objects, food or other mice? These are the once seemingly sci-fi questions that can now be experimentally tackled in the lab."

The research was funded by the RIKEN Brain Science Institute. source - MIT

NTEB News Desk | July 25, 2013 at 10:08 pm | Tags: False Memories, mark of the beast, MIT | Categories: End Times, One World Government, One World Religion | URL: http://wp.me/p1kFP6-3Kt

It is not so far-fetched when we see how close researchers are to finding answers to questions such as 'can we implant false memories into mice?'

As I have mentioned in previous chapters there are many ways we may be controlled, one of which is when, a hypnotist, during a session, may use 'prearranged' signals to induce behaviour. This is what happens at Toronto Blessing or

Pensacola or Prosperity and Miracle Meetings. The religious leader (false prophet) uses specific words or phrases that are implanted into the individual's brain (which is performed collectively over the whole audience at the same time) and when a specific trigger is used, the words are retrieved from the unconscious memory store.   The meetings usually start with worship and praise.   During this time, the preacher uses specific wording and phrases to set the congregations minds into a receptive mood, often the lyrics of the songs also focus on a specific theme i.e. calling down the spirit of fire (which is NOT the Holy Spirit of God).   They know exactly what words to use to reach the searching needs of the people, who are longing for a touch from God and a miracle that will evidence that they belong to him, many Christians and churches wrongly determine a true believer by the level and number of spiritual experiences they have had. Believers have become despondent and entered into severe depression and even left the faith because of these false teachings. The gifts of the Holy Spirit are just that –gifts, not a determinant on level of a believers faith.

God says " *It is by their fruits you shall know them,"* What is meant by fruits is not how many experiences you have had or how many times you have been zapped by the preacher, or how many new recruits you have introduced to Christ! The fruits refer to the believer being obedient to God! The fruits are about having a firm foundation, maturing in the faith (many long standing Christians are still on the milk of learning (baby stage) when they should be on the meat which is a mature adults diet!   The fruits are love, patience, perseverance etc, not the speaking in tongues or gyrating and rolling about the floor or barking like a dog!

Hebrews 5:13 *"Anyone who lives on milk, being still an infant, is not acquainted with the teaching about righteousness.   But solid food is for the mature, who by constant use have trained themselves to distinguish good from evil."*

"Therefore let us leave the elementary teachings about Christ and go on to maturity, not laying again the foundation of repentance from acts that lead to death ...Hebrews 6: 1...

The fruits are as mentioned faithfulness, love, endurance, patience, contentment, joy etc. The key fruits are loving God and others with an unconditional love and a humble heart. These are just a few of the fruits. A fruitful tree is worthy of life whereas a fruitless tree is worth nothing and therefore should shrivel up! Being fruitful is to produce an abundance of fruit and plenty of helpful blessings. When you eat a juicy fruit you feel refreshed, and it satisfies a hunger and you feel you have been nourished! That is how a person with fruit from the spirit should be - nourishment to others!

However, at these Miracle Meetings the preacher an expert hypnotist works the congregation up to the point whereby they are excited and the idea of miraculous events soon to take place makes them even more excited, so that their adrenaline levels are almost at bursting point! Also their perception and anticipation of what is to come, has been implanted in their minds so this too increases the chemical levels (the neurotransmitters – increase the amount of endorphins secreted which produces a 'euphoric feel good situation, so that people are ready to open their minds and submit to what is offered)'. Once the preacher has worked the people into a frenzied state, he then moves into the final capture of his prey! The music during the worship session is selected to stir up the emotions to fever pitch that simulate a pagan dance. People start to shake profusely to the point beyond normal human ability. The building would be considered filled with the holy fire. What this really means is the demons are present and satan's fire of hell is present!

When you have a large hall full of excited people jumping up and down, dancing in frenzy and speaking in a gibberish tongue, (God's Holy Spirit gift of tongues is quite different) there is going to be the production of body heat. The audience would be informed by the preacher that this heat is the spirit of god at work. Many naïve people believe and accept this explanation. This is viewed as another miraculous event drawing the audience in even further. It is the preacher who is guiding the people through autosuggestion that implants specific perceptions.

They have been conditioned like the Pavlov dogs; salivating at the thought of the promises given to them about the miracles they are about to witness. To build up the people's faith, so that they believe the preacher will instigate a miracle, the preacher starts with a healing session. He invites people up onto the stage, he then would ask about the problem that needs healing. He then laid hands on the person, followed by a proclamation that a healing miracle has occurred. This is followed by the preacher laying his hand on the forehead of the victim and immediately the person reacts in a frenzied manner and usually falls to the floor! Other behavior may be to bark like a dog, roll about on the floor, laugh hysterically (completely out of control in a demonic, supernatural manner) or act like a chicken flapping their wings, whatever, triggers the hypnotist uses, the victim complies, even though that person may be elderly, a young child or a disabled person. Some of the leaders of these meetings do weird things that are obviously demonic. The victims may demonstrate behaviour completely out of their normal range of ability, supernatural phenomena may occur. Old people may have super energy.

These are NOT DEMONSTRATING THE FRUITS OF THE SPIRIT OF GOD! These events are demonstrating the actions of occult, witchcraft which is rebellion! These are deceiving spirits, deceiving wolves in sheep's clothing!

There are many YouTube videos demonstrating these meetings, one of these showed a woman who claimed to be a prophet, before she could prophesy, she went into a strange trance then suddenly her head started spinning from side to side at a high velocity, way beyond human ability, and it continued for a very long time, again it would be humanly impossible to do this for such a long time at that rate of spin, even with years of practice- it was an impossibility for a human to perform like that, therefore it could only be DEMONIC! While her head was spinning rapidly from side to side it distorted her facial expression and she spoke the prophecy. These are the sort of events that are attracting millions of viewers who long for the excitement of the unusual!

Many innocent people who attend these meetings and agree to have the preachers lay hands on them (whereby the preacher lays his hand on the front of the forehead, where the third eye is situated and where the mark of the beast will be applied) also become demonic, they are taken over by a demon in their body which causes them to be able to perform unusual behaviour such as the excessive laughter. Old people have been seen rolling about the floor with huge force without injury; it appears that they are being thrown across the floor sometimes. Others stand on the same spot constantly moving about in a jerking movement that would normally dislocate the neck and back. These are people who have had their bodies, minds and souls taken over by demonic beings!

The ultimate purpose of hypnotizing people is to show, through humiliation, that the person is totally under the hypnotist's control. The ghastly thing about such shows, is they influence the most unlikely people, rational, intelligent people, people of position in society i.e. doctors, solicitors, old people and young children with parental consent! Audiences see these events as 'entertainment,' totally unaware of the dangers involved. People queue up eagerly, in readiness, to be the next chosen person to be used and humiliated-all in the name of 'fun' with unsuspecting Christians hoping for a miracle which is actually a counterfeit spirit not the Holy Spirit indwelling the person. They are being possessed by a demon. That demon then controls the life of the person in every way! So much so that there is a personality change, the person becomes hardened to world events, towards religion, and instantly has allegiance to the devil! This may be at a subconscious level; the person may be totally unaware of these consequences. The person's heart becomes hard and cold, the soul has been completely taken over. There is usually no return to their old self or freedom, except by a true miracle from God.

There is a link between Prosperity Preaching and Baal worship! Matt Barber on WorldnetDaily, Feb 16 2009 said he visited Rivermont Evangelical Presbyterian church. He heard a sermon on Baal worship by Pastor John Mabray. He described Baal as a half bull, half man god of fertility and that baal worship still happens today!

He went on to say that the key to Baal worship is child sacrifice and sexual immorality (heterosexual and homosexual) and pantheism which are the reverence of the **created** rather than the **Creator** [God]. The rituals involve burning infants as sacrifices and indulging in sexual orgies. These rituals are performed to produce economic prosperity; Baal is called upon to bring rain to fertile the earth.

Prosperity preachers talk of 'latter-day rain' and promote economic prosperity IF you donate to their organization. Naively many people believe this and part with their money to these 'millionaire' conmen!

Religious cults all have something in common which links to satan (the devil-lucifer) –sex is the dominating factor! God demonstrates in his word that sex is for the procreation of children and sexual activity is to be enjoyed by heterosexual married couples only.

In opposition and rebellion to God, satan encourages immorality, sexual perversion and sex out of marriage or within same sex marriages – hence the society we live in today is in direct rebellion to God's Laws! And follows the lawlessness of satan!

A sure sign that a person is involved in a religious cult or under a satanic influence is when sex becomes a major part of a person's life 'outside of marriage'. Marriage between a man and a woman is the most blessed thing that can happen in God's eyes. It is precious! Yet there is a massive rebellion against this Godly institution, in favour of illicit sex with anyone. Soft pornography as shown in advertising with subliminal messages of hard porn, under age sex, co-habiting, same sex marriages, gay relationships, extramarital sex and ritualistic sex as found in cultic and satanic meetings, which is also the same as the dancing performed by singers such as Lady Gaga and Madonna. These dances are typically pagan and satanic! All of these are an abomination to God who created marriage between a man and a woman. All of the above mentioned behaviour is typically found in the world of satan!

Baal worship is seen to occur in Illuminati or satanic rites or the higher level of freemasonry meetings. It can be seen that these things are taking place on a much grander scale than ever before.

It has been mentioned in previous chapters that a witness, Arizona, who was born and raised in the Illuminati circles, mentioned many children were born specifically to be sacrificed. Babies in particular were used. It is taking place on a larger scale now that there are many more inhabitants of the world who are part human and part demonic [through the thousands of years interbreeding], this has become world-wide, hence the encouragement for abortions!

The author, as a young naive trainee, in a hospital theatre, where abortions were performed (many years ago before the author was a believer), asked a senior member of staff what happens to the foetus after it's removed from the mother's womb? The answer was to flush it down the toilet! But the mind boggles as to whether they are sold off to feed the appetites of these half human half animal species! It is not so far-fetched when you think of past pagan tribes who sacrificed humans on a regular basis. Paganism has always existed and therefore it is logical to assume that sacrificing of children also still exists because paganism is rife today therefore sacrifices would be part of their practice!

Read the article below of how far we have come in the 'civilized' world. Even today babies are being sacrificed (aborted) to be used as a commodity!

Aborted baby's tissue to be used in stroke trial
Posted by Assistant Editor in Abortion Articles, Abortion Law, News on 18 January 2009.
BBC News Online is reporting that the company ReNeuron has been given the go-ahead to use tissue taken from an aborted baby in a clinical trial for stroke. The report attempts to justify this absolutely abhorrent action, by glossing over the origin of the stem cells, with the headline "Stroke therapy assessed". The truth is that this is no reputable report – it is about using an aborted baby brain in research – there can only be one response to this story – it is absolutely despicable and unacceptable. The scientist interviewed tries to justify it saying that it is only one child – what kind of appalling justification is this? What kind of grotesque level of inhumanity has this country reached when an aborted baby's body can be used in this despicable way, and scientists champion it as an exciting moment which may put Britain at the forefront of science? Has the regulator who approved this proposal and the scientists involved lost all sense of humanity and medical ethics? There happens to be perfectly

ethical sources of stem cells from bone marrow – but even if there were no ethical alternative, it will never be acceptable to use a baby's body in this way. It is a disgusting form of cannibalism to kill a baby in a method which is designed to enable harvesting of its cells for research. We should be ending abortion altogether, not coming up with ever more despicable practices. –

See more at: http://prolife.org.uk/2009/01/abhorrent-aborted-babys-tissue-used-in-stroke-trial/#sthash.SLEcp5Dk.dpuf

And yet another horror story!

15 March 2009 by Professor Naomi Pfeffer
London Metropolitan University Appeared in BioNews 499

This January, ReNeuron Group Plc. Announced that the UK Medicines and Healthcare Products Regulatory Agency (MHRA) had granted permission for a Phase I clinical trial of its ReN001 stem cell therapy in the treatment of patients left disabled by an ischaemic stroke, the most common form of the condition. The trial, which involves injecting ReN001 directly into the subject's brain, is expected to start this summer at the Southern General Hospital, Glasgow.

ReN001 is derived from human aborted foetuses. A well-kept secret is that many stem cell scientists use aborted foetuses in their research. Scientists and policy makers tend to shy away from drawing the public's attention to this because abortion and aborted foetuses are political minefields. However what this means is no-one has canvassed the views of women who undergo a pregnancy termination who may be asked to agree to the foetus being used in stem cell research. Source ESRC.

More horrifically!

Obama agency rules Pepsi's use of aborted fetal cells in soft drinks constitutes 'ordinary business operations'

Saturday, March 17, 2012 by: Ethan A. Huff, staff writer
(NaturalNews) The Obama Administration has given its blessing to PepsiCo to continue utilizing the services of a company that produces flavor chemicals for the beverage giant using aborted human fetal tissue. LifeSiteNews.com reports that the Obama Security and Exchange Commission (SEC) has decided that PepsiCo's arrangement with San Diego, Cal.-based Senomyx, which produces flavor enhancing chemicals for Pepsi using human embryonic kidney tissue, simply constitutes "ordinary business operations."

The issue began in 2011 when the non-profit group Children of God for

Life (CGL) first broke the news about Pepsi's alliance with Senomyx, which led to massive outcry and a worldwide boycott of Pepsi products. At that time, it was revealed that Pepsi had many other options at its disposal to produce flavor chemicals, which is what its competitors do, but had instead chosen to continue using aborted fetal cells – or as Senomyx deceptively puts it, "isolated human taste receptors" (http://www.naturalnews.com).

A few months later, Pepsi' shareholders filed a resolution petitioning the company to "adopt a corporate policy that recognizes human rights and employs ethical standards which do not involve using the remains of aborted human beings in both private and collaborative research and development agreements." But the Obama Administration shut down this 36-page proposal, deciding instead that Pepsi's use of aborted babies to flavor its beverage products is just business as usual, and not a significant concern.

"We're not talking about what kind of pencils PepsiCo wants to use – we are talking about exploiting the remains of an aborted child for profit," said Debi Vinnedge, Executive Director of CGL, concerning the SEC decision. "Using human embryonic kidney (HEK-293) to produce flavor enhancers for their beverages is a far cry from routine operations!" To be clear, the aborted fetal tissue used to make Pepsi's flavor chemicals does not end up in the final product sold to customers, according to reports – it is used, instead, to evaluate how actual human taste receptors respond to these chemical flavorings. But the fact that Pepsi uses them at all when viable, non-human alternatives are available illustrates the company's blatant disregard for ethical and moral concerns in the matter.

Back in January, Oklahoma Senator Ralph Shortey proposed legislation to ban the production of aborted fetal cell-derived flavor chemicals in his home state. If passed, S.B. 1418 would also reportedly ban the sale of any products that contain flavor chemicals derived from human fetal tissue, which includes Pepsi products as well as products produced by Kraft and Nestle (http://www.naturalnews.com).

Sources for this article include:
    http://www.lifesitenews.com
http://www.naturalnews.com/035276_Pepsi_fetal_cells_business_operati ons.html#ixzz2Zl0lIMbT

http://www.naturalnews.com/035276_Pepsi_fetal_cells_business_operation s.html#ixzz2ZI0R045a

Further information written by Dr Mercola (ironic name considering the article mentions Pepsi (Pepsi Cola).

For several years anti-abortion advocates have been warning that a new technology for enhancing flavours such as sweetness and saltiness uses aborted foetal cells in the process. The biotech company using this novel process, Senomyx, has signed contracts with Pepsi, Ajinomoto Co. (the maker of aspartame and meat glue), Nestlé and other food and beverage companies[2] over the past several years.[3]

The primary goal for many of these processed food companies is to make foods and beverages tasty while reducing sugar and salt content.

While Senomyx refuses to disclose the details of the process, its patent applications indicate that part of the secret indeed involves the use of human kidney cells, known as HEK293, originating from an aborted baby.

It's worth noting that no kidney cells, or part thereof, are actually IN the finished product.[4] Rather they're part of the process used to discern new flavors, which will be discussed below. That said, to many, this is still "over the line." Two years ago, anti-abortion groups launched boycott campaigns against Pepsi Co., urging them to reconsider using flavorings derived from a process involving the use of aborted embryonic kidney cells.

Whatever your personal convictions might be on the issue of using biological material from an aborted foetus, the issue of whether or not biotech-constructed flavor enhancers are safe or not remains...

Biotech Cooks Up New Flavors

Senomyx[5] is a high tech research and development business that is "dedicated to finding new flavors to reduce sugars and reduce salt." These include new flavors such as Savory Flavors and Cooling Flavors, as well as flavor modulators such as Bitter Blockers and enhancers of Sweet and Salt tastes.[6] Senomyx is also engaged in a new effort to discover and develop high-potency sweeteners to replace high fructose corn syrup, artificial sweeteners, and natural herb sweeteners like Stevia, which some people object to due to its aftertaste.

To accomplish this, Senomyx has developed patented "flavor enhancing" compounds using "proprietary taste receptor-based assay systems." It's a taste testing system that provides scientists with biochemical responses and electronic readouts when a flavor ingredient interacts with their patented receptor, letting researchers know whether or not they've "hit the mark" in terms of flavor. As described by Senomyx: [7]

"Flavors are substances that impart tastes or aromas... Individuals experience the sensation of taste when flavors in food and beverage products interact with taste receptors in the mouth. A taste receptor functions either by physically binding to a flavor ingredient in a process analogous to the way a key fits into a lock or by acting as a channel to allow ions to flow directly into a taste cell.

As a result of these interactions, signals are sent to the brain where a specific taste sensation is registered. There are currently five recognized primary senses of taste: umami, which is the Savory taste of glutamate, sweet, salt, bitter and sour.

Senomyx has discovered or in-licensed many of the key receptors that mediate taste in humans. We created proprietary taste receptor-based assay systems that provide a biochemical or electronic readout when a flavor ingredient interacts with the receptor."

According to an article in The New Yorker[8] published in May 2011, Pepsi's New York plant has a robot fitted with human taste buds to reliably "predict" what humans might like. To create this robotic taste tester, Pepsi Co. scientists injected the genetic sequences of the four known taste receptors into cultured cells, and then hardwired the cells to the robot's computer. The robot (which has replaced human taste testers for the initial taste trials) can sample some 40,000 flavor assays per day.

What are These Genetically Engineered 'Flavor Enhancers,' and are They Safe?

According to a CBS News report from June 2011, 70 out of 77 Senomyx patents[9, 10] filed at that time referred to the use of HEK 293.[11] These are human embryonic kidney cells originally harvested from a healthy, electively aborted fetus sometime in the 1970's. The "HEK" identifies the cells as kidney cells, and the "293" denotes that the cells came from the 293rd experiment.

These cells have been cloned for decades, as they offer a reliable way to produce new proteins using genetic engineering. Senomyx has engineered HEK293 cells to function like human taste receptor cells, [12] presumably such as those used in Pepsi Co's taste-testing robot. This was done by isolating taste receptors found in certain cells, and adding them to the HEK cells.

HEK cells are also widely used within pharmaceutical and cell biology research for the same or similar reasons. It is however the first time HEK cells have been used in the food industry, which carries a certain "ick" factor for many. There's also the issue of just not knowing how these new flavors are created. As stated in another CBS news report: [13]

"So what exactly is this magic ingredient that will be appearing in a new version of Pepsi, and how is it made? Unfortunately, those questions are hard to answer. Senomyx... refers to them only as 'enhancers' or 'ingredients'... The products work by triggering receptors on the tongue and tricking your taste buds into sensing sweetness — or saltiness or coolness, in the case of the company's other programs...

So are Senomyx's covert ingredients safe? That, too, is anyone's guess... many of its enhancers have 'been granted' GRAS (Generally Recognized As Safe) status, but all that means is that the company did its own assessment and then concluded everything was fine. We don't know whether Senomyx did any testing since the company isn't required to submit anything to the FDA.[14]

There's no reason to think that Senomyx's products will cause harm, but until or unless Pepsi decides to share details about how exactly it's achieving a 60 percent reduction in sugar while keeping the taste the same, customers will be drinking their 'scientifically advantaged' sodas completely in the dark."

Since these compounds (whatever they are) are used in such minute quantities, they don't have to be listed on the label. They'll simply fall under the generic category of artificial and/or natural flavors. What this means is that the product will appear to be much "healthier" than it might otherwise be, were a flavor enhancer not used.

According to a 2010 CBS report,[15] Senomyx's flavor enhancers were already being sold outside the US at that time. For example, Nestle was by 2010 using an MSG flavor enhancer in its Maggi brand soups, sauces, condiments and instant noodles, and Ajinomoto was also using a similar ingredient in products for the Chinese market. This means less of the artificial sweetener is needed to create the same sweet taste as before, but while one could argue that this is a good thing, I suspect we will ultimately learn that this flavor enhancement method has multiple unforeseen adverse consequences — metabolically, and biologically.

Consequences of Food Alteration are More the Rule than the Exception...

There are many reasons why you're better off choosing natural whole foods in lieu of processed alternatives, but one of the primary ones is that junk foods contain additives that increase your toxic load, which in turn may increase your tendency to develop cancer. As of yet, there is NO medical research to back up the assertion that manipulating your taste buds in the way Senomyx' products do is safe and healthy in the long term. As an example, I would point to the evidence now available showing that one of the reasons why artificial sweeteners do not work as advertised is because the taste of sweet itself is tied into your metabolic functioning in a way that we still do not fully understand... As a result, artificially sweetened products, oftentimes boasting zero calories, actually result in greater weight gain than sweetened products when used "in the real world."

It's easy to forget that the processed, pre-packaged foods and fast food restaurants of today are actually a radical change in terms of the history of food production. Much of what we eat today bears very little resemblance of real food. Many products are loaded with non-nutritive fillers — purposely designed to just "take up space" to make you think you're getting more than you really are — along with any number of additives. Many additives have been shown to have harmful effects on mood, behaviour, metabolic functioning and biochemistry.

Now, with the introduction of untested engineered flavor enhancers, you're left wondering whether processed foods with "cleaner" labels really are safer and healthier or not... Remember, because Senomyx' flavor enhancers are used in such low concentrations they are not required to undergo the FDA's usual safety approval process for food additives.

The disease trends we're now seeing are only going to get worse as much of the processed foods consumed today are not even food-based. Who knows what kind of genetic mutations and malfunctions we're creating for ourselves and future generations when a MAJORITY of our diet consists of highly processed and artificial foods that contain substances never before consumed by humans in all of history.

How to Enhance Your Food's Flavor, Naturally

When choosing what to eat, I highly recommend you focus your meals on real food, and remember "food" equals "live nutrients." Nutrients, in turn, feed your cells, optimize your health and sustain life. To help you along, I've created a free optimized nutrition plan, which takes you step-by-step from the beginner's through the advanced level.

When you eat real foods as opposed to "food products" like the ones being "enhanced" by Senomyx' technology, you don't need artificial, lab-created flavors or flavor enhancers, because real foods taste delicious. The fact that processed foods taste good is the culmination of a profitable science of artificial flavors, enhancers and additives, without which most processed food would taste and look like shredded cardboard.

Real food naturally has vibrant colors, rich textures, and is authentically flavorful. For times when you want to add even more oomph to your meals, nature has provided herbs and spices, which are not only incredibly tasty but also will make your real food even healthier.

Aborted Foetus is used for vaccination against childhood diseases such as measles, mumps and rubella.

(EWTNews) - The Washington Post announced the award of a contract for the development of a new smallpox vaccine to Oravax/Acambis Corporation. The proposal presented to the CDC and FDA would encompass using "human fibroblasts." In checking the proposed ingredients through the CDC it was found that they intend to use aborted fetal cell line MRC-5 as the cell substrate for growing the virus. The CDC report also stated that other established animal substrates such as chick embryo, (used in Rabies vaccine) Vero Cell Lines and FRHL-2 Cell lines were viable alternatives as well. The FDA stated that they have verified the reports, but also indicated they would most likely use more than one manufacturer and no final decisions have been made. "We do know that testing has already begun using MRC-5 in Phase 1 trials." Says Debi Vinnedge, spokesperson for the Children of God for Life, a Pro-Life

outreach source. *"For over 30 years, our country has been quietly producing vaccines from human cell lines derived from abortion. There are six commonly used vaccines: Polio, Rabies, Mumps, Rubella (MMR), Chickenpox and Hepatitis-A all of which were propagated from the lung tissue of two aborted babies, one male, one female. Of these, three have NO ALTERNATIVE SOURCE: Rubella (MMR-Measles, Mumps, Rubella), Chickenpox and Hepatitis-A. It is not that the pharmaceutical companies had to use aborted children as their source; they simply opted to do so. The United Kingdom was successful in obtaining alternatives for both Rubella and Hepatitis-A, but these products are not available in the United States and unless there is a market, there is little incentive for the pharmaceutical companies to respond." " Immediate action is needed now!" states Debi. " We do not want our families being forced by the government to use a critical vaccine that is derived from aborted fetal tissue." "If there is an epidemic or national crisis, you will NOT be able to use religious exemptions. Please express your concern. Ask that the policy makers consider the moral consciences of hundreds of thousands of Americans who have already voiced their objection to the currently used vaccines derived from aborted fetal tissue."*

MATTERS OF LIFE AND DEATH

Coast Guard forces vaccine derived from aborted child Catholic officer sues to prevent injection – top brass disputes theology, demands

Posted: January 13, 2008
1:00 a.m. Eastern

© 2008 WorldNetDaily.com

A U.S. Coast Guard officer and devout Catholic has filed suit to prevent being forced to receive a vaccination derived from the lung of an aborted child after a higher ranking officer disputed his understanding of Church theology.

The Alliance Defense Fund filed a complaint last week in the U.S. District Court for the District of Columbia on behalf of Lt. Cmdr. Joseph Healy, charging the government with using its own arbitrary judgment of what constitutes Catholic theology while permitting religious exemptions to others, effectively discriminating against Healy's sincerely held religious beliefs.

Healy's request for religious exemption cited a 2005 letter from the

Vatican's Pontifical Academy for Life which condemned the use of cell lines from abortions in vaccines and supported Catholics' right to refuse them while not requiring them to reject the medicines. In May, 2007, Capt. Brent Pennington rejected Healy's request, saying Catholic teaching "does not state that these immunizations are against the religious tenets of the Catholic Church."

"Please note that the refusal to be vaccinated or failure to comply with a lawful order to be vaccinated is a violation of Coast Guard regulations," Pennington wrote Healy. "Any member who refuses to be vaccinated or fails to comply with a lawful order to be vaccinated is subject to military proceedings under [the Uniform Code of Military Justice] or other appropriate administrative proceedings at the unit commander's discretion." All members of the Coast Guard must be vaccinated against a broad spectrum of diseases. The requirement for all active-duty personnel to be inoculated against Hepatitis A was instituted in May 2006. While a vaccine derived from animal sources is awaiting FDA approval, the immunization procedure currently available in the U.S. is based on lung cells taken from an elective abortion performed at 14 weeks approximately 40 years ago.

"Those who lay their life on the line to defend our shores are entitled to the same religious freedoms as anyone else," said ADF attorney Matt Bowman, according to the Philadelphia Evening Bulletin. "Members of the U.S. military should never be forced to make an unconstitutional choice between honouring their country and honouring their faith." Healy is a long-time opponent of abortion and is listed on a Coast Guard website as the contact for an October 2006 pro-life awards banquet held in Glen Burnie, Md. Healy is stationed at the Coast Guard facility in Alexandria, Va.

(Story continues below)

ADF argues that Pennington's refusal of a religious exemption amounts to a governmental definition of Roman Catholic theology. The letter submitted by Healy from the Pontifical Academy for Life was prompted by an inquiry from a Florida Catholic group concerned that the Church had no formal statement in opposition to such vaccines – a fact that could be used by schools to deny religious exemptions for Catholics who refused to vaccinate their children.

The academy's paper, "Moral Reflections on Vaccines Prepared From Cells Derived From Aborted Human Fetuses," was published in May 2005 after having been approved by the Vatican's Congregation for the Doctrine of the Faith. While the document condemned "every form of formal cooperation" – the original abortion 40 years ago and the development of the vaccine – as well as the "passive material cooperation" of those marketing it four decades on, it distinguished the "very remote mediate material cooperation" of doctors and parents who, through lack of options, resort to the medicines for reasons of health – particularly public health – even though they know their origin.

"We are responsible for all people, not just ourselves," Msgr. Jacques Suaudeau, a medical doctor and official at the Pontifical Academy for Life, told Catholic News Service. "If it is a question of protecting the whole population and avoiding death and malformation in others, that is more important," he said. According to Debi Vinnedge, head of the Catholic group, Children of God for Life, "members of the Lutheran Church" are more likely to be given exemptions for their children in Florida schools because their denomination has "a stronger statement" concerning the immorality of using such vaccines.

"We need a stronger statement" if Catholics are to get the exemption, she said. While the Academy's ambiguity and failure to forge a stronger statement may have contributed to Pennington's denial, he also cited the opinion of the National Catholic Bioethics Center that receiving such a vaccine does not constitute cooperation with abortion. Healy's attorney notes his client never cited NCBC, a non-authoritative Catholic group, and argues Pennington, in his governmental capacity, was defining what constitutes orthodox Catholic theology. It's "most troubling that the government would decide some religions get exemptions and others do not based on their own arbitrary judgments," said ADF's Bowman.

"We asked the court to step in because, at any moment, he could be ordered to be vaccinated, Bowman told the Washington Times." He is not asking for special treatment – he is simply saying the Coast Guard cannot disfavour his religion over the beliefs of others when it offers religious exemptions."

***

Obviously abortions have become 'Big Businesses. Why?

Arizona, in her statement, mentioned that the illuminati, many of which are reptilian, must consume aborted babies blood, which contains a specific ingredient necessary for the reptilian's survival!

Is it starting to make sense now? Can you see the links?

It is obvious why there is a desperate need to continue with the abortions in order to feed their insatiable appetites! It is done of course under the disguise of doing it for medical reasons to prevent disease and save people's lives! It is important at this stage to remind the reader not to be alarmed by the mention of reptiles. It is a term used for the dragon mentioned in the book of Revelation and describes the dragon that was originally from heaven but cast out because of His rebellion and cast down to earth along with his followers (other reptile looking beings). These reptile beings have a different diet to humans, their scaly body's need a particular chemical ingredient found only in blood of a certain type and is abundant in foetus blood supply. This is horrific information for any normal sane person to stomach, yet it makes absolute sense when you read scripture!

One of God's Noachide commandments is '**you must not eat meat that has its lifeblood still in it. And for your lifeblood I will surely demand an accounting.**

"Whoever sheds the blood of man, by man shall his blood be shed; for in the image of God has God made man" Gen 9:4-7

So not only are those reptilian beings breaking God's Law by eating the blood of the foetus, they are also committing an abhorrent sin by committing murder, and therefore, shedding innocent blood! This is pure evil! Lucifer is the ultimate lawless one described in **2 Thessalonians 2: 3 -5'**

When the reader appreciates that God's heavenly world is quite different to our world, then we can acknowledge that there are differences between the heavenly host and humans. The heavenly host are all different shapes, sizes and types. We know from scripture that the archangels have a human appearance when seen by mankind. Cherubs have different forms some of which are difficult to comprehend as they have wheels and wings and different faces. Others who were heavenly angels transformed into ugly beings because of their rebellion against

God, so you have the dragon and the demons. We know from scripture that during the Great Tribulation there will be demonic forms like locusts that come out from the Abyss to torment those remaining on earth who have the mark of the beast! See Revelation 9.

We have now read evidence and a witness testimony for the number of reasons why abortions are so important to the illuminati.

People of the Church of Christ recognise the sin of abortion and I am sure non-believers who still own their own minds also recognise this as an abhorrent sin. However, many people have been conditioned to accept these sins.

When you understand that the world is soaring to its end because of the atrocities taking place in it (as it's at the same stage of the Judgement of God which brought on the flood at the time of Noah) then it is easy to realise that lucifer is also anxious to move fast to achieve his 'take over.' He believes he is able to stop God's plan to bring about the final end to this world. Lucifer's initial plan was and still is, to gather as many loyalists to form his army against God. This army will be led by lucifer against Christ Yeshua and His army – the final battle between good and evil which is known as Armageddon!

Lucifer is aware of the end time battle to come, therefore he is recruiting constantly! Because his army of fallen angels and offspring of half human fallen angels and loyal humanists, has increased. This means there's a greater need for this foetal blood for survival and to remain covert until the time arrives to reveal his true identity. It is because of this urgency that abortion is vital to lucifer for his purpose, to feed his and his henchmen's needs!

Therefore all effort is made to condition people to accept him and his deceptive, enticing promises i.e., the promise of good health if you allow unborn babies to be used for research purposes! Just as it is important for people to accept homosexuality as a positive part of life. To encourage the sin of homosexuality is important to the dragon. If he can convince men they are free and safe from condemnation, if they openly have a gay relationship and seal it with a gay couple marriage ceremony, this would persuade the world population that it is safe to commit other sins, entrapping the victim in a web of sin.

Returning to the false evangelists and preachers who practice hypnotism to capture and entice their pray (the audience) into the web of deceit. Like the illuminati, they also use occult methods, i.e. channeling demons (calling demons into play from the underworld). These demons provide them with prophetic information and information about the victim under hypnosis or the person about to be zapped by the unholy fire! These meetings are highly dangerous and have claimed the souls of innocent children and believing men and women because of their naivety and desire for a miracle from God! These false preachers however are working in the demonic world as false prophets for satan.

Sadly many people who have attended these meetings believe they are 'born again' some may well be and protected by God so that they remain unharmed by the deceiver, but many are not! They are being misled and given a false Christian experience that will lead them into death instead of eternal life unless they repent from their involvement, with the occult and witchcraft, and turn to Christ Yeshua for forgiveness!

These false preachers are not the only people to use hypnotism as a means of controlling someone. There are those of course who use hypnotism for altruistic purposes such as those hypnotists who work in healthcare. They may hypnotize someone as a means of improving a patient's health i.e. to stop smoking cigarettes. The technique used is called 'post hypnotic suggestion' it does not take affect at the time of the autosuggestion but after the session is over.

Hypnotists also work in the entertainment business, similarly to the above Pensacola/Toronto preachers; it is made into entertainment to lure the naïve but is highly dangerous as they play with the person's mind.

Another important concept is desensitization, which has already been mentioned a few times (also called inurement) it is defined, by Wikipedia, an online free dictionary,

"As the diminished emotional responsiveness to a negative or aversive stimulus after repeated exposure to it. It also occurs when an emotional response is repeatedly evoked in situations in which the action tendency that is associated with the emotion proves irrelevant or unnecessary".

Desensitization is a process primarily used to assist individuals to unlearn phobias and anxieties and was developed by psychologist Mary Cover Jones.[1][2] Joseph Wolpe (1958) developed a method of a hierarchal list of anxiety evoking stimuli in order of intensity, which allows individuals to undergo adaption.[3] Although medication is available for individuals suffering from anxiety, fear or phobias, empirical evidence supports desensitization with high rates of cure, particularly in clients suffering from depression or schizophrenia.[4] Wikipedia.

To conclude on hypnotism, not only are individuals controlled by influences mentioned in the previous chapter but also in the entertainment sector. People will accept anything and willingly place themselves into a position (not realising the danger) of vulnerability, all in the name of 'laughs, to have a laugh, a bit of fun etc).

The Harry Potter films have had a huge influence on children and adults alike. The popularity of the Harry Potter books and the massive sales the author has made from the series demonstrates the 'mindset' of the nations, Having been so successful in drawing innocent young minds into occult and witchcraft they follow this up with a book of spells! This is a seriously dangerous path!

Adults are encouraging their children to become involved with [desensitized to] evil, occult and witchcraft practices, and with the addition of the 'The Spell Book' by J K Rowling, they can become actually 'hands on' involved in witchcraft. Ironically, many 'so-called' Christians have purchased the Harry Potter books or taken their children to see the movies. Harry potter films are regularly repeated on TV.

Disney World has now incorporated Harry Potter into their Theme Park.

The Spell book has on the front page a dragon and an owl, both of these are important symbols within the illuminati and therefore in the N.W.O. This is to be explained later in the book.

To put all of this information into perspective, the N.W.O leader, to take control of the world, must cause chaos; he must unsettle the world so that the people will welcome him; relying on him to sort things out, to bring about peace. Now this chaos has already started with the various worldwide terrorist acts that have taken place. The key attack was the 9/11, thought to be a conspiracy, and when you piece together the facts it seems very possible. What better way to unnerve the Americans than the 9/11. It worked!

There is fear everywhere! Fear of terrorist attacks! No one wants to challenge the terrorists. The terrorists run freely, unchallenged. They run riot causing worldwide havoc!

To make his way easier this leader of the N.W.O., who is antichrist/anti sematic and generally anti- people, started many years ago to force and organise groups of men (gangsters, prisoners, terrorists) to raise fear within society, to recruit more members, men with a lust for violence. The point was to instil hatred between different communities, i.e. blacks, whites, Jews and seculars, police and protestors, the people and the leaders of nations etc. The violent act would start by this terrorist group or they would infiltrate peaceful demonstrations and goad others into riotous behaviour. Others would join in or attempt to defend themselves and chaos would develop. The general public would be led to believe that the protestors were violent so that public opinion would condemn them and their protest, while the real perpetrators go undetected to work again.

As you can see by the news reports daily, this strategy has worked very well. This is what happened in the previous propaganda report on the George Zimmerman Trial.

There's civil unrest in many European countries i.e. Greece, Italy, Spain. The Middle East are taking turns to fight against each country and within these countries civil unrest is happening against their own people. The instilling of this worldwide chaos consists of a short term and a long term plan.

The short term plan is to cause chaos, to rid the countries of those who follow the faith of the Creator God and His son .i.e. Christians and Jews, and to instil fear and compliance of all people. The long term plan is to reduce the populations of each nation, to change the leadership of these countries by replacing the leaders with N.W.O leaders, and finally to take control of the countries and form a great army!

There is a third reason, recent news states that the unrest amongst the Muslim countries has come about because the 12th Imam is to lead the Muslim countries under one leader and one Muslim religion (under Sharia Law) and all others are to become Sharia Muslims or die! This is a foreshadow (and a reality check) on the future 7 year Tribulation. This is exactly what will happen (very soon) in the latter three and half years (Great Tribulation period). All Muslims will be at that point under Sharia Law. They will then demand all non -Muslim's to become Sharia Muslim's or be killed! This is when the **Mark** of the Beast will be allocated to those who comply! And the rest will be beheaded! See Revelation.

Recently, on the 700 Club (American TV) an author and Terrorism Reporter Erick Stakelbeck researched the Muslim Brotherhood, an Islamic Organisation that appears to be democratic, non-violent and politically correct yet behind the scenes they are linked to terrorist attacks and organised plans to produce worldwide unrest and the murderous atrocities of all who oppose them.

Erick discovered the Brotherhood is embraced by the CIA, FBI and Obama. There has been an exchange of information and support between these three.

To find out more see Erick's book 'Muslim Brotherhood, America's Next Great Enemy. The book would evidence that the Brotherhood was one of those small groups sent out to recruit, cause chaos and fear. The group has now grown and spread throughout the Middle East. They had for many years worked covertly, now they have proudly exposed their identity and claiming their powerful stance as the world's feared aggressors!

To conclude this chapter 'Are we being controlled?' It would seem that there are many forms of control taking place to shape our world, society and individuals, towards a specific goal! Behaviour and thinking has gradually adapted to the 'Status Quo' which has been fashioned and put into place covertly, so that we accept certain things as the 'norm'. Most of the control mentioned in this chapter has been mildly applied at a low level, so that it was hardly noticed. It was introduced through the normal channels of debate, i.e. the abortion debates. Involving the public in such debates puts the sole accountability on the people not on government leaders, as they transfer the issues over to the public for debate yet orchestrate the proceedings and results. The public are always seen to protest yet the protests never seem to have a successful conclusion but end the way the Government or more accurately, how the N.W.O. intended.

CHAPTER 6

ARE WE SUBCONSCIOUSLY CONTROLLED?

The previous chapter introduced the obvious form of mind control which people are aware of and many agree to or accept and even desire! These people who search for and desire to be hypnotized or zapped by false preachers have made their choice. So the reader exclaims, 'but how could we make a choice? We were not to know that these preachers were false and dangerous!' Well in answer to that, the person who is involved in these activities is accountable for their actions because God has forewarned against these things long ago! The reader then says, 'But where were we forewarned?' People were forewarned in the bible and within society (by believer's testimony) as well as in the various signs which have existed for centuries. The fact that you chose NOT to read the bible or to seek the truth, to ignore bible prophecy and God's warnings suggests you were in rebellion! Matthew 24 & 25:31-46.

So the reader then protests that they were persuaded by the serpent like Adam and Eve, they were misled. Adam and Eve attempted to blame the serpent and each other for their disobedience , however, God ignored their claims, he looked beyond that to their rebellious hearts that preferred to rebel against God's world and choose the way to materialism, seeking knowledge outside of the realm of the Garden. In other words they stepped out of God's kingdom of safety, provisions and love, into the world of hardship, insecurity and sin! They made a choice and with that choice there is always consequences!

Of course there are millions of people in this world who were and still are unable to read a bible simply because they do not have access to one for various reasons. But most of these people have God's hand on them anyway, because Yeshua is concerned for the poor, the suffering and the needy, therefore he would guide them to salvation. He knows the hearts of men and women, he knows who is in rebellion and whose heart is seeking or calling out to Him! But those who have the opportunity to read the bible and the freedom to seek out the truth but choose not to, have already rebelled and therefore are susceptible to deception! They are easy fodder for their minds, bodies, souls to become the property of an unscrupulous world leader who desires total domination of this world!

In this chapter we will look at the less obvious types of mind control. These forms are so well disguised by a morally acceptable cover that the underlying schemes are undetectable by the majority. It also consists of mild control that is camouflaged by something else or the sort that is not always noticeable, therefore difficult to accept as being in existence at all. Many of the mind control projects were and are top secret!

Unfortunately, humans will usually look for reasonable explanations for strange phenomena, closing their minds to unusual unexplained concepts or things that threaten their security and peace of mind. It is because of this built- in safety net that controllers can perform these pilots undetected. People rationalize everything, placing what they see into 'safe boxes' of rational thought. To step outside these boxes is far too painful and scary so they keep the lid on the boxes! Some people have blindness, or selective eyesight, whereby they see only what they want to see cutting off any unpleasantness from their sight. This is quite understandable but also puts people into a vulnerable position. Another safety net is to use the word 'coincidence' to cover up any acts of God.

This chapter may prove difficult for the reader, as it discloses a deeper form of mind control, one that attacks the subconscious mind. The chapter also contains information that's difficult to comprehend – the unusual, phenomena that doesn't come into the 'normal' realm of rational concepts. It may be difficult to accept these things are happening around us, and as previously mentioned, there is evidence to back up this information. A lot of this mind control was done covertly, much of it was underground. Secret research and experiments took place without authorization or public awareness or permission. Many of the experiments ignored the Code of Ethics or were performed prior to the amended Ethics Code in the 1990s.

A book entitled 'Mind Controllers, 'written by Dr Armen Victorian was published in 1999 by Vision Paperbacks Company. He wrote some interesting information regarding mind control activities performed by the CIA, which has led onto new research being practiced today that stem from those earlier studies.

In Chapter 11 of his book, he wrote about Electronic implants. It was called a Stimoceiver created by Jose Delgado in the 1950's. He described this implant as a miniature electrode capable of receiving and transmitting electronic signals by FM radio which was to be used by intelligence agencies to control human behaviour. It could be placed within an individual's cranium. Once in place, an outside operator could manipulate the subject's responses.

Dr Victorian claimed to have met people with these implants in their heads, so placed without their consent and certified by independent doctors and radiologists.

Dr Victorian wrote the following: "*Delgardo demonstrated the potential of his Stimoceivers by wiring up a fully- grown bull. With the device in place, Delgado stepped into the ring with the bull. The animal charged towards the experimenter and suddenly stopped, just before reaching him. The powerful beast had been stopped with the simple action of pushing a button on a small black box held in Delgado's hand*".

Dr Victorian wrote Delgado stated that "emotion, motion and behaviour can be directed by electrical forces and that humans can be controlled like robots by pushing buttons".

Delgado's claims above have become a reality and other claims he has made are probably also to be just as realistic in the future if they are not already covertly occurring! He claims that eventually it would be possible to control a human mind using a two-way radio communication between the implanted brain and a computer. Delgado wrote a book 'Physical Control of the Mind: Towards a Psychological Civilized Society', mentioning the use of implants for electronic stimulation of the brain (ESB).

In 1967 a report was released by CIA on experiments with placing the stimoceiver to the tympanic membrane of the ear to transform it into a microphone, so anything whispered in the ear was heard over a loudspeaker. The hidden purpose of this experiment was to study electromagnetic communication between living organisms; one of the ultimate goals was to create an electronic hypnotizer and thought transference over distances.

In 1961 a record was released on Stimoceivers and subproject 94 which was part of MKULTRA. This project involved research on conditioning and controlling animals using implants in various brain areas using remote control. Ultimately the objective is to use these methods on humans. All of this was done with TOP SECRET APPROVAL.

According to Dr Victorian's book, James Olds suggested the hypothalamus, when electronically stimulated, would produce 'rewarding' and 'aversive' effects.

Dr Victorian wrote about a lot of points which have now come into use and far more advanced. Today people have willingly requested the implants on the misunderstanding that it is to help them medically.

Dr Victorian's book is well worth reading as it contains in depth information of research performed leading up to our current situation.

He wrote about hypnotism, electromagnetic and microwave use for mind control as well as LSD and other drugs.

What has all this to do with apostasy? Well, in many cases inhabitants have and will continue to accept anything they hear or are offered that would give credence to wickedness – it is in the hearts of these people to rebel against anything good, particularly God and Yeshua. However, there are also many people who are naïve, innocent, sitting on the fence and not sure whether there is a God or whether God is good! Some people may not be purely evil but lack knowledge or understanding or the ability to research the truth or even care, they just live day by day, hoping all will go well for them and their families and whatever happens in the world does not affect them. These people may need a bit of coercion to accept what is to come in these last days! Others who do believe there is a God but have not accepted Yeshua (Christ) as their savior will be vulnerable to' covert' mind control to move their allegiance from God towards acceptance of satan (Lucifer).

This has already been achieved, through the false religious leaders that have infiltrated the Christian and religious sector. There remains the scholars, the intellectuals, the students who have minds of their own to think, rationalize and revolt against elitist control, these have to be conditioned into submission and compliance – these are much more difficult to program.

The following extract is from a news article on a new study, which demonstrates how close we are to being controlled biologically!

Biological transistor enables computing within living cells, study

BY ANDREW MYERS

The biological transistor developed by Jerome Bonnet and colleagues could be used inside living cells to record when cells have been exposed to certain external stimuli, or even to turn on and off cell reproduction as needed.

When Charles Babbage prototyped the first computing machine in the 19th century, he imagined using mechanical gears and latches to control information. ENIAC, the first modern computer developed in the 1940s, used vacuum tubes and electricity. Today, computers use transistors made from highly engineered semiconducting materials to carry out their logical operations.

And now a team of Stanford University bioengineers has taken computing beyond mechanics and electronics into the living realm of biology. In a paper published March 28 in Science, the team details a biological transistor made from genetic material — DNA and RNA — in place of gears or electrons. The team calls its biological transistor the "transcriptor."

"Transcriptors are the key component behind amplifying genetic logic — akin to the transistor and electronics," said Jerome Bonnet, PhD, a postdoctoral scholar in bioengineering and the paper's lead author.

The creation of the transcriptor allows engineers to compute inside living cells to record, for instance, when cells have been exposed to certain external stimuli or environmental factors, or even to turn on and off cell reproduction as needed.

Related News

» Bioengineers introduce "Bi-Fi" — the biological Internet

» Totally RAD: Bioengineers create rewritable digital data storage in DNA

"Biological computers can be used to study and reprogram living systems, monitor environments and improve cellular therapeutics," said Drew Endy, PhD, assistant professor of bioengineering and the paper's senior author.

The biological computer

In electronics, a transistor controls the flow of electrons along a circuit. Similarly, in biologics, a transcriptor controls the flow of a specific protein, RNA polymerase, as it travels along a strand of DNA.

"We have repurposed a group of natural proteins, called integrases, to realize digital control over the flow of RNA polymerase along DNA, which in turn allowed us to engineer amplifying genetic logic," said Endy.

Using Transcriptors, the team has created what are known in electrical engineering as logic gates that can derive true-false answers to virtually any biochemical question that might be posed within a cell.

They refer to their transcriptor-based logic gates as "Boolean Integrase Logic," or "BIL gates" for short.

Transcriptor-based gates alone do not constitute a computer, but they are the third and final component of a biological computer that could operate within individual living cells.

Despite their outward differences, all modern computers, from ENIAC to Apple, share three basic functions: storing, transmitting and performing logical operations on information.

Last year, Endy and his team made news in delivering the other two core components of a fully functional genetic computer. The first was a type of rewritable digital data storage within DNA. They also developed a mechanism for transmitting genetic information from cell to cell, a sort of biological Internet.

It all adds up to creating a computer inside a living cell.

Digital logic is often referred to as "Boolean logic," after George Boole, the mathematician who proposed the system in 1854. Today, Boolean logic typically takes the form of 1s and 0s within a computer. Answer true, gate open; answer false, gate closed. Open. Closed. On. Off. 1. 0. It's that basic. But it turns out that with just these simple tools and ways of thinking you can accomplish quite a lot.

"AND" and "OR" are just two of the most basic Boolean logic gates. An "AND" gate, for instance, is "true" when both of its inputs are true — when "a" and "b" are true. An "OR" gate, on the other hand, is true when either or both of its inputs are true.

In a biological setting, the possibilities for logic are as limitless as in electronics, Bonnet explained. "You could test whether a given cell had been exposed to any number of external stimuli — the presence of glucose and caffeine, for instance. BIL gates would allow you to make that determination and to store that information so you could easily identify those which had been exposed and which had not," he said.

By the same token, you could tell the cell to start or stop reproducing if certain factors were present. And, by coupling BIL gates with the team's

biological Internet, <u>it is possible to communicate genetic information from</u>
<u>*cell to cell to orchestrate the behavior of a group of cells.*</u>

<u>*"The potential applications are limited only by the imagination of the*</u>
<u>*researcher," said co-author Monica Ortiz, a PhD candidate in*</u>
<u>*bioengineering who demonstrated autonomous cell-to-cell* communication</u>
<u>*of DNA encoding various BIL gates.*</u>

Building a transcriptor

<u>*To create transcriptors and logic gates, the team used carefully calibrated*</u>
<u>*combinations of enzymes — the integrases mentioned earlier — that*</u>
<u>*control the flow of RNA polymerase along strands of DNA. If this were*</u>
<u>*electronics, DNA is the wire and RNA polymerase is the electron.*</u>

<u>*"The choice of enzymes is important," Bonnet said. "We have been careful*</u>
<u>*to select enzymes that function in bacteria, fungi, plants and animals, so*</u>
<u>*that bio-computers can be engineered within a variety of organisms."*</u>

On the technical side, the transcriptor achieves a key similarity between the
biological transistor and its semiconducting cousin: signal amplification.

With transcriptors, a very small change in the expression of an integrase
can create a very large change in the expression of any two other genes.

To understand the importance of amplification, consider that the transistor
was first conceived as a way to replace expensive, inefficient and
unreliable vacuum tubes in the amplification of telephone signals for
transcontinental phone calls. <u>Electrical signals traveling along wires get</u>
<u>*weaker the farther they travel, but if you put an amplifier every so often*</u>
<u>*along the way, you can relay the signal across a great distance. The same*</u>
<u>*would hold in biological systems as signals get transmitted among a group*</u>
<u>*of cells.*</u>

"It is a concept similar to transistor radios," said Pakpoom Subsoontorn, a
PhD candidate in bioengineering and co-author of the study who
developed theoretical models to predict the behavior of BIL gates.
"Relatively weak radio waves traveling through the air can get amplified
into sound."

Public-domain biotechnology

168

To bring the age of the biological computer to a much speedier reality, Endy and his team have contributed all of BIL gates to the public domain so that others can immediately harness and improve upon the tools.

"Most of biotechnology has not yet been imagined, let alone made true. By freely sharing important basic tools everyone can work better together," Bonnet said.

The research was funded by the National Science Foundation and the Townshend Lamarre Foundation.

Information about Stanford's Department of Bioengineering, which also supported the work, is available at http://bioengineering.stanford.edu. The department is jointly operated by the School of Engineering and the School of Medicine.

PRINT MEDIA CONTACT Andrew Myers | Tel **(650) 736-2245** admyers@stanford.edu .

BROADCAST MEDIA CONTACT M.A. Malone | Tel **(650) 723-6912** . mamalone@stanford.edu

Stanford University Medical Center integrates research, medical education and patient care at its three institutions - Stanford University School of Medicine, Stanford Hospital & Clinics and Lucile Packard Children's Hospital. For more information, please visit the Office of Communication & Public Affairs site at http://mednews.stanford.edu/.

The previous clip introduced the beginning of the implanting of the microchip into animals. It has now developed to not only work inside a human body but also can transmit across long distances!

Now the final stage to the Mark of the Beast has begun and the equipment is here and ready to go, during year 2017 (see reference section for YouTube title).

The equipment is the microchip implant discussed in previous chapters. There has been many pilot studies and research projects as well as many improvements made over the years but now it has reached its final stage.

American citizens will be the first to have this microchip implant, the rest of the world will follow gradually. This will be initially, a negotiable event, then it would eventually become compulsory!

Below is an extract explaining the microchip, currently used on animals, and soon to be used on humans, as shown by the human hand with the implanted microchip.

Microchip implant (human) _Wikipedia, free encyclopedia_

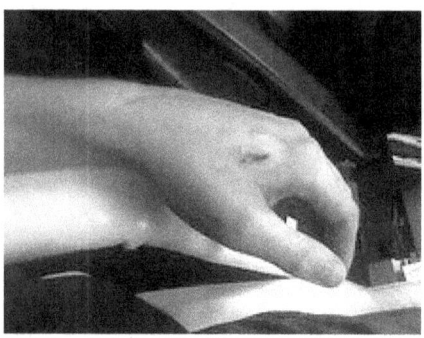

The hand of microchip implant hobbyist Amal Graafstra, just after an operation to insert an RFID tag. The yellow coloration comes from iodine used to disinfect the hand for surgery.

A human microchip implant is an identifying <u>integrated circuit</u> device or <u>RFID</u> transponder encased in silicate glass and implanted in the body of a human being. A <u>subdermal implant</u> typically contains a unique ID number that can be linked to information contained in an external database, such as personal identification, medical history, medications, allergies, and contact information.

Hobbyists

The first reported experiment with an <u>RFID</u> implant was carried out in 1998 by the British scientist <u>Kevin Warwick</u>.[1] As a test, his implant was used to open doors, switch on lights, and cause verbal output within a building. The implant has since been held in the <u>Science Museum (London)</u>. [

Since that time, several additional hobbyists have placed RFID microchip implants into their hands or had them placed there by others.

Amal Graafstra, author of the book "RFID Toys," asked doctors to place implants in his hands. A cosmetic surgeon used a scalpel to

170

place a microchip in his left hand, and his family doctor injected a chip into his right hand using a veterinary Avid injector kit. Graafstra uses the implants to open his home and car doors and to log on to his computer.

Mikey Sklar had a chip implanted into his left hand and filmed the procedure. He has done a number of media [2] and personal interviews [3] about his experience of being microchipped.

Commercial implants

In 2002, the VeriChip Corporation (known as the "PositiveID Corporation" since November 2009) received preliminary approval from the United States Food and Drug Administration (FDA) to market its device in the U.S. within specific guidelines. The device received FDA approval in 2004, and was marketed under the name VeriChip or VeriMed. In 2007, it was revealed that nearly identical implants had caused cancer in hundreds of laboratory animals, [4] a revelation that had a devastating impact on the company's stock price. Some time between May and July 2010, the Positive ID Corporation discontinued marketing the implantable human microchip. [5]

In January 2012, the VeriTeQ Acquisition Corporation acquired the VeriChip implantable microchip and related technologies, and Health Link personal health record from PositiveID Corporation. VeriTeQ is majority owned and led by Scott R. Silverman, former Chairman and CEO of PositiveID and VeriChip Corporation. PositiveID has retained an ownership interest in VeriTeQ. [6]

Medical records use

The PositiveID Corporation (previously known as The VeriChip Corporation; Applied Digital Solutions, Inc.; and The Digital Angel Corporation) distributed the implantable chip known as the VeriChip or VeriMed until the product was discontinued in the second quarter of 2010. The company had suggested that the implant could be used to retrieve medical information in the event of an emergency, as follows: Each VeriChip implant contained a 16-digit ID number. This number was transmitted when a hand-held VeriChip scanner is passed within a few inches of the implant.

Participating hospitals and emergency workers would enter this number into a secure page on the VeriChip Corporation's website to access medical information that the patient had previously stored on file with the company.

According to some reports, in 2006 80 hospitals had agreed to own a VeriChip scanner provided by the company and 232 doctors had agreed to inject the devices into patients who requested them.[7] However, the VeriChip Corporation/Applied Digital Solutions was sued by its shareholders for making "materially false and misleading statements" regarding hospital acceptance figures. According to Glancy & Binkow, the law firm that filed the class action suit:

"...on May 9, 2002, defendants [the then Applied Digital Corporation] claimed that nearly every major hospital in the West Palm Beach, Florida area would be equipped with VeriChip scanners, an indispensable component of the Company's VeriChip technology. However, one day later on May 10, 2002, the truth was disclosed that no hospital had accepted a scanner, an essential device for retrieving the VeriChip's information. Following the May 10, 2002, disclosure, the price of Applied Digital stock again fell sharply, dropping nearly 30% in a single day."[8]

Building access and security]

The VeriChip Corporation has marketed the implant as a way to restrict access to secure facilities such as power plants. Microchip scanners would be installed at entrances so locks only work for persons whose chip numbers are entered into the system. Two employees of CityWatcher, an Ohio video surveillance company, had RFID tags injected into their arms in 2007. The workers needed the implants to access the company's secure video tape room, as documented in USA Today.[9] The company closed, but there is no word on what happened to the employees or their implants.

A major drawback for such systems is the relative ease with which the 16-digit ID number contained in a chip implant can be obtained and cloned using a hand-held device, a problem that has been demonstrated publicly by security researcher Jonathan Westhues[10] and documented in the May 2006 issue of Wired magazine,[11] among other places.

The Baja Beach Club, a nightclub in Rotterdam, the Netherlands, once used VeriChip implants for identifying VIP guests.[12]

Possible future applications

Theoretically, a GPS-enabled chip could one day make it possible for individuals to be physically located by latitude, longitude, altitude, speed, and direction of movement. Such implantable GPS devices are not technically feasible at this time. However, if widely deployed at some future point, implantable GPS devices could conceivably allow authorities to locate missing persons and/or fugitives and those who fled from a crime scene. Critics contend, however, that the technology could lead to political repression as governments could use implants to track and persecute human rights activists, labor activists, civil dissidents, and political opponents; criminals and domestic abusers could use them to stalk and harass their victims; slaveholders could use them to prevent captives from escaping; and child abusers could use them to locate and abduct children.[citation needed]

Another suggested application for a tracking implant, discussed in 2008 by the legislature of Indonesia's Irian Jaya would be to monitor the activities of persons infected with HIV, aimed at reducing their chances of infecting other people.[13][14] The microchipping section was not, however, included into the final version of the provincial HIV/AIDS Handling bylaw passed by the legislature in December 2008.[15] With current technology this would not be workable anyway, since there is no implantable device on the market with GPS tracking capability.

The pilot study was on animals in A microchip implant is an identifying integrated circuit placed under the skin of a dog, cat, horse, parrot or other animal. The chip, about the size of a large grain of rice, uses passive RFID (Radio Frequency Identification) technology.

Externally attached microchips such as RFID ear tags are commonly used to identify farm and ranch animals other than horses. Some external microchips can be read with the same scanner used with implanted chips.

Uses and benefits

Animal shelters, animal control officers and veterinarians routinely look for microchips to return lost pets quickly to their owners, avoiding expenses for housing, food, medical care, outplacing and euthanasia. Many shelters place chips in all outplaced animals.

Microchips are also used by kennels, breeders, brokers, trainers, registries, rescue groups, humane societies, clinics, farms, stables, animal clubs and associations, researchers, and pet stores.

Microchips can also activate some pet doors[1] programmed to recognize specific animals.

Some countries require microchips in imported animals to match vaccination records. Microchip tagging may also be required for CITES-regulated international trade in certain rare animals: for example, Asian Arowana are tagged to limit import to captive-bred fish.

How microchips are used

Information about the implant is often imprinted on a collar tag worn by a pet

Microchips can be implanted by a veterinarian or at a shelter. After checking that the animal does not already have a chip, the vet or technician injects the chip with a syringe and records the chip's unique ID. No anesthetic is required. A test scan ensures correct operation.

An enrollment form is completed with chip ID, owner contact information, pet name and description, shelter and/or veterinarian contact information, and an alternate emergency contact designated by the pet owner. Some shelters and vets designate themselves as the primary contact to remain informed about possible problems with the animals they place. The form is sent to a registry, who may be the chip manufacturer, distributor or an independent entity; some countries have a single official national database. For a fee, the registry typically provides 24-hour, toll-free telephone service for the life of the pet. Some veterinarians leave registration to the owner, usually done online, but a chip without current contact information is essentially useless.

The owner receives a registration certificate with the chip ID and recovery service contact information. The information can also be imprinted on a collar tag worn by the animal. Like an automobile title, the certificate serves as proof of ownership and is transferred with the animal when it is sold or traded; an animal without a certificate could be stolen.

Authorities and shelters examine strays for chips, providing the recovery service with the ID number, description and location so they may notify the owner or contact. Multiple registries may have to be consulted; see Pet recovery service for further discussion of related issues. If the pet is wearing the collar tag, the finder does not need a chip reader to contact the registry. An owner can also report a missing pet to the recovery service, as vets look for chips in new animals and check with the recovery service to see if it has been reported lost or stolen.

Many veterinarians scan an animal's chip on every visit to verify correct operation. Some use the chip ID as their database index and print it on receipts, test results, vaccination certifications and other records.

Components of a microchip

A microchip implant is a passive RFID device. Lacking an internal power source, it remains inert until it is powered by the scanner.

Most implants contain three elements: a 'chip' or integrated circuit; a coil inductor, possibly with a ferrite core; and a capacitor. The chip contains unique identification data and electronic circuits to encode that information. The coil acts as the secondary winding of a transformer, receiving power inductively coupled to it from the scanner. The coil and capacitor together form a resonant LC circuit tuned to the frequency of the scanner's oscillating magnetic field to produce power for the chip. The chip then transmits its data back through the coil to the scanner.

These components are encased in biocompatible soda lime glass and hermetically sealed. Barring rare complications, dogs and cats are unaffected by them.

Implant location

In dogs and cats, chips are usually inserted below the skin at the back of the neck between the shoulder blades on the dorsal midline. According to one reference, continental European pets get the implant in the left side of the neck.[2] The chip can often be felt under the skin. Thin layers of connective tissue form around the implant and hold it in place.

Horses are micro chipped on the left side of the neck, halfway between the poll and withers and approximately one inch below the midline of the mane, into the nuchal ligament.

Birds are implanted in their breast muscles. Proper restraint is necessary so the operation requires either two people (an avian veterinarian and a veterinary technician) or general anesthesia.

Implanted microchips can distort magnetic resonance imaging (MRIs), including those of the spinal cord.[3]

***

How close are we to seeing these microchips useable on humans? We know that it will come to pass as in Bible Scripture that all will receive the Mark so that no one could buy or sell, however, whether this microchip is the actual mark or a part of the initial process remains to be seen, but it certainly appears to be associated with the mark, Revelation 13:16.
All accept those belonging to God will take the mark!

In Texas a law was passed giving schools authority to enforce children to wear a microchip badge, which must be worn at all times. If the child did not wear this badge they would not be able to buy their lunch or hire library books etc. The microchip in the card held all personal information and a tracking system see the YouTube video by 'infowars.com' and the Hernandez Family. 7 Sept 2012.

This is typical mind control, focusing on the children to instigate change. Why are children always the focus? For several reasons, one because they ARE THE LAST HUMANS ON THIS EARTH that may experience the whole of the Tribulation period! They also may be the ones who are likely to turn to God for help! These young people are very susceptible therefore it is easy to instil fear and compliance!

Hitler used children as a tool for adult compliance. Children are precious to us so when they are used for negative purposes we adults are emotionally affected therefore we weaken our defences. Feeling defenceless therefore leads to susceptibility to compliance! Child prisoners are also targets for GPS devices.

The overview of all of this is that gradually people are becoming like the Jews in WW2 becoming just a number. Every person in the world is to have an ID of some sort which holds a microchip that reveals data about the person. Eventually that ID data will be transferred onto a microchip and placed under the skin of each individual!

The Jewish people were the PILOT SCHEME during the Second World War, by wearing the yellow star and the number tattooed on their arm! Now it is the real thing on a GLOBAL SCALE!

People are gradually being programmed into becoming a commodity – a product as in a stock room of a warehouse or a cattle market! You, as a commodity will be recorded on a computer system which includes every detail of your life, it will include your bank details, whether you pay your taxes, where you work, your health records and your family details (they too can be tracked). This then will develop into your chip as your ID card that will allow you to buy or sell goods. Because of this, many will comply and take this chip rather than starve their families. The need to be able to purchase food and to sell goods will be a key bargaining chip, literally, as people have become so reliant on commerce to survive! People have become so materialistic and reliant on luxury living that hardship will take its toll. It has already begun to a lesser degree, middle classes/affluent groups have found their lifestyles have been reduced because of financial constraints affecting all the nations.

When you look at it logically, to be controlled in this way, means a return to slavery!

Humanity is not new to slavery it has existed since the Israelites (Jews) were slaves to the Egyptians centuries ago and again we are aware of the slavery of black people which existed in many nations. And already in this century we have heard many times of child slavery, and women enslaved in Arab countries. The future enslavery of the world will consist of individuals being called on demand. It is not so farfetched when you see films being made of Zombies. What else is a slave but someone who has no mind of their own and under the power of others! Their emotions are controlled, their thoughts are controlled, the irony of this, is that each individual will still believe they have individuality and free will! They still believe they are making their own decisions because they are bombarded with pleasures and lies, to convince them. Again this is the reality today. People have been encouraged to indulge in sexual activity i.e. sexual promiscuity with no limits as this instils a 'feel good factor', which is essential to pacify people so they ignore the bad things occurring around them!

It is so easy to control a mass, as it's the mass that submit like sheep!

It is those who stand alone – the objectionists! The speakers who refuse to become a sheep, they are the key threat and it is why so many Christians, Jews etc are being massacred! In the hope that they will be stopped from informing people what is really going on! What is not realised is people will continue fighting against the controllers and refuse to become Zombies no matter how many are massacred because God is with them. As one is massacred so ten more will arise to take their place! Until God says' ENOUGH! Then Yeshua will come and settle it once and for all – the battle between good and evil will commence and like all good movies, Good overcomes evil! Only it won't be a movie! It will be for real!

Always before any long term permanent plan is put into place a pilot study is performed. This allows researchers to identify problems, or the need for amendments and to sort out any issues that may arise.

During the 1950's, the CIA studied mind control techniques to find ways of interrogating prisoners of war for information. Many experiments took place and the records were destroyed so that this could not be evidenced. However, financial records relating to these experiments were discovered and through these records it became evident that these experiments on mind control took place.

For some years the CIA has kept a low profile on this experimentation research on mind control. However there is no reason to assume that they would stop research in this area, particularly as war has continued through terrorist attacks and the threat of WW3 hanging over the world!

The CIA studied ways to control the mind; these studies were called 'The Clandestine Projects, whereby they were given code names. LSD was used a lot in these experiments to unlock mysteries of the mind and to give others control as controllers. When LSD is used it takes a person into a world of hallucinations and sometimes a 'bad trip'. During these periods, the person's mind is far removed from reality. It is under the control of the events taking place within the hallucination that becomes the reality emotionally and can invoke certain behaviour in the person depending on the type of hallucination. If it is possible to implant into the mind a particular scenario, while having hallucinations from LSD, then it would be possible to get them to do anything without them knowing. A particular test was done on soldiers, trained to be obedient, to obey orders at all times. An experiment whereby a soldier was told to run an obstacle course did so to the very end, his progress was recorded. What the soldier did not know was that he had been given LSD in his drink prior to starting the course. He had become more and more sluggish as he went through the course, yet he struggled to the end as he had been ordered.

Soldiers, students and prison drug addicts are used to test LSD and how it can disturb brain function and may ultimately lead the user to suicide.

The CIA opened covert experimental centres and are paying students and mental institutions to research on mind control.

Between the years 1953-1964 a 149 researches were performed using drugs as well as other mind control techniques such as hypnosis, pain, sleep and sensory deprivation and electric shock.

In 1957 a new method was performed by a DR Cameron under the guise of 'treatment for mental disorders' it was called Depatterning. It was a horrific method and holds a dangerous threat to naïve people who innocently seek help for mental issues such as hurtful memories that have caused emotional traumas. These traumatic experiences cause such emotional turmoil that it interferes with daily life.

Such a mental health issue would cause a person to seek help which only needs a few counselling sessions to work through the key emotional issues using basic common sense cognitive behavioural therapy (CBT) methods to bring the individual back to a more healthy outlook. However, many such people had been sent to a specific clinic and subjected to unethical and permanently damaging methods that negatively altered their lives permanently!

These people were subjected to 'Depatterning'; this involved wiping the person's mind of all thoughts and memories and depatterning the person's behaviour and placing new thoughts. When the patients returned to consciousness they could remember nothing of their past life. These people had to reinvent a new life. One woman gave her testimony on this and said when she came round from the procedure she was like a vegetable, she was as a baby. She was incontinent; she could not speak and did not know how to read. Her husband and her children had to retrain her in the basics like a child. Prior and during the process she had no idea what was happening, she had become a guinea pig. She had thought she was getting treatment for her mental issue and instead her life had been turned upside down. She had lost her identity and memories from her childhood and early adulthood.

There are three particular parts to achieving this Depatterning of the brain:

Phase one is to use LSD and electric shocks to depattern, clean out the brain – wash it out.

Phase two replaces the brain with new recorded messages which was played over hundreds of times. The purpose of this phase was to implant new behaviour and thoughts. CAN YOU SEE THE DANGER IN THIS?

Phase three is to put the patient to sleep for 3-4 weeks so that they forget what has happened to them, this is done by giving them barbiturates.

Dr Cameron continued this horrendous treatment until 1964 and he died in 1967.

Now the reader may be thinking this is unreal it cannot be done. It's too fictional to be true. In answer to these doubts it would be suggested that the reader do their own research into the testimonies of these victims, see for yourself how convincing they are, then look at the past and latest psychological research taking place.

A milder form of this depatterning of the mind is ECT. Originally ECT (Electroconvulsive Therapy) was used for people with Post Natal Depression, It was intended to produce a convulsion in the brain that would then remove the negative thoughts and replace them with a 'good feeling, therefore removing the depression. The convulsion would alter the electrical impulses in the brain which ultimately effected mood. In the 1970's it was used to erase negative memories or thoughts. Today it is used to alter mood by manipulating the brain chemicals in the neurotransmitters.

The NHS website describes ECT below: www.nhs.uk

Electroconvulsive therapy (ECT) may be recommended if you have severe postnatal depression, but is only used when antidepressants and other treatments have not worked. If ECT is recommended, you will be given a general unaesthetic and medication to relax your muscles. Electrodes are placed on your head and a pulse of electricity passed through your brain.

Most people have either six or twelve sessions of ECT, normally with two sessions a week.

For most people, ECT is effective in relieving severe depression, but it is necessary to take antidepressants afterwards to keep symptoms under control. It's unclear how ECT works, but the generally agreed view is that electricity changes the chemical composition of the brain in such a way as to elevate mood.

Some people experience unpleasant side effects after having ECT, including headaches and both short-term and long-term memory loss. Due to the risk of memory loss, your memory will be assessed at the end of each ECT session.

If it looks like your memory is being affected, or you experience other adverse side effects, then the ECT sessions will be stopped

Many subjects in the psychology curriculum cover research projects that discuss how memories can be recalled artificially or how a scientist can enter the brain and alter behaviour just by cutting or damaging a particular area. Also recent research is on detecting brain defects that produce aggressive behaviour. There are many brain experiments taking place that can alter a person's personality, thought processes and memories. Brainwashing has been used for many years during both World wars. Put these together and we have a lethal concoction of methods to rid us of our own minds and replace the content with a completely different one!

Project MKUltra Wikipedia, free encyclopedia

Project MKUltra is the code name of a U.S. government covert research operation experimenting in the behavioral engineering of humans (mind control) through the CIA's Scientific Intelligence Division. The program began in the early 1950s, was officially sanctioned in 1953, was reduced in scope in 1964, further curtailed in 1967 and officially halted in 1973.[1] The program engaged in many illegal activities; [2][3][4] in particular it used unwitting U.S. and Canadian citizens as its test subjects, which led to controversy regarding its legitimacy.[5][2][6][7] MKUltra involved the use of many methodologies to manipulate people's mental states and alter brain functions, including the surreptitious administration of drugs (especially LSD) and other chemicals, hypnosis, sensory deprivation, isolation, verbal and sexual abuse, as well as various forms of torture.[8]

The scope of Project MKUltra was broad, with research undertaken at 80 institutions, including 44 colleges and universities, as well as hospitals, prisons and pharmaceutical companies.[9] The CIA operated through these institutions using front organizations, although sometimes top officials at these institutions were aware of the CIA's involvement.[10] As the Supreme Court later noted, MKULTRA was: concerned with "the research and development of chemical, biological, and radiological materials capable of employment in clandestine operations to control human behavior." The program consisted of some 149 subprojects which the Agency contracted out to various universities, research foundations, and similar institutions. At least 80 institutions and 185 private researchers participated. Because the Agency funded MKULTRA indirectly, many of the participating individuals were unaware that they were dealing with the Agency.[11]

Project MKUltra was first brought to public attention in 1975 by the Church Committee of the U.S. Congress, and a Gerald Ford commission to investigate CIA activities within the United States. Investigative efforts were hampered by the fact that CIA Director Richard Helms ordered all MKUltra files destroyed in 1973; the Church Committee and Rockefeller Commission investigations relied on the sworn testimony of direct participants and on the relatively small number of documents that survived Helms' destruction order.[12]

In 1977, a Freedom of Information Act request uncovered a cache of 20,000 documents relating to project MKUltra, which led to Senate hearings later that same year.[2] In July 2001 some surviving information regarding MKUltra was officially declassified

MKUltra has now been replacing by MKSearch since 1972.

There is no reason to think that the CIA has discontinued their research unless the research stage is over and they now have enough knowledge to put the research findings into action. If they are still doing research on mind control then it will be covert and probably still funding schools and colleges to do the experimentation and research.

However it is more likely that now we are nearing the Tribulation period and lucifer is soon to take on his role as world dictator through his servant the antichrist (first beast) we can assume that the previous research findings have now been collated and are covertly in use! We know that mind control is in existence in its various forms through subliminal messages found in the various media sectors, fashion industry, music industry, business and trade, food industry to mention just a few.

Mind control has been working amongst our youth and taken hold of their minds in a big way. It has directed their minds, through subliminal technology, to accept **Marijuana and other drugs, indulge in immoral sexual behaviour, demonstrate allegiance to lucifer (satan), rebellious behaviour, denounce and reject God, Christ and Christianity, proclaim openly that atheism (humanism) is the way, use satanic symbolism, hand signals and clothing, mark themselves with tattoos to identify themselves against those 'puritans' [rest of the population] ready for the receiving of the true mark of the beast and the giving over of their soul to him forever!**

Heavy stuff! Hard to accept? Yes it is! But it is reality! Therefore it must be dealt with before it's too late!

God offers life in the spirit. The Holy Spirit fills the believer with a new born holiness so they are able to live a righteous life as God intended. God offers Life!

Lucifer however, does the opposite! He brainwashes the person so they are empty and bound by sin! Lucifer offers death!

What the reader needs to understand is that lucifer has no regard for human life! His aim is to control not please, he will perform any devious act of deception to win souls into his domain but he will have no respect for those people! His agenda is about power and control so that he can sit on God's throne as the god of the world and to be worshipped as such!

Lucifer as satan has worked discreetly through his servants to achieve that control! He has worked through every sector of society, in every nation. He is now at the stage where he has all of his chosen team of leaders ready to take their position of authority, he has the religious leaders in place to instigate the world religion, the World Bank is already in situ and functioning, the world currency is ready and the mark of the beast is ready.

Many people, particularly the young, are compliant and ready to receive this mark of allegiance and some have already done so.

The allocation of specialist production and distribution of goods is being organised ready for the restrictions to buying and selling of goods and services. Communication systems are already in place in every home or on every individual that hold every person's details and tracking data.

Currently there are still countries remaining that need to go through the 'financial crash followed by civil unrest and the take -over of that country to put the country under the control of the N.W.O.

The scriptures forewarned that the end times would see another take over, but this time it would be different to all previous ones. Daniel 7: 23 *"It will be different from all the other kingdoms and will devour the whole earth, trampling it down and crushing it….."*

Daniel 7: 25, *"He (the beast) will speak against the Most High and oppress his saints and try to change the set times and the laws."*

Once he has control over the countries of the world and altered their thought patterns (which is already happening) to oppose all things good and to opt for him as their leader, then he will formulate his army ready to attack Israel (therefore attempt to attack God – as the land of Israel is God's chosen land and peoples!)

We are seeing this gradually take place; many countries have been in crisis financially and politically. It is a take -over that is subtle, the weapons consist of mind control, it is a war of the minds not weapons!

Over the past 10 years, the author (as a watchman of the world) has noticed a change of behaviour of employees within large organisations in the UK and USA and other universal companies. In the UK for example, the large communications companies British Telecom and Virgin Media, have robotic like employees who have been trained to speak in a tone and a mindset that can only be described as inhuman or robotic. This also takes place (but less obviously so), within Local Council departments and the National Health Service. The latter is less obvious because they have to deal with the public face to face. But if you contact BT or Virgin for example with a problem they will first go through the ritual of asking security questions, if you deviate from answering these questions in a set manner I.e. if you say you have changed your email address they go into override where they are unable to digest or accept your words of explanation. If you tried to deviate into a conversation without going through the rigid security questions even if it is just to ask them what time it is , they would shut down! It is as though they are unable to step out of the box to deal with anything that deviates from the norm!

At one time the author challenged a telephone operator by asking a question but instead of responding to the question the operator repeated her request for a security answer, she did this several times, chanting 'word for word' in the same order each time until the author responded by asking her if she could stop talking like a robot and respond as a human being, person to person. Her voice softened slightly at this and answered my question. My question was 'who do I call to acquire a National Insurance number for someone new who is about to start work?' The telephone assistant could not answer this question without my full five security questions being answered, the first of her questions was what is the national insurance number of the person and after several attempts to explain that the purpose of the call was for the person (a young adult) to <u>acquire</u> a National Insurance number, therefore the person did not have a NI number which meant I could not answer the assistant's security question. After explaining this several times without success, I ended the call!

This whole scenario is very real and has happened several times with different organisational employees. Occasionally I have come across an individual who remembered what it was like to be human and was able to talk as a human being, entering into a little social conversation. It was obvious by the voice and manner that the person was of a mature age, as this age group remember how it used to be when people conversed with each other and how it should be today; they have not been influenced by subliminal messages in music and horror films, unlike the young generation. Therefore they have managed to retain their humanity.

Many of the young generation show evidence of being 'mind controlled', they are already programmed to respond in a negative way to serious situations. Many young people lack the ability to empathise, they cannot show compassion, and show no desire to be helpful. Usually they also lack the ability to rationalise their thinking, to absorb what is being said even though the query was spoken clearly and offered concise information.

It is a concern when so many people have no compassion to help those in need or to offer time to older people who do not understand the modern systems that are highly complex to the unlearned.

The author has been personally involved and assisted many older people who have spent a good hour speaking on the telephone trying to resolve an issue, such as an excessive gas bill that could not possibly be correct for an old lady on her own in a bungalow. Many of these people have had difficulty resolving such issues for fear of these robotic beings who lose patience with elderly and find it difficult to answer their questions, particularly if the older person has a memory problem. Often the 'robotic' telephone operative just does not listen or comprehend the simplicity of the older person's explanation. These telephone operators working in 'Customer

Care' usually have no idea what Customer Care is! These robotic employees have become brainwashed into speaking in a certain manner (by rote) and to ask specific questions then to give specific answers. Every day these employees have to repeat the same thing over and over again hundreds of times a week. This kind of repetition is unhealthy and is used as a form of mind control.

It was used in the 'Depatterning' treatment mentioned earlier. While the patient was under anaesthetic, the brain was being washed out, after which repetitive messages were being played into the mind of the victim, over and over again for long periods of time, this method is called indoctrination. Religious cults use this method to indoctrinate a victim with their particular religious doctrines.

Prisoners of war were also given this treatment, a tap dripping for long hours, music playing constantly or the interrogator asking the same questions over and over again, are all methods used to control the mind, to weaken resistance and to attain compliance.

Other mind controlling methods used are sensory deprivation and solitary confinement.

This is probably what happens with the telephone operators. They are subtly trained (conditioned by indoctrination) to respond to calls in a specific manner. They also are so busy, so over worked that they have no time for friendly banter with the customer or their colleagues and in some cases they are under such pressure and stress they are totally absorbed in their job, particularly if jobs are hard to find, so that to lose their current job would turn their world upside down. Poverty and debt is a great incentive to work even if it means losing your identity in the process.

The fact that these staff members have no time to socialise during working hours and often have a number of responsibilities or are too tired to socialise when they go home, all contribute to the trapping of the mind, it is taking away the liberties of a human being to breath normally, without stress and take stock of their lives, they lack opportunity to relax. To enjoy their work and to feel no pressure in their head is something of a luxury for employees today. This is a lesser form of sensory deprivation. Within the workplace usually staff these days do not have time to stop for lunch but eat while working, usually their eyes and ears and mind are firmly fixed on the job and dare not deviate from it for fear of being seen as slacking in the job.

Lack of sensory and social interaction is harmful to humanity- socialising is what makes a human being! Socialising, and experiencing the pleasurable sensations that come from eating, drinking, smelling pleasant odours, feeling different textures and reacting to lovely things we see are all part of being a person!

When these are removed, and that is often the case in many workplaces, employees suffer deprivation of these things. Many employees are working 50 hours a week in an environment that has no windows, lack fresh air and often a dismal environment. Music used to be a welcome comfort but in many large organisations the radio is forbidden. Many employees work in silence surrounded by other staff members but rarely exchanging pleasantries except to do the tea round.

Thirty years ago work was enjoyable; many long standing friendships could be made at work, unlike today when employees do not even know the names of those who work in the next office or the other shifts. There used to be regular social events and sometimes coaches to go on day trips or holidays. Not anymore! Instead, couples go home to their television and a glass of wine. Young people go out binge drinking in order to forget work, while others find consolation in sexual activities or drugs.

It is thought and reasonably so, that these mind control experiments continue even today. They are done in covert ways using energy and radiation, sound waves, electromagnetic forces, beamed at targets such as the head or body, to make them feel sick without killing them.

Such an experiment was used on an elderly couple in their cottage in Kent, UK. The Verney's, were subjected to weeks of torment in their retirement cottage where they had hoped to have a happy retirement, instead they were subjected to very low frequency sound waves.

It all started when they heard a buzzing and other noises coming from a distance, it became a regular occasion during all hours, even at night. They became deprived of sleep and peace. These sound waves can cause serious disturbances in the blood cells and attack the nervous system affecting the lower lumber region. It can cause serious disorientation, headaches and ringing in the ears. Depression and irritability are obviously going to be present, as well as the loss of memory and confusion.

Electromagnetic pulses can cause excruciating headaches described as an electric drill boring into the head. When the noise stops disorientation occurs. Radiation can produce severe stomach cramps. The verney's experienced various symptoms which were recorded on their medical records.

Initially Mr and Mrs Verney did not know what was causing the noise pollution and their ailments. However, eventually after many weeks of investigation it became known that it was electromagnetic forces and radiation emissions that caused their symptoms. They also discovered that they were being used as involuntary guinea pigs in an experiment.

Their symptoms led to multiple serious illnesses in both Mr and Mrs Verney, whereas prior to their retirement they were both extremely healthy. Mr Verney eventually died of cancer and Mrs Verney had acquired Leukaemia both of these illnesses were, according to professionals, the result of the torture this couple had been subject to. Interestingly, they both acquired some of the same symptoms such as; they both had difficulties with walking and balance. Both acquired cancer and both had problems around the abdominal areas. Mr Verney lost all of his teeth, they just crumbled and fell out which apparently is a well-known symptoms of ionising radiation.

David Icke is an investigator of activities of the Illuminati and the N.W.O. He is considered to be unreliable by many, as a conspiracy theorist, particularly as he announced on TV many years ago that he was the messiah. He has since announced that he was wrong and was going through a difficult time when his mind was affected. Who knows? His mind may have been infiltrated at some point to cause him to make this statement in order to discredit himself. He had disclosed to the world some major investigations regarding the Illuminati at a time when they were not ready to be exposed, so to discredit him in the public domain would ridicule any reports that he made from that point on.

However, the reason he has been included in this book is because his investigations have disclosed information that link to many other phenomena mentioned in this book, including, worldwide mind control. And because he has researched the same subject, as those covered in this book, and he has come up with the same answers which supports and provides extra evidence. His investigations answer many questions and link also to biblical prophecy. He has done a great deal of research on the N.W.O and mind control, his work can be found on You Tube videos and worth having a look at.

On David's videos he discussed London's influence on British people and nations worldwide, he also pointed out the various statues and symbols found in the area not far from Trafalgar Square. There were statues of dragons and serpents everywhere, particularly on entrances and gates. These serpents and dragons are significant in identifying the Illuminati as will be discussed later. In Washington there are also Freemasonry symbols everywhere. So we have two key cities and leaders in worldwide affairs being controlled by the Illuminati from London and Washington.

This same area of London David discovered is also involved in mind control and N.W.O activities. He particularly mentioned the Tavistock Institute in London which is a centre of Mind Control Research! The Tavistock institute used to be part of Psychological Warfare. Sanford USA also has such a centre.

David suggested London is the centre of a Global Web – A spider web. It seems from this analogy he is implying that the web of deceit spreads and extends worldwide from London which is the headquarters.

Within the area of London are various banks that control world finance, as part of the 'world bank' system. They created the crash in order to increase their wealth. They created a panic situation so that companies would sell up their stock at a low price, then the banks would buy up these stocks and resell them later at a profit, after declaring they had made an error of judgement about the financial situation that caused the crash.

Major Insurance companies were also linked to these financial scams.

David's views fit in with the context of previous chapters in this book, that show the key to the New World Order systems is a centralised power. One of the tricks used to deceive the public is to involve them in decision making so they feel in control, when in reality it is a farce! This was seen to be done in UK during a period when 'Consultations' were introduced.

This was used to initiate change with the consent of the people who were made aware of all the details and then offered an opportunity to voice their views. However, the people's views were never acknowledged unless they were in agreement with the planned changes. These changes were introduced, in a covert manner, regardless of the opposing public opinion. This attitude of government organisations still continues today. People have given up voting or taking an interest in voting for their political party at elections because they have lost faith in ALL leadership. Political parties do not regard public opinion and continue to introduce new policies regardless. There is now a huge division between leadership and the people, leaders today do as they please, public demonstrations have become criminalised and controlled by threats of military intervention and police are automatically an opposing force during the demonstrations regardless of how peaceful the demonstrations are.

If you look at this in the light of the subject matter in this book so far, it becomes obvious that this division between the public and politicians was inevitable as a means of preparing people for a future world dictatorship!

The method of applying these pre-planned government (that came through the EU but originally from N.W.O. Elite) policies was by holding these 'consultations and to get feedback on public thoughts etc regarding the change in policy i.e. reducing a service to save money even though the public still paid the same amount for this reduction in service. The public would complain bitterly, so it would be put to vote. At a later date, after people gave up hope of being heard and their protests were ignored or talked down, they withdrew from negotiations. Eventually, the voting was done by a minority who were left and who were in agreement with the changes so that the vote was unanimously in favour of the changes! This meant that they could manipulate the votes to their advantage –always they would follow up with a report stating votes positively agreed with the changes. People eventually became despondent and abstained from further 'consultation' meetings on other planned changes, so again misleading reports would be disclosed giving authority to implement the changes according to public agreement. And the scam went on and on and is still used by government to get their own way!

It must be understood that not all senior management are devious or corrupt (the majority are), but some are just doing what is necessary to keep their jobs. Some are just sheep blindly following their shepherd, not really understanding the bigger picture.

This scam began when people became despondent about the political voting system; there were so many abstentions that the voting system has become a sham. All of this had to take place to introduce centralisation, to gain power over the different sectors within a country,

Centralisation means power!

When you look at this concept from a global perspective it can be seen that the New World Order – a centralised one world power is the ultimate goal!

Each Member State must pay contributions to the UN and the same applies to EU members and because the World Bank control all the finances which has produced world economic problems for many countries, these countries are left with increased debt so that panic and civil unrest breaks out. The issue over not enough money for pensions or the NHS are red herrings, they are just the tip of the iceberg, there are much deeper reasons for the world financial crisis and the predicted 'crash', as already described above and in previous chapters.

The financial burden of UK and US to provide military support to Afghanistan, Falklands and Iraq over the years has also contributed to the debt situation.

Israel stands alone, surrounded by enemy nations. They receive no support from any country! They have to defend themselves against a number of Arab countries, this has drained resources and the financial costs have been high, so much so that the people are suffering as a result. Just as the countries of the world watched while Hitler and his men massacred 6 million Jews during WW2 so it is again, this time the Jewish people have placed themselves into their own ghetto but this time it is God's Ghetto, this time God himself is overseeing events and ultimately the people will be set free from oppression for ever!

The plan of the N.W.O. is to prevent the Jewish people from having all of the land of Israel and Jerusalem as their capital, because the Messiah is to return to take his place on the throne as the King of Kings to rule over the earth! Lucifer therefore must not allow this to happen! So a subtle war was necessary, to subconsciously direct the inhabitants of this earth to reject God and Yeshua as the coming Messiah, become part of satan's army to take over Jerusalem and submit to Lucifer's (satan) leadership. Lucifer needs to:

*Have control of the nations and the leaders.
*Send out deceiving messages via the communication systems to persuade and deceive the people, to keep them within his grasp.
*Control the money system, the political system and other systems worldwide.
*He must have his own wealth which he acquired and accumulated over the past few decades from contributions made by all the countries to the EU etc but also from scams and schemes such as that used in the banking system which acquired assets i.e. shares. But also from civil unrest, support wars and so on.

This was the N.W.O plan! War cost money! Britain and America and Israel have been placed in a position of huge military expenditure. The armies reduce their size and cut costs in specific areas, as well as increased taxation so that everyone is under pressure. The Enemy States know this is what will happen. It is like watching a massive chessboard in play.

While America, Britain and Israel suffer under pressure, the enemy becomes stronger acquiring greater wealth from allied nations who are able to offer financial and armoury support.

Wars create massive debt which = Massive Control by the enemy.

The enemy are those pulling the puppet strings to orchestrate the New World Order!

Another form of control is military training set to condition the recruit's minds to total obedience without question, through this regimental training they are forced into compliance. This is also a form of 'reverse psychology'. As these recruits have so much pent up anger against their treatment, when they enter a war zone or public domain they display aggression!

Mind control is to manipulate how people behave and think and this can be seen to effectively take place within the military forces.

However, a few controllers can only control a small population at a time so for control of a mass population i.e. worldwide mind control requires worldwide controllers and to achieve this, it is essential to have total control of the worldwide communications systems.

This is called 'Collective Consciousness'.

Wikipedia defines this as: Various forms of what might be termed "collective consciousness" in modern societies have been identified by other sociologists, such as Mary Kelsey, going from solidarity attitudes and memes to extreme behaviors like group-think or herd behavior. Mary Kelsey, sociology lecturer in the University of California, Berkeley, used the term in the early 2000s to describe people within a social group, such as mothers, becoming aware of their shared traits and circumstances and as a result acting as a community and achieving solidarity. Rather than existing as separate individuals, people come together as dynamic groups to share resources and knowledge. It has also developed as a way of describing how an entire community comes together to share similar values.

This falls in line with George Orwell's thinking in his book '1984'.and Animal Farm The concept of 'Group think' and the terms solidarity and collectivity referred to the people (or animals) herding together in their specific groups where they all have a common goal.

The study of Group Dynamics produces interesting behaviour when observing different groups of people, in different circumstances. The more the individual's rights are removed, the more the individuals gather together to form groups. This may transform into gangs, or support groups, or protest groups etc. Groups will automatically enter into a competitive stance with each other and this can lead to discrimination, stereotyping, taunting, bullying and finally aggression, between groups or one group attacks the other. Within the groups there is a strong cohesion and loyalty, even though one member dislikes another member within that group. Regardless of these differences there is a strong bond pulling them together.

Young people again are targeted to form groups causing rivalry between them so that eventually they enter into a gang culture! Over the years this is how ruthless gang culture has developed. Young people innocently formed groups with friends from within their close community. Eventually these different communities would enter into a competitive phase which later became aggressive and led to violent criminal gangs of today. Even the level of aggression and violence has been a gradual change over the years. Aggression would have consisted of verbal aggression, which may become a fist fight. Now however, the aggression has become a war using weapons such as link chain, baseball bat, and knuckle dusters and finally today they manage to arm themselves with flick knives, machetes and hand guns.

Also other groups may form, apart from the various social groups, there are more serious groups with a specific function, usually involving adult members and usually as a means of extra strength to initiate a protest or to stand up for the rights of the people. These groups have been reduced in number by the controlling authorities i.e. police and political intervention and the use of military force or the protests ending in violent aggression.

People power no longer exists!

So control and power came from encouraging the formation of groups which creates a 'collective consciousness and also for the controllers benefit who is able to use group dynamics to segregate people according to their belief systems and culture i.e. religious versus secular groups, compliant and non-compliant and so on.

It has already been mentioned earlier about the effects of trauma on the mind. One method, being subtly used today world –wide, is to produce 'Trauma' individually and collectively.

Trauma based mind control: this method is to create the trauma then shut it down by forming an amnesiac barrier around the trauma after this point it is possible to trigger these traumas, at will, and the emotions that accompany them. This creates a robotic response in the individual or groups as the brain produce the automatic 'amnesic barrier' response. The brain and emotions are subdued and a robotic state takes over. This is when the individual is susceptible to mind control. This method of mind control is used to control the persons mind through these traumatic events – it creates a vulnerable person who has a distressed mind that is easily manipulated. These fragile minds are susceptible to any propaganda, subliminal messages, news reports and community gossip.

It is now possible to systematically traumatise someone, particularly from the age of 5 or 6. Many children are being traumatised daily, through lack of parental discipline, support, love and spiritual guidance. They are being taught that life is meaningless, they will die and that is it! Their parents who are over stressed and overworked and struggling to avoid poverty in western countries (third world countries children are already traumatised by war, hunger and loss of parents etc) that there is little time to teach their children moral standards, to monitor their peer grouping etc. Children are being brainwashed with lies about evolution, religion and conditioned to accept humanism!

Children are being traumatised through television programmes that implant fear i.e. films on witchcraft, horror, murder, violence. Many children are victims of violence, neglect and sexual abuse! Today's society is full of pressure, stress, addictions, contradictions, violence, horror and lack of peace, joy, love and fulfilment because of the lack of God's presence in their lives.. All of this is fodder for a traumatic childhood when the child is left to fend for themselves, to deal with their emotions alone, without parental, love, guidance and protection. Today there is a massive amount of solitude!

These children lost their identities during these traumatic events resulting in a confused state of mind. It is this and social interactions with their peers, that encourage drug taking, binge drinking and sexual promiscuity. Many young people have never spoken about a Creator God! Many do not know that they are eligible for eternal life where they would be safe and secure and loved for ever!

According to David Icke the Tavistock Institute and the American Sanford Institute specialise in co-ordinating Mass Manipulation of humans and co-ordinate mind control around the world.

During the past fifteen or so years there have been some horrific events taking place in USA and Britain. In USA there has been a craze in 'drive by shootings'; People walking into schools to massacre innocent children There's a huge increase in violent crimes of an unusual nature.

In Britain there have been similar unusual crimes of murder and massacres. There could be a number of reasons for these crimes; it could be that people are becoming generally crazy! There is so much pressure on people nowadays that it is easy for someone to just 'snap' yet that don't answer the question as to why these insane people chose to randomly kill innocent children! The obvious answer would be that they are 'out of their mind' and therefore not aware that they have targeted children. A number of these perpetrators have no recollection of their crime or why they did it! This has a hint of suspicious circumstances that could involve 'mind control'. There has been suggestion that experiments have taken place to create mind controlled human assassins. This is a possibility using mass hypnotic methods or even methods used on individuals, placing triggers in their minds as demonstrated by Derren Brown. These triggers are implanted easily into the mind when watching adverts, films, TV programmes, watching videos and DVD's.

Many of the unexplained violent/murderous acts probably could be explained if there was sufficient evidence of mind control. But unless the authorities become aware of this possibility and do the necessary psychological tests to verify this we may never know the truth until the end time when all will be revealed –by God!

Arizona Wilder was programmed as a child, by a German programmer Joseph Mengele (who experimented on Jewish children during WW2). He died which then gave Arizona the opportunity to escape. She spends her time telling the world what happened to her and disclosed secret information on the illuminati.

What Arizona said seems 'far- fetched' yet answers many questions and link to biblical prophecy found in the bible's last book, the book is called Revelation. It mentions the dragon and beasts.

Arizona witnessed the illuminati in action as she grew up within this environment.

She was trained (through traumatisation) to became a goddess once she reached adulthood. She had witnessed some terrible things such as other children being born specifically to be sacrificed later. She had been forced to attend illuminati meetings.

She described the members of the illuminati as reptilian, they are able to transform into humans. There were also human members who could not transform into reptiles. Now when we think about the word 'reptilian' we probably think of a lizard or a chameleon and such like, now these reptiles would have scaly skin, long tails, slit eyes. This also describes the dragon!

God mentions the dragon many times in the bible as a fallen angel, fallen from grace because of his rebellion. Because of this he was cast out of heaven to the earth below, meaning this world! His followers were also cast down to earth. So here we have a clear picture of the devil (as a dragon) and his followers who are also reptilian in look, cast down to earth and now they are working covertly to take control of mankind and rule the world, so that lucifer (the devil) can become the world's new god!

Many older people are aware that there is such a 'being' as satan, the force of evil that is opposite to God the force of Good. However when asked to describe satan it becomes difficult. Yet when asked to describe God the perception is of an old man with silvery hair, a long silvery beard, wearing long robes and sitting on a throne.

The most common perception of satan is almost a cartoon character of a devil, a red creature with two horns, fiery eyes, a long tail and a three prong fork in his hand. Apart from this devil image there has been very little discussion or evidence of the image of satan or lucifer. This cartoon image has overridden any other image in the minds of people; it has kept lucifer pretty much out of the limelight. This has helped to minimise his existence so that he was able to work quietly without suspicion. More importantly when approached people insist there is no such person as satan or lucifer it is all in the mind of people who have created their own satan in their imagination. These people are extremely foolish and will find themselves eating their words when he exposes his identity and power! Many people joke about the devil, it is often a mere game to indulge in Ouija Boards and other occult activities but it will be to their detriment!

Many people have experienced and witnessed to satan as a real entity, active in this world. Satanists claim to have experienced his presence, people have demonstrated in such weird supernatural ways, (such as the woman who spoke out prophecy while her head was spinning at a superhuman rate), that it's evident there's an evil power at work.

Again people have experienced the blessings of God, through his Son Christ, the healing of the sick, miraculous healings and saving from death etc. Many people, hundreds and thousands can witness to his Holy Spirit Presence in their lives which has dramatically changed them so that they have become completely renewed, they know without a doubt their soul is in safe hands. They feel loved more than ever before in their lives, they feel they belong to a heavenly kingdom. And many people witnessed Christ dying on the cross, being placed in the tomb and that he rose up again on the third day (as was prophesied). Witnesses then saw him walking in a heavenly glow with holes in his hands and feet, showing his people that there is life after death! They then witnessed him going up to heaven to be with the Father –God. As He went he promised his disciples the Holy Spirit would come as their counsellor, (John 20).

All of this evidence of goodness and a holy kingdom has been rejected in favour of a fiery red devil image! Yet satan is his true name until the ultimate position is established when he, lucifer, takes the throne. But there is no actual imagery, except the dragon, to associate him as an actual living being. But be assured he is very real, very alive and very active!

In Genesis 6: after Adam & Eve, Cain had been cast out into the world, Noah was born and he became a righteous man who had a righteous family.

In verse 1 & 2, it mentions how the population had grown so that '***sons of God'*** (heavenly angels*) saw that the daughters of men were beautiful, and they married any of them they chose.'* Then in verse 4 *'The Nephalim were on the earth in those days <u>and also afterward</u> – when the sons of God went to the daughters of men and had children by them. They were the heroes of old, men of renown. The Lord saw how great man's wickedness on the earth had become and that every inclination of the thoughts of his heart was only evil all the time. "* Genesis 6: 1 - 2

This is biblical evidence of unusual creatures on earth nephalim and heroes of old (giants and mythical creatures) and also Sons of God (reference to the fallen angels) walking the earth and interbreeding with human women. Now obviously those interbred women had offspring both of which must have been destroyed in the Great Flood. However, the fallen angels who were heavenly beings must have survived by taking residences in the heavenly realms until after the flood, and then returned to earth to continue their work and interbreed once again with human women. There is no biblical evidence of them surviving the flood – it is an assumption as it is obvious there's an existence of an evil presence in the world and it is obvious this evil has multiplied over the years! It also mentions in the previous verse (Gen 6::4) that *"The Nephalim were on the earth in those days and also afterward."*

However, ancient writings indicate the above assumption. In scrolls written by a righteous man of God called Enoch (mentioned in the bible), who never saw death but was taken by God up to the heavens, wrote on the subject of fallen angels. In the Book of Enoch, he was said to be given the role of communicator, on behalf of God, to speak with the fallen angels, particularly about their final destiny. It is this knowledge that gave them the reason to take control of the Earth and its inhabitants in the hope of avoiding their destiny God had decreed for them. According to Enoch's writings, he tells the fallen angels their destiny is an eternal prison. Enoch wrote,

"And it came to pass when the children of men had multiplied that in those days were born unto them beautiful and comely daughters. And the angels, the children of the heaven, saw and lusted after them, and said to one another: Come, let us choose us wives from among the children of men and beget us children." (Enoch VL 1 scroll).

According to Enoch's writings, there were two hundred fallen angels that settled on Mount Hermon and agreed to do as planned. They took themselves human wives and procreated. The book continues to say the angels taught the women about charms and enchantments, astrology and the use of plants for spells and potions. Their offspring became giants. Corruption and evil gradually took over the earth. There was great bloodshed and lawlessness on the earth.

"then said the Most High, the Holy and Great One spake, and sent Uriel to the son of Lamech, and said to him: (go to Noah and) tell him in my name "hide thyself!" and reveal to him the end that is approaching: that the whole earth will be destroyed, and a deluge is about to come upon the whole earth, and will destroy all that is on it. ... the children of heaven (fallen angels) had to watch their loved ones being destroyed.

The watchers were then reprimanded concerning their wickedness. (Enoch scroll)

They had asked for forgiveness and were ashamed of their behaviour.

Enoch went on to explain how '*the fallen angels were once holy, spiritual, living eternal life, then they defiled themselves with the blood of women, and begot children with the blood of flesh...*
Angels were not meant to have wives, this was for humans only. The giant off springs of these women and angels (produced from spirits and flesh) *shall be called evil spirits upon the earth and they shall dwell on earth. The spirits from heaven shall dwell in heaven but the spirits born on the earth she remain on earth. The spirits of the giants afflict, oppress, destroy, attack, do battle, and work destruction on the earth, and cause trouble, they take no food, but nevertheless hunger and thirst and cause offences. . in the hardness of your hearts* (fallen angels) *you have made known to the women the mysteries, so men and women work much on the earth'.* (Enoch scroll)

Enoch referred to the fallen angels as stars – this would explain the choice of name 'illuminati'. The word illuminati is a derivative of illuminate which means to enlighten and links to the enlightenment which is a new age term. Everything has a link to something else – all amount to the beast!

The above scroll writings would suggest the fallen angels survived the flood by being in heaven at the time under judgement. They then repeated their behaviour with human women, producing evil spirits and giants. Also the genetics of the fallen angel's offspring prior to the flood may well have transferred through Ham (one of the sons of Noah who later became the lineage of all the enemies of Israel. The above verses also explain demonic presence in the world and how many people have been born totally wicked!

Enoch also writes of the righteous one (Yeshua) who will save the world, of the New Heaven and Earth and of the eternal life of the righteous chosen.

Another important piece of information from Enoch's writings is about the last days events concerning Israel.

"And in those days the (fallen) angels shall return and hurl themselves to the east upon the Parthians and Medes: They shall stir up kings, so that a spirit of unrest shall come upon them, ...and they shall go up and tread underfoot the land of His elect ones. But the city of my righteous shall be a hindrance to their horses. And they shall begin to fight among themselves, and their right hand shall be strong against themselves, and a man shall not know his brother, nor a son his father or his mother, till there be no number of the corpses through their slaughter, and their punishment be not in vain. (Enoch LV1.1 -scroll)

The above verse is being witnessed right now this day in Sept 2013! The Syrians have murdered many of their own men, women and children using chemical weapons! Prior to this the Egyptians were fighting each other, prior to this Turkey was in the news.

In the writings of Elijah it says, *"Syria and 4 kings will do battle with 3 Spending 3 yrs there looting and plundering in Egypt. Persian king worshiped as a righteous king for 3.5 years. Fourth year false messiah appears, saying he is Christ, and stand in Holy place, perform miracles* (Elijah scroll).

Interestingly, the verse below confirms what many people have been saying to each other over the past few years. That the weather has been changed and the time is moving swiftly!

"The devil has decided to prevent the sun from rising over the earth and prevent the earth from giving produce, wishing to devour men." (Elijah scroll).

It had crossed my mind in the past that satan (who has great powers in the last days to perform miracles, may also have the capability to alter the weather to induce disasters such as famine) may be the instigator of the world problems. It has always been assumed that God is responsible for the disasters because he was involved with the plagues in Egypt. However, the end time's disasters may be something that God has allowed to happen as part of his judgement on the wicked, but he did not induce these disasters. Ironically according to the scroll of Elijah, satan is the culprit and God has been blamed!

We know that it is part of satan's plan to produce a worldwide famine so that he can introduce a solution using Genetically Modified foods. People will then see him as the savior! This all fits together neatly into a pattern or an almost completed puzzle with just a few more pieces left to slot into place for the complete picture!

But God has compassion and will send his son to rescue us. He changed himself into a man. The Lord says 'those who are his, he will put his name on their foreheads and a seal on their right hand, (Elijah scroll).

The Lord God is to place His name on the believer's foreheads in the same way as believers during the first Passover spread blood over the doorposts to protect them from the plagues. God always provided a seal of ownership in the form of a ring which would be placed on the finger of the right hand.

Now we can see where satan acquired the idea of placing a physical mark on the inhabitants of the earth as a seal of ownership.

"Deceivers will multiply at the end times, adopting teachings NOT of God. Setting aside God's Law, people whose god is their own belly, (Elijah).

In the book of Ezra he says, *"Days are coming when those who dwell on earth shall be seized with great terror, the way of truth shall be hidden, and the land shall be barren of faith and unrighteousness shall be increased beyond ...*(Ezra scroll)

"The time is coming when the days will speed on more swiftly than before, the seasons will come on one another more rapidly and years will pass more quickly" (2 Baruch scroll).

Enoch's and Elijah's writings certainly add perspective to the network of interbreeding human reptilian bloodline. And it's these reptiles who want to bring global fascism into play to create the New World Order by producing a structure of world government, world currency (soon to be put in place), world army (expanding NATO) and a microchip population as well as traumatise our minds ready for total control.

In 1989, Arizona, once she was free from their influence, had flashbacks with pieces of missing information, it was difficult piecing together these flashbacks of her past life under Illuminati rule so she sought the support of a therapist. Eventually some of the missing pieces were retrieved from her subconscious brain store. Her mind had been compartmentalised and as a child she was traumatised into "an obedient slave". She suffered sensory deprivation, torture, electric shock to the brain, and she was kept awake by constant noise, usually music or programmed messages. She was forced to drink urine and eat her faeces. (The Jews in the concentration camps were subjected to the same torture).

Arizona witnessed a child being programmed to kill another child. These horrendous events are totalling abhorrent to a child's mind! This is where the reader's empathic skills are important. Imagine Arizona's life as a child, without parental love, without a childhood like other children where they are able to play outside with friends or go to a normal school, feel safe and secure surrounded by responsible adults. Arizona never new this kind of lifestyle, she only knew of darkness, fear, insecurity, pain, suffering, helplessness, deep sadness and despondency. She was controlled daily by this monster of a man who inflicted pain and fear on her. He made her watch horrific scenes and forced her to perform barbaric acts.

Mengele would use colours, as a mind control trigger to program a child and they would perform a certain behaviour according to the colour they were shown. They would be programmed to shoot another child or themselves according to the colour. Children would be forced to watch these events so that they would become traumatised.

Does this explain the many kidnapped and murdered children in recent years? We cannot determine such horror exists in this world. Only God knows the truth and that is why soon he will put an end to it!

Hitler was a student of the illuminati or maybe even an offspring! He may have been a descendant of the half fallen angel and human woman race mentioned in the previous biblical verse 4 of Genesis 6.This would explain his infatuation of a superior race. It would also explain how such evil can come from a human being. How do we know he is linked to the Illuminati? Because he used the same evil psychological methods to torture his victims, to perform the same mind control experiments and because he was determined to exterminate all those who did not belong to the ARYAN RACE! This Aryan race consists of blond haired, blue eyed people – all other types of people were considered obsolete. Hitler's ideal was to have a completely perfect race of superior humans who he considered to be of this Aryan race.

There's the link between the illuminati and hitler! The link is the Aryan bloodline!

Arizona mentioned the illuminati needed a pure race for their blood. The bloodline of the Aryan race contains something in the blood that the reptiles need in order to live in this world! Sounds like a fictional horror film, doesn't it? Yet it links together with facts. The facts here are that we know Hitler favoured the Aryan race; his goal was to preserve and seek out the blue eyed and blonde haired individuals who were considered to be part of this Aryan race!

The author knows a testimony of a person who explained a frightening experience as a child. The young child suddenly woke in the night and felt a hellish presence. The presence was not seen as the child remained under the bedclothes because of fear and the awful smell of putrid flesh that filled the room. After praying constantly to God the presence disappeared but at that young age the child had an image in mind of a reptilian creature! The child, now an adult, telling this story has blue eyes and blond hair. The child was saved on that day under the protection of God! As the child has God's Seal of Ownership and Protection! But it seems that day, an evil presence appeared in the room, to make claim to an Aryan child and failed!

According to Arizona, the Aryan blood contains a drug that keeps the reptilian fallen angels sane by acting in a similar way to endorphins or heroin. Like any heroin addict, if they can't get their fix they become aggressive! This drug can also come via menstrual blood so terrorising women would result in the production of this secretion in the menstrual blood. Is it possible then that this same secretion can be found in a placenta after child birth? Just a thought! It may be another reason for the increased number of aborted foetus.

These reptiles need a continuous supply of this special blood to stay in human form. As these reptiles increase in number through procreation there demand for blood increases, there is short supply, therefore there will come a time soon when the dragon (as the 2nd beast in revelation) will expose his true self to the world, no longer able to remain in human form from lack of the drug and because of the atmospheric changes in the world that also affect their ability to sustain their human identity. Particularly now that he has been exposed to the world through the various witnesses like Arizona!

These changes in the atmosphere and the blood shortage means time is running out and there is pressure for the Illuminati to complete their plans for world domination. This is evidenced by the rapid movement to establish the various world systems, in which most have been put in place 'openly' during the past few years.

All that remains is the world currency and the implanting of the microchip due to take place in 2017 (see Reference section). Although it is already being given to those who willingly request it. Once the population has been implanted and received the mark the reptilian leader will be able to reveal his true identity.

The first part of the 7 year Tribulation, the illuminati is to take control of Jerusalem and this would mean the commencement of building the temple and sacrifices. It would also mean an agreement which brings temporary peace to Israel as the first beast takes up leadership.

In conjunction with this is the false prophet that was prophesied by God to assist the beast. This false prophet is thought to be the 12th Imam soon to be revealed and the new Islamic 'one faith' Sharia leader, who comes into office to replace his predecessor the prophet Mohammad.

So to sum up we have the identity of the biblical beast and the false prophet mentioned in Revelation and Matthew 24.

An interesting point Arizona mentioned is that these reptiles do not have the ability to foresee the future they can only acquire this information by possessing the bodies of those humans who have the ability to foresee the future or by calling on demons. This is called channelling and many false evangelists channel demons to enter into the bodies of people who attend and respond to their call to be 'baptised by fire!' These false preachers practice divination, hypnotism and channelling demons to deceive innocent people who do not realise they are selling their souls for the excitement of taking part in what appears to be, a miraculous event!

Halloween holidays were invented specifically to desensitize people to evil. This has obviously succeeded when you see what goes on at Halloween parties and the way children dress in horror costumes and celebrate witches, and black magic as a normal institution.

During these end times God prophesied an increase in lawlessness (wickedness and evil). This refers to a world without God and His Law. The Law that tells us to worship God only and no other, and to love Him with all of our heart, mind, soul and strength. His law also tells us how to treat others with love, kindness, fairness and to honour our parents. It also tells us to be faithful to him, to our partners in marriage and God provides various ways to solve disputes in a fair and just way as well as providing information on how to look after ourselves and others. His law is of wisdom and guidance for our every need. Christ Yeshua provides all peoples with a way to receive eternal life [and salvation from certain events that are occurring in the world]. He is also the way to receiving forgiveness for our sins; he is the way for atonement! He is the <u>only way</u> to enter into heaven.

Lucifer, on the other hand, is the man of lawlessness; he is the way to eternal damnation! He is the way to destruction! He hates the Law and therefore deceives many believers about God's Law (which actually consists mainly of Guidelines and a few actual laws). Lucifer has managed to whisper in the ears of many so-called Christian believers saying to follow the Law is to be bound in the chains of slavery and legalism. **He has once again put his serpent hat on and managed to deceive the Adams and Eves into disobeying God by rejecting his guidelines for a righteous and holy lifestyle!**

Therefore the end time's apostasy has developed in all sectors of the world and in many forms of gradual manipulation, as well as a mass direction towards humanism and lawlessness.

A program on Revelation TV in year 2000 a guest speaker, Barry Smith spoke on Eschatology (study on End Times) and about the New World Order.

Barry spoke of how *the N.W.O. took control of a variety of institutions by placing them into a weak position so they had no choice but to comply with the N.W.O. demands. He mentioned that this was done by creating a worldwide financial crisis [The Crash] and the N.W.O. institutions came to the rescue, offering financial 'bail outs' in return for certain conditions. These conditions involved a complete restructuring of the nations.* This has already been mentioned early, however below is a true life example of just how such an event took place without too much disruption, so that people were gullible enough to accept the outcome.

The author had a wonderful, enjoyable job for 4 years from 2003 working for the local Council. They were wonderful employers, fair, considerate, compassionate towards staff and customers. They offered them a great service which was value for money. The customers were elderly and they were very happy, until year 2004 when suddenly everything changed. The lives of staff and customers were tuned upside down! The author recalls that suddenly there were threats of redundancy and being made homeless from the house that was tied to the job. Customers were told they would have their service reduced and their site managers (wardens) would no longer be able to support them, they would have to support themselves. We were informed there was to be a '**restructuring** within the organisation leading to **staff redundancies'** and a shuffling around of services that would be a possible transfer of the housing department to a **private housing association.**

All of this happened through 'Consultations' (meetings) these meetings were to inform the people about the plans and why there has to be changes [these are superficial reasons i.e. lack of funding- there's no mention of EU putting the pressure on] and allowing people to make suggestions on how to solve the crisis. At the first consultation the people voted to keep things as they are; they were too old to deal with such issues or to change their lifestyle to include decision-making. However all of their pleas and requests were ignored. No one attended the next consultations except one or two to tell them that the meetings were pointless as it achieved nothing. Staff became very despondent and left on early retirement or found other jobs. Pressure was placed on the remaining staff that had to do the extra work of those who left. It was chaos! The author knew at the time that the New World Order was at work.

What happened within the local council were redundancies, the council was made into a corporation, and the council housing department was then transferred into a housing association. The next stage was to **sell up the housing association to a private company.**

Now read what Barry Smith had to say that agrees with what the author experienced personally and come to your own conclusions! Better still go onto the internet, search for Revelation TV and look for Barry Smith on 3 videos.

Barry's video interview with Revelation TV presenter Howard Gordon was taken in the year 2000 and *he suggested the N.W.O would commence on January 2001.*

The evidence he provides suggest he was right. During his interview he raises many points relevant to subjects mentioned in this book. He evidenced and mentioned biblical prophecies and scriptures of things that have come to pass, happened or are happening now or about to happen! Barry's timing was not correct but that is easily understood when we experience prophesy being fulfilled before our very eyes, it is easy to mistaken the time as being imminent when it could be say 10 years away, as was the case with Barry. This is because the signs occur, so it is assumed that things will happen immediately. In 2000 it was just the start of events; it was also a gradual moving towards completion of events that has led to the current 'rapid' move of these final events. The end times are here but satan is being held back for a period, this period can change at any time depending on God's timing. So although we do not know the time of the end, we must be ready, as it can come upon us within minutes or hours!

So although Barry's timings were not necessarily spot on, his information was totally accurate because the timing depends entirely on God! Here's what Barry said:

"10 Nations join together to control the world's finance etc. President Bush Senior was the political instigator of the New World Order, which is a satanic, luciferian plan for the take-over of the whole world and population and they want to complete it by the end of Year 2000. It all started to roll in January 2001.

How do we know its luciferian? Look at the US Dollar. It has Illuminati symbols and writings that tell us of the plan. Their aim is to put lucifer on the throne.

If you look at the pyramid there is an illuminated eye at the top. This is the third eye called the eye of Horus, as it's known in 'new age religion and occult and witchcraft. It is the eye of Lucifer and it's been on the dollar since 1933. Lucifer is the god of occult, freemasonry, and witchcraft!

How does Egyptian pyramids link to America? Why would they have a pyramid on the dollar? There is no reason at all which makes it all the more interesting and confirms it to be the Illuminati at work.

In 1776 Illuminati secret society set up to put lucifer on the throne. On the dollar there are 13 layers of stone. This links to freemasonry that also have 13 levels of freemasonry.

In 1776 the Illuminati was inaugurated in Bavaria.

On the dollar is written the words 'Novus Ordo Seclorum which literally means New Order absence of God. It is saying a New Order Has Begun and the date given is 1776.

Also on the dollar are two circular seals, one is the mentioned pyramid and the other is what is thought to be an eagle but it is a phoenix which is an ancient symbol [also mentioned by David Ick regarding the symbols in London].

The phoenix has several representations, according to Wikipedia, such as it is a long-lived bird that regenerates from ashes of its predecessor, so it is reborn or regenerated. It generally symbolises 'renewal'. And an 'Empire'. It also symbolises resurrection, consecration and the exceptional man. It used the term metempsychosis which means reincarnation. All of these point to the antichrist. In Revelation 13:13 it states the antichrist had a fatal wound but is reincarnated by the second beast (lucifer).

This is in simulation to Yeshua's death on the cross, his resurrection and second coming. Remember lucifer attempts to simulate Christ Yeshua in every way.

Back to Barry's interview:

There were two settlers in America:
- *The Pilgrim Fathers, for their religious freedom.*
- *Occultists and Freemasons to put lucifer on the throne of the world.*

Bush in Nov 2001 will lead the whole world system into elections to establish a one world government and one world monetary system etc. leading up to the mark of the beast, [these have all be initiated and well established today].

Freemasonry in America, particularly Washington, the evidence of their existence and influence can be seen (as in London) by the symbolism in the streets. There is a huge compass (freemasons compass) and a satanic pentagon with the face of a goat, with horns and beard inside the pentagon. The beard points to the White House. The goat signifies satan (the devil) i.e. lucifer.

Freemasons are dualists and believe the Creator God is darkness and lucifer is the light god.

God has a verse in the bible about this, see Isaiah 5: 20.
"Woe to those who call evil good and good evil, who put darkness for light and light for darkness..."

Back to Barry:

Washington DC has a powerful witchcraft spirit over it, a power group of the New World Order who are pulling the strings of Government.

Now in UK Tony Blair is controlled by a group called 'The City' in London. [Tony Blair was Prime Minister at that time of Barry's report]. Blair had to follow the policies of an organisation called Adam Smith Institute and a Montpelier Society.

Blair was forced to privatise government departments, sell up assets to overseas buyers. This made Britain vulnerable and under control of N.W.O. All the nations were forced to do the same which led to the Global Village.

In 1966 the plan was the N.W.O would send out messages to leaders of the nations to restructure the whole world system ready for one world government. They were to privatise and sell up assets overseas. The nation's leaders then lost their power and they had no assets.

The N.W.O monetary system IMF (International Monetary Fund) was formed in 1961 [possibly established from the assets sold by the nations].

The IMF plan was to lend money to these countries who now struggled financially. But to get this money, they had to sign certain conditions *which later had to be fulfilled. [Author view: These conditions would entrap the leaders into N.W.O control even more].*
It started in New Zealand (Barry's homeland); *New Zealand borrowed money and signed the conditions.*

In 1987 most of the leaders who signed these conditions died and left the problem with the next generation of leaders. To fulfil the conditions.
The conditions were as follows: [notice how these link to the author's personal experience mentioned earlier].

a) **Restructuring** *–sack thousands of government employees.*

b) **Corporation-** *Turn government departments into corporations.*

c) **Privatisation** *– sell those corporations off. This also gets businesses involved with government. [We see this today whereby large organisations are working alongside government i.e. Google, British Telecom, Virgin Media, Barclays Bank etc].*

d) **Shares** *– Sell 49% to overseas buyers, retaining 51% (as false security for the people who feel safe because they hold 51%. However this is short lived as later the country is forced to sell the 51% shares when there is a financial crash), again the shares are sold to overseas buyers (guess who?).*

After the four points above are completed, the N.W.O buys up the countries, because they have no assets, no money, they cannot survive independently. So they are bought and this formulates the Global Village (Globalisation)!
The N.W.O achieves the changes that turned the World into a New World Order by comparing it to building a house.

1. In 1776 the foundation was placed.
2. 1987 Framework was put up
3. 1999 Electrical circuits were installed – this was the Y2K groups who instigated a worldwide scare that all analogue computerised systems would fail. Every country had to become compatible with the N.W.O system. [So that every country would have to convert to the new world order digital system. Everyone had to change over so that N.W.O would have worldwide control over Technology and communications.] It also changed the money system which became electronic i.e. bank cards instead of cash.

Everything became electronic. [As we know today, many companies have closed their buildings to do business online. Many government departments only work online- and they specifically ensure that they are easy to contact when making a purchase but difficult to contact by phone when making a complaint or have a query. Have you also noticed how the numbers for customer sales is usually a free phone number, but all other call numbers are charged? have you noticed that?]

This system transferred the world from individual nations into an electronic one world of governments and electronics. In Jan 2000 the world was 'ONE'.

4. All that was needed to complete the house was to put on the roof. This is to come from the worldwide financial crash. [We know this has occurred during the last few years. Many countries have become angry and revolted against their leaders as a result of this crash].

Biblical verses quoted by Barry: 2 Thess 6 and Rev 17

When the house is completed the antichrist will take over. He will be in charge of the peace treaty. Dan 9:27. Also the Mark of the beast will be administered and the New World Monetary System will commence. [These two latter points has already started since 2010 and continues].

Revelation 18 refers to New York City.
Rev 17 refers to Rome.

Politicians today are ruled like puppets, controlled by N.W.O. They cannot make their own decisions. They are told what to do. Also the political leaders are chosen to be elected by N.W.O not the people. Electronic voting allows potential for hacking and adjusting results to fit with the pre-chosen leader. Always the political leader is chosen because of their involvement with the New World Order or the Illuminati. [Hence the reason for the Middle Eastern countries internal uprisings against leaders. [This was deliberately orchestrated by the Muslim Brotherhood, so that N.W.O. leaders could be put in place. These leaders are selected to produce a 'unity of Islam under one Islamic leader the 12th Imam. This is part of the restructure of world religions into one unified religion.]

Barry also stated that whereas *prior to the N.W.O takeover, countries would grow their own crops and produce their resources. Today, countries are being forced to stop certain production and to focus on one type of product. He used the example of New Zealand was famous for their lamb which was exported to various countries including Britain.* [Lamb was in abundance in the UK. Then over the past 10 years or so it suddenly became rare in Britain.]

The excuse for this was that every sheep and lamb had to be slaughtered because of a sudden onslaught of a disease. Now this may be true, animals catch diseases, but it was too coincidental! Particularly as New Zealand had to slaughter thousands of sheep and lambs because they were ordered to do so. They were told not to sell this meat anymore instead they were to concentrate on producing pine from their pine tree production. Australia also used to produce lamb now focuses on wheat production for the southern hemisphere. [Soon it will be clear what is happening in the countries of the other hemispheres].

The reason for this 'single productivity', that is, every country is to focus on one specific production, was to produce a global interdependency between each nation which again accentuates the Global Village image but also enables control of the countries who depend on each other for their goods. On the surface it is propagated that it is for the benefit of the world to instil world peace.

A recap: Yes it appears that we are being controlled. Every individual and every nation has been manipulated and directed towards a specific goal for many years. Directed and manipulated into performing certain tasks, as puppets, to bring about the situation we find ourselves in. bankrupt, helpless, unaware of the evils going on within our communities, an upside down world where justice is for the perpetrator not the victims. A lawless society, where lawlessness is the norm!

We are being controlled and manipulated by a small powerful group who has acquired worldwide leadership. This elite group works for a dictator who will soon be placed on the throne of this world! This group's leader on the throne is lucifer himself, a fallen angel from heaven! He and his followers are reptilian in form but able to take on human form. This human form may be from possession of a human body or may be also by copying another's identity.

This group control us by placing their own leaders in power and restructuring the nations into a single one world order using their own chosen leaders to rule over certain hemispheres. They control us through their chosen individual 'nation's leadership who apply pressure to our individual lives by 'over work', excessive pressure, traumatisation and stress, by trying to meet our financial commitments that provide us with our basic needs and it is getting harder by the day to acquire those basic needs. Our savings including pensions and investments bring poor returns so that it is pointless saving or investing. In fact many people find it difficult to have any money left to save or invest after meeting their financial commitments. However, those who work for the N.W.O are extremely wealthy and flaunt it- yet the price for all this is their SOUL!

We are also controlled by our minds and soon those who reject Christ will soon be susceptible to the implant of the microchip-a serious form of control that denotes 'you are lost for ever!' Once you accept the mark and worship the beast there will be no turning back! It would be your 'LAST CHANCE TO ACCEPT OR REJECT THE MARK OF THE BEAST! More importantly it will be the 'last chance' to accept Christ, the Messiah to come, as the way to escape this potential slavery! He will be the only way to be saved from the potential hell!

But remember it is not the accepting or rejecting the beast's mark that is as important as it is about accepting lucifer as your god and bowing down to him! Consequently breaking God's commandment that says we are to WORSHIP HIM, THE ONE TRUE GOD AND HIM ONLY AND NO OTHER and to LOVE HIM WITH ALL OF OUR HEART, MIND, SOUL, SPIRIT, BODY AND STRENGTH! If we reject the Creator God of Heaven and Earth we are then LOST FOR EVER! There is no 'Get Out' Clause' there is no opportunity to repent! IT IS FINAL!

Who is this lucifer?

God himself describes lucifer prior to his fall to earth, in Ezekiel 28:11. Lucifer is called the king of Tyre, as this was a city of great wealth and prosperity, it was known as a place of trade and commerce and superior to all other nations! God says about lucifer the following:

"You were the model of perfection,
full of wisdom and perfect beauty.
You were in Eden, the garden of God,
every precious stone adorned you:
ruby, topaz and emerald chrysolite, onyx and jasper,
sapphire, turquoise and beryl.
Your settings and mountings were made of gold;
On the day you were created they were prepared.
You were anointed as a guardian cherub,
For so I ordained you.
You were on the holy mount of God;
You walked among the fiery stones.
You were blameless in your ways
From the day you were created
Till wickedness was found in you.
Through your widespread trade
You were filled with violence and you sinned.
So I drove you in disgrace from the mount of God,
and I expelled you, O guardian cherub, from among the fiery stones.
Your heart became proud on account of your beauty, and you corrupted your wisdom because of your splendour.
So I threw you to the earth; I made a spectacle of you before kings. Ezekiel 28:11

The verse describes the fallen angel satan, it shows he is not equal to Yeshua the Messiah to come! Those who accept the mark of the beast will settle for second best, those who settle for the Son of God will have the cream of the crop! Which do you chose?

It is a decision that must be made whether to turn your back on God and His Son Christ, this also means rejecting the gift of eternal life in a kingdom of safety, joy and peace and instead *choose* to declare open allegiance to lucifer the lawless, evil one who can promise only destruction and an eternity of punishment and suffering [although he rewards you while you are alive, and encourages you to live a sinful life performing immoral, corrupt and evil acts, rewarding you with all sorts of riches to keep you in his snare] is to choose everlasting death! You are being deceived! If you choose the latter you are being led away from the truth! You are being rebellious and deceived!
Hell is real! See Luke 16:22-31.

Many people have experienced 'Near Death Experiences (NDE) where they have experienced the horror of hell [and seen the beauty of heaven] and this experience has altered their lives!

There are many biblical scriptures to evidence that hell is under the earth deep in the centre of earth, including many references where God has opened the mouth of the earth; created an opening in the ground –an earthquake – to swallow up those who have done evil! This is the destiny of satan and all who are his!

God says,

"What good will it be for a man if he gains the whole world, yet forfeits his soul?"
Matt 16:26

CHAPTER 7

HUMANISM AND ONE WORLD RELIGION

Before we turn to the subject of this chapter it is essential we look at what has already been covered.

If the reader hasn't read the author's first book, '**Christ Yeshua Jesus from Genesis to Revelation**' then this should be priority before reading on. As the mentioned book authenticates God, the Bible and Christ, without any doubt. Reading the book essentially will help the reader to have faith and will provide the confidence to accept the contents of this apostasy book, without any fear and dread, it will also offer a resolution to the dreadful things written about. The book is available on Amazon Books.

If you are already a believer then you will be aware that you have eternal life with God through Christ Yeshua and therefore have nothing to fear. You will also know and have faith that God has a plan which involves the Judgement of these evil perpetrators and that God will soon 'call in his time' for this judgment!

Now so far it has been evidenced extensively, using clips from other sources regarding the New World Order and it's leader 'the antichrist' and the covert regime at work, worldwide, to prepare the way for the world to welcome him. Although a lot of the evidence shown sounds remarkably 'farfetched' and too weird or too extreme or too inhumane to accept, the evidence nevertheless has been supplied by responsible and reputable sources such as professional medical/health organisations, professional news reporters, from the very lips of government officials and well known morally upright people. The exception to this may be a couple of examples of personal testimonies by unknown individuals, yet their testimonies fall into place when compared with scripture references found in the book of Revelation.

So although our mind's strongly try to resist the evidence that suggest a worldwide takeover bid and a one world leader, we cannot ignore the fact that it is dangerously true, based on previous events mentioned such as the atrocities of the WW2 holocaust and the more recent evils such as Genocide and ethnic cleansing that has taken place worldwide during the past few decades. If the reader knows about English history, then the mediaeval period and the torture inflicted on those who refused to denounce God should confirm in your own mind, the potential of human beings to inflict pain and enforce control on innocent people by torturing them to produce submission and conversion! This is already happening in Syria in 2013!

People hide behind 'civilised society', but this does not exist anymore. Society is far from civilised when we discover the terrible things taking place such as murdering unborn babies, encouraging under age sex, legalising homosexuality and same sex marriage and prosecuting Christians because they stand up against abominable and murderous atrocities going on worldwide!

It cannot be denied that abortion is a major problem; there is a shortage of babies available for adoption by heterosexual couples, even though it's a fact that there are many young single women indulging in sexual promiscuity and finding themselves pregnant.

A website called 'Mail online' recently produced an article written by Daniel Martin on schoolgirl pregnancies aged 10. Since 2002 63,487 girls under 15 years old were pregnant in the UK and the numbers are increasing daily.

We can see with our own eyes, the daily news reports evidencing European and Middle Eastern countries internal unrest, bankruptcies, violent civil wars and terrorist attacks. These are very real events.

Another reason for reading the book, 'Christ Yeshua Jesus from Genesis to Revelation', is that it provides evidence of fulfilled prophesy and this would help the reader to understand the significance of the book of Revelation and other prophetic books of the bible. Once the reader realises that many events written in the bible pertain to years <u>after</u> the prophecy was written, also many of these prophecies have already been fulfilled, seen and proven, then logically it can be assumed the remaining prophecies would also be fulfilled. The next major prophetic event to occur is the rapture of believers and the revelation of the 'beast,' (the antichrist world leader), which follows the rapture.

Once the reader recognises and accepts that this IS going to happen the reader can then continue the rest of the book with a mind of understanding and belief concerning the danger ahead, so that action can be taken to prepare yourself and your family members with the knowledge and understanding concerning God's intervention in the last days and Christ Yeshua's return as the expected Messiah!

So far it has been established that the inhabitants of this world have become so deceived and corrupt, that evil expounds everywhere in the same manner as the world, prior to its destruction during the flood, which was God's intervention to destroy evil. This world destruction of mankind was a foreshadow and a warning to this world concerning the current end time events!

However, despite the forewarnings many people have once again chosen wickedness instead of righteousness, evil instead of good. And not satisfied with that, the people have also turned the world upside down saying that good is evil and evil is good.

" Woe to those who call evil good and good evil, who put darkness for light and light for darkness, who put bitter for sweet and sweet for bitter. Woe to those who are wise in their own eyes and clever in their own sight. Woe to those who are heroes at drinking wine and champions at mixing drinks, who acquit the guilty for a bribe, but deny justice to the innocent….
Isaiah 5:20-23.

God has written a promise to the world! He says:

"Woe to those who make unjust laws, to those who issue oppressive decrees to deprive the poor of their rights and withhold justice from the oppressed of my people, making widows their prey and robbing the fatherless. What will you do on the day of reckoning, when disaster comes from afar? To whom will you run for help? Where will you leave your riches?..." Isaiah 10: 1-4

God also says: *"Stop trusting in man, who has but a breath in his nostrils. Of what account is he?"* Isaiah 2:22.

God says the above verse to us because mankind has turned their back on the Creator God, the one who created all things. He created the complexity of man, with the intricate design of the brain, the eyes, the cells structure, the DNA that makes us unique, the ability to think and rationalise, to make choices and to speak. Above all God created man with a soul and a spirit. The soul is the human part that holds who we are as a human. The spirit is the part that links us with God, who is also spirit. This spirit is the part that becomes the new 'born again' person. This part is that which becomes holy whereas the soul is worldly.

"What good will it be for a man if he gains the whole world, yet forfeits his soul?" Matt 16:26

God says to love him with all of your heart, mind, soul and strength. All of these, the heart, the mind, and strength and the soul make a <u>worldly</u> human, unless they are focused on God! When you are focused on God and do these things, then you acquire God's spirit in its fullness. This spirit overrides the soul which is placed in the archives of your being with the guarantee of safety in God's hands.

"Do not be afraid of those who kill the body but cannot kill the soul. Rather be afraid of the One who can destroy both soul and body in hell," Matt 10:28.

224

"For the word of God is living and active. Sharper than any double-edged sword, it penetrates even to dividing soul and spirit, joints and marrow; it judges the thoughts and attitudes of the heart. Nothing in all creation is hidden from God's sight. Everything is uncovered and laid bare before the eyes of him to whom we must give account". Hebrews4:12

The spiritual part becomes activated and you find yourself feeling different, more secure, content and uplifted, more importantly you feel loved and at peace! It is God, through His son Christ Yeshua, pouring His Grace upon you. Accepting Christ Yeshua as your Savior and the Messiah to come are all that you need to survive the difficulties ahead! What difficulties? The difficulties concerning the activities of the N.W.O, the worldwide changes and unrest, the increased difficulties of living on a small income, living in an unfriendly world of violence, crime and corruption – until the Messiah returns. The difficulties also pertaining to living in a world full of humanism!

So what is Humanism? It is mankind without God and Yeshua.

The Humanist Journal Jul/Aug 2013 Vol 128 no 4 wrote an article on today's 'Rationalism' and how religion has been taken over by philosophy. Apparently, humanism has two key projects, firstly to change the law on blasphemy so that it is no longer an offence to blaspheme God, (at present in the UK it is illegal to blaspheme). Secondly, the apostasy project involves providing information and support to those seeking to leave religion, what they mean by this is to leave Christianity, not Hinduism or Islam. This journal has a page called Godless Globe.

Humanism is a new religion that incorporates all others. It is the interfaith religion – the ONE WORLD RELIGION, which is being orchestrated by particular 'new world' spiritual leaders ready to be accepted by the people of the whole world. It combines with the new age movement.

The underlying faith of ALL faiths is already humanistic, even though people are worshipping a god! In other words they may be people who attend Christian churches, have a belief in Christ as the savior and accept that God created the world and mankind, however, they may not be born of the Spirit of God but have total faith in mankind, and pursue worldly anti-religious lifestyles.

Some people may have no faith but do not consider themselves 'humanists', rather they either have given the subject no thought or consider themselves agnostic. Many people do not realise that there are only two options in this world; good and evil, God or Satan. There is no in between! Therefore if a person does not belong to God then they are already in the grasp of satan! If a person does not belong in the kingdom of God then they belong in the world.

"No one can serve two masters. Either he will hate the one and love the other, or he will be devoted to the one and despise the other. You cannot serve both God and money." Matt 6:24

How can this be so? People have moved far from God's way and introduced their own religious walk! Christians have chosen to ignore the Noachide Law given to all the inhabitants of the world to follow. Christians have also ignored God's law and ignored Yeshua's teachings on the Law in favour of the teachings Apostle Paul wrote. Which incidentally supports Yeshua's teachings but because Paul, a Rabbi, was a scholar wrote in like manner so that his writings were misunderstood and often taken out of context!

Christian and Catholic churches have a mix of Christian values with pagan rituals. And observe pagan festivals rather than Jewish (apostolic Hebrews) 'God commanded' festivals.

Many religions including Judaism and Christianity use occult symbols, Babylonian symbols and New Age practices.

Many people attending churches and synagogues are devout atheists!

There are many such contradictions and hypocrisies taking place which all point towards Humanism being a faith **in** and dependency **on humans** for salvation, peace, security and material supply!

People prefer what they can see and touch rather than have faith in what they cannot see or touch or feel. They prefer a tangible religious system, therefore worshipping a statue, or a car or a famous footballer or a pop star or a charismatic leader is the new humanistic religion of today!

The many faiths already have filled their lives with and accept the teachings of evolution, many so called believers in God refuse to accept his written word (Bible) as authentic or that the content is to be taken literally, as it is written. Many prefer to believe the Bible to be allegorical or fictional stories or like morality plays. They fail to understand that it is a 'Living Word'. That means it comes to life to those who believe it – God can use the word to speak a message to an individual – it becomes a personal way of communicating with the living God. Humanists speak only to man, they communicate with each other, and they seek wisdom from each other. Therefore they seek human answers to human problems. Humanists believe they acquired their knowledge, skills and abilities all by themselves and praise themselves for their achievements. What they fail to realise is God gave them their abilities, their talents and the tools for their achievements.

Within this chapter there are extracts which evidence the one world religion that consists of a unity of all religions. This one world religion is to satisfy the needs of those who use spirituality as a crutch that need religion as a form of opium!

There are many people who need religion to ease their conscious from the sins they have committed or during a time of crisis when prayer gives them false hope! However there are many more-millions in fact who need a relationship with their Creator and the Messiah, these believers are not 'religious' they have a real living relationship whereby prayers are answered. They are forgiven for their sins and renewed so they have no need to sin anymore; they do not need a crutch as their faith provides them with strength, abilities, courage, and spiritual sustenance to keep them going!

The evidence of a one world religion started with various organisations that have come together and founded an organisation based in Jerusalem (as seen below).

Humanism has developed gradually over the past centuries and is synonymous to the apostate world that exists today.

There are humanistic magazines, humanistic organisations and humanistic churches. Yes, churches! Ironically, in a Humanists Magazine recently it stated that many humanists have requested churches and that humanist churches are being opened around Britain.

Humanism started with various religious and non-religious groups who decided to oppose God choosing independence away from their creator (just as the serpent (satan – who was cast out of heaven and sent down to the earth). The world population (except for true believers) has opted for mankind to be their god! This is what the New Age religion is about – becoming gods ourselves!

"The fool says in his heart, 'there is no God'. They are corrupt, their deeds are vile; there is no one who does good." Psalm 14: 1

"The Lord looks down from heaven on the sons of man to see if there are any who understand, any who seek God. All have turned aside, they have together become corrupt; there is no one who does good, not even one." Psalm 14: 2

"Will evildoers never learn- those who devour my people as men eat bread and who do not call on the Lord? There they are overwhelmed with dread, for God is present in the company of the righteous. Psalm 14: 4

The last bit of the above verse is reference to a prophecy of the final Great Tribulation period when Yeshua returns with all of the true believers to end the evil of this world!

Over the last 2,013 years, the world has become more secular, more pagan and more humanistic and more corrupt than ever before in history! In ancient days many pagan societies were unaware of a God of love who created them and who created the world they live in! However, today there is no excuse! Many have heard the Gospel of Christ, seen miracles performed by Christ and seen how God intervenes in world events! This generation has been given written evidence in historical writings, as well as in the Bible, and witnessed prophecy that has recently past. Many people who have heard the gospel, accepted Christ as their savior and Messiah, only to turn their backs on Him preferring humanistic leaders and teachers, preferring deception and the lie rather than the truth!

As mentioned previously, many groups have attempted to corrupt the true Hebraic Discipleship faith of Christ's followers; they now follow the ways of the pagan churches. Orthodox Rabbis who felt threatened by the Christians of the original church of Christ, and believed Christianity would destroy their Talmudic Pharisaic Judaism, decided to try and put a stop to this new Judeo-Christian faith sweeping across Israel, the persecutions of Christians commenced. They found ways to reject and ostracize those believers who had accepted Christ Yeshua as the son of God and their coming Messiah. These rabbis formed a group in Yavne, Israel, to discuss and plot ways of ridding Israel of these believers, who follow Christ's law (which is based on the Mosaic Law) yet refused to follow the Pharisees and Sadducees manmade torah law – Talmud and Mishnah. These new Christians refused to accept the strict orthodox way. They followed the true 'God given' Judaism as taught by Christ himself! These 'born again' Christians were led by the Holy Spirit to understand the significance of God's Law and His law is still significant to believers today. Unfortunately, fear has entered the church so that many Christians reject the value of the Torah Law (because of false teachings on legalism it has been taken out of proportion).

[Torah Law is found in Leviticus (in bible) and provides guidance on how to live, take care of each other, how to give thanks to God, what foods should be eaten and avoided etc.]

At the same time the Gentiles throughout the last 2,013 years, have been at work annihilating God's name from the world's ears and outlawing the Bible in many countries. In UK for the first time in British history the bible is about to be removed from the Law Courts when previously it was used as a means of acquiring a sworn statement of truth told by the person being questioned in court.

The annihilation of believers also started within the Gentile Nations (non- Jews) whereby philosophers, scientists and pagans also felt threatened and therefore plotted against believers, by focusing on humanistic intellectual reasoning, creating theories and programming minds to accept them as facts, and reintroduce paganism in the form of pagan symbols made into jewelry, re-establishment of old pagan festivals, pagan clothing (re invented through the 1960's flower power and the psychedelic period). But more importantly a jealous roman leader called Constantine decided to create his own pagan form of Christianity! Like today with the many avenues and plots to deceive the people and to control their minds into submission, Constantine and other non-believers plotted to deceive the world to follow a false religion. However, this has escalated rapidly during the past 100 years because time is getting short!

Now we have a division of the world's population between true believers in God and pagans (who also practice religion).The latter have become a mix of beliefs intermingled with ancient paganism, satanism and eastern religions such as hinduism, new age, babylonia and freemasonry.

There appears to be a very definite division of the world into two sectors, secular and religious; the reality however is quite different. People claim to be either one or the other - society has amalgamated both sectors into one without realising it! Therefore the true division is between the apostates and the remnant, the latter being the true believers in Christ.

The following chapter is not applicable to those who truly know and accept God the Father, God the son, and God the Holy Spirit - the true faithful ' born in the spirit' believers. They are in a category of their own -The Kingdom of God category.

This chapter refers to the rest of the inhabitants of this world those that do not come under the title of 'Born in the Spirit believers'.

If you are not religious then you are secular that is, if you reject God or anything to do with him then you are non-religious. That puts you in the category of atheist, pagan, humanistic - secular. If you do not have faith in God then you rely on man (whether it is yourself or others) your faith then is in man.

For example, here is a scenario. You trust the plane you are flying in, built by man's hand and piloted by man, whom you rely on to fly and land you safely at your destination. Yet any hint of problems with the plane and the scenario may change - a possibility of it crashing may bring you into the religious group as you foresee the possibility of your death! At that crucial moment you have two decisions to make, a) you either call out to man, the pilot so that he would somehow perform a miracle and bring the plane down safely (by now the plane's tail - end has blown away; the engines are also on fire). Or alternatively, b) you could pray to the Almighty, all-powerful God to forgive you in your rebellion and cry out for salvation. Of course there is a third option, you could just sit there and say 'oh well, my time is up - that is it! In such a situation most 'so-called' atheist would call out to God in repentance. When they are faced with death and recognize man's limitations in performing miracles, they have a change of philosophy.

Which would you choose?

Humans, up to a point, choose to have faith in man. He wants to go it alone, to show his independence - like the prodigal son. But when he is faced with major problems then he runs back to his father, who forgives him.

That is how it was once, however nowadays, it is different, and mankind has dug his heels even deeper into the ground. Pride will not allow 'Man' to succumb to God, or to admit mankind is wrong or that there is need for God. Pride stands in the way of salvation! It is too much for proud Man to bear. So he continues forward deeper and deeper into the trap of sin and rebellion and onto the wide road that leads ONLY to destruction.

For thousands of years God has forgiven and accepted those who return to Him with a sincere heart. Historically He was graceful to Jews and Gentiles alike. But each has become too proud to acknowledge their Creator in the way He expects. The grace of God turns to anger as man's rebellion increases. Is it any wonder?

There has to be a limit, people cannot continue to increase in wickedness, lawlessness and rebellion and expect to get away with it. God cannot allow the continuation of evil rule over the innocent. God's hand is raised waiting for the 'appointed time' that He has set! The time of judgement on the entire world! The nations are being judged now, but the final judgement that determines the individual's destiny and the destiny of the nations is to come. See The Book of Isaiah for a complete picture of events covering God's plan for the world and mankind.

Here is another scenario to ponder on:

You depend on yourself and others to provide your food and water. When God removes these from you (in line with prophecy when drought, famine and plagues spread throughout the world) will you continue to worship man and ultimately lucifer?

Mankind has contributed to the famines in the world today, through his own greed and selfishness (exception of course is the minority who are doing good works supplying aid to the needy, God remembers their deeds and they will be rewarded accordingly).

Atheists believe there's no God and attempt to convince others of this by blotting out all evidence of His existence. Atheists have also attempted to replace creationism with evolution theory, faith replaced by science and the bible has been replaced by philosophical books. Ironically these atheists take such a lot of trouble trying to prove God doesn't exist! It is futile, as the atheist is a tool of satan yet satan himself <u>knows</u> God exists and that the Son is the Christ! Satan knows of their existence but uses man to deceive each other into believing the non-existence of the Holy Trinity!

"If you do not belong to God - you must belong to satan."
John 8: 42 – 47.

This last generation [people of today] do not know God!

Satan is the prince of this world. God's children do not belong in this world they walk on this world but not in it, they walk in the spirit, in the kingdom of God.

Man = Humanism!

Pagans worship many gods. They perform rituals and gross sacrificial acts to idols. This does not only apply to cannibalistic native tribes; it applies to ordinary people. Idols are anything that is praised highly, which acquires our full admiration. For example, the game of football, it was once harmless fun. Today people have become so obsessed with it, that it has turned into a riotous, violent event. Fans border on hysteria during a match. Individual fans admit to football being their whole life interest, nothing else matters. Money and sexual gratification are other idols. The Lottery has become the latest idol! Money and promiscuity are the two main temptations satan uses to lure the human race into idolatry in a very subtle way. People only associate idolatry with carved wooden images. But by indulging in excessive worship, adoration and obsession with anything other than your creator is idolatry! To devote or worship the things of this world is to worship the one who tempted you - the devil!

There are three main temptations he uses:

1. To tempt people to break the first commandment which is *"to love God only and serve no other gods,"* Deut 5:8 & 6:5 [part of the 10 Commandments] People are encouraged to worship material gods and ' to see themselves as gods. So they see themselves as 'all powerful' able to create their own destiny, reach their full potential by their own merits.

2. To give up your soul in return for wealth, prosperity and success in this world.

3. to encourage people to indulge in wickedness that takes them onto a new level of evil, which then takes them to beyond the ability to return to God (unless a miracle occurs whereby God saves that person before they reach the 'no return barrier)' The sin is so great that the person is unable to recognize his/her sin therefore unable to repent, crossing the barrier of no return is the point of no conscience, no empathy or self- awareness. They are blind to 'wrong and right! Many people are doing many such atrocities today which put them into this position.

In Matthew 4 we have evidence of satan's method of temptation, Verse 3 *"the tempter came to him (Yeshua) and said "if you are the son of God tell these stones to become bread."* In other words satan is suggesting Yeshua misuses God's gifts for his own purposes instead of to glorify God. The serpent in the Garden of Eden again tries to persuade and coerce from Holiness into sinfulness.

Yeshua replies in Matt 4 4,*"It is written, man does not live on bread alone, but on every word that comes from the mouth of God"* that is to say, do God's Will not your own. Yeshua demonstrates to us the need to resist the serpent's attempts to manipulate our minds or to trap us into the world of evil and rebellion!

Matt 4: 6 *"the devil took Yeshua to the highest point on the temple in the city and said "If you are the son of God, throw yourself down".* Satan on every occasion attacks Yeshua's authority and power as the Son of God and uses this to try to work up 'Pride' in Yeshua so that he submits to temptation. But unlike humans, Christ each time returns the attack with a strong defense – He uses the word of God! Christ did not succumb to the temptations because he had nothing to prove! He knew his place in God's overall plan.

Yeshua's reply to this was *"It is also written, do not put the Lord your God to the test"*, Matt 4:7.

Humans, when tempted in this way, should resist! Mankind should not presume to be indispensable. Do not presume God will always protect you; you may not be as righteous as you think. In Yeshua's case he knew God would save him because he was God, he did not have to prove that to anyone, He is the 'I AM', John 8:58, Exod 3:14

In Matt 4:8 *"again the devil took him to a very high mountain and showed him all the kingdoms of the world and their splendor, "all this I will give you, "he said, "If you will bow down and worship me".*
Christ replied " away from me satan! For it is written 'worship the Lord your God and serve him only." Matt 4:10

Christ knew that he already had authority over the whole world; it was already given to him by God. It wasn't satan's world to give away! He is only temporary owner of the world until the time when God says to Christ *"IT IS TIME"*.

Yeshua did not say " I have no need of your gift, it will be mine anyway in the future, no, his response was as ours should be, the first commandment, which is to **'love the Lord your God with all of your heart, mind and soul...**

These three temptations are commonly used by the serpent satan to draw believers away from God.

In summary, satan first dives in when we are at our weakest point, i.e. hungry, alone, frightened or feeling hopeless, our minds will be focused on our desperate situation and not on

God! At these times we are most vulnerable! For example if we suffer hunger our mind would be focused on getting food. Satan steps in subtly to encourage us to take the easy option and either steal the food or perform some behavior to acquire the ability to get food, either by robbing someone or putting an end to our own life! Satan has then robbed YOU of the joy of experiencing God's provision for you, if you ask in prayer!

So in the first temptation satan targets human need.

In the second temptation satan targets faith and in the third temptation he targets human pride! Many people give in to satanic temptations without ever turning to God and experiencing the joy of receiving God's loving care. Today many believers behave the same way as non-believers and fall for these temptations submitting to satan's devious plan and turn to secular means to survive!

During a time of crisis humans tend to return to the safety of human intervention as a resolution to their problems, instead of increasing their faith and turning to God. The human mind relies on what they can see, feel and hear, tangible solutions which provide instant answers rather than prayer that may take a little longer and demand endurance and patience! Therefore it doesn't matter if you are religious or secular it's all the same, there is a blending in of the two! Today there is no difference between the two. How can that be?

We have looked at secular, whereby people choose to reject God. Even though they say they don't believe he exists, they really mean **'he does exist but we do not want to acknowledge his existence'.** Or **'we don't want him as an important part of our lives; we are just fine without him '.**

Religious people however, acknowledge God to be relevant in their lives, choosing openly to acknowledge (openly in most cases, secretly in other cases) his existence, but also like seculars, may not necessarily include God or have anything to do with him, in their daily lives. They may go to church regularly, but if asked to pray to God will shrink away. God is kept at a safe distance where there are no demands or commitment.

Other 'religious' people may pray, go to church and read the Bible, yet acknowledge secular beliefs such as evolution or reincarnation. There is such a mix of beliefs; each intermingled with the other.

Evolution has no place in religion; it is the opposite of God - it is anti - God, so common sense dictates that a religious person is in contradiction when they support evolution! It is like saying Hitler was a catholic! A catholic cannot be a godly person and deliberately murder 6 million Jews! It is a contradiction. A so-called Christian cannot be a Marxist, it is a contradiction -Carl Marx was a recognized atheist, his goal in life was to discredit God. Many people take the name of 'Christian' yet do not accept Christ as the son of God therefore do not follow Christ's teachings! It is all hypocrisy and contradiction!

The title 'religion' covers a wide area.

What is meant by the word 'religion'? When people say "I am religious, or I am not religious" what do they mean? According to the dictionary being religious is a human recognition of a personal God or gods. The religious person is usually pious, God or god fearing, devout or belonging to a sect or order. From this definition, we can see how religion and secularism are the same. The recognition of a personal God or gods and belonging to a sect or order or pagan worship are all intermingled. Freemasons are an 'order' and Jehovah witnesses are a sect. Each of these has their own form of religion. Buddhism is an eastern religion, which worships many gods (paganism). In particular, the buddha idol is central to their worship. This idol can be seen in shops and other public places throughout the UK!

It is easy to see why the world is so confused about the truth when all the world can see is confusion and chaos. How can religion be taken seriously when the world is at war with each other over religion? Catholics fight Protestants, Muslim fight Muslim. Religion is nothing more than a label to classify people it has nothing to do with God! If it did have something to do with God then people would have true peace and security not wars. It is because the religious sector of today, world-wide, consist of hypocrites and Pharisee type religions as Christ referred to in Matthew 23: 13. Hypocrisy does NOT apply only to the Jewish Rabbis who practiced their own extended Judaism 2,013 years ago, it also applies today. The whole world is living under hypocrisy.

Only a remnant are truly faithful to God, those who would lay down their lives for him. Those who openly stand up for his name no matter what the cost. Those who live as Yeshua demonstrated, living a holy life. Giving up their worldly life to walk in 'THE WAY'.

The list is endless whereby religion and secularism are intermingled. A perfect example of mixed beliefs is found in the Catholic Church. Catholics affiliate to Christianity yet worship Mary. She is the key figure in their worship as the mother of God. Worshipping Mary breaks the first commandment which says to *"Love the Lord your God and worship Him only"* Exod 23:25, Matt 4:10.

This lowers the Almighty God to a human level and a human mother is exalted. To put it into its true perspective, yes, Mary deserves recognition. She was chosen just like Moses and King David, just like Apostle Paul or Apostle Peter. All these humans were called by God to perform a specific task. Mary was chosen because she had her heart on God, she was a righteous innocent virgin. God used her as a vehicle, because of her purity, to give birth to Yeshua, OUR LORD. It is because of her purity of body and righteousness of heart and mind that God could place the Holy Spirit conception into her womb. She was also a predestined woman. That is to say, God knew before she was born that this would be her task, as is the case with many of God's chosen. We read of such 'called' as Samson, Daniel and many others, including Judas who betrayed Christ. They all had specific tasks to perform within God's plan. It does not make these people any more special. This becomes clear when we see how God uses animals to perform his work, such as Balaam's donkey.

The same goes for all of us. God has our lives planned. But there is always a choice, we can choose to go his way, safely protected under his loving guidance or we can go our own unprotected way, vulnerable to the perils of life. God never takes choice away. God created humans not robots.

So to finish on Mary, yes it is okay to give her respect as the vehicle chosen by God to carry and give birth to the Messiah. As it is written "people **will call her 'blessed'** because she has been blessed. But it does not give license to give her reverence, especially to revere her above God himself! The church appears to misunderstand the key concept that Christ is the son of God but is also God. They also do not appear to understand that it is God who sent his son Yeshua, as a baby but that the baby grew up into a man and is the Messiah to come. Many Christians still worship the baby! This man had a purpose - to bring the Good News to those who would listen, regarding his gift of salvation, which comes through his death and resurrection.

It is overlooked that Christ died but has RISEN again; people do not understand the concept that HE, THE CHRIST is ALIVE TODAY! John 20

We are to pray to him or the father for our personal needs and for intercession. We are not to pray to any other, not to saints (the term 'saints' was humanly created by the Catholic Church and is not the same meaning as that given by God in the Bible) or Mary! Many Christians have made Apostle Paul their savior, placing more emphasis on his writings rather than on Yeshua's i.e. regarding the significance of the Torah for Christians and the grafting into the Olive tree as adopted children. These two key concepts are rejected by many churches.

I could go on, there are many more things that could be said about the Catholic church but it is not my intention to discredit them as I believe strongly that God can speak through any vehicle including a deceived church, idolatry or even paganism, if he so desires! There are many sincere hearts in all areas, including the Catholic Church and there are many true believers who still loyally attend the Catholic Church yet are reborn followers of Christ!

There are many people who are naive for one reason or another, who know no different than what they are taught. They can be in the wrong environment, worshipping in the wrong way but if God sees a sincere righteous desiring heart and mind then he will bless them. It is only when stubbornness, arrogance and pride is found in the heart, rebellion against the truth, that God removes his blessing. For example, if the Holy Spirit brings to the attention of a (catholic priest that he is leading his people incorrectly and he chooses to ignore God, continues without change, he is in rebellion. But if the priest recognizes he is wrong, corrects his mistakes by leaving the church OR continuing in the church but showing the churches error, then he will be within God's Will, (if it so be). Then he will be blessed, God can and does work even through hypocrisy.

Saying all this however, is not to encourage the religious to continue in hypocrisy, but instead should persuade a person to rethink and revalue their faith. To look towards becoming totally faithful, totally righteous and loyal to GOD.

Returning to the meaning of religion. Some religious groups are pious and God fearing yet not God fearing enough because they easily, without fear of God's judgement, persecute believers. They openly reject Christ Yeshua, as the son of God, believing he would not send His son to die! Therefore they discount Christ as the son of God, or a prophet, or the coming Messiah! Usually the argument is he is just a man!

1 John 4:3

"Every spirit that does not acknowledge Christ is not from God."

"This is the spirit of the ANTICHRIST".

In the book of John he writes about false believers and the theme is about testing the spirits. John says: throughout how we are able to recognize the spirit of truth and the spirit of falsehood, - in summary he says *'Whoever is not from God, does not listen to us'*. 1 John

"So every spirit that acknowledges Christ has come in the flesh is from God, and whoever does not acknowledge Christ, as coming in the flesh is not from God." John 4: 2.

Many religious sectors deny Christ as the Son of God, or that he is part of the Trinity, or that he came as a spiritual being, then became flesh, returning to his spiritual form (after his death) with God in heaven and that he will return again as the Messiah! Many parts of Christ roles as one of the Godhead, Savior or Messiah are denied by the religious and the secular!

This test tells us that the majority of religious institutes are falsehood. This is because they distort the framework of the Holy Trinity one way or another. Only a lack of understanding, not knowing the father could they dare to reject the son. So it has been shown that religious and secular sectors overlap.

The Christian churches are not exempt from scrutiny; individuals within this sector indulge in occult activities, such as astrology, yoga, and new age concepts. All sorts of people will throw up their arms at this statement, shouting excuses for their involvement, but no one will humbly acknowledge that there is a possibility they could be wrong and examine themselves, accordingly as 1 John says, **"test the spirits"**. Or to listen to God's warnings regarding deception in these last days. Yeshua warned that the church could be led astray!

Yeshua warned repeatedly regarding deception to come (which is here now!) Yet Christians today will not accept this as a possibility. Many will cry out saying that yoga, astrology and transcendental meditation has nothing to do with occult practices. They will argue that they use the basic level of Yoga and avoid transcendental meditation or the deeper occult level that is like saying I go to an idol worshipper's temple but I do not go in, I stand at the door and just bow to the idol from there! Well they try to cover up their involvement in occult with excuses because they have one foot in God's direction and the other foot in satan's direction! They would know this if they had done their research.

All of the above mentioned activities are part of the new age religion (which as we have already looked at is also humanistic). This new age has extracted doctrines from the Bible (in order to deceive the elect) and it originated from ancient eastern mystical religions! This mystical religion is the same one mentioned in the book of revelation 'The Mystery Babylon.

Let's look at this further:

Eastern religions and mystical religions are one and the same, and all total to the Babylonian Mystical Religion as mentioned in the Bible. It is a pagan religion. It is based on magic, occult, witchcraft and the worship of statues or idols, baal is the god of this religion.

The religious sector – i.e. the churches, also indulge in idolatry by either worshipping a virgin or a cross symbol or a statue, even the dead are worshiped and prayed to i.e. the apostles are made into saints and prayed to. To pray to saints instead of the true mediator Yeshua is to commit adultery, idolatry and rebellion!

Seculars also use parts of the Bible or duplicate various religious rituals. They deny God's existence yet use his words. They will acknowledge God's existence when it is appropriate, such as to discredit his name, to exalt themselves above him or to blame him for world problems. Seculars also took religious symbols to use, in an attempt to desecrate God's holy objects. For example, the Star of David has been converted to use as a symbol in satanism. God's rainbow and the use of rainbow colors is the main symbol of new age. The rainbow, God's sign to us that he will never again destroy the world by floods, (the next time he destroys the earth will be by fire) has been misused to remove the knowledge and significance of God's promise to us. His sign, which represents a covenant, a promise by God to mankind, has now been taken and used as the insignia for New Age.

Often a symbol is adapted or merely turned upside down. Witchcraft and satanism use this technique with the cross symbol, they use it for various reasons and in various ways, mostly upside down.

The Anker cross worn round many Christian necks is one of the crosses used in satanism and often seen as a tattoo.

Some seculars will go to church on Christmas. The church on Christmas Eve is full of people who never go the rest of the year. Christmas is a mix of paganism and religion. It centers on the birth of Christ (the baby image which never grows up into the man). Christmas although it features on the baby Jesus incorporates pagan rituals, e.g. the Christmas tree.

Incidentally ' Father Christmas' was always a harmless representative of God as a fatherly figure giving his children presents. Today it is a very different story. The key figure at Christmas in these last days is santa instead of Father Christmas (which once was representative of the heavenly father). Now ironically heavenly father has been replaced by santa an anagram for satan. Today everywhere we see satan exalting himself above God. Instead of the Star of David at the top of the tree we see a santa doll. Instead of Christmas lights we see Christmas santa decorating the shelves and window ledges. Instead of the nativity on the Christmas cards we see santa and his reindeer. So the lawless one has already prepared the world to accept him when he reveals himself openly to the world. The Great Apostasy is already here. His work is almost complete and the appointed time for him to exalt himself is almost upon us.

So what is the point in being religious, if it is so hypocritical, pagan and occult? Well correct! There is no point at all! The way it is now, it is useless and serves no purpose at all except to cause confusion and to lead people astray. That was the devil's prime objective and he has succeeded. He will soon be able to claim many souls for himself when he stands amongst the Christians (in the Temple of God - symbolically this has already taken place. The Temple of God being the body of Christian believers and the lawless one is amongst them misleading them), persuading them to worship him totally by receiving his seal of ownership (the mark). This seal of ownership is also in existence symbolically now! The seal of ownership is placed on every man, woman and child who allows a Toronto Blessing leader to touch their forehead ('Zapped 'as it is called). Christians have already accepted the abominable image, to worship. The Toronto Christians do so at every meeting, when they worship the image, the counterfeit Christ and the counterfeit Holy Spirit.

But there is a positive side to all this. If you acknowledge the existence of God, hence labeled religious, you are nearer to the truth than the secular. You are going in the right direction. All is needed is a desire to seek the truth. Ask God to reveal this truth to you. If your intentions are sincere then he will acknowledge your request and promises to answer.

"seek and you shall find, ask and it shall be given"
Matt 7:7

If you ask for the wrong reasons, if you seek power and self-glorification, then you will not be given the truth. It is as simple as that. You need to be sincere, a seeker of righteousness desiring to be obedient to God. You may not have much faith, but a desire for the truth, so that you can follow God's ways.

It is different for the secular however. If they continue in their rebellion they will be destroyed and endure eternal punishment. Don't be deluded by the deception, the lie that when you die that is it. You will die! You WILL be punished!

Unless you are 'Born Again', you will be punished justly and eternally, by the one you have rejected.

If on the other hand the secular person repents and seeks God's truth then he steps on the first rung of the ladder, Jacob's ladder, he has to climb it to get to the gates of heaven. To climb this ladder means to seek, to learn, to grow, to accept righteousness instead of wickedness. The road will be full of obstacles and difficulties as satan struggles to prevent you from returning to God. It is about faith in God instead of man, fear of God instead of the one who can hurt the body.

"Do not fear the one who can hurt the flesh but fear the one who can destroy the soul" Matt 10:28.

God is the one who ultimately decides on the destiny of the soul, he allows a wicked soul to go to the devil but God nurtures and preserves the righteous soul. There will come a time when Yeshua will come to sift the wheat from the chaff. **Matt 3: 12** and the sheep from the goats **Matt 25:31 & Revelation 14:14-20.**

It is okay to celebrate Christmas if it is to celebrate Christ's birth as the BEGINNING of a new era, which includes Christ! Recognising he died for a reason, and 'rose' for a reason. That he is alive and waiting for the 'appointed time' to return as the king. Then with this understanding it is possible to celebrate Christmas. It doesn't matter if you are celebrating on the wrong day (25th is not Yeshua's birth date) it doesn't matter that the original Christmas stemmed from paganism. It is more important what is in the heart - sincerity, compassion, caring. These should be every day fruits of love. Not just to take place at Christmas. Christmas without Christ is the Hypocrisy!

To conclude this summary it has become evident that the world's religions are just secular organizations and institutions - worthless to God!

Having said all that we now can relate to the following article which should clearly show that all these religious can easily unite into one – they are already of 'one mind'.

On July 21 2013 An article was written online in the magazine called Haaretz (digital edition) It stated that the first Interfaith Center promises a new approach to religious study, In cooperation with the University of Cambridge they will conduct research on 3 major monotheistic religions Judaism, Christianity and Islam, to dispel dangerous stereotypes, [in other words they will attempt to find a way to unify these faiths.]

The only way different religions can form into ONE WORLD RELIGION is to find a common ground! There has to be a specific concern or issue that affects and is relevant to all religions. It therefore must be something that affects each of these religions –something that affects the whole world. The key issue is Global Warming!

On YouTube there is an interesting report on the commencement of plans of the NEW WORLD ORDER'S ONE WORLD RELIGION under the disguise of dealing with the problem of global warming. It is known as the:

Interfaith Center for Sustainable Development (ICSD)

As Wikipedia, is a free internet encyclopedia, without issues of copyright, the author has inserted a copy as evidence of the intentions of this organization to bring about unity of religions in order to deal with environmental issues, yet covertly it is the first stages of the unity and acceptance of a one world religion!

The Interfaith Center for Sustainable Development (ICSD*)*** *is a **nonprofit** organization that engages in inter-religious projects on environmental sustainability. Its projects encourage the cooperation and training of religious leaders, teachers, and communities on ecological issues. Founded in 2010, ICSD is based in **Jerusalem**.* [ii] **http://www.interfaithsustain.com**

Panel of religious leaders from the 2012 Interfaith Climate and Energy Conference. From left to right: Orthodox Patriarch of Jerusalem Theophilos III, Rabbi Daniel Sperber, and Sheik Muhammed Amara.

The ICSD and the Konrad Adenauer Stiftung, held the Interfaith Climate and Energy Conference [2] in Jerusalem on March 19, 2012. The Conference featured Jewish, Muslim, and Christian leaders [3] from Israel, and via pre-recorded religious leaders who spoke on the ethical need [4] and religious basis for improvements on climate change and the use of renewable energy. The conference aimed to promote change for environmental sustainability within religious communities in Israel and worldwide. A video was filmed as part of the conference. [5] This conference was reported on from approximately thirty news outlets worldwide.

Interfaith Eco Forum

In July 2011, ICSD held a panel discussion featuring Christian, Jewish, and Muslim religious figures speaking on the importance of environmental conservation and how it relates to their respective religions. [6] One speaker, Auxiliary Bishop to the Latin Patriarch Msgr. William Shomali, stressed, "We are tourists on this land, and we will leave it one day, but we must leave it clean for the next generations, we must be accountable for how we use this common home." [7] These sentiments were echoed by Deputy Minister of the Palestinian Authority's Ministry of Religious Affairs Haj Salah Zuheika and AJC International Director of Inter-religious Affairs Rabbi David Rosen, who agreed that respect for nature is equivalent to a respect for G-d and for G-d's creations. [8][9]

2011 United Nations Climate Change Conference

ICSD collaborated with the Southern Africa Faith Communities Environment Institute and The Interfaith Declaration on Climate Change to organize two events in conjunction with the 2011 United Nations Climate Change Conference. [10] The events featured a number of religious leaders and scientists who called for immediate action to address climate change. [11] The speakers included Bishop Geoff Davis representing Archbishop Emeritus Desmond Tutu, Christiana Figueres, head of the United Nations Framework

Convention on Climate Change, and Ela Gandhi, granddaughter of Mohandas Gandhi and a Member of Parliament in South Africa from 1994-2004.[12]

The Interfaith Declaration on Climate Change issued a statement at the press conference, part of which stated, "We recognize that climate change is not merely an economic or technical problem, but rather at its core is a moral, spiritual and cultural one. We therefore pledge to join together to teach and guide the people who follow the call of our faiths. We must all learn to live together within the shared limits of our planet ... In this spirit, we call upon our leaders, those of our faiths, and all people of Earth to accept the reality of the common danger we face, the imperative and responsibility for immediate and decisive action, and the opportunity to change."[13][14]

United Planet Faith and Science Initiative

The United Planet Faith and Science Initiative aims to shift the consciousness of humanity and the momentum of global society in a more sustainable direction in such critical areas as climate change, environmental protection and biodiversity. This initiative is a joint project of the ICSD and the Interfaith Declaration on Climate Change (IDCC). The United Planet Faith and Science Initiative holds that the failure of governments to protect our ecosphere demonstrates the need for action via other sources of wisdom and authority, namely faith and science. Science provides valuable insights into cause and effect and can help us restore ecological balance on Earth. Science provides valuable insights into cause and effect and can help us restore ecological balance on Earth. Religion has been a channel for moral and ethical instruction across the ages and can help us address the roots of the ecological crisis. The mission of the Faith and Science Initiative is to form a coalition of faith and science that will recognize and solve our ecological problems.

One Home Video Project

ICSD released a video in June 2012 that features world religious leaders, including the Dalai Lama, Patriarch Bartholomew, and Chief Rabbi Sacks, speaking out on environmental sustainability.[15][16] *This is the most recent video produced by the organization in a series of videos featuring faith leaders advocating*

248

action for environmental sustainability. The video was posted on a number of sites including Deseret News[17] and the Huffington Post.[18]

Holy Land Faith Leaders - Religious leaders unite to bless sustainability. From left to right: Sheik Ibrahim Abu El-Hawa, Rabbi Ronen Lubitch, Orthodox Patriarch of Jerusalem Theophilos III, Rabbi Daniel Sperber, and Sheik Muhammed Amara

The ICSD submitted a statement to the Council of Religious Institutions of the Holy Land pertaining to the Rio +20 United Nations Earth Summit.[19] CRIHL represents the highest religious authorities in Israel. The statement by the ICSD proposed that inter-religious strife should be put aside so that people can work together to better the future of future generations. The statement also called on leaders everywhere to adopt science based targets that society as a whole can work towards.

In May 2011, The Council of the Religious Institutions of the Holy Land endorsed a statement submitted by ICSD calling for religious and political leaders and faith communities to act to curb climate change. Some of the statement read, "We call on adherents of our faiths in the Holy Land and worldwide to address this crisis by undertaking a deep reassessment of our spiritual and physical relationship to this God-given planet and how we consume, use and dispose of its blessed resources ... We hope that environmental challenges in our common home of the Holy Land and Planet Earth move religious adherents to overcome inter-religious strife and work together for ours and our children's common well-being."[20]

***

Another YouTube video worth watching is entitled '**Vatican, Third Temple, United Nations, Mark of the Beast**', by Purvigiggle. It provides evidence on all of these subjects.

Once these three religious groups unite, the next stage will commence. This is when the Sharia Muslims will rise up in dominance! Gradually over the past 10 years Muslims have been smuggled into British towns, villages and cities during the night. One day there were no muslims and then suddenly several families appears! Mosques have appeared everywhere and many muslims work in high status jobs with authority to make decisions. Many muslims I have found, to be very friendly and polite who also seek a peaceful existence; they are totally unaware of the underground plots within terrorist's organizations to control or kill these muslims and their families. All it takes for these friendly, peace loving muslims is for mind controllers to trigger them into action against the non-muslim communities. These muslims during the Tribulation will be forced to convert to Sharia Law or die! To convert to Shia Law will involve taking the Mark of the Beast! If they convert they will then willingly become assassins of their own people and of Christians and Jews by forcing others to convert or die!

What we need to understand and grasp with our every being is that the beast (the antichrist) is going to look and behavior like a normal rational human being. He will be a great communicator; he will have persuasive abilities, and a charismatic or strong personality. He will/does say all the right things to encourage the people's trust in him to deliver solutions to the world's problems of financial issues including national debt, problems with shortage of resources and environmental issues including threats of disasters such as water and food shortages, oil, and pending catastrophes, including possible WW3, comet or asteroid showers etc. He will also be the one to bring in a Middle East solution to peace concerning Jerusalem.

This leader will be as a friend and savior (on the surface) yet covertly, he has another personality and another agenda.

The various stages mentioned will eventually unite the religions and prepare the people for the ultimate religion of Babylon!

The author is not suggesting who the 'beast' (antichrist) might be, however the following news clip which has just been brought to light offers thought provoking evidence:

By <u>NTEB News Desk</u> -A shocking video featuring a child seemingly praying to the commander-in-chief is sparking outrage from conservatives, as well as more religious members of the public who see the boy's actions as blasphemous.
"Barack Obama, thank you for doing everything and all the kind stuff," the little boy, who identifies himself as Steven, says as he kneels down in typical praying fashion.

"You are good, Barack Obama. You are great and when you get older you will be able to do great things. Love, Steven," the boy concludes.
Fox News Radio reporter Todd Starnes questioned, "What kind of a parent would allow their child to blaspheme God?"

"Let's clear this up. The child is NOT praying to God. He IS praying to Obama," a commenter in Starnes' thread declares.

In the past, we have documented how Obama's image in the mind of children has been elevated to a "messianic" cult-like status, promulgated through indoctrination facilities better known as public schools.

In 2009, for instance, Infowars writer Steve Watson detailed several disturbing stories wherein children attending public schools were made to "pledge allegiance every day at school to a huge projected image of the new president."

We've also documented Obama's manufactured ascendance to a cult of personality figure, and the dangerous slippery slope America begins down when it starts lifting presidents up as idols.

"The Orwellian nature of what is going on in American schools should at least send a shiver down the spine of all those who are aware of what has happened historically when leaders carefully groom a cult of personality and create a generation of mindless sycophantic followers who are unaware they are pledging allegiance to a dictator," Prison Planet editor Paul Watson wrote in September 2009.

The controversial prayer video is just the latest example of the type of feverish leader worship historically only witnessed in communist and totalitarian regimes, such as North Korea, Mao's China and Nazi Germany. source - InfoWars. *And* NTEB News Desk | August 12, 2013 at 11:57 pm | Tags: Prayer To Obama | Categories: Emergent Church, End Times, Headline News, Obama | URL: http://wp.me/p1kFP6-3Nf

Watch the video of the little boy praying to Obama! The video can be seen on **www.infowars**

The N.W.O. influence children to pass messages onto the parents. Children can reach adults like no other can! This child praying and worshipping Obama as a messianic figure is an example of what is to come when the beast will command ALL to kneel and worship him!

The mark of the beast and the beast (world leader and nations that equal the New World Order) may not yet be blatantly obvious until he proclaims his position openly! But he will behave in a diplomatic manner, politically correct, appearing to act on behalf of humanity's best interest. The hidden agenda is that the intentions is to defy, ignore, reject God's prophecies relating to the end times and to openly encourage people to trust in him for their security and protection. This act means to defy, ignore, and reject God's prophecies.

The Interfaith centre mentioned previously will be the instigator for imparting the beast's mark on individuals. It will be the centre (and many centres are already being established worldwide) for implanting the RFID microchip. This microchip will be used as a tool, for instigating peace among the nations. It is said to be the "key driver for implementing ICT Solutions (a communication corporation). It will be used to monitor an individual's carbon footprint i.e. it will be able to monitor CO_2 through the use of this microchip that is in each individual. The microchip is presently being used by many people to monitor their personal health, therefore it is equally possible to use it (overtly) for any reason they state to the public to encourage compliance.

The author tried to find information on ICT Solutions, on the internet, many websites were unavailable, some referred to schools and training companies that specialise on computer courses. But many web links had been removed. For some reason it appears ICT has gone undercover by changing the company name or hiding behind another company.

The World Health Organisation is governed by the UN guidelines, therefore under the control of the N.W.O. This would explain the changes taking place in USA and Britain regarding the health system. It is being changed in readiness for the coming focus on medical 'mind control' through the microchip. It is interesting to note that the symbol for the World Health Organisation is a serpent coiled around a staff.

Another organisation set up recently is CRIHL Council of Religious Institute of the Holy Land. The Chief Rabbi is working with the Pope; they are linked to the Temple Institute and the rebuilding of the Jewish Temple on the Holy Temple Mountain. Watch the news on this subject and you will see prophecy fulfilled before your very eyes!

On a YouTube video Yishmael *Ariel (April 2012) said Sacrifices will be resumed a.s.a.p. over a Passover festival.*

Before this can happen a sacrifice has to be performed outside of the temple walls to consecrate the area from the Gentile Occupation. The temple cannot be built until this purification takes place to make the mountain 'Holy and acceptable to God'. The temple may not necessarily be built on the same spot on the Temple Mount. Enoch wrote about a new area that would be chosen for the temple which I am not prepared to disclose in print, although I can say the Temple Mount is situated in the North and Enoch's map concerns the East.

This consecration sacrifice consists of a perfect, spotless red heifer. The orthodox Jews have been breeding for the perfect Red Heifer in readiness for this time. In line with prophetic timing determined by God himself, this heifer will have been born and reared! In readiness for the opportunity to perform the purification of the land ceremony. However, at present Jerusalem is still being trampled by the enemies of Israel.

The following article introduces for the first time in modern history the start of the 12th Imam influence on the Islamic nations and explains the true reason for the civil unrest going on in the Islamic nations!

By NTEB News Desk
At a gathering on the Temple Mount in Jerusalem marking the first Friday of the Muslim month of Ramadan, an imam from the Islamist Hizb ut-Tahrir organization incited a crowd of hundreds of Muslims calling for the destruction of America, France, Britain and Rome.
The fiery speech was made on July 12, 2013. The original Arabic video was translated by the Clarion Project.

The imam, Ismat Al-Hammouri, said a number of times, with the crowd repeating after him:

"Allah is Greater! Let America be destroyed!"
"The Caliphate is the answer!"
"Listen, Obama, we are a nation that does not bow down, and the Caliphate will return!"
"Listen, Obama, and the Caliphate will return!"
Source – Clarion Project, *NTEB News Desk | July 22, 2013 6:04 pm*

The Caliphate is an Islamic State (Empire) led by a supreme religious, as well as a political leader, known as a caliph – a successor to the previous prophet mohammad. Caliphate calls for political unity of the entire community of muslim faith ruled by this one leader and under religious Sharia law that appears to be under the elements of direct democracy and elective monarchy, which is a deception.

It is thought this leader (to be elected by muslims) will be the 12th Imam (chosen by God) chosen from the purified muhammad's (prophet) progeny. Watch for further news reports on this subject as this Caliphate (Empire) is growing rapidly. Mosques are being erected everywhere in the world, particularly USA and Britain! They are rapidly spreading worldwide, why? There is an agenda – a worldwide agenda to become the One World Religion! However, these do not plan to unite the religions (which is just a ruse) but to cause forced conversions or death! This has been witnessed in Syria recently as many have been beheaded because of their refusal to convert to Islamic Sharia Law! However, the current movement to a one world religion is being manipulated into place so that all peoples will be ready and willing to convert!

We are actually seeing prophesy taking place! The world is becoming a one world religion! People of different faiths for the first time in history are coming together, working together under the guise of resolving world issues yet forming into 'one' consolidated consensus which will eventually be manipulated into a 'one world religion'. As with all previous plans it is being fashioned into a particularly required structure ready to be announced officially! It is a gradual persuasion of minds to unite, it is the gentle manipulation of common goals, and it is the formation of cohesive groups using every mind controlling psychological trick in the book! And it is all done in such a way that people eventually adapt and comply willingly, innocently and foolishly until one day –when it's too late, they will realise what they have done! One day God himself will open their eyes! One day they will see Christ Yeshua return and regret what they have done! This is prophesied!

When did the New World Order begin? Like the mind control pilot studies it was all introduced slowly and subtly by a gradual introduction to certain concepts, gaining worldwide control and power through subtle takeovers that were barely noticed. It's rather like parents adding a bitter medicine to a chocolate bar to disguise the taste of the medicine, in order to entice the child to take it!

The New World Order was first noticed when President Bush mentioned it in one of his speeches. It later came to light that he was involved with one of the first key stages of the N.W.O. He worked alongside a group who formulated the UN. The first key country targeted to be used as a starting point for the N.W.O.'s United Nations Peace initiative was the attack on Iraq!

The following news clip summarises the activities of the N.W.O.

Our founding fathers perceived the states to be the sovereign foundation of the United States of America, with the central government only exercising control over those areas allowed by the states. But, as time passed and the central government grew in power and size, the states lost more and more of their sovereignty.

Each successive gain of authority at the central level was justified on the basis of altruistic motives. But, one day the country wakes up to discover that the altruistic piecemeal expansion has resulted in a bloated bureaucracy that consumed countless valuable resources, limited state freedoms, and created a debt structure that no generation is likely to recover from.

What is to say that the same will not happen at the international level?

The nation states are espoused by the likes of Boutros Boutros-Ghali as the sovereign foundation of the New World Order just as our country's states were the sovereign foundation of America. But as with our federal government, achievement of the New World Order is contingent upon shifting that sovereignty from the state to central level.

Again, the justification is righteous - peace and prosperity for all mankind. What will be the end result, though? Bloated bureaucracy, limited freedoms, and international debt?

Many internationalists argue that the only way to end wars is through the creation of a New World Order based on world authority and collective security. The trouble that comes with that New World Order will be overshadowed by the benefit of peace and prosperity. The problem is that all governmental entities are run by people.

And not all people have the purest of motives. International "peacekeeping" may not always be used in an altruistic manner. Hundreds of years ago, the Old Testament prophet, Daniel, prophesied that in the end times,
> *"A king of fierce countenance... shall stand up... and by peace shall destroy many."*

Source: Online website by Maj. Bart R. Kessler

March 1997 from OldThinkerNews Website

http://www.bibliotecapleyades.net/sociopolitica/esp_soci opol_nwo72.htm

An extract from Wikipedia on the N.W.O.

Post–Cold War "New World Order

The phrase "new world order", as used to herald in the post–Cold War era, had no developed or substantive definition. There appear to have been three distinct periods in which it was progressively redefined, first by the Soviets, and later by the United States before the Malta Conference, and again after Bush's speech of September 11, 1990.

1. *At first, the new world order dealt almost exclusively with __nuclear disarmament__ and security arrangements. Gorbachev would then expand the phrase to include UN strengthening, and __great power__ cooperation on a range of North-South, economic, and security problems. Implications for NATO, the __Warsaw Pact__, and __European integration__ were subsequently included.*
2. *The Malta Conference collected these various expectations, and they were fleshed out in more detail by the press. __German reunification__, __human rights__, and the __polarity__ of the international system were then included.*
3. *The __Gulf War__ crisis refocused the term on __superpower__ cooperation and regional crises. Economics, North-South problems, the integration of the Soviets into the international system, and the changes in economic and military polarity received greater attention*

When did the new age religion start?

Alice Bailey a new age occultist and false prophet (not a prophet of God), in 1940 predicted that there would be a victory over WW2 and an establishment of a political and religious N.W.O. which will be guided by MASTERS OF ANCIENT

WISDOM intent on preparing humanity for the mystical second coming of Christ and the dawning of the Age of Aquarius. The Great White Brotherhood (this sounds rather like the 'Muslim Brotherhood') oversees transition to N.W.O. (a small group). Later, nearer the time they increase their involvement in the plan, this is called the "externalisation of the hierarchy" everyone will know of their presence on Earth.

If you have read all the previous chapters then you should be able to make sense of Alice's prophecy involving the masters of ancient wisdom as being the Illuminati i.e. the dragon and his fallen angels.

David Rockefeller on June 19 1991 spoke at the Bilderberger meeting in Germany stating there are plans for a N.W.O. which was kept quiet by the press for 40yrs and this made it possible for the N.W.O to develop. He continued by stating that everything is in place after 500 years to build a true 'New World' in the Western Hemisphere. (D Rockefeller Wall st Journal Oct 1 1993).

George Bush said on 11 Sept 1991, 'A new partnership of Nations has begun and the fifth objective is the N.W.O.

In year 2005 Canada, Mexico and USA merged into becoming the NAU (North American Union). Bush signed an agreement which ended USA as we know it. Other nations were also merged into Unions: Asian Union, African Union, and European Union this all equate to a N.W.O. of Nations.

Since year 2000 the N.W.O. has increased its activities, particularly propaganda.

New agers said 21 Dec 2012 is the date of the start of the N.W.O. overt activities IN LINE WITH THE Mayan prophecy.

The Mayan's actually said the world would end in 2012. Some mocked this prophecy while others feared the end of the world! But what people did not understand was that any prophecy not of God is never 100% although there is also a high percentage of the prophecy that is true. In the case of the Mayan prophecy it was a matter of translation. The stated date 21 Dec 2012 was indeed the end of the world- AS WE KNOW IT TODAY! In Dec there was a change – it was the commencement of the N.W.O. in full force! Things started to move forward, mind control activity increased, takeover of the nation's began, financial crises increased worldwide and the plans for a One World Religion became overt along with many more events such as riots, national unrest etc. Everything has become more open, more obvious such as corruption amongst leaders, banks and other professional organisations and prominent individuals have become the key focus in a variety of scandals.

***

A website called 'Light for The last Days (17.9.2009) Wrote an article about Interpol's Biometric Database.
It mentions Global security authorities are pushing for biometric facial scanning of international travellers so security can scan for terror suspects, criminals and fugitives. http://www.wps6.co.uk

Now you can see how this is a pilot for the end time fugitives (Christians and Jews and those who refuse to accept the 'Mark of the Beast'). You can also see that these facial scans are already in operation at airports and security buildings. However, it is soon to change to more complex surveillance such as eye recognition and eventually the implanted microchip which will include all of the above and more!

The same website wrote about other interesting subjects which has either come to pass already or due to take place in the near future. One such article is for the registration of churches. Whereby every religious organisation is to go on a register. That was the first thing the Jewish people had to do at the start of the persecution during WW2.

Another of the websites articles are on 'Religion in the Last days'. It writes about biblical prophecies relating to religion in last days before the Messiah's return. It mentions what will happen to believers, **"The true church will be a remnant saved by grace amidst a majority who are in apostasy'. The true church will be saved from wrath to come by the blood of Christ Yeshua (Jesus) and be caught up to meet Him as He comes in the air."**

(This is the rapture and will be covered in Part 2).

On the other side of the coin are those who are left behind. **These will be the apostate church,** [but of course it will include all peoples who are apostates; it includes those who have taken the mark of the beast],

All those left behind that denied Christ's crucifixion and the shedding of his blood for atonement of their sins as a means of their forgiveness choose to either accept the mark of the beast or settle for the false church of the 'one world religion- the interfaith religion or they remain on the fence –indecisive. However, following this rapture event many people's minds will change, they will become believers, those not marked with the mark of the beast. But for those who accept the mark there's no turning back to God. They are doomed to destruction!

This new one world religion according to the article is known as *Babylon which cooperates with the antichrist during the first half of the tribulation.* The antichrist will use this religion to gain power. (Revelation 17:1-6). From this last statement it is easy to see that the antichrist will soon identify himself because the interfaith religion has already started in 2010.

Further into the article it also mentions that, *the Babylon world religion will hate these disciples of Christ Yeshua and brand them 'fundamentalists who are seen as the enemies of global harmony and therefore of humanity. Babylon will promote a religion based on new age and occult, which will be tolerant of any lifestyle and belief, but intolerant of true believers in Christ. Backed by the media, educational system, government, and especially by the UN, this organisation will support the Antichrist in his rise to absolute power.*

[I would like to add to the above by saying Islam is the army of satan who will be used to execute punishment on Christians and others that refuse to accept satan's mark.]

This article was written in Year 2009 and now most of this is happening 4 years later. Are we almost on the brink of the Tribulation or are we perhaps entering it now? It certainly seems that way when we read of people being beheaded (an end time execution method) and killed by muslims for their faith! Also we know that the interfaith movement has already begun.

Recently on the news (Aug 2013) an Imam has come into public limelight leading the Islamic religions into a one world Islam religion based on Sharia Law.

The Maitreya is also expected by the new agers as their religious leader. So although people have believed the Pope to be the world religious leader it appears there will be many key religious leaders for particular religious fractions and these will all work together.

We already know that humanists are producing their own churches. These will probably be used to (for those who have received the mark of the beast), worship the beast and his image.

In Texe Marrs book on new age, he refers to the pre tribulation period when all believers and the Holy Spirit have been taken out of this world. He states that all churches and temples will be unified in doctrine and rituals [this is not hard to visualise when we see how the protestant state churches perform the same rituals and the clergy dress in the same style robes as the catholic churches. Also many churches and temples already have new age and occult symbols in them.

Texe quotes Daniel 8:23 regarding the antichrist,

'And in the latter times ...when the transgressors are come to the full, A King of fierce countenance' **and** *'understand dark sentences' shall stand up'.*

This suggests the antichrist will have an uncanny ability to deliver powerful evil speeches that have dark meaning and contain untruth after untruth.

This is one of the ways to identify the antichrist. He will be able to hold an audiences 'spell bound' says Texe. Now this could be literal, it could mean held by his hypnotic gaze or it could mean he has a strong charisma. This antichrist may well be able to hold an audience hypnotically through mind control techniques which would certainly put them into a trance like state.

The antichrist's profile is quite extensive. Biblically we are told he has the following traits:

He is boastful

He is blasphemous

He is arrogant

He is an excellent speaker.

He will say one thing but mean another.

He is a liar

He will attack and destroy Christians and Jews.

He shall prosper in all that he does.

He will corrupt people through his flatteries.

He will be very powerful

He will become a world dictator.

Then after three and half years he will declare himself as god. Daniel 8:8-14

The ultimate goal of satan (the beast) is for the world to be of 'one mind'. A ONE WORLD MIND. At this point all the individual religions which have merged to worship the new age/humanistic god, will be forced to worship him 'only' as their god. The false prophet of the beast (who may be the 12th Imam- the Islamic Sharia leader or some other religious leader) will supervise this unification of all worship.

So far a few key controllers have been mentioned, illuminati was one of them.

Another webpage written on the illuminati, during Dec 2009 by Truthwillrise's Weblog. http://nwoobserver.wordpress.com

It states:

"The illuminati operate their evil agenda by using secret societies like Skull & Bones, The Freemasons, Bohemian Grove, The Trilateral Commission and the Bilderberg Group. The illuminati have big influence and control over mainstream media, political parties, governments, religions, banking and big business organisations. These people use secret societies to carry out their satanic agenda for the New World Order consisting of a totalitarian,

Orwellian police state that is controlled by unelected criminally-minded bureaucrats."

The website says it is all happening now. So it can be assumed that the N.W.O. was in action and at these stages during 2009."

The New World Order was also mentioned on a website by Melvin Sickler It refers to animal's being microchipped in many countries i.e. Canada, Quebec. [We know it is also in action in UK and USA.]

It also mentioned that in May 2002, in Texas that Kroger store customers were getting their groceries without cash, check, nor credit cards, but were using 'Secure Touch–n-pay', a finger–image machine known as biometric electronic financial transaction processing system. The fingerprint is scanned and purchases automatically charged to their account.

In May 2002 discussion was taking place to implant electrodes no bigger than the width of a hair in rat's brains. U.S scientists created remote controlled rodents they could command to turn, jump, etc. A news report on Aug 2013 stated a food inspector put some chicken nuggets under the microscope and discovered a minute wire in it. Further investigations found these in other foods. People could be eating these implants (as a pilot test) without knowing it.

The same year (2002) the new ID smart card was introduced to US citizens and now they are used worldwide. Also the VeriChip was made available to use in humans, (since then it has been discovered that the chip may cause cancer). This VeriChip has been superseded by the RFID implant which has a tracking system. (2007)

The article had an interesting paragraph on the Global plan. It mentioned that a few months prior to Dec 2009, a Hollywood director and filmmaker Aaron Russo stated on a radio interview that he was approached by Nick Rockefeller who asked to join the Council on Foreign Relations (CFR). Russo refused, but asked Rockefeller, *"What's the point of this? You have all the money in the world you need, you have all the power you need, and so what's the point, what's the end goal?"* Rockefeller replied (paraphrasing). "The end goal is to get everybody chipped, to control the whole society, to have the bankers and the elite people control the world."

One of the questions asked by people is how will people be willing to accept the chip under their skin. Well this book has already covered how this will be achieved through mind control, food etc which would bring about a submissive and compliant nature to many, however, others will accept it because of its health benefits i.e. tracking wandering Alzheimer's patients so that many people who do not have this disease but potentially may have later in years would opt for it. Others will accept it because they have a serious medical condition that needs urgent attention during an emergency so again this is said to provide immediate medical access to patient details by medical staff. Also children and employees would be introduced to this after piloting a Smart Card that allows them to purchase their meals etc. Eventually businesses will also offer within the system, a means of a cashless society whereby the chip would charge purchases to customer's bank account. Finally the article suggests it will start with prisoners, they will be tagged and allowed to go on parole as they can be tracked. [This is already happening in UK and USA] The next step is to implant the prisoners who will willingly take the chip as a means of early release or community sentences. [Prisoners are already being chipped in USA and let out on parole].

When you realise that a great deal has changed within four years from 2009 to 2013 then it is easy to see how quickly things are moving towards receiving the mark and the implant of the microchip universally!

The N.W.O. has focused on a variety of segments of society and each of these will eventually draw people to accept the mark. Already discussed is the health segment, the retail segment and the criminal segment. Below is a list of potential ways people will be convinced to accept the microchip:

- Health and contact details held on the chip, providing medical services details during a crisis and a tracking system. Health Insurance may also be a requirement entered onto the chip. People worldwide are being pushed into online shopping or doing their banking online so that it has become a requirement for all people of all ages to have a computer and purchase a broadband provider. Therefore the same force will be used to get people to accept the chip, particularly for insurance purposes.

- Retail businesses and service industries will make it a requirement to have a microchip implant in order to use their services. The microchip would be a means of avoiding the use of cash which helps to reduce identity theft or other credit card or banking fraud. It introduces the cashless society which also means no queues. You can walk into a shop pick up goods and walk out again.

- Criminals, terrorists, etc will be microchipped and allowed out on community service so they can be monitored and traced. The public will happily consent to this as a means of feeling safe, it will also solve the problems of 'so-called' overcrowded prisons which have contributed to the financial crisis, (created by government and corrupt judges who imprison innocent people and minor offenders and yet parole murderers and rapists).

- Welfare benefits; attempts are made to discredit many people on benefits, accusing struggling people of fraudulent behaviour. All of this has been exaggerated, fabricated, or the facts twisted to deceive the public so they willingly agree to use microchip technology to solve the problem. They would have to be chipped to reduce the level of fraud. Which would ultimately control those who live below the poverty level, categorising them as 'low consumer contributors' and therefore the 'weak links' in society. This labelling already exists covertly! Employees will have to comply or lose their jobs. Or told they must be chipped to get the job. The Pope, only this year (2013) said he was going to microchip his staff to stop the level of thieving taking place in the Vatican.

- Military and police service etc will be chipped so they can monitor their safety, and check they are following correct orders. They can also be traced if they are killed in action.
- Social services and other responsible people will also be expected to be chipped as a security checking system to replace the CRB checks (UK) and the equivalent in other countries.
- All children will be chipped as a precaution against kidnapping and abduction which has been on the increase during the past few years. Kidnappings have been orchestrated as part of a pilot to prepare the minds of parents to accept the chip i.e. the Madeleine McCann case.
- There will be great incentives to being chipped in the same way as loyalty cards that give special reductions, or vouchers.

Once the main population has received the microchip all that remains is the faithful who will reject the mark of the beast and have the seal of God on their foreheads. These will be obvious to all and there will be attempts to force them to deny Christ and swear allegiance to Lucifer or die! These sealed and beloved will lay down their lives for Christ and are the tribulation martyrs who will receive a crown of righteousness!

The uncanny thing about all of this is those who have taken the mark of the beast will assume they are safe, prosperous and all is well! However, what they do not realise is they have sold their souls to Lucifer and there is no turning back. There will come a point when Lucifer will show his true colours. People will regret taking his mark but it would be too late! Eventually satan has to reveal his true evil nature and this means even those with his mark will experience his evil. He has no loyalty or compassion or love for anyone, his sole ambition is to supersede the true God and to attempt to rob Yeshua of his place on the throne of Israel as King of the World. Anyone who challenges him or stands in his way whether his marked subjects or

Christian/Jewish dissidents it doesn't matter he will destroy them.

A website called Wordpress posted an article on Dec 2009 about the cashless society. It said in 2018 the chequebook could be abolished. We know this has already happened in some banks. In the UK a few years ago shops refused to accept cheques so banks have reduced the number of cheque books issued and only issued when requested, in some banks.

The Nexus Journal June/July 2013 Vol 20 No4 wrote an article on Mind Control entitled THE NEW DIRECTIONS OF MIND CONTROL. Written by Richard A. Miller.

His definition of true mind control is the exploitation of individuals by tampering with their memories, dreams, emotional experiences, their imagination, idea association and creativity. He also includes subliminal info. We have covered most of this already, including evidence in the form of pilot trials, experimentation, use of electromagnetic sound waves on a retired couple, drug and food additives, and other methods. The article also mentions unethical and systematic use of manipulating methods to produce conformity. He mentions brainwashing, coercive persuasion, mind abuse, thought control and thought reform. Although the terms he uses are different to the terms used in this book the concepts match those already discussed.

It seems there are a number of professional media organisations including television, newspapers, and journals etc that are becoming acutely aware of the mind controlling world we live in!

Richard Miller argues that mind control consists of "any tactic, psychological or otherwise, subverting an individual's sense of control over their own thinking, behaviour, emotions or decision-making" interestingly, he also suggests this is achieved by food, water, and air.

GM foods consist of toxins, additives and opiate additives to induce passivity.

Water consists of Chlorine which forms Trihalomethanes (THMs), one of which is chloroform. THMs increase the production of free radicals in the body and are highly carcinogenic (cancer causing). Chlorine and THMS have been linked to various types of cancer, kidney and liver damage, immune system dysfunction, disorders of the nervous system, hardening of the arteries, and birth defects.

Air is polluted by sprayed pesticides and more recently by chemtrails from jets flying over specific land areas, spraying toxic substances such as arsenic into our food chain and altering the weather (see chemtrails on internet for more information).

The author agrees with Richards's suggestion that people are being separated into passive and dominant. It is so obvious when we see the aggressive and violent individuals or groups actively causing chaos in the world, and then we also see the compliant people who either disagree with what they see or accept what they see, because they have learnt to keep a low profile, to say nothing! Many people have allowed themselves to become victims!

He mentions that there is a flickering rate on the television and the computer which alters brain waves, producing a type of hypnosis. This seems feasible!

Other areas he mentioned is cults, religious and political extremists, stimulants such as caffeine, education, drugs, advertising, propaganda, promoting consumerism, encouraging addiction.

Everything he has written about adds confirmation to the evidenced supplied in this book. Finally an important point he mentions is the effect of electromagnetic forces producing mind altering waves. These electromagnetic forces are at low frequency (ELF). It alters behaviour of human cells, tissues, organs, hormone levels and immune system. These ELF could be responsible for many diseases and illnesses affecting the population today.

Another form of subtle world control is seen in political affairs during the past few years. It all started with the overthrown leadership of Iraq and Saddam Hussein. Gradually there has been a planned orchestrated overthrow of each Middle East nation's dictatorship/ leadership.

Saddam Hussein was the most significant major example of this long line of politically motivated assassinations/exiled leaderships. Saddam was a threat to IRAN who is a key investor into the planned N.W.O. Hussein was removed from power so that he could be replaced by a N.W.O leader.

Gradually over the past few years this same principle has occurred within other organisations and nations. If you research the past few years you will find a large number of nations have changed their leadership, many Arab nations have 'supposedly' changed to a more democratic leadership or more accurately have come under extreme Islamic rule. Whether it becomes more democratic or Islamic has no real significance, these are just words -'labels'. Ultimately the new leadership of those countries are just pawns in the N.W.O system, chosen specifically to become part of the world leadership under a totalitarian rule!

Even the Vatican changed their pope suddenly, just recently and this is very significant in order to bring about the New World Religion!

Over the years a gradual move of the power of the Roman Church has subtly been introduced. There has always been a division between Catholics and Protestants worldwide (excluding Ireland, they have their own agenda). Gradually over the years there has been a covert merging of the two divisions, so that the Catholic Church has become accepted and the pope acknowledged as the leader of not just Catholism but Protestants (unofficially) also acknowledge him as a leading figure of religion.

When Christianity is mentioned today it almost always refers to the Catholic Church and the Pope. When the Pope is in the news he is represented and accepted as the world spiritual leader, he is given a major position on the media and he has a major input into religious affairs.

It has been witnessed on many occasions whereby secular people, not associated with religion or Rome, also respect and give credence to the Pope! It has also been observed that non – Catholic Christians reference the Pope as leader. It is an implied assumption!

It is also interesting to read or hear different nations or religions, including the Pope, turn to the USA for approval or to request authority or agreement regarding their decision making. It has been particularly noticeable since Obama became the new leader of America.

The United Nations has become a powerful influence in world changes.

United Nations - Wikipedia, free encyclopedia

The United Nations is an <u>international organization</u> whose stated aims include promoting and facilitating cooperation in <u>international law</u>, <u>international security</u>, <u>economic development</u>, <u>social progress</u>, <u>human rights</u>, <u>civil rights</u>, <u>civil liberties</u>, <u>political freedoms</u>, <u>democracy</u>, and the achievement of lasting <u>world peace</u>. The UN was founded in 1945 after World War II to replace the <u>League of Nations</u>, to stop wars between countries, and to provide a platform for dialogue. It contains multiple subsidiary organizations to carry out its missions.

At its founding, the UN had 51 <u>member states</u>; there are now 193. From its offices around the world, the UN and its specialized agencies decide on substantive and administrative issues in regular meetings held throughout the year. The organization has six principal organs: the <u>General Assembly</u> (the main <u>deliberative assembly</u>); the <u>Security Council</u> (for deciding certain resolutions for peace and security); the <u>Economic and Social Council (ECOSOC)</u> (for assisting in promoting international economic and social cooperation and development); the <u>Secretariat</u> (for providing studies, information, and facilities needed by the UN); the <u>International Court of Justice</u> (the primary judicial organ); and the <u>United Nations Trusteeship Council</u> (which is currently inactive). Other prominent <u>UN System</u> agencies include the <u>World Health Organization</u> (WHO), the <u>World Food Programme</u> (WFP) and United Nations Children's Fund (<u>UNICEF</u>). The UN's most prominent position is that of the office of <u>Secretary-General</u> which has

**been held by <u>Ban Ki-moon</u> of <u>South Korea</u> since 2007.
<u>NGOs</u> may be granted <u>consultative status with ECOSOC</u>
and other agencies to participate in the UN's work.**

**The <u>United Nations Headquarters</u> resides in international
territory in New York City, with further main offices at
<u>Geneva</u>, <u>Nairobi</u>, and <u>Vienna</u>. The organization is financed
from assessed and voluntary contributions from its member
states, and has <u>six official languages</u>: Arabic, Chinese,
English, French, Russian, and Spanish**

The UN is a smoke screen for the N.W.O. it is evidenced by the lack of success with its role as peace maker! However, in these last days and particularly with regards to God's Holy Land, the UN will have significant input with the prophecy of the peace treaty in Israel. The UN will be directly involved with Jerusalem and have substantial control over it and the Temple Mount!

This in itself should be obvious to the most naïve reader that something big is happening in our world!

The recent events whereby in Egypt the military suspended the constitution and overthrew President Mohamed Morsi in the hope it would put an end to the Muslim Brotherhood colonization (unfortunately this hasn't worked out), things have become a whole lot worse!

The excuse for these leadership changeovers is the removal of tyrannical rulers. Whereas the real underlying reason is for the N.W.O to put their own chosen 'compliant' leaders into power.

It is quite obvious to the discerning eye that over the past year the news has consisted of the same internal civil unrest occurring in Greece, Italy, Syria, Turkey and other nations. All of them were about the people revolting against their country's leadership, who has led the country into poverty and excessive debt. This is because the N.W.O orchestrated the economies of these countries so that the leadership was unable to resolve the issues of the country's debt without it affecting the people. The leader was placed in such a position that he was either forced to comply with the N.W.O or be ousted out! It is the sycophants chosen as N.W.O. leaders, those that are controllable and controlled!

A Newspaper article on 17th July 2013 stated that 800 murderers have escaped prison and still at large. Now how could that be possible? Well if you think about the previous discussion where mobs, gangsters etc were brought together to form riot groups or to instigate and gather new recruits to work around the different nations, then it is easy to see why. What better than to trade with murderers in prison who are on a life sentence? To form an agreement which offers freedom, in return for creating chaos and violent episodes when called upon to do so. See Clip by **NTEB News Desk**

Tell me what on earth a roaming pack of criminals, randomly beating innocent people on the street of Hollywood, has to do with the Trayvon Martin case that occurred 3,000 miles away in Florida? Here's a hint: there is no connection other than vandals using the case as an excuse to terrorize and hurt people who had nothing to do with it.

From Breitbart: On Tuesday night, a flash mob of some 40 to 50 teenagers invaded the busiest and most tourist-centric part of Hollywood, smashing windows, stealing cell phones, and assaulting passers-by. The police described the incident as a "rolling crime wave." One police official said that the George Zimmerman acquittal provided the flash point excuse for the flash mob. "They're using Trayvon as an excuse," the official said to local media. "They were saying, 'Let's go mess up Hollywood for Trayvon.'"

Here is a recent news report to confirm the above exist. *Mind Control: America's Secret War*

It is one of the ill-kept secrets of America's intelligence agencies–for decades, they have worked virtually non-stop to perfect means of controlling the human mind. But while many have suspected the existence of these projects, the details have long been preserved.

Mind Control blows the lid off years of chilling experiments, drawing on documents reluctantly released through the Freedom of Information Act and interviews with some of the victims, including a woman whose past was literally taken away.

Hear from John Marks, the author of In Search of the Manchurian Candidate, who broke the story of the CIA's abuses by unraveling the mysteries contained in financial records. All the other records pertaining to the experiments were destroyed by the agency in an attempt to prevent the details from ever being known.

After viewing this important program, you'll have reason to wonder about your own thoughts.

Source: Bloomberg.com 26 March 2013, http://tinyurl.com/cqvfpub

Another unknown group with involvement is the BRICS Nations consisting of Brazil, Russia, India, China and South Africa, these were chosen to approve the establishment of the New Development Bank, the purpose of which is to hold currency reserves of US Dollars and 43% of the world populations who are seeking global finance to match the rising economic power.

BRIC *Wikipedia, free encyclopedia*

In economics, BRIC is a grouping acronym that referred to the countries of Brazil, Russia, India and China, which are all deemed to be at a similar stage of newly advanced economic development. It is typically rendered as "the BRICs" or "the BRIC countries" or "the BRIC economies" or alternatively as the "Big Four". It has been replaced by BRICS since the 2010 inclusion of South Africa in the bloc.

The acronym was coined by Jim O'Neill in a 2001 paper entitled "Building Better Global Economic BRICs".[1][2][3] The acronym has come into widespread use as a symbol of the apparent shift in global economic power away from the developed G7 economies towards the developing world.

Projections on the future power of the BRIC economies vary widely. Some sources suggest that they might overtake the G7

273

economies by 2027.[4] *More modestly, <u>Goldman Sachs</u> has argued that, although the four BRIC countries are developing rapidly, it was only by 2050 that their combined economies could eclipse the combined economies of the current richest countries of the world.*[5]

In 2010, however, while the four BRIC countries accounted for over a quarter of the world's land area and more than 40% of the <u>world's population</u>,[6][7] *they accounted for only one quarter of the world gross national income.*[8][9]

According to a paper published in 2005, <u>Mexico</u> and <u>South Korea</u> were the only other countries comparable to the BRICs, but their economies were excluded initially because they were considered already more developed, as they were already members of the <u>OECD</u>.[10] *The same creator of the term "BRIC" coined the term <u>MIKT</u> (or MIST), that includes <u>Mexico</u>, Indonesia, <u>South Korea</u> and Turkey.*

Several of the more developed of the <u>N-11</u> countries, in particular <u>Turkey</u>, <u>Mexico</u>, <u>Indonesia</u> and <u>Nigeria</u>, were seen as the most likely contenders to the BRICs. Some other developing countries that have not yet reached the N-11 economic level, such as <u>South Africa</u>, aspired to BRIC status. South Africa was subsequently successful in joining the bloc. This was despite economists at the <u>Reuters</u> 2011 Investment Outlook Summit, held on 6–7 December 2010, dismissing the prospects of South African success .[11] *Jim O'Neill, for example, told the summit that South Africa, at a population of under 50 million people, was just too small an economy to join the BRIC ranks.*[12] *However, after the BRIC countries formed a political organization among themselves, they later expanded to include South Africa, becoming the <u>BRICS</u>.*[13]

Goldman Sachs did not argue that the BRICs would organize themselves into an economic bloc, or a formal trading association, as the <u>European Union</u> has done.[14] *However, there are some indications that the "four BRIC countries have* *been seeking to form a 'political club' or 'alliance'", and thereby converting "their growing economic power into greater geopolitical clout".[15][16] On June 16, 2009, the leaders of the BRIC countries held their first summit in Yekaterinburg, and issued a declaration calling for the establishment of an equitable, democratic and multipolar world order. Since then they have met in Brasília in 2010, met in Sanya in 2011 and in New Delhi, India in 2012.[17]*

In recent years, the BRICs have received increasing scholarly attention. Brazilian political economist Marcos Troyjo and French investment banker Christian Déséglise founded the BRICLab at Columbia University, a Forum examining the strategic, political and economic consequences of the rise of BRIC countries, especially by analyzing their projects for power, prosperity and prestige through graduate courses, special sessions with guest speakers, Executive Education programs, and annual conferences for policymakers, business and academic leaders, and students.[18]

***

The reader should study the youth of today, they provide a lot of information about these end times and the mind of the youth! Most young are aware that the world is corrupt and many young people of school age and college students go through a phase where they protest about something. There peer groups encourage them to be involved in anti-establishment protests i.e. against any system except those in the youth culture. They protest against rules, set structures and uniformed behavior. Yet if you examine the youth culture they do exactly the same things as those they are protesting about, they wear specific styles of clothing that identify with youths that have specific ideals or objections, particularly within youth gang culture. This gang culture has spread rapidly throughout the world; it started innocently as a means of self- preservation when individuals were attacked in the streets, and now no young person feels safe walking alone, especially as news regularly reports on increased fatal knife crimes.

If you observe the youth gang culture you will note they have their own language, full of code words, they also communicate to each other through hand signs and gesturing. They all have tattoos .and hatred towards 'normal society'. They have an intolerance of 'nice' people. They are only interested in people who have the same values and show power and a hardness of the heart! There is no place for sentiment, compassion or feelings (other than rage and hatred) in a gang! A lot of the gang culture has spread rapidly throughout the UK, particularly in the large cities and follow the lines of American gang culture using guns and knives.

Many non-gang youth form their own 'safety net' groups, these young people are not full of hate, and rage, but do normal things like play football, attend youth clubs and discos with their friends. However, they have adapted some of the culture of the hardened criminal gangs, such as the tattoos and hand gestures and the style of clothing.

The hoodies for example are worn by both groups, and both groups use the coding system and hand signals. Some of these hand signals and gestures are also used by Freemasons and occultists to give allegiance to the devil (lucifer). The hand signal where the fingers are separated to look like the devil's horns and beard are obvious. Just as the common tattoos seen on many youth, of the pentagram (the 5 pointed star) which is a well- known satanic symbol and when the star is inverted it becomes the goat's horns and beard. The goat denotes the devil's face which is the same symbolism with the hand signal. It is used specifically among secret societies and mystery groups. Gangs have their secret codes and practices.

New Age which is affiliated to occult, satanism and witchcraft, plans to use the pentagram as part of its initiation ceremony during which all of mankind is to be

demonized and obey the image of the beast to receive the mark on the forehead or right hand."

The above statement was written in a book called 'Mystery Mark of the New Age' by Texe Marrs. It was published in 1988. If you can get hold of his book it is well worth it!

Texe has been labeled as an extremist and therefore his writings and statements were rejected as radical. People were not ready to receive such information at that time, it was too soon. However, much of what he wrote in the book has actually occurred or taking place now! He predicted the New World Order, the Illuminati, Freemasonry and New Age influences on the world. He also wrote of the introduction of the One World Religion! His book illustrated the various symbolism used by these satanic groups. He discusses the mark of the beast and how it would come about.

Texe's blurb on the back page of his book says: satan, the prince of this world, is unleashing a campaign of wickedness the likes of which have never before been seen on earth….includes a worldwide initiation into his service through the imposition of a Mark on the forehead or right hand.

Texe is a strong believer in Christ and provides biblical references to help the reader to avoid taking the Mark.

He starts his book by saying " satan has a Mark he wants to give you. If you take his Mark, he will own your mind, your body, and your spirit". What he did not say is that satan would also own your soul!

The soul is the part that is you! Your personality, the part that allows you to feel, think and make decisions! It is this part that is crucial if you are not a believer! It is this part that satan wants to own so that he can make your decisions for you, so that you cannot think rationally, so that you do not feel guilt or shame, so that you become confused about what is good and start to see it as evil.

Then you start to see evil as being good! Once your soul has been taken over you would not be able to feel compassion, love, contentment or peace. You will not be able to feel at all! You certainly would not have free will or the ability to make decisions unless those decisions are implanted. The microchip would probably have the ability to implant false memories and decisions as well as trigger specific behavior!

It all sounds 'far- fetched', of course it does! It is meant to; if it was rational then people would not submit to it!

It is because it's far-fetched that people are gullible, they do not believe these things could happen so they are off guard when it does!

As you have read in the evidence throughout this book, everything that is done to change the world, society, nations and individuals, is done covertly and subtly and over a gradual period with the aim of desensitizing people and to introduce changes in stages so that it is not noticed. Everything that is done is not from a rational stance and has a superficial purpose different from the dangerous hidden agenda. The superficial reason is always acceptable by people and therefore encourages compliance! The Mark will be developed and applied in the same manner!

Going back to Youth culture, their selection of tattoos cannot be coincidence. If you go into a tattoo shop most of the tattoos are a combination of skulls, serpents, dragons, Egyptian or Greek letters or occult symbols. These tattoos already distinguish the goats from the sheep! The goats are those who choose to follow satan and the sheep are those who have chosen to follow the Lamb of God –Yeshua!

In Texe's book he also talked about the purpose of the New Age Movement. They had a five year plan to gain credibility, and momentum towards its goal of world domination. And the following stages were part of the five year plan:

- ❖ They would instigate the start of the removal (start the apostasy) of people from the Christian churches towards new age churches, to form a united religion, this is the first stage.
- ❖ Secondly, take control of all media so that they can introduce propaganda in favour of new age.
- ❖ Thirdly, dismantle national governments and set up a one world order based on global units.
- ❖ Fourth is to purify the earth and abolish the true Christianity/Judaism which is based on the Hebraic lifestyle as Christ and the disciples 2000 yrs ago. Satan will attempt to destroy these believers.
- ❖ Fifth, possess human beings on a mass scale by demons. (This is done today through Toronto blessing and Pensacola meetings).
- ❖ Six, encourage mankind to find their own god within themselves, many of which display superhuman feats. Have you ever wondered how people can perform horrendous feats in talent shows and circus acts etc? Some of the acts are beyond 'normal' human possibilities and therefore must be supernaturally demonic.
- ❖ Seven, seize world resources and redistribute them, through a sharing principle. (This is the Global Village mentioned in earlier chapters).
- ❖ Eight, bring in the new age messiah. He waits the time when international crisis takes place then he can assume his place as world leader.

Does all this sound familiar? Isn't it what we have already experienced?

ALL OF THE ABOVE POINTS HAVE ALREADY TAKEN PLACE, EXCEPT POINT EIGHT. WE ARE IN BETWEEN

STAGE SEVEN AND EIGHT WHERE THE FALSE MESSIAH IS TO REVEAL HIS IDENTITY AND TAKE HIS PLACE AS WORLD LEADER OFFICIALLY!

WHAT NEXT?

The next key political development in biblical prophecy is to watch for is the signing of the resolution to the problem of Jerusalem between the Jewish people and the Palestinians. It is thought that this will be resolved by going back to the 1947 agreement and the UN General Assembly Resolution 181. To return to this agreement would mean Israel is to give up (yet again) land to Palestinians and Jerusalem would not belong to Jew or Palestinian, but as an International City supported by Russia, EU, and USA.

Resolution 181 would declare Jerusalem as a separate body to be run under an International UN administration and includes all of Jerusalem, Bethlehem and other Christian Holy sites. The next stage of the takeover plan is to put the world dictator on the worldwide throne!

Up till now everything discussed has been pretty depressing and negative, everything looks bleak. Sadly many people, young, middle aged and old, have chosen to take their own lives rather than turn to God for help! That is the saddest thing ever. It should not have happened! Unfortunately, there are not enough true believers available and willing to tell them about the saving Christ who cares about those who are suffering! There are plenty of 'worldly' people to help them but they help them from a humanistic point of view, which is why they fail to prevent the suicide from occurring. Even counsellors speak as evolutionists and new agers. Many Christian counsellors are too afraid of the consequences to speak about God as a comforter and savior! It is easy to understand why they think this way, people in this apostate age seem to have a built in defence system that enables them to switch off, shut down their senses i.e. close their ears and eyes, close their minds and their heart at the mere mention of God!

What can we do to escape the threat of the beast and the dragon's world control? What can we do to avoid God's wrath and Yeshua's Judgement?

Can we save ourselves? Who is really in control? How will it all end?

The reader will be pleased to know that there is a positive ending.

Every human being has a choice to make. Understand this no person can save themselves!

"See the Lord is going to lay waste the earth and devastate it" Isaiah 24.

"See, the Lord is coming out of His dwelling to punish the people of the earth for their sins". Isaiah 26'

God is annoyed with all nations and will destroy them all! Isaiah 34.

But he or she who believes Christ Yeshua is the Son of God and asks for His forgiveness and choose to follow Him will be saved!

The reader can avoid the above outcomes mentioned in the verses!

Part 2 of this book provides positive solutions!

CHAPTER 8

MIND CONTROL AND CONTROLLERS

So far we have read the evidence of extreme activity taking place worldwide which has altered the fabric of society! Much of what has been read is just unbelievable, outrageous, mind boggling and defies all logic as we know it from the rational human perspective. Yet there is something in all of this that has a reality about it, especially when we read of incredible things that have already taken place. Things we know to be true because it was predicted many years ago and we have witnessed and are still witnessing these prophesied events, particularly events in the Middle East.

When something is prophesied and actually takes place, it becomes an 'occurred' fact, it has happened and therefore cannot be denied as truth! When an event is described in detail and expected to happen in a future period, when it actually happens and comes to pass and the details are correct, then it becomes historical fact. Those who read my first book, 'Christ Yeshua Jesus from Genesis to Revelation' will know that many such prophecies took place and now can be classified as fact!

It is essential for the reader to acknowledge the existence of God and Satan. They are real, they are fact!

There is an invisible spiritual war going on, a battle between good and evil. The great thing is, the battle ground has been set, the armies are being prepared and the final outcome already written in God's Diary of Events! He has already assigned the victor of the battle, the conqueror who will disable the evil leader, binding him in chains as he slays the evil ones with the sword of the Spirit! Yeshua the Messiah is the name! Revelation 19: 11-21. He is the conqueror, the savior and the Messiah soon to come [after the false messiah reveals his identity!]

Much of the contents of this book are also based on fact. The holocaust for example is fact; terrible experiments were performed on Jewish victims during this period. Testimonies from victims, diaries, photos etc all evidence the existence of the Massacre of Jewish people in appalling circumstances. We also know that since WW2 there has been ethnic cleansing and genocides throughout the world as well as many Christians and Jews targeted by terrorist's attacks. These events are facts! They are historical facts because they have occurred. We also know that diseases have increased worldwide, many new diseases and many old ones have made a comeback but more virulent! We also know that cancer is caused by death of cells in the body and often caused by hidden forces such as large amounts of radiation or other chemicals. We also know it is a fact that the world has become more Godless, more evil and more violent.

Now another fact is that God chose several righteous men to become his prophets. These prophets wrote scrolls according to God's directive. They also performed certain duties as instructed by God throughout the Old Testament period. Although there are specific books in the bible written by prophets such as Isaiah, Ezekiel, and Daniel there were many more prior to these such as Elijah and Jonah.

Many of these biblical prophets have written prophecies of the End Times, even though they knew the end times weren't for their generation, they all wrote something about end time events! God inspired them to write about these end time events so that believers would know what is to take place. But more importantly, many of the end time prophecies are written in the Old Testament books. This suggests God intended for everyone to know what the future holds so that we may make decisions regarding our destination and to learn the purpose of life!

We are seeing these prophecies being fulfilled in our lifetime, before our very eyes! Also in the New Testament, Christ himself speaks of these end times and warns us of false teachers, preachers, antichrists and dark forces of evil! Apostles Paul and Peter and others also wrote of prophecies some of which have come to pass already.

Paul writes in Ephesians 6: how to put the full armour of God on to protect us from the devil's schemes! He also warns we are fighting a battle against evil.

"Put on the full armour of God so that you can take your stand against the devil's schemes. For our struggle is not against flesh and blood, but against the rulers, against the authorities, against the powers of darkness and against the spiritual forces of evil in heavenly realms. Therefore put on the full armour of God, so that when the day of evil comes, you may be able to stand your ground... Eph 6: 10-14

Now if you can accept that there are dark forces of evil at work that go beyond flesh and blood (human) as described in the above scripture, then you will understand the following clip: This clip is 'extreme' and totally against all logic, yet there is something about it that makes it a reality! It very much links to what has already been covered in previous chapters. It therefore supports what has been covered so far but it also provides an alternative view point on some issues mentioned. You should be able to pick out certain pieces of information such as 'implants' and this can be linked to the RFID implant of today (see Appendix 5). Electromagnetic exposure and ELF (extremely low frequency forces) used in mind control. The clip also mentions the use of food and water and many other resources and methods that coincide with the contents of these chapters.

It is an article written on a website called Bariumblues. com. I agree with his disclaimer, that these clips need further investigation as to the authenticity of these claims and the people making them. The reader should research further and come to their own conclusions.

Electromagnetic Mind control

Disclaimer: This article is really sketchy. I'm posting it despite my reservations because aspects of it are fascinating and may encourage further investigation. Please trust your own judgment and do more research.

I question most everything in this article: the references to Andrija Puharich, the "pendulum expert", the "Extraterrestrials", and also the "vaccine implants", nature of GWEN etc.

It's hard to find answers about these things!

But, here are a few things I have learned:

Andrija Puharich was a brilliant but questionable (even sinister) character. I include him in a special category with other shadowy types such as Steven Greer, Ingo Swann, Courtney Brown, Timothy Leary, and Thomas Bearden and many, many more. You really can't trust these guys.

Some are probably aware that they spread disinformation, while others naively let themselves be used as "assets". Maybe they were just really brilliant guys and going down the rabbit hole screwed them up too much. Often they are sort-of in-the-military, but also sort-of not-in-the-military. They may dabble in drugs or the occult. They may be interested in mind control. They may seem to work for the government and also against the government.

Sometimes they are being duped and used by nonhuman entities. Andrija Puharich was influenced by such entities. These beings have had many names: aliens, spirits, Etherians, Extraterrestrials, etc. I prefer to identify them as Jinn.

In modern times we naively assume that these beings come from other planets, but they've always visited us and they come from another "dimension" or "space" that is a part of this world we call Earth.

The entities may pretend that they come from another planet. Or they may refer to themselves as Space beings. "Space" doesn't necessarily mean the "Outer Space" of NASA. "Space" is also defined as: "the unlimited expanse in which everything is located", or "the boundless regions of the infinite". Well, that pretty much includes everything -- including those realms and dimensions which modernized western society is amazingly ignorant about. Seems like those jinn are having another big laugh at our expense. They do that all the time.

The jinn are quite often tricksters and liars. Some are demonic and like to frighten or debase and corrupt. They have free will like humans, so they can range from good to bad. However, the ones who confuse and mess around with us aren't likely to be good. The best approach is to avoid them. They love to pose as gods or masters-of-the-universe and create followings. They often make predictions (which don't come true). They are channeled by people who are willing to go into a trance and let strange, unknown entities take over their bodies and minds.

In the case of Andrija Puharich the entities were called "The Nine".

The extra-terrestrials mentioned in this article were undoubtedly jinn.

There really is no such thing as a "pendulum expert". Pendulums can't be trusted for consistent, truthful or scientific responses.

I'm posting this article despite serious reservations. Please trust your better judgment and do more research!! ~Lydia

Total Population Control

An overview of the ELF, GWEN towers, and HAARP inter-
connection. By Nicholas Jones From http://educate-
yourself.org/mc/mctotalcontrol12jul02.shtml

*Earth is wrapped in a donut shaped magnetic field. Circular lines of
magnetic flux continuously descend into the North Pole and emerge from
the South Pole. The Ionosphere, an electromagnetic-wave conductor, 100
kilometres [62 miles] above the earth, consists of a layer of electrically
charged particles acting as a shield from solar winds.*

Earth Resonant Frequency
*Natural waves are created which result from electrical activity in the
atmosphere. They are thought to be caused by multiple lightning storms.
Collectively, these waves are called 'The Schumann Resonance', with the
strongest current registering at 7.8 Hz. These are quasi-standing [scalar],
extremely low frequency (ELF) waves that naturally exist in the earth's
electromagnetic cavity which is the <u>space between ground and the
Ionosphere</u>. These 'earth brainwaves' are identical to the frequency
spectrum of our human brainwaves.*

*[Frequency nomenclature: 1 hertz = 1 cycle per second, 1 KHz = 1000cps,
1 MHz =1 million cps. Wavelength: A 1 Hertz wave has a wavelength that
is 186,000 miles long, A 10 Hz wave is 18,600 miles long, etc. Radio-waves
move at the speed of light (186,000 miles per second)]*

HAARP
*The Creator designed living beings to resonate to the natural Schumann
Resonance frequency pulsation in order to evolve harmoniously. The
Ionosphere is being manipulated by US government scientists using the
Alaskan transmitter called HAARP, (High-Frequency Active Auroral
Research Program) which sends focused radiated power to heat up
sections of the Ionosphere, <u>which bounces power down again</u>. ELF waves
produced from HAARP, when targeted on selected areas, can weather-
engineer and create mood changes affecting millions of people. The
intended wattage is 1,700 billion watts of power.*

Geomagnetic Waves & GWEN
*Sixty four elements in the ground modulate, with variation, the
geomagnetic waves naturally coming from the ground. The earth's natural
'brain rhythm' above is balanced with these. These are the same minerals*

287

found in red blood corpuscles. There is a relation between the blood and geomagnetic waves. An imbalance between Schumann and geomagnetic waves disrupts these biorhythms. These natural geomagnetic waves are being replaced by artificially created low frequency (LF) ground waves coming from GWEN Towers.

GWEN (Ground Wave Emergency Network) transmitters placed 200 miles apart across the USA allow specific frequencies to be tailored to the geomagnetic-field strength in each area, allowing the magnetic field to be altered. They operate in the LF range, with transmissions between LF 150 and 175 KHz. They also emit waves from the upper VHF to the lower UHF range of 225 - 400 MHz. The LF signals travel by waves that hug the ground rather than radiating into the atmosphere. A GWEN station transmits in a 360 degree circle up to 300 miles, the signal dropping off sharply with distance. The entire GWEN system consists of, (depending on source of data), from 58 to an intended 300 transmitters spread across the USA, each with a tower 299-500 ft high. 300 ft copper wires in spoke-like fashion fan out from the base of the system underground, _interacting with the earth_, like a thin shelled conductor, _radiating radio wave energy for very long distances through the ground_.

The United States is bathed in this magnetic field which can rise from ground up to 500 ft, but goes down into basements, _so everyone can be affected and mind-controlled_. The entire artificial ground-wave spreads out over the whole of the USA like a web. It is easier to mind-control and hypnotize people who are bathed in an artificial electromagnetic-wave.

GWEN transmitters have many different functions including:

1. controlling the weather,
2. mind control,
3. behavior and mood control, and
4. sending synthetic-telepathy as infrasound to victims with US government mind-control implants.

GWEN works in conjunction with HAARP and the Russian Woodpecker transmitter, which is similar to HAARP. The Russians openly market a small version of their weather-engineering system called Elate, which can fine-tune weather patterns over a 200 mile area and have the same range as the GWEN unit. An Elate system operates at Moscow airport. The GWEN towers shoot enormous bursts of energy into the atmosphere in conjunction with HAARP. The website www.cuttingedge.org wrote _an expose_ of how the major floods of the Mid-West USA occurred in 1993.

288

Atmospheric Vapor Rivers
Enormous, invisible rivers of water, consisting of vapors that flow, move
towards the poles in the lower atmosphere. They rival the flow of the
Amazon River and are 420 to 480 miles wide and up to 4,800 miles long.
They are 1.9 miles above the earth and contain a volume of water
equivalent to 340 lbs of water per second. There are 5 atmospheric rivers in
each Hemisphere. A massive flood can be created by damming up one of
these massive vapor rivers, causing huge amounts of rainfall to be dumped.
The GWEN Towers positioned along the areas north of the Missouri and
Mississippi Rivers were turned on for 40 days and 40 nights, probably
mocking the Flood of Genesis. (This was in conjunction with HAARP, that
creates a river of electricity flowing thousands of miles through the sky and
down to the polar ice-cap, manipulating the jet-stream , like the Russian
Woodpecker.) These rivers flooded, causing agricultural losses of $12-15
billion. HAARP produces earthquakes by focusing energy along fault
lines. GWEN Towers are located on the fault lines and volcanic areas of
the Pacific Northeast.

In 1963, Dr Robert Beck explored effects of external magnetic-fields on
brainwaves showing a relationship between psychiatric admissions and
solar magnetic storms. He exposed volunteers to pulsed magnetic-fields
similar to magnetic-storms, and found a similar response. US 60 Hz
electric power ELF waves vibrate at the same frequency as the human
brain. UK 50 Hz electricity emissions depress the thyroid gland.

Dr Andrija Puharich in the 50's/60's, found that clairvoyant's brainwaves
became 8 Hz when their psychic powers were operative. He saw an Indian
Yogi in 1956 controlling his brainwaves, deliberately shifting his
consciousness from one level to another. Puharich trained people with bio-
feedback to do this consciously, making 8 Hz waves. A healer made 8 Hz
waves pass into a patient, healing their heart trouble, her brain emitting 8
Hz . One person emitting a certain frequency can make another also
resonate to the same frequency. <u>*Our brains are extremely vulnerable to*</u>
<u>*any technology which sends out ELF waves*</u>*, because they immediately*
start resonating to the outside signal by a kind of tuning-fork effect.
Puharich experimented discovering that:

A) 7.83 Hz (earth's pulse rate) made a person feel good, producing an
altered-state.
B) 10.80 Hz causes riotous behavior and
C) 6.6 Hz causes depression.

Puharich made ELF waves change RNA and DNA, breaking hydrogen
bonds to make a person have a higher vibratory rate. He wanted to go

beyond the psychic 8 Hz brainwave and attract psi phenomena. James Hurtak, who once worked for Puharich, also wrote in his book The Keys of Enoch that ultra-violet caused hydrogen bonds to break and this raised the vibratory rate. [The keys of Enoch – is the mirror image (counterfeit) of the biblical Enoch I mentioned in earlier chapters]

Puharich presented the mental effects of ELF waves to military leaders, but they would not believe him. He gave this information to certain dignitaries of other Western nations. The US government burned down his home in New York to shut him up and he fled to Mexico. However, the Russians discovered which ELF frequencies did what to the human brain and began zapping the US Embassy in Moscow on 4 July 1976 with electromagnetic-waves, varying the signal, including focusing on 10 Hz. (10 Hz puts people into a hypnotic state. Russians and North Koreans use this in portable mind-control machines to extract confessions. A machine was even found in an American church to help the congregation believe!) The Russian "Woodpecker" signal was traveling across the world from a transmitter near Kiev. The US Air Force identified 5 different frequencies in this compound harmonic Woodpecker signal that was sending signals through the earth and the atmosphere.

Nikola Tesla revealed in 1901 power could be transmitted through the ground using ELF waves. Nothing stops or weakens these signals. The Russians retrieved Tesla's papers when they were finally returned to Yugoslavia after his death.

Puharich continued to monitor the Russian ELF wave signal while in Mexico and the higher harmonics produced in the MHz range (5.340 MHz). He met the CIA and started working for them. He and Dr. Robert Beck designed equipment to measure these waves and their effect on the human brain. Puharich started his work by putting dogs to sleep. By 1948/49 he graduated to monkeys, deliberately destroying their eardrums to enable them to pick up sounds without the eardrum intact. He discovered a nerve in the tongue could be used to facilitate hearing. He created the dental tooth implant which mind-control victims are now claiming was surreptitiously placed in their mouth by controlled dentists causing them to hear 'voices in their head.' The implant was placed under dental caps or lodged in the jaw.

Vaccine Implants
Implants are now smaller than a hair's width and are injected with vaccine and flu shots. Millions have had this done unknowingly. These 'biochips' circulate in the bloodstream and lodge in the brain, enabling the victims to hear 'voices' via the implant. There are many kinds of implants now and 1

in 40 are victims from 'alien abduction' statistics, though 1 in 20 has also been gauged. The fake alien abduction event, revealed to be actually the work of US military personnel using technology to make hologram spaceships outside, virtual reality scenarios of going onto a spaceship with humans in costumes, has been astutely perceived. Though real alien abductions do occur, the 'alien abduction' scenario has been useful to stop any further investigation or accountability of government authorities by poor victims who would face mockery and appear silly.

Are we being forced to respond to an artificially induced vibratory rate by global masters who want this planet to have a sudden leap in evolution, populated by the psychically aware and therefore a superior class of humans or is the agenda designed to eliminate billions of people who are 'useless eaters', deceptively being disposed by electro magnetically-induced cancers and diseases?

Electromagnetic Disease Transmission, ELF, & Chemtrails
The physics and engineering behind electromagnetic disease transmission are frightening. Diseases can be reproduced as 'disease signatures' in that the vibration of a disease can be manufactured and sent on to be induced. (The brainwave pattern of hallucinogenic drugs can also be copied and sent by ELF waves to induce 'visions'.) Once diseases are sprayed in the air, electromagnetic-waves attuned to the disease, using harmonics and sub harmonics, will make them more lethal and infectious by sending particular disease frequency death-patterns.

Chemtrails are being sprayed daily all over USA (and other countries too) in a white crisscross pattern. They contain diseases and chemicals which affect our state of consciousness. They can produce apathy which works in conjunction with fluoridation of the water, as well as aspartame and drugs. Fluoride disables the willpower section of the brain, impairing the left occipital lobe.

Fluoride and selenium enable people to 'hear voices'. ELF waves create disturbances in the biological processes of the body and these can be activated in the population once the diseases are introduced into the body from the chemtrails.

Some chemtrails have been analysed and shown to be creating cleavages in spacial perceptions, <u>blocking the interaction of various amino-acids that relate to higher-consciousness</u> and to increase dopamine in the brain producing a listless, spaced-out state of lower reactive mind. Basically, the goal is to fog the difference between the real and unreal and some of this could be connected with the many UFO abductions occurring en-mass.

Hundreds have been witnessed laid out on tables and implanted. Intelligence agencies are in league with each other behind this disablement of the masses to such a point that they can't even fight back. In order for the perpetrators to do what they want, they need the overall 'frequency' of each victim to function at a specific rate below the threshold of awareness.

Could this be part of a greater plan with mind-control transmitters covering the whole of USA and England, cleverly disguised as cell phone towers and trees? The power from microwave towers may be turned up to such a level that people can die.

A brain functioning at beta-level (above 13 Hz) is agitated and can't change its perceptions, if it is artificially maintained by technology to that frequency. This may increase body electricity in others, giving them psychic powers. Is this linked to the New-Agers claim of a rising 12-14 Hz Schumann Resonance, inching us towards the 4th dimension? Stimulants ingested globally from caffeine genetically-modified plants, may also produce an impact on the 'global-brain' in the ionosphere collecting our brainwaves. New-age channellers say we are going into 4th dimensional frequency. They 'heard' the voice of some 'ET' who told them.

However, some 'ETs' may be local boys. Voices in the head were produced in prisoners in Utah prisons using Tesla technology. Each of the prisoners received the same message from an 'ET'. Today, it seems, it's easy to produce 'voices in the head' without implants.

A prisoner called David Fratus in Draper Prison, Utah in 1988 wrote: "I began to receive, or hear, high-frequency tones in my ears. When I plug my ears, the tones are still inside and become amplified. It's as if they had become electrified echo chambers with the sounds coming from the inside out.. I began to hear voices.. into my inner ears as vivid as though I were listening to a set of stereo headphones with the end result being that I am now having my brain monitored by an omnipotent computerized mind reading or scanning machine of some sort "

Hundreds of inmates at the Gunnison Facility of the Utah State Prison, and the State Hospital were subject to this brand of mind-control in order to test it. In the early 1970s, this was brought out in the Utah U.S. District Court, because inmates who had been subjected to this Tesla-wave mind-control in prison had tried unsuccessfully to fight back in court. The University of Utah researched how Tesla-waves could be used to manipulate the mind into hearing voices, overriding and implanting thoughts into the mind, and reading the thoughts, as well as developing eye-implants.

Cray computers, using artificial-intelligence, monitor the victims of government implants sending pre-recorded sound-bytes or occasional live messages. They are picked up by satellite and relayed to whatever large TV broadcasting antenna, GWEN tower or other microwave antenna is near the victim. It's believed that some type of body implants pick up the signal and broadcast the correct Tesla-wave pattern to create voices within the victim.

The tracking implant keeps the staff and the satellite system informed every few minutes as to exactly where to send the voice signals. The master computer and central HQ for this is reported to be in Boulder, CO. It is thought that transponders are being made there as well. The central cellular computer is in the Boulder, CO National Bureau of Standards building. AT&T is also cooperating in this project. Several government agencies work together on this.

Tim Rifat of UK wrote that "this inter-cerebral hearing is used to drive the victim mad, as no one else can hear the voices transmitted into the brain of the target. Transmission of auditory data directly into the target's brains using microwave carrier beams is now common practice. Instead of using excitation potentials, one uses a transducer to modify the spoken word into ELF audiograms, that are then superimposed on a pulse modulated microwave beam."

The Sydney Morning Herald on <u>21 March 1983</u> published an article by Dr Nassim Abd El-Aziz Neweigy, Assistant Professor in the Faculty of Agriculture, Moshtohor Tukh-Kalubia, Egypt. It stated:

"Russian satellites, controlled by advanced computers, can send voices in one's own language interweaving into natural thoughts to the population of choice to form diffused artificial thought. The chemistry and electricity of the human brain can be manipulated by satellite and even suicide can be induced. Through ferocious anti-humanitarian means, the extremist groups are fabricated, the troubles and bloody disturbances are instigated by advanced tele-means via Russian satellites, in many countries in Asia, Africa, Europe and Latin America."

Another source says that these have been fed with the world's languages and synthetic telepathy will reach into people's heads making people believe God is speaking to them personally to enact the Second Coming, complete with holograms! The Russians broke the genetic code of the human brain. They worked out 23 EEG band-wave lengths, 11 of which were totally independent. So if you can manipulate those 11, you can do anything.

NSA Cray computers can remotely track people just knowing the specific EMF waves (evoked potentials from EEGs in the 30-50 Hz, 5 milliwatt range) of a person's bioelectric-field. Each person's emissions are unique and they can remotely track someone in public.

Maxwell's 'Hidden' Etheric Component
Evoked-potentials officially don't exist in physics, but in 1873 a Scotsman, James Clerk Maxwell, <u>discovered electromagnetic waves have 3 components:</u>

He discovered waveforms which exist at a certain number of right-angled rotations away from the electromagnetic-field. These are hyperspacial components, not subject to constraints of time and space. He claimed that electromagnetic-radiation waves were carried by the ether and the ether was disturbed by magnetic lines of force. The hidden component is called only 'potential' now and <u>not normally used except for covert hyper dimensional physics and to manipulate consciousness itself via electromagnetic-waves covering vast areas of the planet.</u>

Approx. one person in 3000 is naturally sensitive to this magnetic-waveform component, the telepathic types (according to a writer called "Majix"), but we are all capable of tuning into this magnetic component by tuning our subconscious to it. Maxwell's successors thought potentials were akin to mysticism, because they believed fields contain mass which cannot be created from apparently nothing, which is what potentials are, both literally and mathematically - they are an accumulation or reservoir of energy; but this hasn't been taught in mainstream physics.

Thought Control
Subliminal words in the correct electromagnetic-field that expresses human consciousness, attuned to the human brain, can enter our minds at a subconscious level. Our brain activity patterns can apparently be measured and stored on computer by super-computers. If a victim needs subliminal-thoughts implanted, all that is necessary is to capture, save on computer, and target the person's brainwave pattern to send them such low frequency subliminal-messages that they actually think it is their own thoughts [confirmed by Al Bielek and Preston Nichols with the Montauk Project in Long Island]. The researcher Majix says our brains are so sensitive that they are like liquid-crystal in response to the magnetic component of the earth.

We are sensitive to earth's magnetic changes, changes in the ionospheric cavity and re-resonate those frequencies ourselves. We are incredibly complex, beyond comprehension and a type of biocosmic transducer.

He adds:

"Physicists in Russia correlate the mean annual magnetic-activity, electro-magnetic and electro-static fields on human behavior and medical indications. They are similar to biorhythms. These magnetic frequencies can be manipulated. Our brain waves can mimic magnetic frequencies from very simple equipment at extremely low power levels. From half a second to 4 seconds later, the neurons and brainwaves are driven exclusively by the device, with power levels almost non-existent. All one needs is a circularly polarized antenna aimed up at the ionospheric cavity and they can manipulate the moods of everyone within a 75 sq. mile area. The body picks up these "new" manipulated waves and begins to correspond immediately. "Sleep" frequency will make everyone become tired and sleep."

In 1967, an "internationally renowned scientist" and Christopher Hills, a pendulum expert, communicated with some ETs. (It is not known who the scientist was, but at one time both Hills and Puharich were with the medium Eileen Garrett at a time when Puharich was communicating with ETs.)

In short, ETs communicated with us via modulated radio-waves, between 10,000 and 20,000 cycles below the known electromagnetic-spectrum. In the carrier-wave by amplitude modulation, mixed with frequency modulation. Single band energy, transmission power less than 25 watts. A naturally present wave on earth, the brain modulated - <u>a wave that resonates between the earth and the ionosphere</u>. All humans influence the ionosphere in this manner. A reflecting technique is involved. The brain modulation consisted of pulses, akin to those known from neuro pulses. Two humans can use this. It's related to something akin to low frequency radar and to ultrasonic techniques, but qualified. A mixed electro-acoustic wave function. The electromagnetic-wave induced an ultrasonic transduction in human tissue. The brain radiation has a sonic component to it as well as an electromagnetic component. Electromagnetic-radiation has a sonic component and it's dependent on the medium through which it travels.

The scientist cut through months of work. Now HAARP is slicing up the ionosphere, the world-brain, like a microwave knife, producing long tear incisions destroying the membrane which holds the reservoir of data accumulated by all earth's history. A healer called Mr. "A" claimed to receive "Ancient Wisdom" from this protective Magnetic-Ring of energy which stores within it all knowledge since time began. Ruth Montgomery wrote about him in Born To Heal. [Ancient Wisdom was mentioned in an earlier chapter as a term used by the new ager Alice Bailey.]

He claimed that if our energy flow is cut off from this magnetic-field, the Universal-Supply is obstructed and we are no longer in tune and start to get sick. The Power from this travels in split-seconds around the world and is available to anyone who is capable of receiving it and handling it. The waves from The Ring automatically translated into words in his mind, as wisdom to diagnose and heal others, coming from the storehouse of knowledge here since the beginning of time. He produced instant miracles, knitting broken bones and removing arthritis. A photo caught forked lightning coming from his fingers. [This is to imitate Yeshua and the Holy Spirit who are able to provide sound everlasting healing. The above is to fool the public into accepting the production of satan's artificial healing to the nations]

In Let's Talk MONTAUK, Joyce Murphy shows that experiments on the 410-420 MHz cycle have been done which could affect the "window frequency to the human consciousness" as a whole:

"He (Preston Nichols) used his. radio equipment to learn that whenever a 410-420 MHz signal appeared on the air, the psychic's minds would be "jammed." Tracing the signal to Montauk Point and the red and white radar antenna on the Air Force Base.."

In Encounter in the Pleiades by Peter Moon and Preston Nichols, http://www.time-travel.com/skybooks/ Preston wrote that: "Dr. Nicholas Begich has picked up 435 MHz signals connected to HAARP and that a mind control function is being employed. He says that 400-450 MHz is the window to human consciousness because it is our reality's background frequency."

Tim Rifat wrote in his Microwave Mind Control in the UK article http://www.brazilboycott.org/ that cellular phones use 435 MHz. UK police use 450 MHz exclusively. Dr. Ross Adey used this for CIA behavioral modification experiments. Police have a vast array of antennae to broadcast this frequency all over the UK. Adey used 0.75mW/cm2 intensity of pulse modulate microwave at a frequency of 450 MHz, <u>with an ELF modulation to control all aspects of human behavior</u>. 450 MHZ radar modulated at 60 Hz greatly reduced T-lymphocyte activity to kill cultured cancer cells. A study of USA 60 Hz power lines repeated this finding.

<u>*Dystopian visionary quotes from Brzezinski's book*</u> *written back in 1970: "a system that would seriously impair the brain performance of very large populations"*

More about Puharich: from
http://www.theforbiddenknowledge.com/hardtruth/council_of_nine_fort
ean.htm

Perhaps the most disturbing aspect of the history of The Nine is its
relationship to the career of Andrija Puharich. Recent research has
revealed Puharich to have a distinctly sinister side. As an Army doctor
in the 1950s, he was deeply involved with the CIA's notorious
MKULTRA mind control project (see panel). He - together with the
infamous Dr Sidney Gottlieb - experimented with a variety of techniques
to change or induce actual thought processes. even to creating the
impression of voices in the head. These techniques included the use of
drugs, hypnosis and beaming radio signals directly into the subject's
brain. And, significantly, he was engaged in this work at exactly the
same time that The Nine made their first appearance at the Round Table
Foundation. The Foundation itself is now known to have been largely
funded by the Pentagon as a front for its medical and parapsychological
research. Puharich was still working for the CIA in the early 1970s,
when he brought Uri Geller out of Israel. Puharich's use of hypnosis is
particularly interesting in The Nine circle. In the case of Uri Geller and
Bobby Horne, he first hypnotised them and then suggested that they
were in touch with The Nine - and lo, they were! Ira Einhorn - a close
associate of Puharich's during the 1970s - confirmed to us that he
believed that Puharich was "humanly directing" The Nine
communications. from
http://64.233.167.104/search?q=cache:vu7Tv44XhP8J:www.timboucher.
com/journal/2005/11/09/andrija-puharich-yeh-
hoova/+puharich+extraterrestrial&hl=en&ct=clnk&cd=5&gl=us

"To quickly summarize, Puharich was involved on the one hand with
ELF (extremely low frequency) transmissions, and even supposedly
invented a radio receiver which could be inserted into tooth fillings. And
then on the other hand, he has this history of alleged UFO contact, and
a series of channellers who claimed to be in communion with ancient
Egyptian gods. Here are a couple pieces I've written about him, which
you might want to explore:
He's one of these malleable characters who flit in and out of other
people's life stories, such as Gene Roddenberry, creator Star Trek, and
psychic Uri Geller, who in turn is connected to Michael Jackson, John
Lennon, Dodi Fayed's father and more. Further, Puharich seems to
have been very much treading the line between working for the
government and working against the government at various times, which
perhaps indicates that there was some deeper hidden agenda at work.
I've encountered fewer figures in the annals of conspiracy research who

seem to have lead more interesting lives, nor left behind more twisted trails.

The Council of Nine

One New Age channeling cult, above all the rest, has had a huge - very disturbing influence on hundreds of thousands of devotees worldwide. Known as 'The Nine', its disciples include cutting edge scientists, multi-millionaire industrialists and leading politicians. This exclusive extract based on The Startgate Conspiracy by Lynn Picknett and Clive Prince looks at the sinister origins of The Nine

I am the beginning. I am the end. I am the emissary. But the original time I was on the Planet Earth was 34,000 of your years ago. I am the balance. And when I say "I" - I mean because I am an emissary for The Nine. It is not I , but it is the group. We are nine principles of the Universe, yet together we are one.

The declaration above is typical of the channelled pronouncements of the Council of Nine - or just 'The Nine'. They contain all the usual New Age ingredients of grandiose statements, shaky grammar and unprovable predictions. But unlike all the other channelling cults, that of The Nine has serious clout. Perhaps the reason for this is that they claim to be the Ennead, or the nine major gods of ancient Egypt (see panel). Or could there be another reason, one that owes more to The X-Files than the Pyramid Texts? Although The Nine may appear to be quintessentially a modern phenomenon, our research uncovered its truly astonishing pedigree. In fact, the story begins nearly 50 years ago, in a private research laboratory in Glen Cove, Maine, called the Round Table Foundation, run by a medical doctor named Andrija Puharich (also known as Henry K Puharich).Set up in 1948 to research the paranormal, among the noted psychics studied at the Foundation were the famous Irish medium Eileen Garrett and the Dutch clairvoyant Peter Hurkos (Pieter van de Hirk).Prominent members included the influential philosopher and inventor Arthur M Young and the socialite Alice Bouverie (née Astor).

In December 1952, Puharich brought into his laboratory an Indian mystic named Dr D G Vinod, who began to channel The Nine or 'the Nine Principles'. In the months before Vinod returned to India, a group met regularly to hear The Nine's channelled wisdom. Never known for their modesty, The Nine proclaimed themselves to be God, stating "God is nobody else than we together, the Nine Principles of God."

Three years later, there appeared to be independent confirmation of their existence. In Mexico, Puharich and Young met Charles and Lillian Laughead, former Christian missionaries who were by then prominent in the burgeoning UFO contactee movement. (For a description of their involvement in the Dorothy Martin circle, see Jerome Clark's 'When Prophecy Failed' in FT117.) Back in the States a few weeks later, Puharich received a letter from the Laugheads containing messages received by their group's channeller. This message also claimed to come from the Nine Principles, even - amazingly - including references to the earlier communications transmitted through Dr Vinod. Could The Nine possibly be for real?

Perhaps the answer is embedded in the career of Puharich himself. After disbanding the Round Table Foundation in 1958, he worked for 10 years as an inventor of medical devices and achieved international recognition as a parapsychologist, most famously studying the Brazilian psychic surgeon, Arigo (José Pedro de Freitas). But all that was to pale into insignificance because, in 1971, Puharich discovered Uri Geller.

At their first meetings in Tel Aviv in 1971, Puharich hypnotised Geller in an attempt to find out where his abilities came from. As a result, the young Israeli started to channel 'Spectra' - an entity which claimed to be a conscious super-computer aboard a spaceship. However, Puharich suggested to him that there might be a connection with the Nine Principles, and Spectra readily agreed that there was. The Nine claimed that they had programmed Geller with his powers as a young child.

Through Geller, The Nine alerted Puharich to his life's mission, which was to use Geller's talents to alert the world to an imminent mass landing of spaceships that would bring representatives of The Nine. However, Geller - by now an international psychic superstar - bowed out in 1973 and has resolutely turned his back on The Nine ever since. Puharich had to find other channels. He joined up with aristocratic former racing driver Sir John Whitmore and Florida-based psychic and healer Phyllis Schlemmer. They found a new channeller - a Daytona cook known to history only by the pseudonym 'Bobby Horne' - who lived to regret his dealings with The Nine. Driven to the brink of suicide by their constant demands, he too dropped out of the scene - his despair being dismissed by Whitmore as "signs of instability". After this, Phyllis Schlemmer was appointed the authorised spokesperson for the entity - known simply as 'Tom' - who represented The Nine.

Puharich, Whitmore and Schlemmer then set up Lab Nine at Puharich's estate in Ossining, New York. The Nine's disciples included multi-

299

millionaire businessmen (many hiding behind pseudonyms and including members of Canada's richest family, the Bronfmans), European nobility, scientists from the Stanford Research Institute and at least one prominent political figure who was a personal friend of President Gerald Ford.

We also know that Lyall Watson (then the darling of the alternative scene because of his seminal 1973 book Supernature) was involved, as was the influential counter-culture guru Ira Einhorn - and Gene Roddenberry, creator of Star Trek.

The key to predicting eclipses is noticing that they occur in cycles, or at more or less regular intervals. The Sun goes round the sky once a year; the Moon once a month. This means that, every month, the Moon 'overtakes' the sun. This happens at the New Moon, and this is when solar eclipses occur. But, of course, we don't get an eclipse every New Moon. This is because the Moon has an elliptical orbit: sometimes it passes above the Sun when it overtakes it, sometimes below. But the Moon's elliptical orbit has its own cycle: it returns to the same place it started from every 18 years or so. Thus - if seen from the same place on Earth - an eclipse will be followed by another one just over 18 years later.

Roddenberry was part of that circle in 1974 and 1975, and even produced the screenplay for a movie about The Nine. How much he was influenced by them is unknown, although it is said that some of their concepts found their way into the early Star Trek movies, and The Next Generation and Deep Space Nine (what a giveaway!) series.

(There is a character named 'Vinod' in one Deep Space Nine episode.) Another key player in Lab Nine was Dr James J Hurtak, who was appointed Puharich's second-in-command by The Nine. In fact, Hurtak had been independently channelling The Nine since 1973. Puharich and Whitmore commissioned British writer Stuart Holroyd to write an account of their adventures, which appeared in 1977 as Prelude to the Landing on Planet Earth (retitled Briefings for the Landing on Planet Earth in paperback)

In this extraordinary book the true identity of the Nine - and of Tom - was finally revealed. Far from being the chummy character that his rather avuncular name suggests, Tom is actually Atum, the creator-god of the ancient Egyptian religion of Heliopolis, and Uncle Tom with his eight mates are none other than the Great Ennead of Heliopolis,

But even with such impressive contacts, all was not well with Puharich. Lab Nine broke up in 1978 after a series of mysterious events that culminated in an arson attack on the Ossining estate, and he fled to

Mexico, claiming that he was being persecuted by the CIA. He returned to the USA two years later, and appears to have played no further part in The Nine story. He died in 1995 after falling down the stairs in his South Carolina home. However, The Nine continued. Not only did Schlemmer and Whitmore continue their mission, but Dr Hurtak has also moved on. He has become a major player in the unfolding millennial drama currently being played out at Giza, but perhaps more importantly he has established himself as a New Age guru par excellence, travelling the world giving workshops on his book of channelled revelations from The Nine, The Keys of Enoch. Written and laid out in classic Biblical style, its darkly apocalyptic vision has huge numbers of influential devotees. This we find very worrying.

Another Nine channel - an Englishwoman named Jenny O'Connor - was introduced to the avant garde Esalen Institute in San Francisco by Sir John Whitmore. She and The Nine became so influential there that they held seminars and - unbelievably - were actually listed on the Institute's staff, even successfully ordering the sacking of its chief finance officer and the reorganisation of its entire management structure..

This should concern us, because many influential people attended The Nine's Esalen seminars, including Russians who were part of the Institute's Soviet Exchange programme. Some of these later rose to prominence in the Gorbachev regime and were instrumental in the downfall of Communism. (The Esalen Institute now runs the US branch of the Gorbachev Foundation.)

The Nine are very much still with us. One of their recent channels, who is also in contact with Tom, is the American writer David M Myers. He is co-author with Britain's David S Percy of that extraordinary tome Two-Thirds, a history of the galaxy and the human race according to Myer's other worldly contacts (who clearly have no sense of the absurd). Percy - best known as a champion of the 'Face on Mars' and the 'hoaxing' of the Apollo moon landings - was at one time part of the Schlemmer circle. Among the other major proponents of the 'monuments' of Mars and their alleged connection with ancient Egypt is none other than Dr James Hurtak - The Nine's great prophet - who has promoted this idea since as long ago as 1973. Richard C Hoagland - familiar to FT readers as another unrepentant 'Mars Face' enthusiast - is also clearly under The Nine's spell. David Myers and David Percy were, respectively, American and European Director of Operations for Hoagland's Mars Mission. In fact, his interpretation of the 'monuments' of Mars comes directly from The Nine. Flake though he may appear (increasingly in these hallowed pages), but his influence over huge swathes of the hungrier mystery seekers is undeniable. This is the man who addresses rapt audiences at the United Nations.

But it is in the New Age channelling circuit that The Nine have truly come into their own. In any other circles their true agenda would no doubt have been rumbled long ago, but this is the New Age. Anything The Nine say must be sweetness and light, right? But an objective reading of their divine pronouncements reveal the first stirrings of something very nasty in Paradise.

Their words appeared in 1992 as the book The Only Planet of Choice, credited to 'transceiver' Schlemmer and edited by Mary Bennett (a one-time member of the Schlemmer circle who also edited Myers and Percy's Two-Thirds). This has had an unprecedented influence over the New Age. According to Palden Jenkins (editor of an earlier edition of Only Planet) more and more New Age channelling groups are 'realising' that the real source of their wisdom is The Nine. In fact, we have discerned what amounts to a campaign by The Nine - or their adherents - to 'take over' the New Age. It would be a mistake to underestimate the economic or even political potential of this vast subculture - rich pickings indeed.

But The Nine's influence does not extend merely to New Age channelling circles. Andrija Puharich, James Hurtak and Richard Hoagland have all lectured at the United Nations in New York. And individuals connected with The Nine are also known to have influence with Vice-President Al Gore. Of course, if The Nine really are the ancient gods of Egypt, then surely there could be fewer more significant events than their return. One may be justified in thinking that the more leading politicians who fall under their influence the better; but are they really the ancient Ennead of Egypt? Can it be that they have actually returned to sort us all out, scattering love and enlightenment from their high moral ground?

Tom, in The Only Planet of Choice, chooses his words carefully as he explains that all the races of the Earth were seeded from space-gods - except one, the "indigenous race", the blacks. He is very careful to urge us not to make an issue out of this. After all, it's not the black race's fault that they have no divine spark like the rest of us.

Perhaps the most disturbing aspect of the history of The Nine is its relationship to the career of Andrija Puharich. Recent research has revealed Puharich to have a distinctly sinister side. As an Army doctor in the 1950s, he was deeply involved with the CIA's notorious MKULTRA mind control project (see panel). He - together with the infamous Dr Sidney Gottlieb - experimented with a variety of techniques to change or induce actual thought processes. even to creating the impression of voices in the head. These techniques included the use of drugs, hypnosis and beaming radio signals directly into the subject's brain. And, significantly, he was engaged in this work at exactly the same time that The Nine made their first appearance at the Round Table Foundation. The Foundation itself is now known to have been largely funded by the Pentagon as a front for its medical and parapsychological research. Puharich was still working for the CIA in the early 1970s, when he brought Uri Geller out of Israel. Puharich's use of hypnosis is particularly interesting in The Nine circle. In the case of Uri Geller and Bobby Horne, he first hypnotised them and then suggested that they were in touch with The Nine - and lo, they were! Ira Einhorn - a close associate of Puharich's during the 1970s - confirmed to us that he believed that Puharich was "humanly directing" The Nine communications.

The evidence we have gathered strongly suggests that Tom and his fellow gods originated, not in the stars, but behind closed doors as part of a CIA mind control experiment. And what happened to that experiment? Now with hundreds of thousands of devotees, some in very high places, can The Nine be deemed a success? Of course, that depends very much on what the CIA had in mind. With their subtle racist propaganda, perhaps the flaky New Age Nine should worry the hell out of us.

The above clips link to many of the subjects mentioned in this book suggesting an element of truth in what has been written, .i.e. Stanford research centre in Florida, CIA involvement in mind control experiments, the microchip that is already in use as an implant in animals and humans. The increase in the number of people with mental illness, unexplained incidences, such as crazed individuals on a shooting rampage, people not being aware they are committing evil acts etc.

The aliens bit sounds weird but when you think of aliens as being the heavenly realm mentioned in the biblical scriptures then it makes sense we are dealing with demonic beings. In the book of Revelation, chapter 9, there is a prophecy of things to come during the Great Tribulation (last 3.5 years) which simulates that of an alien being.

"A star that had fallen from the sky to the earth the star was given the key to the shaft of the abyss. When he opened the Abyss, smoke rose from it like the smoke from a gigantic furnace. The sun and sky were darkened by the smoke from the Abyss. And out of the smoke locusts came down upon the earth and were given power-like that of scorpions of the earth. They were told not to harm the grass of the earth or any plant

or tree, but only those people who did not have the seal of God on their foreheads..... "

It continues to describe these 'beings' looking like scorpions and their function is to torment people for five months. It mentions their king as the king of the Abyss, Abaddon whose other names are Beelzebub or satan or lucifer.

Further articles found in Journals such as Nexus have also verified the existence of electromagnetic forces being used for mind control TODAY! These news clips state the following:

*Electromagnetic Manipulation of our minds and GM foods are being used as mass mind control!
*Chemtrails are seen performing criss- cross patterns for no apparent reason when the sky is clear and blue. After the manoeuvres the sky turns grey and cloudy, screening out the sun. The next day is usually dull, windy or rain. It is thought these planes spray harmful chemicals that cool the atmosphere. It is also thought the chemicals are arsenic (a poison), Lead (damages the brain), Cadmium (shrinks the skeletal bones), and Aluminium (links to Alzheimers). The planes (jets) drop out chemical substances that lie on the ground, fall on the food crops, enter into animals through fodder and ultimately breathed in by humans. Research has suggested these chemtrails are the cause for people becoming sick
   *A recent article in Nexus magazine Global News section, gave an update on GM foods. It stated that rice (named Frankenrice referring to the mad scientist Frankenstein who made a monster); this rice has contaminated global food supply. It may be possible that ALL rice has already become GM. This GM rice comes from an American Multinational Corporation, BAYER CROPSCIENCE. Apparently 3 varieties of GM rice was not approved or authorised for cultivation or consumption anywhere in the world, but has been discovered in 30 countries worldwide. Source: Naturalnews.com 3 July 2013 or http://tinyurl.com/koy7eb3

There is ample evidence available to prove the items discussed in this book.

The reader should visit the local libraries, read newspapers and surf the web for information and subscribe to receive regular news updates.

I would recommend the News websites used in this book as they are probably reliable sources, however, there are many professional news reporting websites.
Also use Christian /Judaic websites to gain the whole picture.

Revelation TV is an excellent television station for information on current events. They are also the best and most spirit filled and therefore the most accurate interpreters of God's word the bible. [Beware they also have franchise TV programs that may not be reliable].

This book has provided tasters of some of the key events to forewarn and bring awareness to people being deceived!

PART 2

PART 2 PROVIDES ANSWERS AS TO WHAT CAN BE DONE ABOUT THE ISSUES IN PART 1 FROM A PRACTICAL AND BIBLICAL PERSPECTIVE.

Psalm 121:7

The LORD shall preserve thee from all evil: he shall preserve thy soul.

CHAPTER 9

A SUMMARY

This chapter will summarise part 1 as a reminder of the key points, so that solutions can be applied accordingly. There's some additional information included.

In part 1 a great variety of evidence was supplied to authenticate current world events and how these events relate to biblical prophecy associated with these end times, particularly concerning the worldwide apostasy and how it came into being.

We have also seen how mind control has played a significant part in this world apostasy. The various mind control techniques used, have influenced different communities and individuals, according to their susceptibility to being controlled. For example, a teenager would be the most easily controllable as they are willing and receptive via their peers, through music, the school curriculum and alcohol or drugs, to mention but a few.

Poor (third world) countries are already susceptible because of their vulnerability while western societies are going through a financial crisis which has created a division between the wealthy and the poor. The poor are bound up by debt, poverty, sickness and homelessness while the majority of wealthy citizens are controlled by their wealth, status, influence and power, their materialism enslaves them and therefore they are easy prey for the web of deception. They are candidates for involvement in corruption which opens doors to susceptibility to mind control and compliance like anyone else!

Evidently, the methods of control used were mostly covert but since year 2010 it has become more overt!

From the various evidence supplied it has been revealed that we can soon expect a total takeover of every nation which has already been divided into hemispheres and our countries are being forced to close specific export products to focus on one allocated export of goods as dictated by New World Order Elite. Each country will specialize in productivity of one product i.e.

one country produces all the wheat for their particular hemisphere, while another country will produce lamb and so on.

The food industry is about to change, a large organisation called Monsanto is in the process of taking control of all the seed production worldwide. All seeds will be genetically modified and many foods will contain drug additives, and other substances that will affect every inhabitant physically and mentally!

David Icke is well known as a conspiracy theorist investigator, as far as is known, he is not a 'Spirit-filled Believer' However, he has contributed to an understanding of the 'behind the scenes activity' of the N.W.O. For many years he has been a watcher of the illuminati activities and how they are linked to the New World Order. He has many videos on the subject, particularly on mind control.

David Icke's YouTube videos, found on the internet, provide additional knowledge of events taking place today, in relation to biblical prophecy. Some of the things he revealed were beyond belief. Yet fall in line with biblical prophecy it was possible to piece the biblical references to the things he was reporting.

David interviewed a woman who was able to provide answers. Arizona Wilder explained she had been involuntary involved with the illuminati since she was a child. She had been born specifically by her illuminati parents as property of the illuminati elite. She testified to being abused and traumatised, a common method of control used so that she would become compliant and obedient (through fear) to do whatever the illuminati members commanded her to do. She had witnessed the killing of children as human sacrifices and other children were trained to kill, programmed to commit murder and other acts of evil. On one occasion a child committed suicide on the command of their programmer.

This programming takes place in America and Britain. Psychologists are used as the programmers. Arizona's programmer was a German who performed scientific experiments on Jewish children during WW2. Because of his knowledge he was asked to join the illuminati as a programmer. After his death Arizona was no longer under his control so she was able to escape and since then she has bravely disclosed the horrors taking place behind the scenes.

The contents are too shocking to report everything however this book has covered snippets of David Ickes discoveries and Arizona's exposure regarding illuminati activities and their ultimate goals. These can be linked to biblical prophecy of these end times. The illuminati have been described as reptiles which also describes the dragon that the bible uses to describe lucifer (the beast to come).

From this we now know that lucifer will be the world leader during the Great Tribulation period. He has many secret organisations working for him, while he hides in the background, waiting for the day when he can come out into the open to claim his throne. We are very close to the start of the Tribulation; lucifer's plans are almost complete! It has been declared that in year 2017 in USA, and may also apply to all nations; the government will require everyone to receive the microchip implant into their body. This will fall in line with the full introduction of the cashless system, the restrictions for purchasing and trading goods and services, and the segregation between those who received the mark of the beast (and/or the microchip) and those who refused. All of these factors will produce the biblically prophesied event whereby those without the mark will not be able to buy and sell. It will be rather like the ghetto Jews during WW2, they were not permitted to work or trade or continue in business. This had dire results! If the microchip is indeed enforced in 2017 it suggests we are already in the first 3 .5 years of the Tribulation! It would coincide with the events of recent years either from 2010 or 2012 as previously mentioned in earlier chapters.

Mind control experimentation has been piloted over the past few decades and now we are entering the period where the mind control is no longer piloted, but now in use! It has been orchestrated according to inhabitant's age and status and level of suggestibility. Derren Brown demonstrated how easy it is to do mass mind control using autosuggestion techniques.

Derren Brown an Illusionist performed experiences on television using mind control techniques. One of his programs was to prove that it is possible to do a mass hypnosis. He did this by hypnotizing the whole audience all in one go. Another time he wanted to prove it was possible to program someone to go out and assassinate a person. Obviously Derren orchestrated this so that no one was hurt but he managed to show that an innocent person could be manipulated by using triggers during a meeting where Derren used subliminal techniques to implant those 'trigger' words into the mind of the potential assassin.

David Icke reported that London Tavistock Institute is the centre of mind control research.

Mind control is about manipulation, controlling how people behave and think, to produce compliance so they 'accept' events that are taking place in the world. For example a few decades ago witches were encouraged publicly to discuss witchcraft and their particular practise. As a result of this publicity people have accepted the practice of witchcraft as normal behaviour and part of 'normal' society. Following on from this came the Harry Potter books and more recently the next stage of the process was to desensitize the world to occult practices by mass film production on the subject and producing spell books etc. There are many such books on sale now!

This witchcraft was never accepted by society before, yet today witches are accepted as part of the community. Satanists walk the streets wearing black clothing, occult tattoos all over their bodies and occult symbols as jewellery, whereas they would have been a secret society who frequented the graveyards during the night, and would only venture out during the day in disguise, for fear of discovery, which meant the ducking stool or burning at the stake or in more modern society –imprisonment. This change, acceptance of evil, demonstrates how people's minds have been conditioned and desensitized to accept evil. Society accepts many things that were once taboo.

No one would have accepted little girls wearing tight miniskirts and make- up but now it is normal practise.

No one would have accepted abortions or hire as employees, men who prefer to dress and behave as a woman, or women who prefer to dress and behave like men, let alone entrust an innocent child into such people's hands!

It is not that difficult to perform a mass hypnotic mind control of the world population once Television, Technology,

Printing Companies, Psychological, Medical Institutions and Computers come under the control of authority figures such as the EU, UN etc who work ultimately for the Illuminati who ultimately control and orchestrate the New World Order!

Psychologists have researched the mind and in 1950s Wilder Penfield performed surgery on an epileptic patient and discovered he could manipulate the brain to produce memories. Stimulation from external stimuli produces our perceptions and therefore our actions, i.e. the hot sun triggers our thoughts into the action of putting on sunglasses to protect our eyes. This was done consciously; however, subconsciously it is possible for someone else to trigger your brain to respond to electrical impulses implanted in your brain.

Psychology has developed rapidly over the past 2 decades, from the initial research on brain functionality, personality traits and memories to knowing how to manipulate memories, to alter behaviour and brain functionality using classical and operant conditioning methods and mind control techniques.

It has been mentioned earlier that control over the mass population has come about from the slow introduction to wickedness and evil by discrediting everything that is good (i.e. God, the Bible, Christianity and Judaism), and to produce a secular, humanistic society. For this to be effective the methods used must guarantee total on-going compliance by the population so that future plans could be set in place without hindrance.

A number of methods were used to produce this result.

Firstly, long term plans which commenced decades ago, to condition the public to accept certain wicked/evil behaviour i.e., abortion, sexual immorality, violent acts. In these end times these acts are considered normal everyday occurrences.

Society often makes judgements about situations and makes excuses for the perpetrators, often accusing or blaming the victim instead! The perpetrators are usually supported in court and often have free legal representation whereas the victims are not offered the same support! An example of this was a case whereby an elderly man confronted two men who illegally entered his property for the second time to rob him. He was ready for these intruders with a gun. In defence he shot one of the intruders. The elderly man was sent to prison for a few years while the intruder was rewarded with injury compensation.

The aim of the overall plan is to desensitize the world; to bring them to a state where they hunger for violence; as evidenced by the TV and Films people prefer to watch, in particular the 'reality' programmes where contestants are judged and phased out according to their popularity with the viewers. This simulates the thumbs up /thumbs down the Romans used in the arena whereby the loser of the fight had his fate, to live or die, in the hands of the people! They would decide his fate, whether the Gladiator should live or die, based on entertainment value and their lust for blood, and they would indicate their choice by a thumb down for death or a thumb up for life! . Life had no value then and the same applies today in many societies.

People have already been conditioned to ignore a person's feelings. Competitive reality television programs contestants are criticized, condemned and character assassinated, voting and booing them off the stage. Programs such as X Factor, Big Brother etc can be quite ruthless. People are already back in the place where Christ Yeshua (Jesus) stood before Pilate the Roman Governor and the people chose a known murderer to be set free rather than an innocent son of God who came to save the people from such evil!

Secondly reduce the population to a more manageable level by controlling the population through disease from chemical pollution in the air (Jet chemtrails), in food (GM Products and additives), excessive stress from daily pressures of overwork, traumatic experiences, excessive debt and financial difficulties etc. Maintaining poverty and famine levels in specific target areas is a key part of the plan. As well as continuing wars and civil unrest which claims many lives as these situations are used to ethnically cleanse non-compliant communities. During Aug 2013 Syria used biological/chemical weapons on its own people killing many!

Thirdly, use leaders of nations to adopt the psychological methods used by hitler, to train their own people ready to administer mind control techniques to their own people.

Fourthly, implant specific mind controlling signals, triggers, and eventually the microchip.

Finally, to induce into all subjects an addiction, deprivation and debts that will guarantee a worldwide 'hopelessness and helplessness, to ensure full dependency, submission and compliance.

The most important point here and must be emphasized is that satan is responsible for all of this yet it is orchestrated to POINT THE FINGER AT GOD! The world blames the Almighty Creator for everything that goes wrong in their lives and in the world! Let it be known that as mentioned before God allows these things to happen for a reason, and there are times when he fulfils His prophesies or exert judgement i.e. earthquakes etc as foretold by Christ in Matthew 24, Isaiah and the other prophets.

It is important that the reader distinguishes between God's judgements and the evil events orchestrated by satan. God's full and final judgements on the world will be put into action during the final seven years (Tribulation Period) similarly, God exerted plagues on the Egyptians through Moses at the early stages of Mankind's existence, as written in Exodus 7. The story is about Pharaoh who enslaved God's people and would not let them go. Pharaoh put enormous pressure on the slaves, through hard work, starvation and cruel punishments. God gave Pharaoh many opportunities to release His people the Israelites, but Pharaoh refused. So God brought down on him and the Egyptians many plagues until Pharaoh let his people go. Pharaoh is a simile of satan. The world is in a similar situation as the Israelites were in Egypt. Once again God uses His chosen people, the Israelites, to foretell the last days scenario! Satan is another Pharaoh who has enslaved not only the Jews (Israelites) but all peoples of the world. He enforces great suffering on the people by starving them, imposing severe punishment and suffering and will not let them go free. Therefore, God brings down terrible plagues worse than the ones in Moses time. These plagues will affect all of satan's army (and those with his mark of ownership) but the plagues will not touch those with God's holy seal of ownership!

The recent internal wars in the Middle East are all part of the global plan instigated by satan but God has also prophesied this would happen and that he would confuse their minds, so there are dual events that occur whereby both satan and God are involved – this is the war that is taking place between God and satan! Countries are fighting within their own country with their own people and killing each other. Many people of all nations are dying of 'HUMAN PRODUCED' starvation, diseases and wars! All of this was foretold by God in His word!

"See, the Day of the Lord is coming – a cruel day, with wrath and fierce anger – to make the land desolate and destroy the sinners within it....I will punish the world for its evil, the wicked for their sins....therefore I will make the heavens tremble; and the earth will shake from its place at the wrath of the Lord Almighty... Isaiah 13: 9-13.

"The oppressor will come to an end, and destruction will cease; the aggressor will vanish from the land.
In love a throne will be established;
In faithfulness a man will sit on it
One from the house of David, one who in judging seeks justice and speeds the cause of righteousness.
Isaiah 14: 4-12 this verse speaks of satan's doom see also Isaiah 14:12-17. It also speaks of Yeshua's reign!

God says in Isaiah 48: 3, *"I foretold the former things long ago, my mouth announced them and I made them known; then suddenly I acted, and they came to pass."*

"For I knew how stubborn you were; the sinews of your neck were iron, your forehead was bronze.
Therefore I told you these things long ago; before they happened I announced them to you so that you could not say, 'my idols did them, my wooden image and metal god ordained them." Isaiah 48:4.

"From now on I will tell you of new things, hidden things unknown to you. They are created now, and not long ago you

have not heard of them before today. You have neither heard nor understood from of old your ear has not been open." Isaiah 48:6-8.

"Return *to me with all your heart, with fasting and weeping and mourning." Joel 2:12*

"Rend your heart and not your garments.

Return to the Lord your God,

For He is gracious and compassionate,

Slow to anger and abounding in love,

and he relents from sending calamity" Joel 2: 13

CHAPTER 10

<u>WHAT CAN BE DONE ABOUT IT?</u>

There are many ways to avoid mind control from an individual's perspective and some of these solutions are provided in this chapter, however, there is not so much that can be done about 'mass mind control' except to encourage people to buy this book and to promote it on the internet so that people become aware. Some would say this is 'scare mongering' but that is just another ruse to prevent people from knowing the truth. Some would say this is a book that is trying to scare people into accepting Christ and Christianity! The time for gentle evangelism has passed; we are now in the phrase of direct evangelism for the saving of souls during a 'Terrible Time of Trouble!' Would you rather be left to your own devices whereby your soul is sent to hell! Or would you rather someone told you the truth concerning these terrible times so that you may make the right decision? There have been ample opportunities during the past decades to listen to gentle evangelism, read books on the Gospel of Christ, to attend church services or meetings! Now with so many people who have been born never to have entered a church or synagogue, who have never heard of Christ nor have any knowledge of God, these people deserve the 'full on' truth!

The only way today to reach an apostate world is by presenting 'full on facts', even though those facts may be frightening! The barriers of desensitization, the hardened hearts and the buried or concrete heads need hard facts to break through –to reach the subdued emotions of guilt and conviction! God will do this in many cases, the Holy Spirit will pierce the soul and convict many, but it is also the duty of believers to attempt to break through by whatever means is necessary to save that soul from perishing!

The two articles below are relative to the contents of this book and very helpful so I decided to enclose them. Permission to include the articles was given by 'Revive Israel Ministries' website.

Don't Harden Your Heart

by Asher Intrater

The Bible warns us not to let our hearts be hardened. Hebrews 3:7-8 (Psalm 95:7-8)

As the Holy Spirit says, "Today if you hear His voice, do not harden your hearts as in the rebellion."

Physically, if even a small piece of a person's heart becomes hard, he is in mortal danger of a stroke. Spiritual hardening of the heart is likewise mortally dangerous. We can hear the voice of God through Scripture meditation and by the still small voice of God within our spirit and conscience (I Kings 19:12, Romans 8:16; 9:1).

When we feel that inner prompting of the Lord, we immediately have a choice: either to submit and obey; or to resist and rebel. We need a soft heart to submit. A hardened heart will cause us to resist.

There are many things that can cause our heart to be stiff and hard, such as anger, offenses, wounded pride, fear, pain, rejection, lies, unforgiveness, lusts, etc. Because of lawlessness in the end times the love of many will "grow cold" (Matthew 24:12), people will become "lovers of themselves" (2 Tim 3:1-8).

We need to guard our hearts from all evil, not allowing our heart to get hard or cold. A soft heart will hear and absorb the spiritual "sound waves" of the voice of the Lord. Those same voice waves will bounce off a hardened heart. The voice of the Lord, when we do receive it and submit to it, will radiate into our inner being like a spiritual "microwave," softening and warming our hearts in love.

This Present Darkness
By Patty Juster,

It does not take great spiritual discernment to see and to feel the present darkness around us in the world today. This darkness at times almost suffocates. All one has to do is to read the newspaper or listen to people on the street to know that the world is in a serious condition.

Isaiah 60:1-2 "Arise, shine, for your light has come and the glory of the Lord rises upon you. See, darkness covers the earth and thick darkness is over the peoples, but the Lord rises upon you and his glory appears over you."

Sometimes we are unaware of how this blanket of darkness can affect even the most mature of believers. Its influence may begin to penetrate our soul. Then, the door is open to despair, disappointment, depression, apathy and complacency. It is as if one has fallen asleep. The disciples could not stay awake even for an hour with Yeshua in the Garden of Gethsemane. They were laden with sorrow, which put them to sleep. The word for "deep darkness" in verse 2 is *araphel*, which means "fog." We may experience this as blurry or confusing thoughts.

The good news is that no darkness can hide us from the presence of the Lord (Psalm 139:11-12). And Isaiah 9:2 speaks of the coming of the Messiah as being a great light to a people living in darkness. As Yeshua was a light shining in great darkness, so are we. It is time to focus on the light so that the glory of the Lord will shine through us to those around us.

The weapons of our warfare are not carnal but powerful through God for pulling down strongholds; casting down imaginations, and every high thing that exalts itself against the knowledge of God, bringing into captivity every thought to the obedience of Christ" **2 Corinthians 10:4-5.**

Do not allow anyone to get into your mind; do not allow anything to distract you from TRUTH and reality! Your mind is an important part of who you are, it allows you to make decisions, and it allows you to think for yourself! It allows you to communicate with the Almighty Creator.

Do not allow anyone or anything to take control of your mind!

Another important aspect is your soul! Your soul is also a very crucial part of you. Your chosen decision for your destiny is the one that decides whether your soul takes precedence in your life or whether your soul is placed in the hands of the savior. It is the savior who is able to replace your soul with the Holy Spirit. When you make the choice to follow Christ, the Holy Spirit is sent to teach you God's ways, to help you through a 'New Birth' into the kingdom of God.

This new birth is a conscious and decisive choice to accept Christ as your Lord and Savior, to denounce evil and wickedness, to ask Christ's forgiveness for your sin, to forgive yourself and accept Christ has forgiven you, to die to self and be reborn into righteousness through water baptism and receiving the baptism of the Holy Spirit as your counsellor and teacher!

It is the soul that is placed in the safety of the Great and Mighty hand of God, so that the devil cannot claim it!

However, the alternative to the above is that the soul is snatched by lucifer to be enslaved for ever in his world of hell! That means, if this is your choice, you will spend the rest of your days under the control of the dragon not only in this world but also after your body dies!

319

It is therefore essential to be covered by the blood of the lamb (Christ) as a means of retaining your freedom OF MIND! Christ promises salvation and eternal life. The Holy Spirit alerts the believer against such things as subliminal messages, hypnotic and mind altering drugs or sound waves. God's gifts of discernment, wisdom, and knowledge protect against being directed away from the path that leads to the Kingdom of God. However, the person who chooses to accept the beast's mark is vulnerable and susceptible to all the evil being used to claim souls.

Although people have been misled, deceived and controlled, this does not excuse them from being sinners and committing sin against God. The fact that an individual choose to ignore God and reject him as well as ignore his signs and warnings suggest rebellion is already in the heart and therefore easy prey for the devil to use the person as a tool in his overall plan! The person will be accountable for their sins even if they are deceived or controlled by satan!

People have gradually been manipulated over the past 20 years or so to accept new technology as a necessity to advancement. The creation of new technology has been welcomed as a means of increasing knowledge and the ability to communication more effectively.

Today people have become conditioned (and desensitised) to the dangers of new technology. People are now eager for the next new invention; there is an eagerness to purchase new technology as soon as it reaches the headlines! The old saying 'keeping up with the Jones' has never been more true than it is today! People have an insatiable, uncontrollable desire to own the latest technology, without questioning the consequences!

It is this readiness to accept anything new that has conditioned, particularly the young, to accept and trust whatever comes next, such as the latest technological breakthrough, the new Google Glasses. These glasses are expected to be introduced to the world in 2013! Then many young people will be totally controlled through this equipment. Their minds would be tampered with in such a way that it would lead to their destruction! All ready young people have lost the ability to converse with others using their mouths! The new form of communication has become a slang language of abbreviations and codes, written within a text or social networking in short coded sentences! Image what a new idea like these glasses will do to their mind. Apparently, these glasses will need a microchip inserted into the head to use the glasses. This will probably start as a pilot (without the implant) then once people have become addicted to the glasses they will take it to the next stage – the implant- which will offer extra capabilities.

These glasses should be avoided at all costs!

Below is a report from NTEB News Desk regarding a Company called 'Googleplex' at Mountain View.

Larry Page, Google co-founder and CEO, rushed out a blog to deny claims in leaked NSA documents that it – in parallel with other American internet giants – had been co-operating with the spying programme since 2009. "Any suggestion that Google is disclosing information about our users' internet activity on such a scale is completely false," he said.
Trust is everything to Google

It stands on the verge of a technological breakthrough that can transform its relationship with us. Already, it is universally recognised as the world leader in searching for information. It handles around 90 per cent of internet searches in the UK: when we want to know something, most of us turn to Google. But it wants more – it wants to become our constant companion.

The rapid evolution of mobile technology has brought new opportunities to a business generating annual revenue in excess of $50bn (£33.7bn). It began, just 15 years ago, as a service that enabled you to type a request into a personal computer and be given links to associated websites. Things have rather moved on. Soon Google hopes to have the ubiquitous presence of a personal assistant that never stops working, capable of conversing naturally in any language. Ultimately, as Page and co-founder Sergey Brin have asserted, the goal is to insert a chip inside your head for the *most effortless search engine imaginable. Some will find this prospect exciting. Others might want to call for Dick Tracy.*

The first stage of this new level of intimacy is Google Glass, which I am invited to trial as part of a briefing on the company's future plans

My first impression is that this revolutionary contraption is remarkably unobtrusive. It looks like a pair of glasses and, at 36 grams, weighs about the same as a typical pair of sunglasses due to its largely titanium frame. Despite the chunkiness of the right temple – made from plastic and where all the technology is stored – there is no sense of imbalance.

The awkwardness only starts when you start to interact. You turn the contraption on by tapping your finger on the right side of the frame, or surreptitiously throwing your head back. On a screen projected a few inches in front of your right eyeball is a digital clock and the magic words "OK glass", the uttering of which takes you to a range of task options: ask a question, take a picture, record a video, get directions to, send a message to, make a call to, make a video call to.

The idea of Google Glass is that you can walk down busy streets receiving helpful facts – without needing to take your mobile phone from your pocket. It could end the urban hazard of pedestrians staring at their mobiles instead of looking where they're going.

At the moment it's a work in progress, which is why the prototype is called the Explorer and the 10,000 American-based pioneers who are trialling the apparatus – mostly web developers and heavy social-media users – are dubbed "explorers".

Does it work? Yes and no. Answering questions is its central feature. It likes straightforward instruction such as "OK Glass... Google – what is the height of David Cameron?", returning within four seconds with an image of the Prime Minister and a computer voice telling me "David Cameron is six feet zero inches tall". But when I ask for the name of the wife of his predecessor, Gordon

Brown, I'm offered details of "Golden Brown", a hit for The Stranglers in 1982.

The camera and video option is novel and discreet, except when you bark out the words: "OK Glass, take a picture!" Three seconds after giving the order, you have a shot (or film) which you can share with friends on the Google+ social network. One Explorer recently used Google Glass to snap a police arrest as it was taking place. The potential is enormous: a proud mum could film her son taking a penalty kick in a football match while dad, abroad but connected through the Google Hangout service, could watch the action live through his wife's Google Glass. The more you hand your life over to Google, the more you get out of this technology.

Google Glass is part of a wider ecosystem and is not currently intended as an alternative to a mobile phone but as a complement to it. Glass needs the mobile in your pocket to locate your position and connect to your contacts via 4G and Bluetooth. Rather than encouraging users to be constantly gibbering in public, the default position for this device is "off", I am told. The screen has been positioned above the eye line and at two o'clock on a clock face to ensure that the people you are with know from your squint when you are consulting Glass.

But none of these caveats can conceal the scale of Google's ambition. It is staking its future on a vast store of information called the Knowledge Graph, which is growing at an exponential rate. When it launched in May 2012, Knowledge Graph was a pool of 3.5 billion facts on 500 million of the world's most searched subjects. In a little over a year the knowledge held on the Google servers has grown to 18 billion facts on around 570 million subjects.

This Knowledge Graph is the base for Google Now, the latest incarnation of Google which is personalising the search engine by giving you a series of bespoke "cards" as you log on. They tell you the local weather, the traffic you might face on the way to work, details of your meetings and restaurant bookings taken from your Google email account, your team's latest result and so on.

In Building 43 of the Googleplex, Ben Gomes talks with barely concealed excitement about a "new epoch". A Google fellow and the company's Vice President of Search he has been working on these technologies for 14 years. "[Knowledge Graph] is everything you have at some point asked a query about – plus everything that everyone else has thought of!" he exclaims. "It's a meld of all the world's interests and information needs."

The future, he says, is for this enormous resource to be "present everywhere". It's a long step from the British Council library in Bangalore, where Gomes used to go to obtain his reading matter. "You borrowed a book – if it was available – and then you read it and got the next book. I got two books and that was all the information that I had for a week," he says. "Today it would be unthinkable for that [information] not to be available in seconds."

Google's options have grown with recent advances in speech-recognition technology (it can now decipher 35 languages) and in natural-language processing, the "holy grail" that means the computer can understand what is being spoken (for example, knowing that "tall" refers to height) and hold a conversation. The "OK Google..." voice-prompted search tool (already installed on mobile apps) is to become standard on the Google Chrome engine.

Scott Huffman, Google's engineering director, says the company's intention is to "transform the ways people interact with Google". That means having conversations similar to those you would have with humans. No longer will we have to go to "settings" to recalibrate our devices – we will simply order them to make the desired changes. And those devices will not be in our pockets – but all around us in every room.

"If you look back 10 years there was a computer on my desk and today there's a computer in my pocket and it still has a screen and a keyboard," says Huffman.

"But fast forward a bit and... I think there is going to be a device in the ceiling with microphones, and it will be in my glasses or my wristwatch or my shirt. And like the Google Glass it won't have a keyboard... you just say 'OK Google, blah-blah-blah' and you get what you want." Where will it end?

Gomes agrees that a chip embedded in the brain is far from a sci-fi fantasy. "Already people are beginning to experiment with handicapped people for manoeuvring their wheelchairs," he says. "They are getting a few senses of direction with the wheelchair but getting from there to actual words is a long ways off. We have to do this in the brain a lot better to make that interaction possible. We have impatience for that to happen but the pieces of technology have to develop."

Any visitor to the Googleplex will testify that this is not a regular company. By lunchtime, Googlers are out on the sand of the beach volleyball court. A statue of a dinosaur skeleton – a pointed juxtaposition of past and future – has been decorated with model pink flamingos, hanging from its bones. Around the central patio there are awnings in Google-style primary colours which add to the impression of a holiday resort.

Building 43 is decorated with a giant model of Virgin Galactic's Space Ship One, donated by Sir Richard Branson, and Building 2000 has a long, silver, swirling slide that allows you to bypass the stairs.

It's no wonder people want to work here. About 10,000 do. But the company gets two million applications a year, a demand reflected in the new Hollywood movie The Internship, which was partly filmed at the Googleplex. . Source - Independent UK . NTEB News Desk | July 22, 2013 at 5:07 pm |

Now the above clip is the very latest evidence of mind control taking place in this world! It doesn't take a genius to understand the implications of such technology in relation to receiving 'the mark of the beast'. People will become conditioned to readily accept this mark without any resistance, because it will be seen as advancement for mankind. Only those 'born of the spirit of God would see its folly and danger!

Understand this! Your mind is a valuable commodity for the beast! He wants to own every person's MIND, body, SOUL and strength. He wants to prevent these minds from focusing on his opposition which is Christ Yeshua and God, so that he (the

Beast – lucifer) can take possession of you totally – lucifer's goal is to enslave, whereas Yeshua's goal is to set you free!

The many types of evidence supplied in Part 1 should have convinced the reader that something terrible is going on behind the scenes! Now the natural, human thing to do is to panic and reach for a bottle of whisky, or go into a deep depression or maybe to shrug your shoulders and carry on partying, living life to the full. However, if the reader would like to turn their life around there are better options than just waiting for death, drinking into oblivion or falling into a depression.

The following clip is an example of a family that turned their lives around when they found what Christ could do for them!

Joy for Mourning

Alon and Hannah were born in Colombia.

They immigrated to Israel and became part of our community. A few years ago, Alon's older brother in Columbia was murdered in cold blood on the street, shot by masked men.

About six months ago, his dear niece was shot on the street, again by masked assailants. The closely knit family was devastated. Last month came yet another call. Alon's younger brother, leaving his business at the end of the day, was shot in cold blood. Alon, a burly man, broke down and cried. As a community we decided to help Alon and Hannah fly to Columbia to visit the family.

Hannah shares "As we visited family members, Alon proclaimed the kingdom of God and exhorted them to repent. He explained that only Yeshua can stop these tragedies."

Repeatedly, individual family members would call and ask to speak with Alon. Their hearts had been softened. By the end of the trip all 60 extended family members had prayed to receive the Lord!

"A touching moment was visiting the family of the brother who was recently murdered. The wife and daughter were distraught, and the son bitter and vengeful. However, upon hearing the good news, all three prayed with Alon, and the son melted in his arms. Yeshua had replaced the anger with healing love.

Alon and Hannah came back to Israel with joy in their hearts. Although the healing will take time, the Lord turned a devastating tragedy into victory.

What can we do about it? What can we do about these world events?

How can we avoid mind control?

And how can we avoid the pending 'Tribulation' period?

There are many approaches to answering this question, three of which are:

- ❖ The spiritual approach,
- ❖ The psychological approach
- ❖ The practical approach

It seems logical to start with the most important and most powerful approach that will equip the reader with all the necessary tools to safeguard against mind control and against the coming influences and forces such as the one world religion and the mark of the beast. It is the first of the three – the spiritual approach.

The other two approaches will blend in with the Spiritual approach as each of these are related to the spiritual resolution.

Up until reading this book, the reader has been either, an atheist, an agnostic or a believer in some sort of spiritual or materialistic concept.

There are different types of believers as listed:

• Someone who believes there is a superior being that is called God. This is most of the population, including atheist, agnostics and pagans.

• Someone who knows there is a God but does not know him personally. There are those who fall into this category that have 'intellectual' understanding of God but does not have His Spirit within them. This type of person are usually puffed up with pride, they know all the answers, read all the books, and debate about truth yet are often way off the truth!

• Someone who says he is a Christian because he lives by

righteous moral standards and therefore believes to be a Christian but is merely a morally upright person.

- Another type tries to achieve salvation and eternal life through good works.
- There is also the part-time believer who accepts there is a God yet prefers to live in the world rather than walk with God in his kingdom,
- There is also a type that serves two masters, it can be God and Satan, or God and materialism, but usually it is God and Humanism!
- There are believers who have backslidden, prodigal sons and daughters, or believers still under the slavery of sin and worldly influences, preferring what the world has to offer because they have not yet discovered the delights of God's Kingdom!
- This is a person who is sitting on the fence not quite sure who is what and what it is all about. Yet believe there is a good force and a bad force at work.
- Ultimately, there are those who believe there is a God yet they openly choose to serve Lucifer!

Many churches put people off becoming believers by saying they will spend the rest of eternity worshipping God! This gives a false picture! Who wants to spend eternity on their knees praising God every minute of their day? This is the picture they are getting! God's kingdom is much more than that!

Adam and Eve are examples of a life in heaven where they did not have to work hard for their food, it was supplied, they did not suffer sickness or pain, and they walked and talked with God. They had a life! They did not worship God all day long!

Obviously worship will be a natural occurrence of the heart and a continuous implicit thankfulness in the person's loyalty and actions. And yes there will be times of explicit adoration and thanksgiving of our God and King Christ Yeshua. In the same way as we show adoration for our Queen and the royal family. Only the praise and adoration will be much greater than that given to a mere mortal and of course will include worship! God would be worthy of such as he provides us with wonderful gifts, a splendid life in safety and his continuous love and care!

The 9 categories or types of believer, demonstrate that to believe in God does not necessarily mean they are true believers. The devil (lucifer) believes there is a God – he knows there is! And he knows that he lucifer, his fallen angels, the rest of mankind and the world were all created by God! Yet he defiantly rejects God!

There may also be readers who are truly born again and therefore already have the knowledge of God's saving power and promises!

Therefore it is important first to define which type of believer you are. Whether you believe there is a good God and an adversary - a force of evil that opposes all things good.

Once you have decided what type of believer you are, you then need to decide whether you want to do something about it, or whether you want to 'take your chances' and plod along as always and hope for the best.

For those readers who have been affected by the contents of this book may be in fear and therefore want to do something about saving themselves, their families and friends from the future Tribulation period.

To be able to do this you need a firm foundation in the true faith! All of the 9 types mentioned in the above list, lack a firm foundation. A firm foundation is essential and will be explained in more detail later.

The Lord shall preserve thee from all evil:
    He shall preserve thy soul.

This is God's promise to those who have a firm foundation in His Son Christ Yeshua! This is the only way to receive this promise and the only way to receive eternal life!

In these end times God will reveal all false hoods to his people. The Jews have been blinded for a while but then

God will remove the scales from their eyes.

He will speak to his people and those who are seeking His way; he will guide them into righteousness and salvation through his son Christ Yeshua. However, this will be during the Tribulation period – the time of real troubles.

I am sure however that you would want to avoid this period and therefore seek a solution prior to this end time period. At this point it is important for you to face your sins, face your rebellion, face your defiance towards God and bring it to the surface of your mind, acknowledge it, recall how you laughed and mocked when people mentioned God or Christ, when you were informed of how he died on the cross for you – you laughed and walked away! Think of the times when you had heard the message of salvation and rejected it! Then ask for forgiveness! Reveal to God your inner fears, your hurts, your disappointments, unburden yourself onto Christ's listening ears!

***

A great deal has been revealed within the public domain. In recent years there has been many disclosures regarding corruption amongst politicians, clergyman, TV and film stars. Secrets have been revealed to the world about child pornography and sexual abuse!

Recently Edward Snowden's revelations about the snooping of the US Government's National Security Agency (NSA) in its Clandestine Electronic Surveillance Programme Prism was well timed and has brought about all sorts of concerns which has now opened doors to further investigations. It has since been discovered that UK is also involved. The USA and UK have access to all of our information and not only that, they are able to zoom into our homes, our computers, our telephones etc to acquire information or to check on our activities!

This is a precedent!

Never before in history has anything like this ever occurred! Never before has governments or leaders ever had such power! This in itself should be enough to make people sit up and realise something is not right in the world!

This is not the time for naivety! It is not the time to bury your head in the sand, or try to romanticise events, or make excuses for events just to make life easier to bear! We all have a responsibility to ourselves and others to do something about it, and to prepare ourselves for the things ahead! WW2 came upon the Nations suddenly because people would not acknowledge it was coming! The same happened just before Noah's flood warnings, everyone chose to ignore his warnings and carried on partying, laughing, drinking, and working and then it happened suddenly!

The world is on the brink of its most evil period ever in all history of this world and the world before it! This evil force is about to take over the world population – its people, its nations and attempt to take over God's holy land and his Holy People. This is where he fails!

The good news is God is in control! However, the bad news is many things are going to happen to the inhabitants of this world before God intervenes and this is why it is important for the reader to take these events seriously and to make a decision to deal with it!

There will be a division of the people as mentioned before and this will determine each individual's destiny. The division will be made by lucifer, and God has allowed this, as it will also cause a division between the goats and the sheep! The goats will be those who have opted and will opt willingly, to follow and worship lucifer, as the god of this world. The sheep will be those who choose not to bow down to lucifer or worship him and have made an open allegiance to Christ!

In Isaiah 40:5 God says,

"And the Glory of the Lord will be revealed, and all mankind together will see it. For the mouth of the Lord has spoken."

When the Rapture occurs believers will be taken away by Christ, they will all be taken. This means that only those remaining, who did not choose to follow Christ, will remain on earth to endure the Great Tribulation period. It is these people who will see Christ return (after the Rapture of believers) as mentioned in the above scripture.

Some of those that are left behind will come to realize their error of not believing who Christ is and therefore make a decision to follow him! These believers will then be blessed and Christ says to them and all believers today:

"Maintain justice and do what is right for my salvation is close at hand and my righteousness will soon be revealed. Blessed is the man who does this, the man who holds it fast, who keeps the Sabbath without desecrating it, and keeps his hand from doing evil." Isaiah 56:1.

Again in Isaiah 56: 6, *" And foreigners who bind themselves to the Lord to serve him, to love the name of the Lord, and to worship him, all who keep the Sabbath without desecrating it and who hold fast to my covenant – these I will bring to my Holy Mountain and give them joy in my house of prayer. Their burnt offerings and sacrifices will be accepted on my altar for my house will be called a house of prayer for all nations." The Sovereign Lord declares – he who gathers the exiles of Israel: I will gather still others to them besides those already gathered."*

This is an interesting verse as it is full of information about God's plans after the Great Tribulation Period, when Christ Yeshua is taking his place as King and conqueror of this world.

Firstly it tells us that the verse applies not only to Jews but Gentile believers – STRANGERS (meaning believers other than Israelites, new to the Laws of God and Jewish Culture) also the passage of scripture reveals the importance of Gentile believers observing the Sabbath and holding on to the Covenant given to the Jews by God. Just like the Jews, the covenant is applicable to adopted children – Christians (strangers). It is these two groups that will be gathered to the Holy Temple on the Holy Mountain of Israel in Jerusalem.

The offerings and sacrifices mentioned are not the ancient sacrifices prior to Christ Yeshua; these are sacrifices of praise and offerings of thanksgiving. As it states it will be a house of prayer for ALL NATIONS. This means Syria, Egypt and all the other nations of the world will come to Jerusalem to the Temple to pray!

Below are some useful bible verses to help you further with your decision-making concerning your destiny.

"Those who live according to the sinful nature have their minds set on what the nature desires; but those who live in accordance with the Spirit have their minds set on what the Spirit desires.
The mind of sinful man is death, but the mind controlled by the Spirit is life and peace; the sinful mind is hostile to God. It does not submit to God's Law, nor can it do so. Those controlled by the sinful nature cannot please God." Romans Chapter 8

"Do not conform any longer to the pattern of this world, but be transformed by the renewing of your mind. Romans 12: 2

"See, the Lord is coming with fire,
And his chariots are like a whirlwind;
He will bring down his anger with fury,
And his rebuke with flames of fire.
For with fire and with his sword
The Lord will execute judgement upon all men,
and many will be those slain by the Lord.
Isaiah 66:15-16

The previous verse refers to those who choose to accept the mark of the beast and reject Christ Yeshua, preferring evil to good!

Revelation 3.5 He who overcomes will, like them, be dressed in white. I will never blot out his name from the book of life…

***

Those who consecrate and purify themselves to go into the gardens, following the one in the midst of those who eat the flesh of pigs and rats and other abominable things – they will meet their end together, declares the Lord.

This verse suggests that there are those believers who are hypocrites! They perform all the duties of the covenant, purifying and consecrating themselves yet indulge in unrighteous manner. They are involved with people who indulge in worldly wickedness! Therefore they will be judged and punished in the same way as the wicked!

The reader should read all of the verses from Isaiah 66: 17 to the end, as it has a promise of a new heaven and a new earth! This cross references with the book of Revelation.

In Revelation 22:7 Christ says, to his followers, ***"Behold, I am coming soon! Blessed is he who keeps the words of the prophecy in this book"***.

"He who overcomes will, like them, be dressed in white. I will never blot out his name from the book of life. But will acknowledge his name before my father and his angels." Revelation 3:5

The above verse is a message for those readers who have decided to follow Christ!

The Lord has done what he planned; he has fulfilled his word which he decreed long ago.

Lamentations 2: 17

The above picture of Proverbs 29:25 is very significant to the person who has become a new creature in Christ. There is no need to fear man, or beast, as neither are more powerful than God himself!

There is a prophecy and a promise that Christ the Messiah will return to rescue His people, to save His people and to take them into heaven after which there will be a new heaven and a new earth, whereby Christ will sit on the throne as the King of the world. He will then dwell with us forever!

There is nothing man or beast or lucifer can do to prevent this prophecy from coming to fruition!

CHAPTER 11

A FIRM FOUNDATION

A firm foundation is required during the difficult times ahead. To be safe from the effects of subliminal and hypnotic messages, and to resist the mind controlling techniques as well as the propaganda or false reporting set out to deceive, it is essential to firstly have God's protection through Christ Yeshua, which would then seal you against all attacks from the evil one!

Once a decision has been made to follow Christ rather than lucifer, there are various steps that need to be taken.

Yeshua says in Matt 7:7 **"seek and you shall find"**
Also in Matt 6:33 **"seek first his kingdom and his righteousness"**

To acquire this firm foundation, firstly acknowledge Christ Yeshua as the Son of God and Savior of the world. Secondly, acknowledge your sinful nature, that you need to be renewed, refined and purified and this comes from Christ as the atoner for our sinful natures. He is able to forgive us when we pronounce and denounce our sins to him.

If you have lied, committed adultery, been involved in pornography, committed a violent or corrupt act, had an abortion, deceived others etc; then you are to give up these sins to Christ who will forgive your sins and cleanse you.

Acknowledge that you are a person who intentionally and unintentionally commits sin; you have sinned against G-d in the past and the present. This sin and the denial of sin in your life is what separates you from G-d, it is preventing you from being born again and holy enough to enter G-d's future kingdom.

But it is possible to become as white as snow and forgiven of these past intentional sins and the future unintentional ones- in other words- it is possible to be forgiven for all your sinfulness and to become a 'new person' through Yeshua!

It is not necessary to be part of the Great Apostasy that sweeps throughout the world today!

Stand out from the crowd and declare your need to return to the Great God of the Nations!

It is not too late to turn your life around!

No matter how unworthy you feel, no matter how wicked you have been, no matter how rebellious you have been, you can be forgiven! And it is easy!

All you need to do is acknowledge:

Yeshua, son of God is the forgiver of sins
He died for YOU on that cross. He rose again and is **alive today!** He mediates between us and our Heavenly Father – the Creator of the Universe. **State these points as a prayer – speaking it from the heart! Prayer is speaking to God as you normally would speak.**

You then:

1. Tell Yeshua you are aware of the above
2. Confess and release your sins to him
3. Ask for forgiveness
4. Accept that he has forgiven you
5. Forgive yourself

It is as easy as that!

After you pray (speak) to Yeshua, he will acknowledge your sincerity of heart and will direct your path.

You should do the following:

1. Read the Bible.

2. Find a 'Born Again' teacher to help you grow and provide you with a firm foundation in your new faith. You will need sound spiritual support through your walk on the narrow road that leads you to eternal life in the Heavenly Kingdom! To find a good supportive church ask your savior to direct you to one and a person who studies a bible and prays.

3. You will need to acquire other gifts from the Holy Spirit to equip you for this walk.

Gifts such as:

1. Real Love – not the wishy washy love seen through a false smile, but the unconditional love that can love an enemy!

2. Discernment – the ability to understand what is happening around you, the needs of others, to detect liars and false teaching etc.

3. Wisdom - to receive the sevenfold teaching of God.

4. The Holy Armour – to protect you and many more!

These gifts are available to those who through Christ, desire righteousness, a righteous lifestyle and a faith in a living God who provides his people with all their needs. The Holy Spirit is the third person of the Trinity and his role is to teach and counsel you, he is also the provider of the Gifts, therefore if you ask you shall receive!

There are THREE important actions to be taken, to be truly equipped for the walk of salvation:

1. State the prayer to accept the Gospel of Christ, as mentioned above.

2. Be fully immersed in water as a baptism to outwardly evidence your commitment. The procedure cleanses you from your old life, dying to sin and being raised up into a new 'born again' sin forgiven life!

3. Receive the baptism of the Holy Spirit.

Yeshua demonstrated all of these through his ministry. He himself went through the waters of baptism and a dove settled on him. This dove represents the receiving of the Holy Spirit, Matthew 3:13-17

Yeshua says *"Seek and you shall find, Ask and it shall be given"* Matthew 7: 7

Psalm 24: 1 – 5 " *The Earth is the Lord's and everything in it, the World and all who live in it; for he founded it upon the seas and established it upon the waters.*

Who may ascend the hill of the Lord? Who may stand in his holy place? He who has clean hands and a pure heart; who does not lift up his soul to an idol or swear by what is false. He will receive blessing from the Lord and vindication from G-d his Savior."

A firm foundation is to be renewed in Christ – to become a new person, who has received the Holy Spirit gifts, such as wisdom, discernment, love, patience etc, but also endurance! It is the endurance that holds a person firmly in the faith. Enduring hardship until the end. Singing in Psalms, praising and thanksgiving sent up to heaven. These are strong weapons against the enemy.

Yeshua says, "I am the resurrection and the life. He who believes in me will live, even though he dies, and whoever lives and believes in me will never die. John 11: 25

IMITATE CHRIST'S HUMILITY.

If you have any encouragement from being united with Christ, if any comfort from his love, if any fellowship with the Spirit, if any tenderness and compassion, then (says Apostle Peter to you) *then make my joy complete by being like-minded, having the same love, being one in spirit and purpose. Do nothing out of selfish ambition or vain conceit, but in humility consider others better than yourselves. Each of you should look not only to your own interests, but also to the interests of others.*

Your attitude should be the same as that of Christ Yeshua: Who being in very nature God, did not consider equality with God something to be grasped, but made himself nothing, taking the very nature of a servant, being made in human likeness. And being found in appearance as a man, he humbled himself and became obedient to death –even death on the cross!

Therefore God exalted him to the highest place and gave him the name that is above every name, that at the name of Yeshua every knee shall bow, in heaven and on earth and under the earth, and every tongue confess that Christ Yeshua is Lord, to the Glory of God the Father. Philippians 2

The Lord God says *"Do not be anxious about anything, but in everything, by prayer and petition, with thanksgiving, present your requests to God. And the peace of God, which transcends all understanding, <u>will guard your hearts and your minds</u> in Christ Yeshua."* Philippians 4:4

Apostle Paul wrote in Colossians chapter 2: *"Continue to live in Christ, rooted and built up in Him, strengthened in the faith as you were taught and overflowing with thankfulness".*

"See to it that no one takes you captive through hollow and deceptive philosophy, which depends on human tradition and the basic principles of this world rather than on Christ." "For in Christ all the fullness of the Deity lives in bodily form, and you have been given fullness in Christ, <u>who is the head over every power and authority"</u> Colossians 2

THE SUPREMACY OF CHRIST

"He is the image of the invisible God, the firstborn over all creation. For by Him all things were created: things in heaven and on earth, visible and invisible, whether thrones or powers or rulers or authorities; all things were created by Him and for Him. He is before all things, and in Him all things hold together....".Colossians 1: 15-

"Once you were alienated from God and were enemies <u>in your minds</u> *because of your evil behaviour. But now he has reconciled you by Christ's physical body through death to present you holy in His sight, without blemish and free from accusation – if you continue in your faith, established and firm, not moved from the hope held out in the Gospel".* Colossians 1: 21

"Be made knew in the attitude of your minds and to put on the new self, created to be like God in true righteousness and holiness". Ephesians 4:23

"Put to death, therefore, whatever belongs to your earthly nature, sexual immorality, impurity, lust, evil desires and greed, which is idolatry. Because of these, the wrath of God is coming". Col 3: 5 *"Do not lie to each other!"* Col 3: 9

THE RAPTURE

"We who are still alive, who are left until the coming of the Lord, will certainly not precede those who have fallen asleep. For the Lord himself will come down from heaven, with a loud command, with the voice of the archangel and with the trumpet (the seventh trumpet [the silence period] in book of Revelation) call of God, and the dead in Christ will rise first. After that, we who are still alive and are left will be caught up together with them in the clouds to meet the Lord in the air." 1 Thess 4: 15-

THE ARMOUR OF GOD

Finally be strong in the Lord and in His mighty power. Put on the full armour of God so that you can take your stand against the devil's schemes. For our struggle is not against flesh and blood, but against the *rulers,* against the *authorities*, against the *powers of darkness* and against the *spiritual forces of evil in the heavenly realms.* Therefore put on the full armour of God, so that when the day of evil comes, you may be able to stand your ground, and after you have done everything, to stand. Stand firm then.

Put on the armour:

*The Belt of **Truth** buckled around your waist

*The Breastplate of **Righteousness** in place

*Your feet fitted with the **Readiness** that comes from the Gospel of Peace

*Take up the Shield of **Faith**, with which you can extinguish all the flaming arrows of the evil one.

*Take the Helmet of **Salvation**

*And the Sword of the Spirit which is the **Word of God.**

*And **Pray** in the Spirit on all occasions, with all kinds of prayers and requests.

With this in mind, **be alert** and always keep on praying for all the saints.

This was spoken by Apostle Paul in Ephesians 6: 10-18.

PART 3

This section provides further
information on the subjects
covered such as important additional
reading material on the
illuminati, drugs, GM Rice etc.

There is also a list of suggested
further reading.

Further books of the
LAST CHANCE series
are also listed.

APPENDIX 1

Energy Therapy

Most forms of energy psychology have only been known since the mid 1980's, but they derive from Eastern medicine which includes Shamanism (demonic influence) that goes back at least 5000 years. Acupuncture, chakras, the subtle energies, yoga, gi gong, and applied kinesiology are the theoretical underpinnings of this energy therapy.

It is playing with demonic influences using the same methods as the Toronto Blessing Movement which involves channelling demons to enter the body or for a demonic energy to enter the body. This demonic energy is an instrument of satan to gain control of your mind and body and therefore ultimately –your soul!

All of these treatments work by accessing the deeper, subconscious part of the brain more directly than traditional psychotherapy, which relies mainly on the conscious processes that are located in the Prefrontal Cortex.
Hypnosis is the oldest and most established of the new "power therapies" in psychology. The other counselling techniques that make up these revolutionary therapies are EMDR, NET™, TFT, and EFT.

These methods are highly dangerous for those who do not wish to be 'mind controlled'. Avoid these treatments as conventional treatments work well. However, God is a great healer of the mind and the body!

APPENDIX 2

Illuminati Elite Group

New World Order (conspiracy theory)

From Wikipedia, the free encyclopedia
This article is about the use of the term New World Order *in conspiracy theory. For other uses, see* New World Order.

The reverse side of the Great Seal of the United States (1776). The Latin phrase "*novus ordo seclorum*", appearing on the reverse side of the
Great Seal since 1782 and on the back of the U.S. one-dollar bill since 1935, translates to "New Order of the Ages"[1] and alludes to the beginning of an era where the United States of America is an independent nation-state; it is often mistranslated by conspiracy theorists as "New World Order".[2]

As a conspiracy theory, the term *New World Order* or *NWO* refers to the emergence of a totalitarian one-world government.[3][4][5][6][7]

The common theme in conspiracy theories about a New World Order is that a secretive power elite with a globalist agenda is conspiring to eventually rule the world through an authoritarian world government—which replaces sovereign nation-states—and an all-encompassing propaganda that ideologizes its establishment as the culmination of history's progress. Significant occurrences in politics and finance are speculated to be orchestrated by an unduly influential cabal operating through many front organizations. Numerous historical and current events are seen as steps in an on-going plot to achieve world domination through secret political gatherings and decision-making processes.[3][4][5][6][7]

Prior to the early 1990s, New World Order <u>conspiracism</u> was limited to two American countercultures, primarily the <u>militantly anti-government right</u>, and secondarily <u>fundamentalist Christians</u> concerned with <u>end-time</u> emergence of the <u>Antichrist</u>.[8] Skeptics, such as <u>Michael Barkun</u> and <u>Chip Berlet</u>, have observed that <u>right-wing populist</u> conspiracy theories about a New World Order have now not only been embraced by many seekers of <u>stigmatized knowledge</u> but have seeped into <u>popular culture</u>, thereby inaugurating an unrivaled period of people actively preparing for <u>apocalyptic</u> <u>millenarian</u> scenarios in the <u>United States</u> of the late 20th and early 21st centuries.[4][6] These political scientists are concerned that this <u>mass hysteria</u> could have what they judge to be devastating effects on American political life, ranging from widespread <u>political alienation</u> to escalating <u>lone-wolf terrorism</u>.[4][6]

The **United States one-dollar bill** ($1) is a denomination of United States currency. The first *U.S. President (1789–97), George Washington, painted by Gilbert Stuart, is currently featured on the obverse, while the Great Seal of the United States is featured on the reverse. The one-dollar bill has the oldest reverse design of all U.S. currency, while the two-dollar bill has the oldest obverse design currently being produced. The obverse design seen today on the one-dollar bill debuted in 1963 when it first became a Federal Reserve Note.*

The inclusion of the motto, "In God We Trust," on all currency was required by law in 1955, and first appeared on paper money in 1957.

During the 20th century, many statesmen, such as Woodrow Wilson and Winston Churchill, used the term "new world order" to refer to a new period of history evidencing a dramatic change in world political thought and the balance of power after World War I and World War II. They all saw these periods as opportunities to implement idealistic proposals for global governance in the sense of new collective efforts to address worldwide problems that go beyond the capacity of individual nation-states to solve, while always respecting the right of nations to self-determination. These proposals led to the creation of international organizations, such as the United Nations and NATO, and international regimes, such as the Bretton Woods system and the General Agreement on Tariffs and Trade, which were calculated both to maintain a balance of power in favor of the United States as well as regularize cooperation between nations, in order to achieve a peaceful phase of capitalism. These creations in particular and liberal internationalism in general, however, would always be criticized and opposed by American ultraconservative business nationalists from the 1930s on.[9]

Progressives welcomed these new international organizations and regimes in the aftermath of the two World Wars, but argued they suffered from a democratic deficit and therefore *were inadequate to not only prevent another <u>global war</u> but also foster <u>global justice</u>. The United Nations was designed in 1945 by U.S. bankers and <u>State Department</u> planners, and was always intended to remain a free association of sovereign nation-states, not a transition to democratic world government. Thus, activists around the globe formed a <u>world federalist movement</u> hoping in vain to create a "real" new world order.[10]*

British writer and futurist <u>H. G. Wells</u> would go further than progressives in the 1940s by appropriating and redefining the term "new world order" as a synonym for the establishment of a technocratic <u>world state</u> and <u>planned economy</u>.[11] Despite the popularity of his ideas in some <u>state socialist</u> circles, Wells failed to exert a deeper and more lasting influence because he was unable to concentrate his energies on a direct appeal to <u>intelligentsias</u> who would, ultimately, have to coordinate a Wellsian new world order.[12]

During the <u>Red Scare of 1947–1957</u>, agitators of the American secular and <u>Christian right</u>, influenced by the work of Canadian conspiracy theorist <u>William Guy Carr</u>, increasingly embraced and spread unfounded fears of <u>Freemasons</u>, <u>Illuminati</u>, and <u>Jews</u> being the driving force behind an "<u>international communist</u> conspiracy". The threat of "Godless communism" in the form of a <u>state atheistic</u> and <u>bureaucratic collectivist</u> world government, <u>demonized</u> as a "Red Menace", therefore became the main focus of <u>apocalyptic</u> <u>millenarian</u> <u>conspiracism</u>. The Red Scare would shape one of the core ideas of the political right in the United States which is that <u>liberals</u> and <u>progressives</u> with their <u>welfare-state</u> policies and international cooperation programs such as <u>foreign aid</u> supposedly contribute to a gradual process of <u>collectivism</u> that will inevitably lead to nations being replaced with a <u>communist one-world government</u>.[13]

<u>Right-wing populist</u> advocacy groups with a <u>producerist</u> worldview, such as the <u>John Birch Society</u>, disseminated a

multitude of conspiracy theories in the 1960s claiming that the governments of both the United States and the <u>Soviet Union</u> were controlled by a <u>cabal</u> of <u>corporate internationalists</u>, greedy bankers and corrupt politicians intent on using the <u>United Nations</u> as the vehicle to create the "One World Government". This right-wing <u>anti-globalist</u> conspiracism would fuel the Bircher campaign for <u>U.S. withdrawal from the U.N.</u>. American writer Mary M. Davison, in her 1966 booklet The Profound Revolution, traced the alleged New World Order conspiracy to the creation of the U.S. <u>Federal Reserve System</u> in 1913 by international bankers, who she claimed later formed the <u>Council on Foreign Relations</u> in 1921 as the <u>shadow government</u>. At the time the booklet was published, "international bankers" would have been interpreted by many readers as a reference to a postulated "international Jewish banking conspiracy" masterminded by the <u>Rothschilds</u>.[13]

Claiming that the term "New World Order" is used by a secretive elite dedicated to the destruction of all national sovereignties, American writer <u>Gary Allen</u>, in his 1971 book None Dare Call It Conspiracy, 1974 book Rockefeller: Campaigning for the New World Order and 1987 book Say "No!" to the New World Order, articulated the anti-globalist theme of much current right-wing populist conspiracism in the U.S.. Thus, after the <u>fall of communism</u> in the early 1990s, the main demonized <u>scapegoat</u> of the American <u>far right</u> shifted seamlessly from <u>crypto-communists</u> who plotted on behalf of the Red Menace to globalists who plot on behalf of the New World Order. The relatively painless nature of the shift was due to growing right-wing populist <u>opposition to corporate internationalism</u> but also in part to the basic underlying apocalyptic millenarian paradigm, which fed the <u>Cold War</u> and the <u>witch-hunts of the McCarthy period</u>.[13]

In his 11 September 1990 <u>Toward a New World Order</u> speech to a joint session of the <u>U.S. Congress</u>, President <u>George H. W. Bush</u> described his objectives for <u>post-Cold-War global governance</u> in cooperation with <u>post-Soviet states</u>:

351

*Until now, the world we've known has been a world divided—
a world of barbed wire and concrete block, conflict and cold
war. Now, we can see a new world coming into view. A world
in which there is the very real prospect of a new world order.
In the words of Winston Churchill, a "world order" in which
"the principles of justice and fair play ... protect the weak
against the strong ..." A world where the United Nations, freed
from cold war stalemate, is poised to fulfill the historic vision
of its founders. A world in which freedom and respect for
human rights find a home among all nations.*

*<u>The New York Times</u> observed that progressives were
denouncing this new world order as a rationalization for
<u>American imperial</u> ambitions in the <u>Middle East</u>, while
<u>conservatives</u> rejected new security arrangements altogether
and fulminated about any possibility of U.N. revival.[14]
However, <u>Chip Berlet</u>, an American investigative reporter
specializing in the study of <u>right-wing</u> movements in the U.S.,
writes:*

*When President Bush announced his new foreign policy
would help build a New World Order, his phrasing surged
through the Christian and secular hard right like an electric
shock, since the phrase had been used to represent the dreaded
collectivist One World Government for decades. Some
Christians saw Bush as signaling the End Times betrayal by a
world leader. Secular anticommunists saw a bold attempt to
smash US sovereignty and impose a tyrannical collectivist
system run by the United Nations.[13]*

*American televangelist <u>Pat Robertson</u> with his 1991 best-
selling book <u>The New World Order</u> became the most
prominent Christian popularizer of conspiracy theories about
recent American history as a theater in which <u>Wall Street</u>, the
Federal Reserve System, Council on Foreign Relations,
<u>Bilderberg Group</u>, and <u>Trilateral Commission</u> control the flow
of events from behind the scenes, nudging us constantly and*

covertly in the direction of world government for the Antichrist.[6]

Observers note that the galvanization of right-wing populist conspiracy theorists, such as Linda Thompson, Mark Koernke and Robert K. Spear, into militancy led to the rise of the militia movement, which spread its anti-government ideology through speeches at rallies and meetings, through books and videotapes sold at gun shows, through shortwave and satellite radio, and through fax networks and computer bulletin boards.[13] *However, overnight AM radio shows and viral propaganda on the Internet is what most effectively contributed to their extremist political ideas about the New World Order finding their way into the previously apolitical literature of many Kennedy assassinologists, ufologists, lost land theorists, and, most recently, occultists. The worldwide appeal of these subcultures then transmitted New World Order conspiracism like a "mind virus" to a large new audience of seekers of stigmatized knowledge from the mid-1990s on.*[6] *Hollywood conspiracy-thriller television shows and films also played a role in introducing a vast popular audience to various fringe theories related to New World Order conspiracism (black helicopter, FEMA "concentration camps", etc.), which were previously confined to radical right-wing subcultures for decades. The 1993-2002 television series X-Files, the 1997 film Conspiracy Theory and the 1998 film The X-Files: Fight the Future are often cited as notable examples.*[6]

Following the start of the 21st century, specifically during the late-2000s financial crisis, many politicians and pundits, such as Gordon Brown[15] *and Henry Kissinger,*[16] *used the term "new world order" in their advocacy for a comprehensive reform of the global financial system and their calls for a "New Bretton Woods", which takes into account emerging markets such as China and India. These declarations had the unintended consequence of providing fresh fodder for New World Order conspiracism, and culminated in talk show host Sean Hannity stating on his Fox News Channel program Hannity that "conspiracy theorists were right".*[17] *Fox News in general, and its opinion show __Glenn Beck__ in particular, have been repeatedly criticized by progressive __media watchdog__ groups for not only mainstreaming the New World Order conspiracy theories of the __radical right__ but possibly agitating its __lone wolves__ into action.[18][19][20][21]*

American film directors Luke Meyer and __Andrew Neel__ released __New World Order__ in 2009, a critically acclaimed documentary film which explores the world of conspiracy theorists, such as American radio host __Alex Jones__, who are committed to exposing and vigorously opposing what they perceive to be an emerging New World Order.[22] The growing dissemination and popularity of conspiracy theories has created an alliance between right-wing populist agitators, such as Alex Jones, and __hip hop music__'s left-wing populist rappers, such as __KRS-One__, __Professor Griff__ of __Public Enemy__, and __Immortal Technique__, which illustrates how __anti-elitist__ conspiracism creates unlikely political allies in efforts to oppose the political system.[23]

Conspiracy theories- There are numerous __systemic conspiracy theories__ through which the concept of a New World Order is viewed. The following is a list of the major ones in relatively chronological order:[24]

__End Time__ - Since the 19th century, many __apocalyptic millennial__ Christian __eschatologists__, starting with __John Nelson Darby__, have predicted a globalist conspiracy to impose a tyrannical New World Order as the fulfillment of __prophecies__ about the "__end time__" in the __Bible__, specifically in the __Book of Ezekiel__, the __Book of Daniel__, the __Olivet discourse__ found in the __Synoptic Gospels__, and the __Book of Revelation__.[25] They claim that people who have made a __deal with the Devil__ to gain wealth and power have become pawns in a supernatural chess game to move humanity into accepting a __utopian__ world government, which rests on the spiritual foundations of a __syncretic-messianic__ world religion, that will later reveal itself to be a __dystopian__ world empire, which imposes the __imperial__

cult of an "Unholy Trinity" — Satan, the Antichrist and the
False Prophet. In many contemporary Christian conspiracy
theories, the False Prophet will either be the last pope of the
Catholic Church (groomed and installed by an Alta Vendita or
Jesuit conspiracy) or a guru from the New Age movement or
even the leader of an elite fundamentalist Christian
organization like the Fellowship, while the Antichrist will
either be the president of the European Union or the
secretary-general of the United Nations or even the caliph of a
pan-Islamic state.[6][25]

Some of the most vocal critics of end-time conspiracy theories
come from within Christianity.[13] In 1993, historian Bruce
Barron wrote a stern rebuke of apocalyptic Christian
conspiracism in the Christian Research Journal, when
reviewing Robertson's 1991 book The New World Order.[26]
Another critique can be found in historian Gregory S. Camp's
1997 book Selling Fear: Conspiracy Theories and End-Times
Paranoia.[3] Religious studies scholar Richard T. Hughes
argues that "New World Order" rhetoric libels the Christian
faith since the "New World Order", as defined by Christian
conspiracy theorists, has no basis in the Bible whatsoever and
that, in fact, this idea is not only unbiblical; it is anti-biblical
and fundamentally anti-Christian because, by misinterpreting
key passages in the Book of Revelation, it turns a comforting
message about the coming kingdom of God into one of fear,
panic and despair in the face of an allegedly approaching one-
world government.[25] Progressive Christians, such as
preacher-theologian Peter J. Gomes, caution Christian
fundamentalists that a "spirit of fear" can distort scripture
and history by dangerously combining biblical literalism,
apocalyptic timetables, demonization, and oppressive
prejudices;[27][28] while Camp warns of the "very real danger
that Christians could pick up some extra spiritual baggage" by
credulously embracing conspiracy theories.[3] They therefore
call on Christians who indulge in conspiracism to repent.[29][30]

355

Freemasonry - <u>*Freemasonry*</u> *is one of the world's oldest secular <u>fraternal organizations</u>, which arose in late 16th- to early 17th-century Britain. Over the years a number of allegations and conspiracy theories have been directed towards Freemasonry, including the allegation that Freemasons have a hidden <u>political agenda</u> and are conspiring to bring about a New World Order, a world government organized according to Masonic principles and/or governed only by Freemasons.*[13]

The <u>esoteric</u> nature of <u>Masonic symbolism</u> and <u>rites</u> led to Freemasons being first accused of secretly practicing <u>Satanism</u> in the late 18th century.[13] *The original allegation of a <u>conspiracy within Freemasonry</u> to subvert religions and governments in order to take over the world traces back to Scottish author <u>John Robison</u>, whose <u>reactionary</u> conspiracy theories crossed the Atlantic, and during the 19th century influenced outbreaks of Protestant <u>anti-Masonry</u> in the United States.*[13] *In the 1890s, French writer <u>Léo Taxil</u> wrote a series of pamphlets and books, denouncing Freemasonry, charging their lodges with worshiping <u>Lucifer</u> as the <u>Supreme Being</u>. Despite the fact that Taxil admitted that <u>his claims were all a hoax</u>, they were and are believed and repeated by numerous conspiracy theorists, and had a huge influence on subsequent anti-Masonic claims about Freemasonry.*[31]

Some conspiracy theorists eventually speculated that some of the <u>Founding Fathers of the United States</u>, such as <u>George Washington</u>, <u>Benjamin Franklin</u>, were having Masonic <u>sacred geometric</u> designs interwoven into American society, particularly in the <u>Great Seal of the United States</u>, the <u>United States one-dollar bill</u>, the architecture of <u>National Mall landmarks</u>, and the <u>streets and highways of Washington, D.C.</u>, as part of a master plan.[6] *Accordingly, colonial American Freemasons are portrayed as having embraced <u>Bavarian Illuminism</u> and used the power of the <u>occult</u> to bind their planning of a government in conformity with the plan of the "Masonic God" because of their belief that the "<u>Great</u>*

Architect of the Universe" has given the United States the task of eventually establishing the "Kingdom of God on Earth" — a Masonic world government with New Jerusalem as its capital city and the Third Temple as its holiest site — the initially utopian New World Order presided over by a Masonic Messiah.[32]

Freemasons rebut these claims of Masonic conspiracy. Freemasonry, which promotes rationalism, places no power in occult symbols themselves, and it is not a part of its principles to view the drawing of symbols, no matter how large, as an act of consolidating or controlling power.[33] Furthermore, there is no published information establishing the Masonic membership of the men responsible for the design of the Great Seal.[33][34] The Latin phrase "novus ordo seclorum", appearing on the reverse side of the Great Seal since 1782 and on the back of the one-dollar bill since 1935, translates to "New Order of the Ages"[1] and alludes to the beginning of an era where the United States of America is an independent nation-state; it is often mistranslated by conspiracy theorists as "New World Order".[2] Lastly, Freemasons argue that, despite the symbolic importance of the Temple of Solomon in their mythology, they have no interest in rebuilding it, especially since "it is obvious that any attempt to interfere with the present condition of things [on the Temple Mount] would in all probability bring about the greatest religious war the world has ever known".[35]

Although the European continental branch of Freemasonry has organizations that allow political discussion within their Masonic Lodges and a few operate as active political lobbies for secularist causes, as exemplified by the Grand Orient of France, Masonic researcher Trevor W. McKeown argues:

The accusation that Freemasonry has a hidden agenda to establish a Masonic government ignores several facts. While agreeing on certain Masonic Landmarks, the many independent and sovereign Grand Lodges act as such, and do *not agree on many other points of belief and practice. Also, as can be seen from a <u>survey of famous Freemasons</u>, individual Freemasons hold beliefs that span the spectrum of politics. The term "Masonic government" has no meaning since individual Freemasons hold many different opinions on what constitutes a good government.*[36]

Illuminati *- The Order of the <u>Illuminati</u> was an <u>Enlightenment-age</u> secret society founded by university professor <u>Adam Weishaupt</u> on 1 May 1776, in <u>Upper Bavaria</u>, Germany. The movement consisted of advocates of <u>freethought</u>, <u>secularism</u>, <u>liberalism</u>, <u>republicanism</u> and <u>gender equality</u>, recruited in the German <u>Masonic Lodges</u>, who sought to teach <u>rationalism</u> through <u>mystery schools</u>. In 1785, the order was infiltrated, broken up and suppressed by the government agents of <u>Charles Theodore, Elector of Bavaria</u>, in his preemptive campaign to neutralize the threat of secret societies ever becoming hotbeds of conspiracies to overthrow the Bavarian <u>monarchy</u> and its <u>state religion</u>, <u>Roman Catholicism</u>.*[37]

In the late 18th century, <u>reactionary</u> conspiracy theorists, such as Scottish physicist <u>John Robison</u> and French <u>Jesuit</u> priest <u>Augustin Barruel</u>, began speculating that the Illuminati survived their suppression and became the masterminds behind the <u>French Revolution</u> and the <u>Reign of Terror</u>. The Illuminati were accused of being <u>subversives</u> who were attempting to secretly orchestrate a <u>revolutionary wave</u> in <u>Europe</u> and the rest of the world in order to spread the most <u>radical</u> ideas and movements of the Enlightenment — <u>anti-clericalism</u>, <u>anti-monarchism</u>, and <u>anti-patriarchalism</u> — and create a world <u>noocracy</u> and <u>cult of reason</u>. During the 19th century, fear of an Illuminati conspiracy was a real concern of European <u>ruling classes</u>, and their oppressive reactions to this unfounded fear provoked in 1848 <u>the very revolutions they sought to prevent</u>.[38]

During the interwar period of the 20th century, fascist propagandists, such as British revisionist historian Nesta Helen Webster and American socialite Edith Starr Miller, not only popularized the myth of an Illuminati conspiracy but claimed that it was a subversive secret society which serves the Jewish elites that supposedly propped up both finance capitalism and Soviet communism in order to divide and rule the world. American evangelist Gerald Burton Winrod and other conspiracy theorists within the fundamentalist Christian movement in the United States — which emerged in the 1910s as a backlash against the principles of Enlightenment secular humanism, modernism, and liberalism — became the main channel of dissemination of Illuminati conspiracy theories in the U.S. Right-wing populists, such as members of the John Birch Society, subsequently began speculating that some collegiate fraternities (Skull and Bones), gentlemen's clubs (Bohemian Club) and think tanks (Council on Foreign Relations, Trilateral Commission) of the American upper class are front organizations of the Illuminati, which they accuse of plotting to create a New World Order through a one-world government.[6] Skeptics argue that evidence would suggest that the Bavarian Illuminati was nothing more than a curious historical footnote since there is no evidence that the Illuminati survived its suppression in 1785.[38]

APPENDIX 3

DRUGS LSD –Cannabis and others

EFFECTS OF LSD Lysergic acid diethylamide

From Wikipedia, the free encyclopedia

LSD or LSD-25, also known as lysergide (INN) and colloquially as acid, is a semisynthetic psychedelic drug of the ergoline family, well known for its psychological effects which can include altered thinking processes, closed and open eye visuals, synesthesia, an altered sense of time and spiritual experiences, as well as for its key role in 1960s counterculture. It is used mainly as an entheogen, recreational drug, and as an agent in psychedelic therapy. LSD is non-addictive, is not known to cause brain damage, and has extremely low toxicity relative to dose. However, adverse psychiatric reactions such as anxiety, paranoia, and delusions are possible.[3]

LSD was first synthesized by Albert Hofmann in 1938 from ergotamine, a chemical derived by Arthur Stoll from ergot, a grain fungus that typically grows on rye. The short form "LSD" comes from its early code name LSD-25, which is an abbreviation for the German "Lysergsäure-diethylamid" followed by a sequential number.[4][5] LSD is sensitive to oxygen, ultraviolet light, and chlorine, especially in solution, though its potency may last for years if it is stored away from light and moisture at low temperature. In pure form it is a colorless, odorless, tasteless solid.[6] LSD is typically delivered orally, usually on a substrate such as absorbent blotter paper, a sugar cube, or gelatin. In its liquid form, it can also be administered by intramuscular or intravenous injection. LSD is very potent, with 20–30 μg (micrograms) being the threshold dose. New clinical LSD experiments in humans started in 2009 for the first time in 40 years.[7][not in citation given]

Introduced by Sandoz Laboratories, with trade-name Delysid, as a drug with various psychiatric uses in 1947, LSD quickly became a therapeutic agent that appeared to show great promise.[8] In the

1950s, officials at the U.S. <u>Central Intelligence Agency</u> (CIA) thought the drug might be applicable to <u>mind control</u> and <u>chemical warfare</u>; the agency's <u>MKULTRA</u> research program propagated the drug among young servicemen and students. The subsequent recreational use of the drug by <u>youth culture</u> in the <u>Western world</u> during the 1960s led to a political firestorm that resulted in its <u>prohibition</u>.<u>[9]</u> Currently, a number of organizations—including <u>the Beckley Foundation</u>, <u>MAPS</u>, <u>Heffter Research Institute</u> and the <u>Albert Hofmann</u> Foundation—exist to fund, encourage and coordinate research into the medicinal and spiritual uses of LSD and related psychedelics.[10]

* * *

<u>EFFECTS OF MARIJUANA</u>

Revised December 2012
Marijuana is a dry, shredded green and brown mix of leaves, flowers, stems, and seeds from the hemp plant Cannabis sativa. In a more concentrated, resinous form, it is called hashish, and as a sticky black liquid, hash oil. The main psychoactive (mind-altering) chemical in marijuana is delta-9-tetrahydrocannabinol, or THC. Marijuana is the most common illicit drug used in the United States. After a period of decline in the last decade, its use has generally increased among young people since 2007, corresponding to a diminishing perception of the drug's risks. More teenagers are now current (past-month) smokers of marijuana than of cigarettes, according to annual survey data.

How Does Marijuana Affect the Brain?

When marijuana is smoked, THC rapidly passes from the lungs into the bloodstream, which carries the chemical to the brain and other organs throughout the body. It is absorbed more slowly when ingested in food or drink.

However it is ingested, THC acts upon specific molecular targets on brain cells, called cannabinoid receptors. These receptors are ordinarily activated by chemicals similar to THC called

361

endocannabinoids, such as anandamide. These are naturally occurring in the body and are part of a neural communication network (the endocannabinoid system) that plays an important role in normal brain development and function.

The highest density of cannabinoid receptors is found in parts of the brain that influence pleasure, memory, thinking, concentration, sensory and time perception, and coordinated movement. Marijuana overactivates the endocannabinoid system, causing the high and other effects that users experience. These include distorted perceptions, impaired coordination, difficulty with thinking and problem solving, and disrupted learning and memory.

Effects on Life

Research clearly demonstrates that marijuana has the potential to cause problems in daily life or make a person's existing problems worse. In fact, heavy marijuana users generally report lower life satisfaction, poorer mental and physical health, relationship problems, and less academic and career success compared to their peers who came from similar backgrounds. For example, marijuana use is associated with a higher likelihood of dropping out from school. Several studies also associate workers' marijuana smoking with increased absences, tardiness, accidents, workers' compensation claims, and job turnover.
Research has shown that, in chronic users, marijuana's adverse impact on learning and memory persists after the acute effects of the drug wear off; when marijuana use begins in adolescence, the effects may persist for many years. Research from different areas is converging on the fact that regular marijuana use by young people can have long-lasting negative impact on the structure and function of their brains.

A recent study of marijuana users who began using in adolescence revealed a profound deficit in connections between brain areas responsible for learning and memory. And a large prospective study (following individuals across time) showed that people who began smoking marijuana heavily in their teens lost as much as 8 points in IQ between age 13 and age 38; importantly, the lost cognitive abilities were not restored in those who quit smoking marijuana as adults. (Individuals who started smoking marijuana in adulthood did not show significant IQ declines.)

What Are the Other Health Effects of Marijuana?

Marijuana use can have a variety of adverse, short- and long-term effects, especially on cardiopulmonary and mental health.

Marijuana raises heart rate by 20-100 percent shortly after smoking; this effect can last up to 3 hours. In one study, it was estimated that marijuana users have a 4.8-fold increase in the risk of heart attack in the first hour after smoking the drug. This may be due to increased heart rate as well as the effects of marijuana on heart rhythms, causing palpitations and arrhythmias. This risk may be greater in older individuals or in those with cardiac vulnerabilities.

Marijuana and Driving

Because it seriously impairs judgment and motor coordination, marijuana also contributes to accidents while driving. A recent analysis of data from several studies found that marijuana use more than doubles a driver's risk of being in an accident. Further, the combination of marijuana and alcohol is worse than either substance alone with respect to driving impairment.
Marijuana smoke is an irritant to the lungs, and frequent marijuana smokers can have many of the same respiratory problems experienced by tobacco smokers, such as daily cough and phlegm production, more frequent acute chest illness, and a heightened risk of lung infections. One study found that people who smoke marijuana frequently but do not smoke tobacco have more health problems and miss more days of work than nonsmokers, mainly because of respiratory illnesses.

A number of studies have shown an association between chronic marijuana use and mental illness. High doses of marijuana can produce a temporary psychotic reaction (involving hallucinations and paranoia) in some users, and using marijuana can worsen the course of illness in patients with schizophrenia. A series of large prospective studies also showed a link between marijuana use and later development of psychosis. This relationship was influenced by genetic variables as well as the amount of drug used and the age at which it was first taken—those who start young are at increased risk for later problems.

Associations have also been found between marijuana use and other mental health problems, such as depression, anxiety, suicidal thoughts among adolescents, and personality disturbances, including a lack of motivation to engage in typically rewarding activities. More research is still needed to confirm and better understand these linkages.

Marijuana use during pregnancy is associated with increased risk of neurobehavioral problems in babies. Because THC and other compounds in marijuana mimic the body's own cannabinoid-like chemicals, marijuana use by pregnant mothers may alter the developing endocannabinoid system in the brain of the fetus. Consequences for the child may include problems with attention, memory, and problem solving.

Finally, marijuana use has been linked in a few recent studies to an increased risk of an aggressive type of testicular cancer in young men, although further research is needed to establish whether there is a direct causal connection.

Is Marijuana Medicine?

Although many have called for the legalization of marijuana to treat conditions including pain and nausea caused by HIV/AIDS, cancer, and other conditions, the scientific evidence to date is not sufficient for the marijuana plant to gain FDA approval, for two main reasons.

First, there have not been enough clinical trials showing that marijuana's benefits outweigh its health risks in patients with the symptoms it is meant to treat. The FDA requires carefully conducted studies in large numbers of patients (hundreds to thousands) to accurately assess the benefits and risks of a potential medication.

Also, to be considered a legitimate medicine, a substance must have well-defined and measureable ingredients that are consistent from one unit (such as a pill or injection) to the next. This consistency allows doctors to determine the dose and frequency. As the marijuana plant contains hundreds of chemical compounds that may have different effects and that vary from plant to plant, its use as a medicine is difficult to evaluate.

However, THC-based drugs to treat pain and nausea are already FDA approved and prescribed, and scientists continue to investigate the medicinal properties of cannabinoids. For more information, see DrugFacts - Is Marijuana Medicine?

Is Marijuana Addictive?

Contrary to common belief, marijuana is addictive. Estimates from research suggest that about 9 percent of users become addicted to marijuana; this number increases among those who start young (to about 17 percent, or 1 in 6) and among daily users (to 25-50 percent). Thus, many of the nearly 7 percent of high-school seniors who (according to annual survey data) report smoking marijuana daily or almost daily are well on their way to addiction, if not already addicted (besides functioning at a sub-optimal level all of the time).

Long-term marijuana users trying to quit report withdrawal symptoms including irritability, sleeplessness, decreased appetite, anxiety, and drug craving, all of which can make it difficult to remain abstinent. Behavioral interventions, including cognitive-behavioral therapy and motivational incentives (i.e., providing vouchers for goods or services to patients who remain abstinent) have proven to be effective in treating marijuana addiction.

Although no medications are currently available, recent discoveries about the workings of the endocannabinoid system offer promise for the development of medications to ease withdrawal, block the intoxicating effects of marijuana, and prevent relapse.

Cannabis

There is some evidence that <u>cannabis</u> use can contribute to schizophrenia. Some studies suggest that cannabis is neither a <u>sufficient nor necessary</u> factor in developing schizophrenia, but that cannabis may <u>significantly</u> increase the risk of developing schizophrenia and may be, among other things, a significant causal factor. Nevertheless, some previous research in this area has been criticized as it has often not been clear whether cannabis use is a cause or effect of schizophrenia. To address this issue, a recent review of prospective cohort studies has suggested that cannabis statistically doubles the risk of developing schizophrenia on the individual level, and may, if a causal relationship is assumed, be responsible for up to 8% of cases in the population.

Cannabis misuse by young people is suspected of causing schizophrenia in later life by interfering with and distorting <u>neurodevelopment</u> particularly of the <u>prefrontal cortex</u> region of the brain. An older <u>longitudinal study</u>, published in 1987, suggested a sixfold increase of schizophrenia risks for high consumers of cannabis (use on more than fifty occasions) in <u>Sweden.</u>

The hypothesis of causality in relation to cannabis consumption and the development of schizophrenia can be aptly countered by coupling the observations - that cannabis consumption in youth (as in adulthood) is more common in males than in females and - that the prevalence of schizophrenia is equivocal between genders, although an early average age of onset is found in men.

Cannabis use is also suspected to contribute to the hyperdopaminergic state that is characteristic of schizophrenia. Compounds found in cannabis, such as THC, have been shown to increase the activity of dopamine pathways in the brain, [unreliable source?] *suggesting that cannabis may exasperate symptoms of psychosis in schizophrenics.*

Despite increases in cannabis consumption in the 1960s and 1970s in western society, rates of psychotic disorders such as schizophrenia remained relatively stable over time. Also, Sweden and Japan, where self-reported marijuana use is very low, do not have lower rates of psychosis than the U.S. and Canada do. Thus, there remains controversy over whether or not the apparent association between cannabis and schizophrenia is a causal relationship.

Amphetamines and other stimulant

Main article: Stimulant psychosis

As amphetamines trigger the release of dopamine and excessive dopamine function is believed to be responsible for many symptoms of schizophrenia (known as the dopamine hypothesis of schizophrenia), amphetamines may worsen schizophrenia symptoms. Methamphetamine, a potent neurotoxic amphetamine derivative, induces psychosis in a substantial minority of regular users which resembles paranoid schizophrenia. For most people, this psychosis fades away within a month of abstinence but for a minority the psychosis can become chronic. Individuals who develop a long lasting psychosis, despite abstinence from methamphetamine, more commonly have a family history of schizophrenia.

Concerns have been raised that long-term therapy with stimulants for ADHD might cause paranoia, schizophrenia and behavioral sensitization. Family history of mental illness does not predict the incidence of stimulant toxicosis in ADHD children. High rates of childhood stimulant use have been

*noted in patients with a diagnosis of <u>schizophrenia</u> and <u>bipolar</u>
<u>disorder</u> independent of ADHD. Individuals with a diagnosis
of bipolar or schizophrenia who were prescribed stimulants
during childhood typically have a significantly earlier onset of
the psychotic disorder and suffer a more severe clinical course
of psychotic disorder. It has been suggested that this small
subgroup of children who develop schizophrenia due to
stimulant use during childhood have a genetic vulnerability to
developing psychosis. In addition, amphetamines are known to
cause a <u>stimulant psychosis</u> in otherwise healthy individuals
that superficially resembles schizophrenia, and may be
misdiagnosed as such by some healthcare professionals.*

Hallucinogens

*Drugs such as <u>ketamine</u>, <u>PCP</u>, and <u>LSD</u> have been used to
mimic schizophrenia for research purposes. Using LSD and
other <u>psychedelics</u> as a model has now fallen out of favor with
the <u>scientific research community</u>, as the differences between
the drug induced states and the typical presentation of
schizophrenia have become clear. The <u>dissociatives</u> ketamine
and PCP, however, are still considered to produce states that
are remarkably similar, and are considered to be even better
models than stimulants since they produce both positive and
negative symptoms.*

APPENDIX 4

Genetically modified rice

From Wikipedia, the free encyclopedia

> *A major contributor to this article appears to have a __close connection__ with its subject. It may require __cleanup__ to comply with Wikipedia's content policies, particularly __neutral point of view__. (August 2013)*

Genetically modified rice are types of __rice__ that have been genetically modified (also called __genetic engineering__) for agricultural purposes. The rice genome is usually modified using particle bombardment via the use of a __gene gun__ or more commonly, a process known as __agrobacterium__ mediated __transformation__.[1] Rice plants can be modified in DNA to be herbicide resistant, resist pests, increase grain size, generate nutrients, flavours or even produce human proteins.[1] The natural movement of genes across species, often called __horizontal gene transfer__ or lateral gene transfer, can also occur with rice through gene transfer mediated by natural vectors. Some examples of such natural transgenic events in plants through movement of natural mobile DNAs called __MULEs__ between rice and __Setaria__ millet have been identified.[2] The cultivation and use of genetically modified varieties of rice is however controversial and not legal in some countries.

Scientists are genetically modifying rice for several purposes including making rice resistant to herbicides, diseases, and pests, increasing nutritional value, eliminating rice allergies, producing human blood protein, increasing yield; improving tolerance to drought and salinity; and enhancing nitrogen use efficiency.

In 2000, the first two GM rice varieties both with herbicide-resistance, called LLRice60 and LLRice62, were approved in the United States. Later, these and other types of herbicide-resistant GM rice were approved in Canada, Australia, Mexico, and Colombia. However, none of these approvals resulted in commercialization.[3] __Reuters__ reported in 2009 that China had granted biosafety approval to GM rice with pest resistance,[4] but it hasn't been commercialized either. As of December 2012 GM rice had not yet become widely available for production or consumption.[5] A 2013 article calculated that the annual global value of future developments of genetically engineered rice to be US$64 billion. They argued that since *rice is a staple crop for a large number of very poor people in the world, this has enormous potential for alleviating hunger, malnutrition and poverty.[6]*

In order to produce "Roundup Ready rice",[7] Monsanto allowed research into it for one year (2000–2001) but has not developed a variety for market.[8] Bayer's line of herbicide resistant rice is known as LibertyLink.[9] LibertyLink rice is a transgenic variety of rice resistant to glufosinate (the active chemical in Liberty herbicide).[7] Bayer crop sciences is currently attempting to get their latest variety (LL62) approved for use in the EU. The strain has already been approved for use in the U.S. but is not in large scale use. A variety of rice known as Clearfield rice has been bred by selection from variations created in environments known to cause accelerated rates of mutations.[10] This variety is selected for resistance to imidazolinone herbicides and since these are bred by traditional breeding techniques are not considered as genetically modified.[10] Clearfield is cross bred with higher yielding varieties to produce an overall hardier plant.[10]

Nutritional value

Half of the world population's main food source is rice. In Asia, white rice is eaten three times a day. The main concern about white rice is that it has insufficient concentrations of vitamin A.[11] It has been suggested that rice could be fortified to reduce the level of nutritional vitamin A deficiencies. Golden rice was originally created by Dr. Ingo Potrykus and his team in Zurich, Switzerland.[12] This genetically modified rice is capable of producing beta-carotene in the endosperm (grain) which is a pre cursor for vitamin A production.[12] Potrykus's goal is to distribute the rice to poor countries whose citizens suffer blindness and even death from a lack of vitamin A.[12] Syngenta was involved in the early development of Golden Rice and held some intellectual property on Golden Rice,[12] but has since handed it over to non-profit institutes including the International Rice Research Institute (IRRI) to develop on a non-profit basis.[13] The scientific details of the rice were first published in Science in 2000.[14]

The World Health Organization has stated that iron deficiency affects 30% of the world's population. Research scientists from the Australian Centre for Plant Functional Genomics (ACPFG) are helping to address this issue as part of broader program with HarvestPlus and IRRI to increase the amount of iron in rice.[15] They have modified three populations of rice by over expressing the genes: OsNAS1, OsNAS2 or OsNAS3. The research team found that nicotianamine, iron, and zinc concentration levels increased in all three populations of rice relative to the controls.[11]

Ventria Bioscience uses a proprietary system known as Express Tec for producing recombinant human proteins in rice grains.[16] Their most notable variety produces human Lactoferrin and Lysozyme.[16] These two proteins are produced naturally in human breast milk and are used globally in infant formula and rehydration products.[16] The company's primary facility is located in Kansas.[17]

Pest resistance

BT rice is modified to express the cryIA(b) gene of the bacillus thuringiensis bacterium.[18] The gene confers resistance to a variety of pests including the rice borer through the production of endotoxins. The Chinese Government is currently doing trials on insect resistant cultivars.[19] The benefit of this is that the farmers do not need to spray their crops with pesticides to control fungal, viral, or bacterial pathogens. In comparison, conventional rice is sprayed three to four times per growing season to control pests.[19] Other benefits include increased yield and revenue from crop cultivation.[18][20] China has approved the rice for large scale use as of 2009.[20] India, Indonesia, and Philippines are expected to carry out cultivation of genetically modified rice in the future.[19] In a rat model, no adverse effects from Bt rice consumption were observed, supporting the safety of widespread use.[21]

Allergy resistance

Researchers in Japan are attempting to develop allergen free rice cultivars for people who are allergic to rice. Researchers are trying to repress the activity of the formation of allergen, AS-Albumin.[19] Thus far the researchers have not been successful in completely eliminating the formation of AS-Albumin.[19]

Also in Japan, lead researcher Fumio Takaiwa of Japan's National Institute for Agrobiological Sciences in Tsukuba tested a type of genetically modified rice on macaques (monkeys) that would prevent allergies to cedar pollen which causes hay fever. The symptoms a person can get to cedar pollen are itchy eyes, sneezing, and other serious allergic reactions.[22] The modified rice contains seven proteins within cedar pollen to block these symptoms.[22] When this was tested on the monkeys, the monkeys did not have any allergy symptoms to cedar pollen. More importantly, they did not have any side effects; Japanese scientists conclude that these types of rice are safe to use as an antihistamine to control cedar pollen allergy. Takaiwa is already doing clinical trials on patients to see if it works the same for humans. He states that if it works it, it will pave the way for genetically modified based vaccines and decrease the opposition toward genetically modified foods.

Human blood protein

Human serum albumin (HSA) is a blood protein in human plasma. It is used in treatment such as severe burns, liver cirrhosis, and hemorrhagic shock.[23] More importantly, it is used in blood donations and thus is in short supply around the world.[23] In China, the scientists modified brown rice as a cost effective way to produce HSA protein. The Chinese scientists put recombinant HSA protein promoters into 25 rice plants using Agrobacterium.[23] Out of the 25 plants, nine of them breed (brown rice plants), and contained the HSA protein. They confirmed that the genetically modified brown rice had the same amino acid sequence as human serum albumin. They called this protein Oryza sativa recombinant HSA. The modified rice were transparent compared to regular rice. Additionally, they tested this protein on the rats with liver disease. The rats showed improved liver function.[23]

Main article: Genetically modified food controversies

There are controversies around GMOs on several levels, including whether making them is ethical, whether food produced with them is safe, whether such food should be labeled and if so how, whether agricultural biotech is needed to address world hunger now or in the future, and more specifically to GM crops—intellectual property and market dynamics; environmental effects of GM crops; and GM crops' role in industrial agricultural more generally.

Legal Issues US

In the summer of 2006 the USDA detected trace amounts of LibertyLink variety 601 in rice shipments ready for export.[24] LL601 was not approved for food purposes; it was approved only for experimental and research use.[24] Bayer applied for deregulation of LL601 in late July and the USDA granted deregulation status to the strain in November 2006.[25] The contamination lead to a dramatic dip in rice futures along with massive losses to farmers who grew rice for export.[24] Approximately 30 percent of rice production was affected along with over 11,000 farmers.[24] In June 2011 Bayer agreed to pay 750 million dollars for damages and lost harvests associated with the contamination.[24] The affected farmers in the five states, Arkansas, Louisiana, Mississippi, Missouri, and Texas will split the settlement.[26] Furthermore, Japan and Russia have banned U.S. export of the rice, while Mexico and the European Union imposed strict testing.[26] So this had impacted the U.S. agricultural business because the price of rice declined due to the contamination. "The contamination occurred between 1998 and 2001 (Berry 2011)." [26] The exact cause of the contamination has never been discovered.

The Chinese scientists state that human blood protein (HSA) produced in brown rice requires a lot of modified rice to be grown.[23] This raises environmental safety concerns about modified gene transfer during pollination. The Chinese scientists argue that this would not be a problem because rice is a self-pollinating crop, and their test showed less than 1% of the modified gene transfer in pollination.[23] They are still further studying the issue.

Arsenic toxicity

Rice and rice products contain <u>arsenic</u>, a known poison and <u>Group 1 carcinogen</u>.[26] There is no safe level of arsenic, but, as of 2012, a limit of 10 parts per billion has been established in the United States for drinking water, twice the level of 5 parts per billion originally proposed by the <u>EPA</u>. Consumption of one serving of some varieties of rice gives more exposure to arsenic than consumption of 1 liter of water that contains 5 parts per billion arsenic; however, the amount of arsenic in rice varies widely with the greatest concentration in brown rice and rice grown on land formerly used to grow cotton; in the United States, Arkansas, Louisiana, Missouri, and Texas.[27] The U.S. <u>Food and Drug Administration</u> (FDA) is studying this issue, but has not established a limit.[28] China has set a limit of 150 ppb for arsenic in rice.[29]

White rice grown in Arkansas, Louisiana, Missouri, and Texas, which account for 76 percent of American-produced rice had higher levels of arsenic than other regions of the world studied, possibly because of past use of arsenic based pesticides to control cotton weevils.[30] Rice from Thailand and India contain the least arsenic among rice varieties in one study.[31]

Bacillus cereus

Cooked rice can contain <u>Bacillus cereus</u> spores, which produce an <u>emetic</u> toxin when left at 4–60 °C (39–140 °F). When storing cooked rice for use the next day, rapid cooling is advised to reduce the risk of toxin production.[32] One of the <u>enterotoxins</u> produced by Bacillus cereus is heat-resistant; reheating contaminated rice kills the bacteria, but does not destroy the toxin already present.

APPENDIX 5

How RFID (RADIO FREQUENCY IDENTIFICATION) Works by Kevin Bonsor and Wesley Fenlon

Long checkout lines at the grocery store are one of the biggest complaints about the shopping experience. Soon, these lines could disappear when the ubiquitous <u>Universal Product Code</u> (UPC) bar code is replaced by smart labels, also called radio frequency identification (RFID) tags. RFID tags are intelligent bar codes that can talk to a networked system to track every product that you put in your shopping cart. Imagine going to the grocery store, filling up your cart and walking right out the door. No longer will you have to wait as someone rings up each item in your cart one at a time. Instead, these RFID tags will communicate with an electronic reader that will detect every item in the cart and ring each up almost instantly. The reader will be connected to a large network that will send information on your products to the retailer and product manufacturers. Your <u>bank</u> will then be notified and the amount of the bill will be deducted from your account. No lines, no waiting.

RFID tags, a technology once limited to tracking cattle, are tracking consumer products worldwide. Many manufacturers use the tags to track the location of each product they make from the time it's made until it's pulled off the shelf and tossed in a shopping cart. Outside the realm of retail merchandise, RFID tags are tracking vehicles, airline passengers, Alzheimer's patients and <u>pets</u>. Soon, they may even track your preference for chunky or creamy peanut butter. Some critics say RFID technology is becoming too much a part of our lives -- that is, if we're even aware of all the parts of our lives that it affects.

APPENDIX 6

Back masking

(Subliminal messages –Rock Music)

From Wikipedia, the free encyclopedia
Jump to: navigation, search

Back masking is a recording technique in which a sound or message is recorded backward on to a track that is meant to be played forward. Back masking is a deliberate process, whereas a message found through phonetic reversal may be unintentional.

Back masking was popularized by the Beatles, who used backward instrumentation on their 1966 album *Revolver*.[1] Artists have since used back masking for artistic, comedic and satiric effect, on both analogue and digital recordings. The technique has also been used to censor words or phrases for "clean" releases of rap songs.

Back masking has been a controversial topic in the United States since the 1980s, when allegations from Christian groups of its use for Satanic purposes were made against prominent rock musicians, leading to record-burning protests and proposed anti-backmasking legislation by state and federal governments.[2]

History

In 1877 Thomas Edison invented the phonograph, a device allowing sound to be recorded and reproduced on a rotating cylinder with a stylus (or "needle") attached to a diaphragm mounted at the narrow end of a horn. Emile Berliner invented the familiar lateral-cut disc phonograph record in 1888. His design overtook the Edison phonograph in the 1920s, partly because Berliner's patent expired in 1918, leaving others free to use his invention.

In addition to recreating recorded sounds by placing the stylus on the cylinder or disc and rotating it in the same direction as during the recording, one could hear different sounds by rotating the cylinder or disc backwards.[3] In 1878 Edison noted that, when played backwards, "the song is still melodious in many cases, and some of the strains are sweet and novel, but altogether different from the song reproduced in the right way".[4] The backwards playing of records was advised as training for magicians by occultist Aleister Crowley, who suggested in his 1913 book *Magick (Book 4)* that an adept "train himself to think backwards by external means", one of which was to "listen to phonograph records, reversed."[5]

Tape recorders allowed backward recording in recording studios.

The 1950s saw two new developments in audio technology: the development of *musique concrète*, an avant-garde form of electronic music which involves editing together fragments of natural and industrial sounds; and the concurrent spread of the use of tape recorders in recording studios.[6] These two trends led to tape music compositions, composed on tape using techniques including reverse tape effects.[7]

The Beatles, who incorporated the techniques of *concrète* into their recordings, were responsible for popularizing the concept of backmasking.[1] Singer John Lennon and producer George Martin both claimed they discovered the backward recording technique during the recording of 1966's *Revolver*; specifically the album tracks "Tomorrow Never Knows" and "I'm Only Sleeping", and the single "Rain".[8] Lennon stated that, while under the influence of marijuana, he accidentally played the tapes for "Rain" in reverse, and enjoyed the sound. The following day he shared the results with the other Beatles, and the effect was used first in the guitar solo for "Tomorrow Never Knows", and later in the coda of "Rain".[9][10] According to Martin, the band had been experimenting with changing the speeds of and reversing the "Tomorrow Never Knows" tapes, and Martin got the idea of reversing Lennon's vocals and guitar, which he did with a clip from "Rain". Lennon then liked the effect and kept it.[11][12] Regardless, "Rain" was the first song to feature a backmasked message: "Sunshine ... Rain ... When the rain comes, they run and hide their heads" (listen (info); the last line is the reversed first verse of the song).[13]

Sayings

The Beatles were involved in the spread of backmasking both as a recording technique and as the center of a controversy. The latter has its roots in an event in 1969, when WKNR-FM DJ Russ Gibb received a phone call from a student at Eastern Michigan University who identified himself as "Tom". The caller asked Gibb about a rumor that Beatle

Paul McCartney had died, and claimed that the Beatles song
"Revolution 9" contained a backward message confirming the rumor.
Gibb played the song backwards on his turntable, and heard "Turn me
on, dead man … turn me on, dead man … turn me on, dead man…"
(listen (info)).[14] Gibb began telling his listeners about what he called
"The Great Cover-up",[15] and to the original clue were added various
others, including the alleged backmasked message "Paul is a dead man,
miss him, miss him, miss him", in "I'm So Tired".[14] The "Paul is dead"
rumor popularized the idea of backmasking in popular music.[1]

After Gibb's show, many more songs were found to contain phrases that
sounded like known spoken languages when reversed. Initially, the
search was done mostly by fans of rock music; but, in the late 1970s,[16]
during the rise of the Christian right in the United States,[17]
fundamentalist Christian groups began to claim that backmasked
messages could bypass the conscious mind and reach the subconscious,
where they would be unknowingly accepted by the listener.[18] In 1981,
Christian DJ Michael Mills began stating on Christian radio programs
that Led Zeppelin's "Stairway to Heaven" contained hidden messages
that were heard by the subconscious.[19] In early 1982, the Trinity
Broadcasting Network's Paul Crouch hosted a show with self-described
neuroscientist William Yarroll, who argued that rock stars were
cooperating with the Church of Satan to place hidden subliminal
messages on records.[20] Also in 1982, fundamentalist Christian pastor
Gary Greenwald held public lectures on dangers of backmasking, along
with at least one mass record-smashing.[21] During the same year, thirty
North Carolina teenagers, led by their pastor, claimed that singers had
been possessed by Satan, who used their voices to create backward
messages, and held a record-burning at their church.[22]

Allegations of demonic backmasking were also made by social
psychologists, parents and critics of rock music,[23] as well as the Parents
Music Resource Center (formed in 1985),[24] which accused Led Zeppelin
of using backmasking to promote Satanism.[25] On the April 28, 1982
edition of the CBS Evening News, Dan Rather discussed the finding of
possible backmasked messages, and played reversed sections of songs by
Led Zeppelin, Electric Light Orchestra, and Styx.[26]

Legislation

One result of the furore was the firing of five radio DJs who had
encouraged listeners to search for backward messages in their record
collections.[16] A more serious consequence was legislation by the state
governments of Arkansas and California. The 1983 California bill was
introduced to prevent backmasking that "can manipulate our behavior

377

without our knowledge or consent and turn us into disciples of the Antichrist".[27] Involved in the discussion on the bill was a California State Assembly Consumer Protection and Toxic Materials Committee hearing, during which "Stairway to Heaven" was played backwards, and William Yaroll testified.[28] The successful bill made the distribution of records with undeclared backmasking an invasion of privacy for which the distributor could be sued.[21] The Arkansas law passed unanimously in 1983, referenced albums by The Beatles, Pink Floyd, Electric Light Orchestra, Queen and Styx,[17] and mandated that records with backmasking include a warning sticker: "Warning: This record contains backward masking which may be perceptible at a subliminal level when the record is played forward." However, the bill was returned to the state senate by Governor Bill Clinton and defeated.[21] House Resolution 6363, introduced in 1982 by Representative Bob Dornan (R-California), proposed mandating a similar label;[29] the bill was referred to the Subcommittee on Commerce, Transportation and Tourism and was never passed.[30] Government action was also called for in the legislatures of Texas and Canada.[21]

The Compact Disc made finding backward messages difficult, causing interest in backmasking to decline.

With the advent of Compact Discs in the 1980s, but prior to the advent of sound editing technology for personal computers in the 1990s, it became more difficult to listen to recordings backwards, and the controversy died down.[23]

Resurgence

Though the backmasking controversy peaked in the 1980s, the general belief in subliminal manipulation became more widespread in the United States during the following decade,[31] with belief in Satanic backmasking on records persisting into the 1990s.[32] At the same time, the development of sound editing software with audio reversal features simplified the process of reversing audio,[23] which previously could only be done with full fidelity using a professional tape recorder.[18] The Sound Recorder utility, included with Microsoft Windows from Windows 95 to Windows XP, allows one-click audio reversal,[33] as does popular open source sound editing software Audacity.[34] Following the growth of the Internet, backmasked message searchers used such software to create websites featuring backward music samples, which became a widely-used method of exploring backmasking in popular music.[23]

The switch to <u>digital audio</u> made recording backmasked messages quicker and easier.

Backmasking has been used as a <u>recording</u> technique since the 1960s. In the era of <u>magnetic tape sound recording</u>, backmasking required that the source <u>reel-to-reel</u> tape actually be played backwards, which was achieved by first being wound onto the original takeup reel, then reversing the reels so as to use that reel as the source (this would reverse the stereo channels as well). <u>Digital audio</u> recording has greatly simplified the process.[35]

Backmasked words are unintelligible noise when played forward, but when played backwards are clear speech.[22] Listening to backmasked audio with most <u>turntables</u> requires disengaging the drive and rotating the album by hand in reverse[36] (though some can play records backwards).[18] With <u>magnetic tape</u>, the tape must be reversed and spliced back in to the cassette.[36] <u>Compact discs</u> were difficult to reverse when first introduced, but <u>digital audio editors,</u> which were first introduced in the late 1980s and became popular during the next decade,[37] allow easy reversal of audio from digital sources.[23]

Satanic backmasking

In the 1973 film _**The Exorcist**_ a tape of noises from the possessed victim was discovered to contain a message when the tape was played backwards. This scene might have inspired subsequent copycat musical effects. Although the Satanic backmasking controversy involved mainly <u>classic rock</u> songs whose authors denied any intent to promote <u>Satanism,</u> backmasking has been used by <u>heavy metal</u> bands to deliberately insert messages in their lyrics or imagery. Bands have utilized satanic imagery for commercial reasons.[38] For example, <u>thrash metal</u> band <u>Slayer</u> included at the start of the band's 1985 album _Hell Awaits_ a deep backmasked voice chanting "Join Us" over and over.(<u>listen</u> (<u>info</u>)).[39] However, Slayer vocalist <u>Tom Araya</u> states that the band's use of satanic imagery was "solely for effect".[40] <u>Cradle of Filth</u>, another band that has employed Satanic imagery, released a song entitled "Dinner at Deviant's Palace", consisting almost entirely of unusual sounds and a reversed reading of the <u>Lord's Prayer</u>[41] (a backwards reading of the Lord's Prayer is reportedly a major part of the <u>Black Mass</u>).[19][42] Seattle-based grunge band <u>Soundgarden</u> parodied the phenomenon of Satanic backmasking on their 1989 album _Ultramega OK_. When played backwards, the songs "665" and "667" reveal a song about <u>Santa Claus</u>. <u>Marilyn Manson</u> used this way to hide subliminal messages. For example, in the beginning of his song "Tourniquet" when played backwards, his voice is heard saying "This is my lowest point of vulnerability" as explained in his book Long Hard Road Out of Hell.

Some satanic backmasked messages are heard, but later confirmed false. Rihanna's "Diamonds" from her eighth studio album *Unapologetic* contains some believed backmasked messages including *He's my Hindu, he's Satan, Lucifer, He's Eros, hail Satanism, I love Lucifer*. These have been confirmed false. [*citation needed*]

Aesthetic use

Backmasking is often used for aesthetics, i.e., to enhance the meaning or sound of a track.[16] During the Judas Priest subliminal message trial, lead singer Rob Halford admitted to recording the words "In the dead of the night, love bites" backwards into the track "Love Bites", from the 1984 album *Defenders of the Faith*. Asked why he recorded the message, Halford stated that "When you're composing songs, you're always looking for new ideas, new sounds."[43] Stanley Kubrick used "Masked Ball", an adaptation by Jocelyn Pook of her earlier work "Backwards Priests" (from the album *Flood*) featuring reversed Romanian chanting, as the background music for the masquerade ball scene in *Eyes Wide Shut*.[44] At the end of Before I Forget by Slipknot, lead singer Corey Taylor's voice can be heard saying "...You're wasting it" which is in reference to how Rick Rubin, the producer of their album Vol. 3: The Subliminal Verses, wanted Taylor to change the chorus vocal melody because he felt it wasn't catchy; however, Taylor stood his ground and the chorus stayed unchanged.[45]

One backmasking technique is to reverse an earlier part of a song. Missy Elliott used this technique in one of her songs, "Work It",[46] as did Jay Chou ("You Can Hear", from *Ye Hui Mei*),[47] At the Drive-In ("300 MHz", from *Vaya*),[48] and Lacuna Coil ("Self Deception", from *Comalies*).[49] A related technique is to reverse an entire instrumental track. John Lennon originally wanted to do so with "Rain", but objections by producer George Martin and bandmate Paul McCartney cut the backward section to 30 seconds.[9] The Stone Roses have made heavy use of this technique in songs including "Don't Stop",[50] "Guernica", and "Simone",[51] which are all backwards versions of other Stone Roses tracks, sometimes overdubbed with new vocals. Meanwhile, Klaatu used the reversed vocals from "Anus of Uranus" (from their first album, *3:47 EST*) as the vocals for the song "Silly Boys" (on their third album, *Sir Army Suit*). The lyrics for "Silly Boys" on the lyric sheet from *Sir Army Suit* are accordingly printed backwards.[52] And Danish band Mew's 2009 album *No More Stories...* contains a track,

"New Terrain", which, when listened to in reverse, reveals a new song, entitled "Nervous".[53]

Artists often use backmasking of sounds or instrumental audio to produce interesting sound effects.[35][54] One such sound effect is the reverse echo. When done on tape, such use of backmasking is known as *reverse tape effects*. One example is Matthew Sweet's 1999 album *In Reverse*, which includes reversed guitar parts which were played directly onto a tape running in reverse.[55] For live concerts, the guitar parts were played live on stage using a backward emulator.[56] The French House group Daft Punk released a song called "Funk Ad," which is a section of their single, "Da Funk," played backwards.

On the eponymous album *Crosby, Stills & Nash*, Stephen Stills' lead guitar in "Pre-road Downs" is heard in reverse through the entirety of the track.

Humorous and parody messages

The manual for the popular sound program SoX includes the "reverse" option "for finding Satanic subliminals."

A common use of backmasking is hiding a comedic or parodical message backwards in a song. The B-side of the 1966 Napoleon XIV single "They're Coming to Take Me Away, Ha-Haaa!" is a reversed version of the entire forwards record, entitled "!aaaH-aH ,yawA eM ekaT oT gnimoC er'yehT". It reached #3 in the US charts, and #4 in the UK.[57]

Pink Floyd dropped a backmasked message into "Empty Spaces":

The first line may refer to former lead singer Syd Barrett, who is thought to have suffered a nervous breakdown years earlier.[58]

In "Weird Al" Yankovic's "Nature Trail to Hell", from 1984's *"Weird Al" Yankovic in 3-D*, Yankovic's backmasked voice declares that "Satan eats Cheez Whiz" (listen (info)).[23] Another early example can be found on the J. Geils Band track "No Anchovies, Please", from 1980s album *Love Stinks*. The message, disguised as a foreign-sounding language spoken under the narration, is, "It doesn't take a genius to tell the difference between chicken shit and chicken salad."[118] Belgian act Poésie Noire included a satirical backmasked message on their 1988 album *Tetra* saying "You fucking asshole, play the record in the normal way".[59] Tenacious D includes the backmasked message "Eat Donkey Crap" at the end of "Karate" from their self-titled first album.[60]

<u>Styx</u>, after being accused of Satanic backmasking, included an actual backmasked message in *Kilroy Was Here*: "*Annuit cœptis, Novus ordo seclorum*".

<u>Electric Light Orchestra</u> and <u>Styx</u>, following their involvement in the 1980s backmasking controversy, released songs that parody the allegations made against them. ELO, after being accused of Satanic backmasking on their 1974 album *Eldorado*, included backmasked messages in two songs on their next album, 1975's *Face The Music*.[61] "<u>Down Home Town</u>" begins with a voice twice repeating (in reverse) "Face the mighty waterfall".[62] And the opening instrumental "<u>Fire On High</u>" contains the backmasked message "The music is reversible, but time is not. Turn back! Turn back! Turn back! Turn back!" (<u>listen</u> (<u>info</u>)).[63] In 1983 ELO released an entire album, *Secret Messages*, in response to the controversy.[64] Among the many backmasked messages on the album are: "Welcome to the big show" (2x);[118] "Thank you for listening"; "Look out there's danger ahead"; "Hup two three four"; "Time After Time"; and "You're playing me backwards".[62] Styx also released an album in response to allegations of Satanic backmasking:[65] 1983's *Kilroy Was Here*, which deals with an allegorical group called the "Majority for Musical Morality" that outlaws rock music.[117] A sticker on the album cover contains the message, "By order of the Majority for Musical Morality, this album contains secret backward messages", and the song "Heavy Metal Poisoning" does in fact contain the backmasked <u>Latin</u> words "*Annuit cœptis, Novus ordo seclorum*" ("[God] has favored our undertakings; a new order for the ages")—part of the <u>Great Seal</u> which encircles the pyramid on the back of the American <u>dollar bill</u>.[29]

<u>Iron Maiden</u>'s 1983 album *Piece of Mind* features a short backwards message, included by the band in response to allegations of Satanism that were surrounding them at the time.[66] Between the songs "<u>The Trooper</u>" and "Still Life" is inebriated drummer <u>Nicko McBrain</u> doing an impression of <u>Idi Amin Dada</u>: "'What ho', sed de t'ing wid de t'ree bonce [said the thing with the three heads]. Don't meddle wid t'ings you don't understand," followed by a <u>belch</u>.[67] <u>Prince</u>'s controversial song "<u>Darling Nikki</u>" includes the backmasked message, "Hello, how are you? I am fine, because I know that the Lord is coming soon."[68] <u>The Waitresses</u>' 1982 EP *I Could Rule the World if I Could Only Get the Parts* included a backwards masking warning on the cover and a message masked within the song "The Smartest Person I Know": "Anyone who believes in backwards masking is a fool."

Some messages chastise or poke fun at the listener who is playing the song backwards. One such message was included by "Weird Al" Yankovic in "<u>I Remember Larry</u>", from the 1996 album *Bad Hair Day*, on which Yankovic lightly chastises the listener with the backmasked remark, "Wow, [you] must have an awful lot of free time on your hands" (listen (info)).[69] Similarly, the B-52's song "Detour Through your Mind", from the 1986 LP *Bouncing off the Satellites*, contains the message, "I buried my parakeet in the backyard. Oh no, you're playing the record backwards. Watch out, you might ruin your needle."[70] Meanwhile, Christian rock group Petra included in their song "Judas Kiss", from the 1982 album *More Power to Ya*, the message, "What are you looking for the devil for, when you ought to be looking for the Lord?"[18] Bloodhound Gang's 1996 controversy-begging track "Lift Your Head Up High (And Blow Your Brains Out)" mocked the Judas Priest controversy directly, and included the backmasked phrase "Devil child, wake up and eat Chef Boyardee Beefaroni".[71] The band Mindless Self Indulgence released a song titled "Backmaskwarning!", which contains the forward lyrics "Play that record backwards / Here's a message yo for the suckas / Play that record backwards / And go fuck yourself". The backwards messages in the song include, "clean your room", "do your homework", "don't stay out too late", and "eat your vegetables".[48][72]

Backmasking was also parodied in a 2001 episode of the television series *The Simpsons* entitled "New Kids on the Blecch." Bart Simpson joins a boy band called the Party Posse, whose song "Drop Da Bomb" includes the repeated lyric "Yvan eht nioj." Lisa Simpson becomes suspicious and plays the song backward, revealing the backmasked message "Join the Navy", which leads her to realize that the boy band was created as a subliminal recruiting tool for the United States Navy.

Critical or explicit messages

Frank Zappa used backmasking to avoid censorship.

Backmasking has also been used to record statements perhaps too critical or explicit to be used forwards. Frank Zappa used backmasking to avoid censorship of the track "Hot Poop", from *We're Only in It for the Money* (1968). The released version contains at the end of its side "A" the backmasked message "Better look around before you say you don't care. / Shut your f...ing mouth 'bout the length of my hair. / How would you survive / If you were alive / shitty little person?" This profanity-laced verse, originally from the song "Mother People", was censored by Verve Records, so Zappa edited the verse out, reversed it, and inserted it elsewhere in the album as "Hot Poop" (though even in the backward message the word "fucking" is censored).[73] Another example is found in Roger Waters' 1991 album *Amused to Death*, on which Waters recorded a backward message, possibly critical of film director Stanley Kubrick, who had refused to let Waters sample a breathing sound from _2001: A Space Odyssey_.[74] The message appears in the song "Perfect Sense Part 1", in which Waters' backmasked voice says, "Julia, however, in light and visions of the issues of Stanley, we have changed our minds. We have decided to include a backward message, Stanley, for you and all the other book burners."[75]

Censorship

A further use of backmasking is to censor words and phrases deemed inappropriate on radio edits and "clean" album releases.[176] For example, The Fugees' clean version of the album _The Score_ contains various backmasked profanities;[176] thus, when playing the album backwards, the censored words are clearly audible among the backward gibberish.[177] When used with the word "shit", this type of backmasking results in a sound similar to "ish". As a result, "ish" became a euphemism for "shit".[178]

In Britney Spears' 2011 song "Till The World Ends", Spears says "if you want this good shit". However, on the official version, "shit" is reversed, creating the "ish" sound; therefore, the official version says "if you want this good ish". Backmasking is also used to censor the word "joint" in the video for "You Don't Know How It Feels" by Tom Petty, resulting in the line "Let's roll another tnioj".[79]

Accusations

Artists who have been accused of backmasking include Led Zeppelin,[80] The Beatles,[80] Pink Floyd,[80] Electric Light Orchestra,[80] Queen,[80] Styx,[80] Judas Priest,[80] The Eagles,[80] The Rolling Stones,[80] Jefferson Starship,[80] AC/DC,[29] Black Oak Arkansas,[29] Rush,[81] Britney Spears,[82] and Eminem.[23]

Electric Light Orchestra was accused of hiding a backward Satanic message in their 1974 album _Eldorado_. The title track, "Eldorado", was said to contain the message "He is the nasty one / Christ, you're infernal / It is said we're dead men / Everyone who has the mark will live."[29] ELO singer and songwriter Jeff Lynne responded by calling this accusation (and the related charge of being "devil-worshippers") "skcollob",[64] and stating that the message "is absolutely manufactured by whoever said, 'That's what it said.' It doesn't say anything of the sort."[70] The group included several backward messages in later albums in response to the accusations.

In 1981, Styx was accused of putting the backward message "Satan move through our voices" (listen (info)) on the song "Snowblind", from

Paradise Theatre.[17] Guitarist James Young called these charges "rubbish,"[83] and responded, "If we want to make a statement, we'll do it in a way that people can understand us and not in a way where you have to go out and buy a $400 tape player to understand us."[65] In 1983, the band released a concept album, *Kilroy Was Here*, satirizing the Moral Majority.

A well-known alleged message is found in rock group Led Zeppelin's 1971 song "Stairway to Heaven". The backwards playing of a portion of the song purportedly results in words beginning with "Here's to my sweet Satan" (listen (info)).[84] Swan Song Records issued a statement to the contrary: "Our turntables only play in one direction—forwards."[19] Led Zeppelin vocalist Robert Plant denied the accusations in an interview: "To me it's very sad, because 'Stairway To Heaven' was written with every best intention, and as far as reversing tapes and putting messages on the end, that's not my idea of making music."[85] Another widely-known alleged message, "It's fun to smoke marijuana," in Queen's song "Another One Bites the Dust", is similarly disclaimed by the group's spokesperson.[23]

Fundamentalist Christian groups

Various fundamentalist Christian groups have declared that Satan—or Satan-influenced musicians—use backmasked messages to subliminally alter behavior. Pastor Gary Greenwald claimed that subliminal messages backmasked into rock music induce listeners towards sex and drug use.[86] Minister Jacob Aranza wrote in his 1982 book *Backward Masking Unmasked* that rock groups "are using backmasking to convey satanic and drug related messages to the subconscious."[16] Christian DJ Michael Mills argued in 1981 that "the subconscious mind is being successfully affected by the repetition of beat and lyrics—being affected through a subliminal message."[87] Mills has toured America warning Christian parents about subliminal messages in rock music.[21]

In 1985, Dr. Joe Stuessy testified to the United States Congress at the Parents Music Resource Center hearings that:

The message [of a piece of heavy metal music] may also be covert or subliminal. Sometimes subaudible tracks are mixed in underneath other, louder tracks. These are heard by the subconscious but not the conscious mind. Sometimes the messages are audible but are backward, called backmasking. There is disagreement among experts regarding the effectiveness of subliminals. We need more research on that.

ADDITIONAL USEFUL INFORMATION

The following information may be useful to the reader. The first three definitions are fashionable words used today in general conversation yet fit in with the contents of this book. The information was obtained from Wikipedia the free online encyclopaedia.
http://www.religioustolerance.org/chr_symb.htm

Or other online dictionaries as stated.

Definition of Machiavellianism

It is the art of **manipulation** in which others are socially manipulated in a way that benefits the user, whether it is to the detriment of the people being used. The user would feel little to no remorse or empathy when their actions harm others.

Definition of draconian (adj)

Bing Dictionary **dra·co·ni·an** [drə kő́nee ən]
There are two meanings:

1. too harsh: unjustly harsh or severe
2. of Draco: relating to the Athenian legislator Draco or his wide-ranging and harsh code of laws

Synonyms: **harsh, severe, strict, strong, austere, ruthless**

Notice the letters simulates Dragon who will rule the earth harshly!
He is very ruthless, and severe with harsh laws!

Definition of clandestine (adj)

Bing Dictionary **clan·des·tine** [klan déstin]

Secret: needing to be concealed, usually because it is illegal or unauthorized

Christian Symbol Fish (Ichthus)

The history of the Christian fish symbol:

The fish outline is a logical symbol for the early Christian church to adopt. Fish are often mentioned in the gospels. This is what one would expect, if Jesus did most of his teaching in the Galilee. The synoptic gospels state this, although the Gospel of John denies it. Fish were a staple in the diet of Galilee.

The symbol was simple to draw and was often used among Christians as a type of password during times of persecution by the Roman government. If two strangers met and were unsure whether each other were a Christian, one would draw an arc in the earth like a fish). If the other were a Christian, they would complete the symbol with a reverse arc: ( ), forming the outline of a fish.

According to Albatrus.org: "When threatened by Romans in the first centuries after Christ, Christians used the fish [symbol to] mark meeting places and tombs, or to distinguish friends from foes."

In modern times, the fish outline symbol is experiencing a comeback. It is commonly seen in the form of a bumper sticker or casting mounted on the trunk lids of cars. The body of the symbol may be empty, or may contain a name ("Jesus" or "ICTUS").

We also found a satirical essay *"Experts concerned about backward Jesus fishes"* which suggested, with tongue in cheek, that fish swimming to the right is *"a duplicitous tool of Satan, the Lord of Lies...Our children are viewing these fish and are losing their grip on morality....These backwards fishes, and all their inherent evils could destroy a society."* [13]

The most meaningful orientation is probably to have the fish swimming to the left. The symbol then resembles the first letter of the Greek alphabet, alpha. That recalls Revelation 1:8:

CONCLUSION

This book is one of a series called **'Last Chance Series'**. The series was written for a number of reasons. Firstly there are many books written about the End Times, Biblical Prophecy and Apostasy, however, not from the Psychological Perspective.

Secondly, many books of this kind are written in complex language. My books are written in ordinary simple English so ALL people can read and understand!

In all of my books my goal is to enable readers to look at how they themselves think, feel and behave and then to look at how they have been <u>conditioned</u> to think, feel and behave. It is very easy to assume that everything we see and do is okay, acceptable and true therefore we assume ourselves to be immune to any 'comeback' or 'retribution'. This may not necessarily be the case.

People are under a Great Delusion and a Great Lie! People are being misled, misdirected and lied to by those who are in authority and leadership. We put our trust in these people who are misleading us and yet they themselves are also being misled!

On the other hand many people have knowingly chosen to be misled, deceived and controlled because they are already filled with rebellion and wickedness in their hearts, deliberately choosing to rebel against all that is good!

This book is for the innocent and the deceived! So they become aware of the Great Lie and choose the safety net of God to lead them to the narrow path that leads to eternal safety!

These are the words of Yeshua, the Saviour and Messiah soon to come!
"Do not be afraid. I am the first and the last. I am the Living One; I was dead, and behold I am alive for ever and

ever! And I hold the keys of Death and Hades." Revelation 1:17

"For God so loved the world that He gave His one and only son that whoever believes in Him shall not perish but have eternal life. John 3:16

The book series has a rolling theme and follows a connecting pathway. My first book of the series called *'Christ Yeshua Jesus from Genesis to Revelation'*, introduces the reader to evidence of Christ found throughout the whole bible from beginning to the end – from Genesis the first book in the Old Testament, to the last book of the New Testament, the book of Revelation. Genesis was written thousands of years ago in the BC (before Christ) era. Revelation was written AD (after Christ).

The books in between Genesis and Revelation were all written during different historical periods of time and therefore by different writers. Yet all through these books are references to Christ as the Lord of Salvation and the Messiah to come! Many of these books hold witness testimonies to biblical characters such as Elijah and Moses actually speaking to Christ!

The book is full of evidence to link Christ to the Creator God and the Holy Spirit, which makes up the Trinity (Triune God).

"All scripture is God –breathed and is useful for teaching, rebuking, correcting, and training in righteousness" 2 Timothy 3:16.

The psychological aspect for the reader is to come to understand just how much people have been directed away from the truth of the bible's content and how valuable it is for directing our path in life. It also tells us the purpose for our existence! He has specific guidelines to help us achieve a satisfying life while on this earth. It directs us to the pathway that takes us back to our roots – the Garden of Eden where we humans fellowshipped with God himself on a daily basis!

Our minds have been invaded; our thoughts have become twisted and turned upside down so that our loyalties have changed! Over the past 100 years or so we have allowed ourselves to be deceived into accepting myths and theories that hold no truth! Mankind has strayed from the truth, from the reality- to the point of denying the Triune God!

God prophesied what is taking place today!

"For the time will come [has come already] when men will not put up with sound doctrine. Instead, to suit their own desires, they will gather around them a great number of teachers to say what their itching ears want to hear. They will turn their ears away from the truth and turn aside to myths." 2 Tim 4:3

This book is the second of the series and continues from the first book **'Christ Yeshua Jesus from Genesis to Revelation'**, which introduces the series to evidence of how the world has been deceived and manipulated 'psychologically' into denying the Triune God.

My next books in the series will continue the psychological theme linking to God's prophecies and these end times:

Worldwide Delusion

A book about the previously mentioned 'GREAT LIE and DELUSION. It discusses how we now have achieved what our hearts desired – A Godless society based on myths and stories! The people chose to reject truth and therefore were given the Lie!

End Times –Last Days

It is a book that doesn't hold back the truth; it gives full details of events that will take place in the very near future! It delves into biblical prophecy and links to ancient scrolls such as those written by Elijah and Baruch to reach a full understanding of these pending times.

Last Chance

This book discusses the time is now to make a decision for your destiny! If the reader reads all of the book series they should have acquired enough evidence to convince them of a loving God who offers them a sanctuary away from the pending Great Tribulation!

The reader will also by the end of the book series have enough knowledge to convince them Satan, the Biblical Serpent, the Devil and Lucifer are not myths but reality and therefore what has been foretold by God throughout the books of the bible (particularly the prophet's books and the book of Revelation) is happening and going to happen very soon. Therefore it is decision – time!

If you care about your future, the future of your children, family members and close friends you would think seriously about the contents of these books. It may be your last chance!

FURTHER READING/REFERENCES

Christ Yeshua Jesus from Genesis to Revelation by M.A.Noble (2013)
 ISBN 13- 9781484136386, www. Createspace and Amazon.com (online)

Combatting Cult Mind Control by Steven Hassan (1988), ISBN 1-85538-025-0, Park
Street Press, USA, division of Inner Traditions International Ltd.
[A book on exit counselling]

Mind Controllers by Dr Armen Victorian (1999)
ISBN 1-901250-26-1, Vision Paperbacks, division of Satin Publications Limited.

Muslim Brotherhood, America's Next Great Enemy, by Erick Stakelbeck (2013),
purchase on Amazon or Bing his Blog.

Mystery Mark of the New Age by Texe Marrs (1988)
ISBN 0-89107-479-1, Crossway Books, a division of Good News Publishing, Illinois
60153.

Pilgrim's Progress. By John Bunyan DVD and books can be purchased from
amazon.co.uk/Pilgrim**'s** Progress DVD.

For evidence of Microchip implanting for year 2017 see NBC You Tube, entitled
" NBC Prediction That We Will All Have RFID Chip".
Also look on Infowars.com OMG (must see !!!) Titled "In 2014 by 2017 The
Mark of the Beast".

Websites

Bing or Google the following for relevant subjects:

*Globalresearch.ca
*WorldnetDaily for Matt Barber on Baal Worship.
*Infowars.com for latest on world unrest.
*Clarion Project for latest on Islamic activity.
*NTEB News Desk – for current news updates.
*Light for the last days – various relevant articles.
*Truthwillrise's weblog
*Wikipedia, **www.**wikipedia**.org**

www.ingramcontent.com/pod-product-compliance
Lightning Source LLC
Chambersburg PA
CBHW070626290526
45790CB00001B/12